1999

CREATING THE NATIONAL PASTIME

ALSO BY G. EDWARD WHITE

The Eastern Establishment and the Western Experience (1968)

The American Judicial Tradition (1976) (Expanded Edition, 1988)

Patterns of American Legal Thought (1978)

Tort Law in America: An Intellectual History (1980)

Earl Warren: A Public Life (1982)

The Marshall Court and Cultural Change (1988)

Justice Oliver Wendell Holmes: Law and the Inner Self (1993)

Intervention and Detachment: Essays in Legal History and Jurisprudence (1994)

CREATING THE NATIONAL PASTIME

BASEBALL TRANSFORMS ITSELF

1903–1953

G. Edward White

PRINCETON UNIVERSITY PRESS · PRINCETON, NEW JERSEY

Published by Princeton University Press, 41 William Street,
Princeton, New Jersey 08540
In the United Kingdom: Princeton University Press,
Chichester, West Sussex

Library of Congress Cataloging-in-Publication Data

White, G. Edward.
Creating the national pastime : baseball transforms
itself, 1903–1953 / G. Edward White.
p. cm.
Includes bibliographical references (p.) and index.
ISBN 0-691-03488-5 (cl : alk. paper)
1. Baseball—United States—History—20th century. 2. Baseball—
Social aspects—United States—History—20th century. I. Title.
GV863.A1W447 1996
796.357'09'041—dc20 95-20743

This book has been composed in Palatino

Princeton University Press books are
printed on acid-free paper and meet the guidelines
for permanence and durability of the Committee
on Production Guidelines for Book Longevity
of the Council on Library Resources

1 3 5 7 9 10 8 6 4 2

For Elisabeth McCafferty Davis White

Contents

List of Illustrations ix

Preface xi

Introduction 3

Chapter One
The Ballparks 10

Chapter Two
The Enterprise, 1903–1923 47

Chapter Three
The Rise of the Commissioner: Gambling, the Black Sox, and the Creation of Baseball Heroes 84

Chapter Four
The Negro Leagues 127

Chapter Five
The Coming of Night Baseball 160

Chapter Six
Baseball Journalists 190

Chapter Seven
Baseball on the Radio 206

Chapter Eight
Ethnicity and Baseball: Hank Greenberg and Joe DiMaggio 245

Chapter Nine
The Enterprise, 1923–1953 275

Chapter Ten
The Decline of the National Pastime 316

Notes 331

Index 355

Illustrations

Hilltop Park, New York, about 1912 14

Shibe Park, Philadelphia, 1913 25

Aerial view of Shibe Park, around World War I 28

Scorecard for a 1914 Chicago White Sox game 31

Yankee Stadium, New York, 1928 43

Napoleon Lajoie in 1909 51

Ben Shibe and Garry Herrmann in the early 1920s 62

Albert Goodwill Spalding in 1915 68

The 1919 Chicago "Black Sox" 94

Charles Comiskey and William L. Veeck in 1920 100

Judge Kenesaw Mountain Landis at the 1922 World Series 109

Adrian ("Cap") Anson and Andrew ("Rube") Foster 132

The East Negro League All-Stars, 1937 140

A Negro League game in 1942 145

A May 2, 1930, night game, Des Moines, Iowa 165

The first major league night game, May 24, 1935, Cincinnati 177

The first night game at Ebbets Field, Brooklyn, June 15, 1938 183

Press box at Ebbets Field, 1940s 202

Graham McNamee broadcasts World Series game, October 5, 1924 210

Broadcast of Cleveland Indians game heard by fan at game, 1937 221

Hank Greenberg and Joe DiMaggio at 1937 All-Star Game 267

Branch Rickey in the early 1940s 287

National League owners Philip Wrigley, Emil Fuchs, and Sam Breadon 296

Larry MacPhail at the 1951 Celler Subcommittee Anti-Trust Hearings 300

Milwaukee County Stadium in the 1950s 311

Preface

WHEN I began work on this book, the issues that had led to the 1994–95 baseball strike were still unresolved. I had already decided to confine my coverage of baseball in America to a period ending in the 1950s, because I believed that after that decade forces had begun to have an impact on major league baseball that would fundamentally transform the nature of the enterprise. I sketch out some of those forces in the last chapter of the book. I want to note here that none of the original fundamental "rules" of Organized Baseball—a "reserve clause" system for player contracts, the collusive blacklisting of players who did not abide by that system, and sanctions against any competitive challenges to the "territorial rights" of the original franchises—is currently in existence. Baseball is now like other American professional sports in having free agency for players and a fluid, shifting map of franchises, one significantly affected by media markets as well as gate receipts.

The irony of baseball's current situation, in light of these fundamental changes, is that its franchises still retain immunity from antitrust laws and it still claims to be the "national pastime." I believe that in one sense that claim is valid: baseball has been an especially meaningful sport for Americans because of its association with the past, and past time.

A fair inference to be drawn from that conclusion is that baseball's claim for special status and its uniquely evocative character as an American sport are tied to its early twentieth- century history and may well not survive its altered character as an enterprise. I myself am inclined to draw that inference, but at the same time to caution against drawing it too hastily or categorically. This book suggests that baseball as an economic and civic institution may have fundamentally changed; but it also suggests that baseball's connection to the past—even, in some instances, a benighted and insular past—has been of compelling power. Americans may forgive baseball its current transgressions and restore it to its privileged place among professional sports, because they find it so compelling a link to history.

◆

A number of persons, in the course of reading early drafts of this book, corrected errors and disabused me of suspect interpretations. Thanks to Robert Bluthardt, Alan Boyer, Richard Crepeau, Michael Klarman, Alfred S. Konefsky, Lawrence Ritter, Michael Seidman, Paul Stephan, Spencer Waller, and the unidentified readers of Princeton University Press for their comments. Thanks also to Bing Devine and Robert Payne for supplying helpful information, to Walter Lippincott of Princeton for his interest in the project, to the Park Lane Swim Club for inspiration, and to Eric David Schramm for his thoughtful editorial suggestions.

The illustrations in this book are based on photographs in the collection of the National Baseball Library and Archive, Cooperstown, New York. My thanks to Pat Kelly of the Library and Archive staff for her help in assembling photo subjects and in securing the access to archival collections. Thanks also to Robert Payne and to the Bettmann Archive for permission to use photographs of Crosley Field and Branch Rickey. The excerpt from Edgar A. Guest's poem "Speaking of Greenberg," in Guest's *Collected Verse* (1934), is reprinted by permission of Contemporary Books, Inc.

A special thanks to three people who coped with the very long first draft of the book: my father-in-law, John F. Davis, who knows even more about baseball than he does about hockey; my research assistant for this project, Michael D'Agostino of the class of 1996 at Virginia Law School, who provided indefatigable research help and moral support; and Frederick Payne, in many respects the guiding spirit behind the whole effort. Fred Payne is a lawyer, linguist, and player-manager of the Charlottesville Blues baseball team (to mention only his politically correct talents), who somehow found time to read every line of the first draft and to improve it with his knowledge of baseball and his stylistic skills. When Fred talks baseball, Peter Gammons and Tom Boswell ought to listen.

This book was written over a period of time in which my teaching responsibilities were reduced, with two effects on internal relations within the White household. First, I got very little sympathy from

Susan Davis White, whose law practice is busy and stressful and who does not have the luxury of staying home and reading or writing about something she loves. I love Susan anyway. Second, having a more open-ended schedule enabled me to drive around the Northeastern and Middle Atlantic states attending athletic contests and making college visits with my younger daughter, Elisabeth McCafferty Davis White, who I hope will enjoy college academics and athletics as much as I did. The experience also enabled me to spend some unanticipated time with Elisabeth, which helped make up for the too infrequent company of her older sister Alexandra White-Ritchie, who lives farther away from Virginia than her parents like.

Even the anguish of having to eliminate cherished details from the manuscript failed to detract from the pleasure of writing this book. I hope a little of that rubs off on readers.

G.E.W.
Charlottesville
April 1995

CREATING THE NATIONAL PASTIME

Introduction

THERE IS A body of literature on baseball that takes for granted the special cultural resonance of the sport for Americans: the status of baseball as America's "national pastime." In that literature several interesting and suggestive themes have been introduced, such as the "pastoral" dimensions of a game played on green spaces in the midst of urban centers, or the distinctive mix between individual accomplishment and team play that marks the game. Among other things, the literature demonstrates the hold baseball has had on Americans who regard themselves as intellectuals. But although I found the literature on baseball's cultural appeal important, I did not find it persuasive in demonstrating why baseball had emerged, among other competing sports, as the game in which Americans, for at least the first fifty years of the twentieth century, made their largest collective investment.

In particular, I found the assertion that baseball outdistanced other sports in appeal because it was "there first," developing as a national professional sport prior to football, basketball, golf, tennis, or ice hockey, unreflective. Baseball had not in fact preceded those sports in time: all of them were in existence in the nineteenth century. Baseball had simply outdistanced them in popularity in the fifty years after 1903. The reasons for baseball's eminence lay elsewhere than in chronology. Yet there had been little discussion of how baseball emerged as America's "national game."

The emergence of baseball as a "national pastime" was doubly interesting to me because, from a contemporary perspective, the game does not seem particularly well suited for widespread public acclaim. To the extent that the spectator appeal of a sport is tied to participation in that sport, baseball would appear unpromising. The game is quite difficult to play, especially at a young age. It uses a hard ball, thrown and hit at considerable speed, making play potentially frightening and dangerous. It is not particularly good aerobic exercise when compared with other sports, such as basketball, tennis, or ice hockey. Moreover, the game is not particularly exciting to watch, at least for the uninitiated. Large portions of time go by without any action; the game seems disproportionately centered on the pitcher and batter to the exclusion of other players; most of the celebrated strategizing that takes place among fans in the stands during delays in the action presupposes a detailed knowledge of the game. The inaccessible quality of baseball was even more acute during its early twentieth-century history, when players were not given numbers or otherwise identified to spectators, no public address systems existed, and in-the-stands home runs, one of the most attractive features of the game to today's fans, were quite rare. Yet it was in this period that baseball became the sport that nearly every American schoolboy was introduced to early in his life.

I wondered how this emergence of baseball as the national pastime came about. Baseball had started in America as a working-class sport, played by Irish, German, and British immigrants in large cities. Its early history included close connections with gambling, drinking, and general rowdiness. Its early owners were not, for the most part, representatives of the wellborn classes, but entrepreneurs seeking upward mobility and public recognition. Yet by the 1920s baseball had clearly become the favorite sport of the American middle-class family.

I resolved that to understand the special role of baseball in America one had to look within the structure of the game as an enterprise as well as in the larger culture in which baseball was played. In the course of that exploration I discovered some features of baseball history that I found, from a contemporary perspective, anomalous to the point of being mysterious. Most obvious of those involved the nature of baseball's economic structure and labor relations. Not only was the game organized around legal and economic principles that were clearly inconsistent with those existing in other early twentieth-century American industries, the courts and Congress, who were well aware of that inconsistency, declined to force baseball to conform its labor relations to those of other interstate enterprises or even other professional sports. Moreover, the individuals most severely disadvantaged by the "laws" of baseball, the players, showed very little dissatisfaction with a system that by depriving them control over their wages, working conditions, or terms of employment, essentially reduced them to a species of peonage.

Indeed, for an industry that seemed as driven by economic motives as any of its counterparts in the world of American business, Organized Baseball* maintained some policies, and engaged in some practices, that appeared to be inefficient or counterproductive on their face. One such policy was resisting the opportunity to stage major league games at night for at least twenty years after baseball under the lights had been demonstrated to be technologically feasible and economically profitable. Another was adopting an extremely cautious attitude toward the broadcasting of games on the radio, even though such broadcasts provided considerable publicity and income to the clubs and cost them nothing in terms of dollars and cents. Another was not embracing air travel for teams after such travel had become widespread and relatively inexpensive for commercial enterprises. Still another was dogged resistance to potential changes in the geographic map of franchises, which had been established in 1903. Even after demographic and economic trends in the twentieth century had made it clear that some cities with two major league teams could not support them, and other cities without any teams could, large potential markets were frozen out of major league baseball.

A final anomaly was the persistent exclusion of black players from the game, not only at the major league level but throughout the minor leagues, for nearly the first fifty years of the twentieth century. In those years, of course, racial segregation was a pervasive feature of American life, so that baseball's exclusionary practices tracked ones throughout the nation. But baseball's segregationist practices were additionally peculiar in two respects. First, baseball included players from all other ethnic groups, including Latins, Asians, and Native Americans, three groups that faced persistent segregation and discrimination elsewhere in American culture. Only "the wooly-headed Ethiopian," as an editorial in *The Sporting News* characterized him, was banned from Organized Baseball. Second, baseball conspicuously publicized itself as a "democratic" game, one personifying the "melting pot" theory of ethnic assimilation in America. Under that theory representatives of diverse nationalities were expected, over time, to shed their ethnic distinctiveness and blend into American society. Blacks, however, were not treated as capable of "melting."

The total exclusion of blacks from Organized Baseball seemed par-

* The term *Organized Baseball* refers to the established, "official" major and minor professional leagues in the years covered by this study. It is meant to exclude "unofficial" leagues not "recognized" by baseball's establishment, such as the Federal League, the Negro Leagues, and the Mexican League.

ticularly curious in light of the fact that by World War I leagues of black baseball players, called Negro Leagues, were established, and exhibition games between white and black players were common. Given the reserve clause structure of Organized Baseball, which bound players to their teams year after year, player development was the central focus of club executives. The reserve clause made it exceptionally difficult for major league clubs to staff their rosters by obtaining players from other big-league teams: they were constantly looking at the minor leagues, colleges, and semi-pro leagues in search of talent. They knew that a pool of black ballplayers existed that could add considerably to the talent level in the major leagues. Yet they were willing to send scouts to Canada or Latin America in search of ballplayers, but not to the Negro Leagues.

I also wondered, as have many contemporary observers of baseball, what has happened to the special lure baseball has held on the American public. How was the centrality of baseball to followers of sports in America somehow lost, so at this writing baseball does not appear fundamentally different, in its institutional practices, economic organization, labor relations, and arguably in its cultural appeal, from other established professional sports? I concluded that perhaps the clearest way to see baseball's loss of its unique cultural role was to explore how that role had been gained in the first place.

That effort has taken me into a number of facets of early and mid-twentieth-century baseball history, some of them comparatively well traveled, others virtually unexplored, that form the basis of my narrative. Rather than previewing the subjects of my coverage at this point, I want to sketch out my central argument and its conclusions.

Baseball, as a "national game," came of age in the first two decades of the twentieth century, a period of time framed by the interleague "wars" of the 1900s, which resulted in the National Agreement of 1903 and the birth of the modern economic and organizational structure of Organized Baseball, and the residue of the 1919 Black Sox scandal, which produced the installation of a commissioner of baseball, with autocratic supervisory powers, in 1921. The time frame of baseball's emergence as America's most popular and evocative sport had decisive effects on its character for at least the next thirty years.

Baseball was launched as a national sport, and a cultural icon, in the Progressive Era. Its internal legal and economic structure, its business expectations, its conception of city ballparks, its attitudes on race and ethnicity, its myths, its aspirations, and its idealized image of itself as a sport and a "pastime" for its followers were characteristic of that era. Those in its inner circles held conventional early twentieth-century attitudes toward labor relations, ballpark construction, corruption, entertainments staged at night, and urban and rural life. The policies they fashioned for the sport reflected those attitudes.

Over the course of the twentieth century, the close connection between baseball's coming of age and the Progressive ethos in which that coming of age took place had two quite different effects. First, the Progressive ethos framing baseball's emergence as a national sport was of inestimable value in establishing baseball's status as a cultural icon. Baseball grew up with America's cities, its teams becoming a focus of civic pride and energy. At the same time baseball's fields and parks, the leisurely pace of the game, and its being an outdoor, daytime spectacle invoked rural and pastoral associations that were particularly evocative to a generation of Americans confronting an increasingly urbanizing and industrializing environment. The Progressive Era's linking, in its aspirational literature, of the values of morality and "progress" provided an impetus for baseball to engage in a ritualistic self-cleansing after the Black Sox scandal, in which it purged itself of gamblers and "crooked" ballplayers, hired a Progressive Republican judge as commissioner, and began to promote itself as a model for America's youth.

Baseball was Progressive in other respects. Its new "permanent" ballparks in major league cities, built between 1908 and 1923, were part of the City Beautiful movement sponsored by Progressives. Its symbiotic relationship with the growing American newspaper industry was launched in the Progressive Era, the time period of the newspaper's greatest dominance among American media. Its simultaneous adoption of an integrationist stance toward American ethnics, justified in the name of democratic theory, and of exclusionist policies toward blacks tracked mainstream Progressive responses to the issues of ethnicity and race in America. Its successful insulation of itself from both the courts and Congress, despite the fact that its monopsonistic labor practices appeared to violate antitrust laws, took advantage of the comparatively archaic legal definitions of "trade" and "commerce" that were still extant in the Progressive Era. Even its self-conscious effort to transform its image from a working-class, urban sport to one that would appeal to all sectors of America's youth, and American families of all classes, was in keeping with the Progressives' championing of middle-class values.

Thus a remarkable synergy existed between the game of baseball and the aspirations of Americans in the first two decades of the twentieth century. This synergy helped propel baseball from one among many sports and recreational pursuits to America's national pastime. At the same time, however, another effect of the time frame of baseball's emergence was taking place, an effect that became more marked as the twentieth century evolved. The governing policies of baseball and the assumptions behind those policies were decisively those of a particular period in time. As that period passed into history, those policies and assumptions remained largely intact, creating a collective enterprise that was sometimes unconscious of change and sometimes deliberately resistant to it.

The most telling aspect of this set of effects was not, however, that it made baseball an anachronistic and reactionary sport, increasingly out of touch with twentieth-century America. It was that, paradoxically, the anachronistic dimensions of baseball helped cement its image as the national pastime, fostering a mythology that the game, instead of reflecting the historical and cultural context in which it came to prominence, was a timeless, even magical, phenomenon, insulated from the rest of life. When it became obvious, in the 1950s, that some baseball franchises in the original major league cities were nearly moribund, that the first generation of "permanent" steel and concrete ballparks was decaying, that there were many population centers in America that were larger than some major league cities, that major league baseball had no team west of St. Louis or south of Washington, and that baseball was the only professional sport still exempt from the antitrust laws, Congress held hearings about the franchise map and the reserve clause and took no action, and the Supreme Court upheld baseball's antitrust exemption. It was as if the status of baseball as America's national pastime meant the sport had become a metaphor for the past itself.

So the subtitle of this book is used in a double sense. It represents the extent to which baseball's emergence as a cultural icon was self-consciously fashioned by those within the center of Organized Baseball. It also represents the extent to which the idealized image of baseball as the national pastime was a product of a particular point in time. Baseball transformed itself in the years from 1903 to 1953, and in that time interval baseball also tried hard, and failed, to stay the same.

Despite the troubled status of baseball in contemporary America, this book has not been conceived as an exercise in recreating a nostalgic, purer past. It is, rather, an effort to understand how baseball's past history was far more complex, and far less heroic, than romanticized treatments of the game might suggest. It is an effort to demonstrate that the evolution of baseball from a marginal urban sport to the national pastime took place in a circumscribed moment in time and combined a series of historical factors that were both time-bound and fortuitous. It can also be seen as an attempt to distinguish baseball's past from its future.

1

The Ballparks

ON APRIL 14, 1911, shortly after midnight, a fire swept through the wooden grandstand of the Polo Grounds, the field where the New York Giants baseball club of the National League of Professional Baseball Clubs played its home games. The Polo Grounds, which at the time had a capacity of 31,316 seats, was the largest structure of its kind in major league baseball. It was located in the north Harlem area of Manhattan Island, in a meadow framed by a large bluff on the west and the Harlem River on the east. The bluff and the meadow, at the time of the fire, were owned by Mrs. James J. Coogan, whose husband had originally leased the property to the Giants for a baseball park in 1889.

At the time of the 1911 fire the owner of the Giants was John T. Brush, who had been previously known in baseball circles for his determined opposition to the city of New York's acquiring a second baseball team. After establishing themselves in the Coogan's Hollow site, Brush and his associates sought to acquire an interest in any other vacant parcels of Manhattan land that they thought might lend themselves to the location of a baseball park. Once they reached Coogan's Hollow, near 155th Street, they concluded that the Manhattan land to the north was too hilly and rocky to be suitable. In 1903, however, Frank Farrell and Bill Devery, two New Yorkers who between them had close connections to city politics and the real estate market, bought the Baltimore Orioles of the rival American League of Professional Baseball Clubs for $18,000 and moved the club to New York. They built Hilltop Park, so named to reflect its high vantage point, in the Washington Heights section of Manhattan, north of the Polo Grounds. Brush responded, a year later, by pointedly snubbing the league in which his new competitors played. His Giants had won the National League championship in 1904, but he declined to accept the then-informal challenge from the American League champion Boston Red Sox to participate in a "World Series," which had taken place the year before between the Red Sox and the National League champion Pittsburgh Pirates.[1]

On the night of the 1911 fire, however, Frank Farrell called Brush from Atlantic City, New Jersey, and offered the Giants the opportunity to complete their season in Hilltop Park. Remembering the incident, Brush spoke of the wooden grandstand of the Polo Grounds having "vanished in fire and smoke" and of the "dismay, despondency and regret depicted upon the faces of the multitude of fans" when they learned that the park had been destroyed. "While the flames were raging fiercest and the embers glowing," Brush recalled, Farrell phoned him, "tendering the use of his American League Park to the Giants as long as they might need it to carry out their schedule." Overwhelmed by the offer, Brush described his longtime antagonist as a "baseball philanthropist" who "deserves a monument" for his gesture.[2]

A year after the destruction of the Polo Grounds John Brush was able to write, in *Baseball Magazine*, that "upon the ruins of the old historic stand . . . there rises majestic, 100 feet above the ground and more than a thousand feet in length, the latest contribution to the comfort and convenience of the baseball fan." A new steel and concrete Polo Grounds had been built on the Coogan's Hollow site, complete with Italian marble boxes around the front of the upper deck of its grandstand, a balustrade ornamented with American eagles, reinforced Roman-style pylons flanking each end of the balustrade, and a cantilever roof with masts, from which blue and gold banners were displayed, projecting up every thirty feet. A writer in the same journal called the new Polo Grounds "the greatest ball park in the world," noting, among other things, that on the frieze of the grandstand, running below the balustrade, were male and female figures, "the perfect idealization of national manhood and womanhood," supporting shields that contained emblems of the eight National League teams: New York, Brooklyn, Boston, Philadelphia, Pittsburgh, Chicago, Cincinnati, and St. Louis. "There is nothing like it in baseball," the writer concluded, "and even New York, with all of its marvels, pauses a moment to take a fresh breath and brag about the 'biggest baseball yard in the world.'"[3]

The new Polo Grounds was ready to host baseball games as early as June 28, 1911, and was nearly completed by October 14 of that year, when the World Series opened with the Giants hosting the American League's Philadelphia Athletics. Ten thousand seats had survived the fire and were retained, with 6,000 new ones having been added by June 28 and another 18,000 by the opening of the World Series, now made a formal part of baseball in the aftermath of the National Agreement of 1903, in which the National and American Leagues agreed to recognize each other as equals. A 1912 commentator anticipated that the seating capacity of the park would eventually reach 60,000, and over the years, as a double-decked roofed grandstand was extended around nearly the entire circumference of the park, it did reach 55,000.[4]

The most impressive feature of the new Polo Grounds, however, was neither its seating capacity, which varied over the years, nor the elaborate ornamentation of its grandstand walls, which required frequent repainting and which was eventually discarded, nor even the strikingly irregular dimensions of its horseshoe-shaped playing field, featuring very short foul lines and a huge centerfield. It was the apparent permanency of its structure, which symbolized the apparent permanency of baseball as a game that would be forever identified with a large American city. To get a sense of the symbolic meaning of the 1911 version of the Polo Grounds, one has to consider the new ballpark in the context of other older and newer ballparks, in other major league cities, in the early years of the twentieth century.

The Polo Grounds was by no means unique in being a steel and concrete stadium that replaced an older wooden structure in the years between 1908 and 1915. In that time period a concrete and steel ballpark was either built from scratch, or remodeled from a wooden park on the same site, for every team in the major leagues, with the exception of the Philadelphia Phillies and the St. Louis Cardinals, who continued to play in primarily wooden parks. Moreover, after this five-year interval only one new baseball park was built in the major leagues until the 1950s, Yankee Stadium, which opened in 1923.[5] Just as the composition of major league cities and the identity of major league franchises did not change from 1911 to the early 1950s, so too the places where major league baseball was played remained almost exclusively constant. The ballparks represented by the new Polo Grounds were assumed to have become, on their completion, enduring civic symbols.

◆

The new Polo Grounds was one of three major league ballparks that existed in the New York area at the same time. The more proximal of those to the Polo Grounds, and the more controversial from John Brush's point of view, was Hilltop Park, the home of the transplanted Orioles, the New York Highlanders. Hilltop Park was built six weeks after the American League approved Farrell's and Devery's purchase of the Baltimore club, opening on April 30, 1903. Its structure and dimensions spoke volumes about the state of major league baseball at the time, as well as the state of building construction.

Hilltop Park, when it opened, had a single-decked wooden grandstand encircling the area behind home plate and extending a few feet past first and third bases on either side. The grandstand had a roof, which was supported on wooden pillars, spaced evenly throughout the structure. On the third base and first base lines, extending into the outfield in foul territory, were single-decked bleachers with no roofs. There were no seats in fair territory in the outfield, which was surrounded by a fence of a height ranging between fifteen and twenty feet, much of which was covered by advertising signs. The original distances of Hilltop Park were 365 feet from home plate to the left field foul line, 542 feet from home to dead center, and 400 feet to the right field foul line. The grandstand and bleachers, taken together, seated 16,000 fans. The cost of the park was $200,000 in excavation fees, a result of the rocky soil on which the field was built, but only $70,000 in construction fees because of the single deck and the fact that wood was the primary material.[6]

A number of features of Hilltop Park were symptomatic of the state of ballparks in the era just preceding the emergence of their concrete and steel "permanent" successors. First, the capacity of most of the wooden ballparks was comparatively small, especially when measured against structures such as the new Polo Grounds. That capacity was primarily a function of the fact that major league baseball, at the time of its "official" beginnings in 1903, was not very far removed from the game that had first started on a professional basis in the

Batting practice at Hilltop Park, New York, about 1912. Note the reporters interviewing players on the field, the single-decked wooden grandstand and open outfield seats, and the large crowd. (National Baseball Library and Archive, Cooperstown, N.Y.)

1860s.[7] An experiment increasing the number of umpires from one to two had ended in 1902, and would not be revived until 1911.[8] Baseballs, even when hit into the stands, were returned and kept in play wherever possible. Catchers wore no shin guards, and few wore masks. Gloves were little more than slightly padded versions of ordinary hand gloves. Pitchers had an unlimited license to scuff, spit on, or otherwise alter the surface of baseballs, which did not have cork centers until 1910. Each of these features meant that hitting a baseball for great distances was an extraordinarily difficult thing to do, but fielding a batted ball was not easy either.

As a result, most professional teams adopted the strategies of the "deadball era," encouraging their hitters to take short, choppy swings at pitches, designed to spray the ball around all the dimensions of the field; to bunt; to steal bases as much as possible; and generally to attempt to score runs by putting pressure on the other team's fielders rather than by hitting the ball long distances. Given this focus, most of the action of a baseball game, from a fan's point of view, was in the infield, and so there was no particular reason for those who built ballparks to locate seats in the outfield. At the same time, however, there was reason to make the outfield dimensions of a park large: a larger expanse of outfield meant a greater opportunity for a ball to roll through fielders or to a distant fence, thereby increasing the possibility of triples or inside-the-park home runs, which spectators found to be exciting plays. Thus few prospective builders of ballparks contemplated placing seats in the outfield in fair territory. Instead they allowed fans, on days when demand exceeded the seating capacity of a ballpark, to bring their own seats or to stand in the outfield, or even to drive their carriages up to the outfield fences. On such occasions ropes separated the fans from the players, and balls hit into outfield sections where fans had gathered were treated as doubles.

On October 10, 1904, for example, Hilltop Park's seating capacity was expanded from 16,000 to 30,000 as fans lined the foul lines and stood several rows deep in the outfield, watching the New York Highlanders (later to become the Yankees) face the Boston Red Sox (also known as the Puritans). The Red Sox had gone into that day's play in first place in the American League, leading the Highlanders by half a game, and the two teams were scheduled to play a doubleheader. October 10 was the last day of the season, so if the Highlanders won both games they would win the pennant. The scores in the games were 3–2 and 1–0, characteristic of the deadball era. The Red Sox won the first game when Highlander pitcher Jack Chesbro, who had already won forty-one games that year, threw a spitball over his catcher's head with two out in the Red Sox ninth, a man on third, and an 0–2 count on the batter. The low scoring games, the spectators on the field, Chesbro's choice of a spitball, and Chesbro's incredible won-loss record (he figured in fifty-three decisions that year, with fifty-one games started and forty-eight completed) all gave evidence that professional baseball was in the heart of its deadball era, when, among other things, relief pitchers were nonexistent.[9]

By the end of the 1912 season, however, Hilltop Park was regarded as sufficiently obsolete by its owners that they agreed to pay John

Brush a sum so that the Highlanders could play their home games in the new Polo Grounds.[10] The move of the Highlanders from Hilltop Park to the Polo Grounds signified a recognition by two of the three baseball club owners in the New York area that a commodious steel and concrete ballpark was an essential part of a major league baseball franchise. And even before the 1911 fire at the Polo Grounds, the third New York area club owner, Charles Ebbets of the National League's Brooklyn Superbas—also known as the Dodgers—had come to that same conclusion.

On April 9, 1913, in connection with the opening of Ebbets Field, the *Brooklyn Daily Eagle* ran a story on the process of its construction. "Planning and carrying through the deal for the buying of the site of Ebbets Field," the *Eagle* noted, "occupied President Ebbets two years and was a remarkable piece of the suppression of news."[11] Ebbets had actually announced the fruition of his plans to acquire a site to build Ebbets Field on January 2, 1912; those plans had been in operation since 1910. To understand what the *Eagle* meant by "a remarkable piece of the suppression of news," some brief history of Ebbets Field's predecessor structure is necessary.

Ebbets's club had been playing their games in Washington Park, in the Red Hook section of Brooklyn near the Gowanus Canal. By 1910 Ebbets had concluded that Washington Park, which had been built in 1898 for $60,000, was an inadequate facility. Its wooden stands made it a fire hazard, it was located close to a can factory and a coal yard, which emitted smoke and unpleasant odors, and its proximity to the Gowanus Canal often resulted in stenches permeating the ballpark. Moreover, as the popularity of baseball and the population of Brooklyn increased in the first decade of the twentieth century, Washington Park became overcrowded. A vivid demonstration of that fact came on the Superbas' opening day game on April 12, 1912. An overflow crowd of spectators resulted in fans lining the foul lines and standing in the outfield, obstructing the views of others in the seats and interfering with play. The private security guards hired by Ebbets proved inadequate to control the crowd, and the Mayor of Brooklyn, William Gaynor, who was present at the game, eventually had to order city police, stationed outside Washington Park, to attempt crowd control. When the police arrived the crowd attempted to scatter, but there was so little room that a crush of bodies was feared. Eventually the game was called after six innings when it became apparent that the playing field could not be cleared of fans.[12]

An attraction of Washington Park's had been its relatively central location in Brooklyn and its proximity to trolley lines; two trolley car companies had even contributed to its construction costs, hoping to induce ridership.[13] Ebbets noticed that an area of Brooklyn at the southeast corner of Prospect Park between the Bedford and Flatbush sections, colloquially known as "Pigtown," was adjacent to the tracks of nine separate trolley car lines. Pigtown was currently occupied by squatters, and not regarded as desirable property, but Ebbets believed that the growth of Brooklyn's population, the proximity of Pigtown to Prospect Park, and the fact that Bedford and Flatbush were becoming upscale residential areas would eventually result in a boom in land values in Pigtown itself.

Ebbets set about to acquire a five and a half acre site in Pigtown through individual purchases of lots by a dummy corporation not linked to the Superbas. The *Eagle* reported that "it was necessary to buy the [lots] individually without letting [the lot owners] know that the purchasers desired a large plot, otherwise some of the owners might have 'hung up' the purchaser, who would have been helpless, as he could not have brought condemnation proceedings."[14]

The dummy corporation created by Ebbets to make the purchases was called the Pylon Construction Company, and the negotiations were conducted by one Edward Brown, "who had never figured in baseball and was not known to be associated with Ebbets." Ebbets managed to acquire the entire site for the remarkably low price of $100,000. The eventual realization of his ambition to build a modern steel and concrete, fireproof stadium on the Pigtown site, however, eventually cost Ebbets another $750,000, which forced him to take in his contractors, the brothers Edward and Stephen McKeever, as business partners. When Ebbets announced the purchase of the site in January 1912, he anticipated the new ballpark being ready for the opening of the season, but, "as he himself expressed, Ebbets found he had bit off more than he could chew." The *Eagle* applauded his and the McKeevers' decision "to take their time and have the park even better than originally planned." It claimed, on the day Ebbets Field opened, that the ballpark was "the handsomest and best-arranged home of the national game in these United States."[15]

Contemporary comments on Ebbets Field at the time of its opening in 1913 convey a sense of what was then found noteworthy about the park. First was its enhanced safety and security. The *Eagle* noted that Ebbets had hired "members of a newly-organized special police force," known as "The Doughertys," who "will be on the job throughout every minute of play to suppress disorder by ejecting the perpetrator." Each member of "The Doughertys," the *Eagle* added, "formerly was in the military service and is more than six feet tall." The presence of "The Doughertys" was a reminder of the crowd problems accompanying the 1912 Washington Park opener and a signal of Ebbets's interest in attracting "respectable people" to baseball games. "Of course it's one thing to have a fine ball club and win a pennant," *The Sporting News* quoted Ebbets as saying after revealing his plans for "the new plant for the Brooklyn fans" in 1912, "but to my mind there is something more important. . . . I believe that the fan should be taken care of." He then particularized: "A club should provide a safe home for its patrons. This home should be in a location that is healthy, it should be safe and it should be convenient. The safety of the public should be looked after, and risk of accident or loss of life should be eliminated."[16]

Ebbets's references to a "healthy" location, to the convenience of the site, and especially to the "safety of the public" suggest that he was making a conscious effort to enhance the image of baseball by assuring prospective fans that no longer would a journey to the ballpark be an assault on their senses or a dangerous experience. He constructed a massive rotunda inside the main entrance with the ticket booths, with a floor of Italian marble and a large chandelier hanging from the ceiling, comparable to the main lobbies of operas or theaters. He painted the brick wall encircling the outfield dark green and planted ivy seeds at its base. He introduced seats with curved backs and one armrest, designed to resemble those at opera houses and to provide more comfort than the narrow, straight-backed seats common to grandstand sections of early twentieth-century ballparks. He provided women's "comfort rooms," coat-checking rooms, and a small parking lot for carriages or automobiles, complete with valet service.[17]

Contemporaries reacted to these features of Ebbets Field and associated the aesthetic features of the ballpark with the fostering of civic pride. The *New York Times* sent a reporter to cover an exhibition game between the Highlanders and the Superbas on April 6, 1913, two days before Ebbets Field's official opening. The reporter mentioned the marbled rotunda, describing it as "similar to a theatre lobby only very much larger." He also alluded to the parking lot, checkrooms, and women's bathrooms. He then turned to the atmosphere of the park itself:

> The inside of the park was a picture. The grandstand of steel and concrete loomed high in the air, holding its admiring thousands. The upper and lower tiers of boxes held the galaxy of Brooklyn's youth and beauty embellished by a glorious display of Spring finery and gaudy color. The girls of Brooklyn never turned out to a ball game like this before, and it's too bad they never did, because from now on they will always be considered a big feature of a ball game at the new park.[18]

After his first impressions—those of the size and scope of the steel and concrete grandstand—the reporter began to focus on the fact that among the spectators in the crowd were a number of finely dressed young women. This struck him as a novel feature of ball games in Brooklyn, and one likely to be common in the new Brooklyn ballpark. It was as if by constructing a baseball field that resembled a theater or an opera house, Ebbets and the McKeevers had transformed the audience for Brooklyn baseball games into one more resembling the audiences for those events. The "galaxy of Brooklyn's youth and beauty" now frequented the boxes of Ebbets Field.

The *Eagle*, two days later, took the impressions of Ebbets Field a step further. Not only had the new ballpark upgraded the audience for baseball, it had enhanced the image of Brooklyn itself. "Ebbets Field offers unusual opportunities for an extensive view of the borough and its suburbs," the *Eagle* suggested, in an article entitled "Ebbets Builded Better Than He Knew In Giving Ebbets Field To Brooklyn." Whether a fan came to the site of the ballpark from Manhattan or elsewhere, the *Eagle*'s correspondent pointed out, the trolley car lines took him "along the outer edge of one of the most beautiful enclosures in the country—Prospect Park." Once he was seated in the grandstands, "the eye is attracted by the surrounding country, a better view of which could not be obtained from any other spot." Beyond the centerfield fence was a "rolling stretch of hills known as Crown Heights"; close to the ballpark lay Eastern Parkway, "a boulevard famed for its unequalled roadbed and unexcelled scenery." To the right and in the rear of the field was the Flatbush section, "with its thousands of pretty homes and its network of immaculate streets, set off in bold relief against the verdant clusters of trees and foliage." In sum, the *Eagle* concluded, "[a]s a booster for Brooklyn Mr. Ebbets has worked better than he knew in giving to the borough so handsome a baseball park."[19]

Contemporary commentary on the opening of Ebbets Field furnishes an impression of the symbolic meaning of the early concrete and steel ballparks. They were perceived by those who first encountered them as more than improvements over the small, crowded firetraps that had preceded them. They were seen as signals that the game of major league baseball had evolved from its amateurish beginnings to become a sport that could serve as the basis for civic identification and pride. The new ballparks were more than technological achievements; they were architectural landmarks in a growing urban landscape. Their steel and concrete character suggested that they were intended to be permanent features of city life in twentieth-century America.

The remarkable transformation of the ballpark from a temporary, cramped, wooden structure to the new "permanent," relatively commodious steel and concrete structures built between 1908 and 1915 did much to cement baseball's image as an enduring, "national" game. Only two of the original concrete and steel structures, Fenway Park in Boston and Navin Field (now Tiger Stadium) in Detroit, now remain primarily in their original state, but as late as 1947 just two of the original structures, Baker Bowl in Philadelphia (which had been built in the nineteenth century and was only partially of steel construction), and League Park in Cleveland, completely supplanted by Municipal Stadium in that year, were no longer in use. From World War I to 1947 Shibe Park in Philadelphia, Forbes Field in Pittsburgh, Crosley Field in Cincinnati, Wrigley Field and Comiskey Park in Chicago, League Park (later Griffith Stadium) in Washington, League Park in Cleveland, and Sportsman's Park in St. Louis joined the Polo Grounds, Ebbets Field, and after 1923 Yankee Stadium in hosting major league baseball. This meant that three generations of Americans, in several cities, had the opportunity to watch baseball games in the same park.

The sense of continuity, even timelessness, created by the presence of a "permanent" ballpark located in the same city for at least a forty-year period cannot be underestimated. Part of the hold major league baseball has had on Americans seems traceable to the fact that for many years, in many cities, going to a ball game in a particular park, in a particular location, with a distinctive ambience, was an experience that crossed generational lines. But one cannot assume, as one might be tempted to do, that in their years of "permanence" the steel and concrete ballparks were islands out of time, immune from change, or that the game played in them was likewise a timeless, universal spectacle. Indeed one of the more fascinating dimensions of the history of the early "permanent" ballparks involves the subtle ways in which the ballparks changed alongside changes in the game, in ballpark construction, and in the culture of American cities.

◆

When John Brush and Charles Ebbets decided to build, or rebuild, ballparks in the years just before World War I, they did so for at least two common reasons that can be discerned. First, they found the existing structure that housed their ballclub "inadequate." In Brush's case inadequacy was dramatically obvious: regardless of the Polo Grounds's impressive size and aesthetically attractive location, it was susceptible to fire. In Ebbets's case inadequacy was communicated more subtly, in a combination of locational, size, and risk factors, symbolized by the near-riot at Washington Park in April 1912. But inadequacy also presupposed that Brush and Ebbets had a clear sense of what was adequate. We can assume that they did, based on what was going on in other major league baseball cities with respect to ballpark construction at the time.

In April 1909 Shibe Park in Philadelphia opened, the first of the steel and concrete ballparks. Ben Shibe, its owner, had followed a pattern similar to Ebbets in acquiring land for a square block in an undeveloped section of the city north of the Pennsylvania railroad tracks, using his general contractor, Joseph Steele, as a front for a series of transactions with individual landowners. The site was near a hospital for contagious diseases, filled with smallpox victims, which helped lower the price of the land. Through connections Shibe learned that the hospital, owned and operated by the city, was going to be closed and dismantled; closing took place three months after the first game in Shibe Park.

Shibe had been involved with baseball since 1900, when he and Connie Mack invested in the Philadelphia Athletics, a new franchise in the emerging American League. Eight years later Shibe was the majority owner of the Athletics, and had become a wealthy man from his sporting goods business, which, under the name of A. J. Reach & Co., had the exclusive rights to furnish baseballs to the American League. He was also aware of Joseph Steele's expertise in constructing steel and concrete buildings, many of which he had erected for manufacturers in the Philadelphia area in the first years of the twentieth century. Moreover, Shibe was experiencing problems with the Athletics' existing park, Columbia Park, similar to those Ebbets had experienced with Washington Park. Columbia Park was not fireproof and could hold only 28,000 persons if the crowd was allowed to reach overflow proportions; it appeared that baseball was getting too popular for such facilities.[20]

Shibe thus knew, by at least 1907, that Columbia Park was "inadequate." But he also had a vision of what was "adequate": a large, double-decked, concrete and steel ballpark, built on a site that could be acquired cheaply, at a location convenient to trolley car lines, that would serve as a monument to its owner and a symbol of the upgrading of the city in which it was located. In one form or another, Shibe's vision became that of all the men who built ballparks in the years between 1908 and 1915. All of them wanted to build concrete and steel structures or rebuild wooden structures using new construction techniques. Nearly all of them double-decked, or even tripled-decked, their stadiums. All of them built new ballparks in locations convenient to subway or trolley lines. All of them designed the appearance of their parks as Brush and Ebbets had designed the new Polo Grounds and Ebbets Field: to look like "palaces." For some owners this meant the creation of ornate structures with decorative friezes and imposing lobbies, often sporting neoclassical motifs; for others it meant less elaborately decorated, but nonetheless imposing, "plants." Finally, all of them thought of their ballparks as architectural symbols of the commercial and cultural vitality of urban twentieth-century America.[21]

In addition to having an expansive vision of what an "adequate" ballpark entailed, Brush, Ebbets, Shibe, and the other owners of new twentieth-century ballparks had a second common reason for deciding to build. They believed that a major league baseball club had the prospect of evolving from a kind of luxury item, comparable to the polo ponies and yachts of gentlemen "sportsmen," to a solid business enterprise that would earn a profit. A characteristic of the generation of owners that built or rebuilt early twentieth-century ballparks—James

Gaffney (Braves Field) and John Taylor (Fenway Park) in Boston, Barney Dreyfuss (Forbes Field) in Pittsburgh, Jimmy Manning and Frederick Postal (League Park, later Griffith Stadium) in Washington, Julius and Max Fleischmann (Redland Field, later Crosley Field) in Cincinnati, Frank Navin (Navin Field, later Briggs Stadium, finally Tiger Stadium) in Detroit, Ernest Barnard (League Park) in Cleveland, Charles Comiskey (White Sox Park, later Comiskey Park) and Charles Weeghman (Weeghman Park, later Wrigley Field) in Chicago, and Robert Lee Hedges (Sportsman's Park) in St. Louis, in addition to Brush, Ebbets, and Shibe—was that none was a member of an established late nineteenth-century upper-class family.[22] They were former ballplayers, brewery owners, liquor manufacturers, former bookkeepers, contractors, urban real estate speculators, and entrepreneurs in the sporting goods industry. They were not interested in owning a baseball club in order to demonstrate that they were members of the idle rich. On the contrary, they were interested in owning a baseball club in order that they might someday become members of the idle rich, and social lions in the process.

The construction of new ballparks thus symbolized that major league baseball had come to be regarded as a potentially lucrative business, as distinguished from a diversion from the business world. And yet the central attractions of baseball as a spectator sport, the generation of new owners realized, lay in the fact that it *was* a diversion from the business world, a game echoing the associations of childhood play and leisured, sporting pursuits. Paradoxically, the more baseball was thought of as a pastime, a retreat from urban life as much as a confirmation of its vitality, a vicarious experience as much as an observational experience for the "cranks" and "bugs" (later "fans") who attended games, the more it appeared to become a spectacle that was socially desirable, as well as emotionally uplifting, to attend. From its earliest modern decades, baseball was thought of as a business, a form of entertainment for profit, but implicitly presented as a much more engaging spectacle than a circus or an opera or a play. It conjured up idyllic rural and pastoral associations, although staged in an urban setting.

Brush, Ebbets, and Shibe probably did not consider the extended cultural meanings of major league baseball when they decided to build new concrete and steel ballparks. Their first concern, once having acquired the land for a site and resolved to proceed, was very probably with techniques of construction. In venturing into ballpark construction they were functioning as technological and architectural pioneers.

The inadequacy of the older ballparks, to their owners, had rested principally on two factors: their wooden composition, which made them susceptible to fire and decay, and the fact that their seating capacity had not kept pace with the growth of urban populations and the related growth of interest in major league baseball as a spectator sport. Two technological developments in place in the first decade of the twentieth century made a dramatic response to these problems possible. One was the capacity to build upper decks to grandstands; the second was the capacity to replace wooden structures with steel and concrete structures that served the same function. Both developments emanated from the same engineering and architectural innovation, the "ferro-concrete" building process.

Even though the process of converting iron to steel had been available in America well before the first decades of the twentieth century, and steel had a number of properties that seemed ideal for ballparks—it could be shaped to fit the intricate patterns of intersecting materials required by ballpark design, it was strong enough to bear enormous weight, and it lasted longer and was more fire-resistant than wood—no steel-based, stone-covered ballparks were built in the late nineteenth century, although steel and stone houses and buildings began to appear in cities in that period. The reason was simple enough: steel-based, stone-covered ballparks were too expensive because of the massive amounts of steel they required and the fact that the stone facings, to be regarded as attractive, had to be cut and carved.

By the early twentieth century, however, contractors such as Joseph Steele had begun to perfect the "ferro-concrete" process of building large structures. The process required no new materials, only an ingenious combination of existing ones. It consisted of framing the weight-bearing portions of a structure in wood, pouring concrete into the frame, and then inserting steel rods in the concrete while it was still soft. The wooden frames kept the concrete from spreading; the steel rods prevented the concrete from cracking and added strength of their own; and the concrete encased the steel rods and prevented them from exposure to fire or other elements. Once the concrete had hardened, it could only be blasted apart. Wood could also be attached to the con-

Shibe Park in Philadelphia, the first steel and concrete ballpark, in 1913. The steel posts were necessary to support the upperdeck, but they significantly obstructed views. Notice the policeman stationed along the field and the mixture of hats and caps worn by spectators. (National Baseball Library and Archive, Cooperstown, N.Y.)

crete in places (such as seats) where its comparative softness and flexibility made it superior to the other materials. In some areas, eventually, a version of steel ("structural" steel) was used without being mixed with concrete. Structural steel was more fireproof and stronger than wood and over time became less expensive to use. It could not be carved on, and was not regarded as attractive in the early twentieth century, so it was reserved for those areas (such as supports under stands) that were not in the line of sight of most spectators.[23]

Ferro-concrete and the expanded use of steel solved the problems of fire and decay, making the conception of a ballpark as a "permanent" structure feasible. They also helped solve the problem of seating capacity. In dealing with that problem, however, early twentieth-century owners had faced some complexities engendered by the fact that a baseball "plant" was not just a large arena; it was a structure designed to offer spectators the distinctive experience of watching baseball games. Where one sat when watching a baseball game mattered in a way that seating did not matter, or mattered less, when one watched a track meet or a boxing match. Those sports lent themselves to circular or spheroid seating around an oval or square. If the seating was angled, spectators traded off closeness against an improving angle of vision; where one sat around the oval or square arguably made little difference. The earlier descriptions of Hilltop Park and Washington Park make it clear, however, that the proprietors, players, and fans of early baseball recognized that baseball was a different spectator sport. It was played on a large circular or oval-sized field, but most of the action took place in one area of that field, the infield.

Thus most everyone associated with major league baseball in the era of the wooden ballparks knew that some seats were more desirable than others at a baseball game. The early parks, including the Polo Grounds, typically did not offer extensive seating anywhere but in the semicircular grandstand. Adding seats in the outfield was regarded as perhaps a necessary concession to spectator demand, but they were priced lower and were typically not roofed. Almost no early ballparks had seats in fair territory in the outfield. Thus when population growth and an expanding economy contributed to increased spectator demand in the early twentieth century, the owners of Hilltop Park and Washington Park, as well as owners in other cities, responded by allowing standing room along foul lines and in the outfield.

There was another response, that of the owners of the Polo Grounds. Most early wooden ballparks had single-decked grandstands with roofs; the Polo Grounds grandstand was double-decked. Wood pillars could be fashioned that were strong enough to support wooden decks filled with people, so long as a sufficient number of pillars were used. Upper decks could be set back from lower decks so that not all the spectators in the lower deck had their aerial views restricted by the upper deck. Double decking could thus increase capacity without requiring spectators to sit outside the infield-oriented grandstand. Double decking, however, was rare in the era of the wooden ballparks. In the age of the first steel and concrete ballparks it became the norm, and triple decking eventually followed.

One may wonder why there was not more double decking in the

wooden ballpark era. The answers this time are not so straightforward. Wood is not as strong as steel and obviously less resistant to decay, so an investment in wooden pillars meant an ongoing investment in maintenance. The owners of the Polo Grounds, however, were prepared to make that investment in order to service the crowds they anticipated. They were perhaps unusual in anticipating crowds of that size. Hilltop Park was built after the old Polo Grounds, yet its owners, bringing a new franchise in a new league into the New York area, did not double-deck their grandstand. It seems likely, in fact, that the owners of Hilltop Park were more conventional in their expectations about spectator demand. None of the wooden parks of the early twentieth century had a seating capacity of greater than 20,000 except for the Polo Grounds.[24]

When the concrete and steel ballparks were built, however, all except the two constructed in Boston were double-decked, and one, Forbes Field in Pittsburgh, which opened in 1909, was triple-decked in a limited portion of the grandstand. Contemporaries regarded the fact that Fenway Park and Braves Field were not double-decked as sufficiently unusual to comment upon.[25] It thus appears that Ben Shibe and Joseph Steele—who double-decked the grandstand at Shibe Park, provided seats for a total of 23,000 persons, and made room for an additional 7,000 standees—were trendsetters.[26] And it further appears that the Shibe-Steele partnership assumed that ferro-concrete stands, supported by structural steel and ferro-concrete pillars, were significantly stronger than wooden stands supported by wooden pillars. Not only would they not burn, they would not collapse.

The shells of the new concrete and steel ballparks, then, were remarkably similar to those of the old wooden ballparks, with the important exception of double decking. Outside the grandstand area the new ballparks tended to have more seats than the older ones, but not significantly more. Of the ballparks built or refurbished between 1909 and 1915, only the Polo Grounds, Shibe Park, and Braves Field anticipated a capacity of more than 30,000, and that was, in the last two instances, through overflow, on-the-field arrangements comparable to those in Hilltop or Washington Parks.[27] None of the new ballparks provided extensive seating behind the outfielders in fair territory, and many ran their outfield fences very close to the property line of the site, a practice that indicated that the owners had not even anticipated expanding seating capacity through outfield seats in fair territory.

An aerial view of Shibe Park around World War I. Notice the elaborate domed central entrance, the lack of automobile parking, the proximity of trolley car lines to the park, and the fact that the ballpark was wedged within adjacent residential areas in the city. (National Baseball Library and Archive, Cooperstown, N.Y.)

Here was another example where construction practices, assumptions about spectator preference, and the style of play in major league baseball in the early twentieth century complemented one another. "Deadball baseball" was a game of subtleties, such as stolen bases, doctored pitches, bunts, and angled chop hits, all of which could be more easily observed from the grandstand. Thus it was not at all implausible, as curious at it may seem to the modern observer, for ballpark owners and designers to build elaborate, ornate grandstands and at the same time allow their outfields to end at fences bordering on urban streets or houses. Such was the configuration in Shibe Park, Ebbets Field, Redland Field, and many other of the steel and concrete structures. That configuration was no more remarkable, or short-sighted, than the absence of significant parking lots at any of the early twentieth-century steel and concrete ballparks. Although the ballparks were designed to be permanent, they were not built for a future that could not be fully imagined.

◆

The construction of an early twentieth-century steel and concrete ballpark also involved a construction of the ambience within that structure. Here again one makes a mistake if one too readily accepts the view that baseball has been a changeless sport, capable of eluding time. To get a sense of the ambience of a ball game in one of the early "permanent" ballparks, one needs to reconstruct what it would have been like actually to attend one. Fortunately, such a reconstruction is not particularly difficult.[28]

On Saturday, August 15, 1914, the New York Giants played the Boston Braves in the third game of an important series. The Braves were to become the "Miracle Braves" later that season, when they completed a journey from last place in the National League on July 15 to first place on September 8, and then hung on to win the pennant over the Giants, who had won the National League championship the previous three years. On the morning of August 15, however, they were four and a half games behind the Giants in second place, in the midst of a second-half streak in which they were to win fifty-one of sixty-seven games. The Giants had disposed of August challengers in the 1912 season and had overwhelmed their competition in 1913; New York sportswriters expected them to respond in similar fashion to the Braves.[29]

Most fans attending the game arrived on foot or on the Sixth Avenue Elevated line, which stopped at 155th Street, adjacent to the Polo Grounds. Even though it was a Saturday, the game started at 3:30 P.M., Saturdays still being working days for many prospective baseball fans. On arriving at the 155th street station, fans would immediately become aware of the Polo Grounds, looming up to the north. On their way down ramps to the stadium, the fans would have quickly recognized that the crowd that day was going to be large. A number of seats in the grandstand and the bleachers had been put on sale on the day of the game, and long lines of people waited for the chance to buy tickets. Thirty-three thousand people attended the game, the largest crowd in major league baseball that year.

Once inside the turnstiles, many fans purchased scorecards for five cents. Those scorecards were the only way fans could identify the players on either team. There were no numbers on the players' uniforms, and there was no public address system announcing the names of the starters, new players coming into the game, or players coming to bat. Instead there was a rudimentary scoreboard, hanging on a section of the grandstand (and thus not visible to everyone in the park), which listed "New York" and "Visitors," with nine rectangular spaces in a vertical line below those categories, anticipating numbers for a nine-man lineup. The scoreboard also had a horizontal series of squares, prefaced by "Visitors" and "New York" and divided into nine innings, each identified by numbers above the square spaces. After the number "9" were six more squares arranged in two vertical groups of three, designated "Runs," "Hits," and "Errors" and following the same horizontal line as "Visitors" and "New York."

The paper scorecards contained a list of the last names and positions of players on each team, except when two players had the same last name and therefore were also given first initials. The scorecard numbers assigned to the players were based on a player's place in the batting order for the game, with pitchers and substitute players receiving numbers higher than nine. The scoreboard numbers corresponded to numbers eventually posted on the scoreboard.

Batting practice thus would not enable fans to learn the identity of the players on either team, since the scoreboard numbers had not yet been posted. In some respects pregame batting and fielding drills resembled those rituals before a major league game today. There were, however, no portable screens protecting the pitchers throwing batting practice or the infielders fielding balls. In fact batting practice and infield or outfield workouts did not take place simultaneously, although infielders and outfielders assumed fielding positions during batting practice, retrieved balls, and threw other balls back and forth among themselves. When batting practice stopped, infield and outfield practice began.

The Braves' uniforms were a dull gray, plain without any piping, with high collars that the players buttoned up, even though the uniforms were flannel and the day was reported to be hot. Teams of the day did not carry multiple sets of uniforms, and when doubleheaders

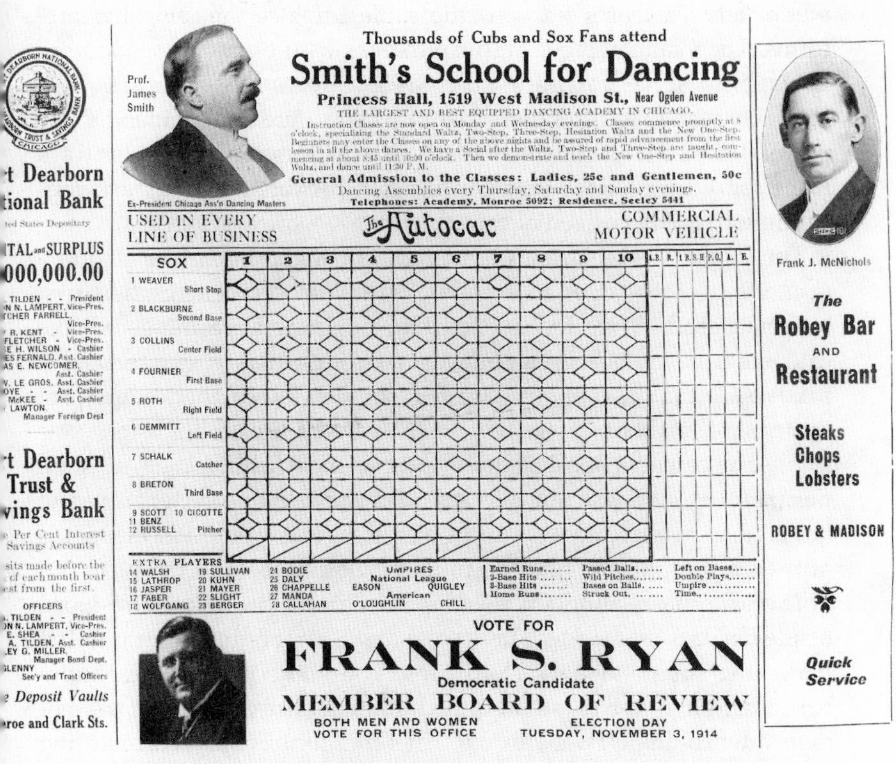

A scorecard for a 1914 Chicago White Sox game. The numbers assigned to players matched their positions in the batting order. Nonstarting players were given higher numbers than pitchers. The scorecards changed every day and were dotted with advertisements. (National Baseball Library and Archive, Cooperstown, N.Y.)

were played the players did not change between games. The teams' caps had no prominent bills or shape, resembling the cloth caps of early twentieth-century laborers. The uniforms had three-quarter-length sleeves and were made of durable flannel. The pants, which the players rolled high up on their calves in the fashion of knickers, were secured with wide belts. The Braves wore blue-gray caps, without any insignia, and dark blue socks.

The Giants' uniforms were a contrast to those of the Braves, white with thin violet stripes, violet piping up the sides of the pants, and a violet "NY" on the caps. The violet was a color introduced by Giant manager John McGraw out of affection for New York University, whose athletic teams featured the same color scheme on their uniforms. The Giants wore dark purple socks with two wide white horizontal stripes. Neither team wore white cotton socks under their colored socks, so that on a hot day wool socks would be worn next to the players' skin. The baseball shoes of both teams resembled older track shoes, slim in the heel, better structured for forward and backward running than for horizontal movement.

The players' baseball gloves had only a slight amount of padding and were barely larger than today's durable work gloves. The first basemen used gloves that looked like small catcher's mitts, and the catchers used mitts with significant padding at the circumference, a small pocket in the center, and little flexibility. The catchers wore chest protectors, smaller and less flexible than the current major league versions. The catchers' masks barely covered their faces, lacked substantial padding, and did not overlap with the chest protectors, leaving large areas of the catchers' necks and throats exposed. Catchers did not wear shin guards, and the umpire standing behind the plate did not wear a mask, although he wore a catcher's chest protector worn inside his dark suit jacket. There were only two umpires, both wearing dark blue suits and dark cloth caps. The home plate umpire, who called balls and strikes, stood quite far behind the catcher and did not crouch when a pitch was thrown. The other umpire stood behind first base when no offensive players were on the basepaths, and then moved behind second base to follow the action on the basepaths. He was also responsible for calling plays in the outfield, although the home plate umpire was responsible for calling the foul lines.

About ten minutes before 3:30 P.M. a man with a megaphone strode to the area of home plate and announced the starting lineups for each team. The announcer gave only the last names of the players who were starting, noting their positions in the batting order and their fielding positions. "For Boston, Devore, right field; Evers, second base; Connolly, left field; Maranville, shortstop; Schmidt, first base; Smith, third base; Mann, center field; Gowdy, catching; Tyler, pitching. For New York, Bescher, center field; Doyle, second base; Burns, left field; Snodgrass, right field; Merkle, first base; McLean, catcher; Stock, third base; Mathewson, pitcher." The announcer then walked down the third base line and repeated the lineups, subsequently repeating them again from a position on the first base line. As the players were being announced, an invisible presence behind the scoreboard placed a number in the batting order of "Visitors" and "New York." Those numbers were keyed to the numbers on the paper scoreboards. Now the fans were able to discern the identities of the starting players for both teams.

The game began, proceeding at a very brisk pace. Several features of the game contributed to the speed with which it progressed. The pitchers were rarely visited at the mound by their teammates or by the managers. George Stallings, the manager of the Braves, made a practice of not appearing on the field at all (he did not wear a baseball uniform), and John McGraw of the Giants coached third base when his team batted, wearing a fielder's glove and yelling encouragement at his players.

The pace was also affected by the short time pitchers took between pitches. Pitchers seldom shook off catchers' signs, and did not, as a rule, go through elaborate warm-up rituals before delivering the ball (nor did batters in the batter's box step out between pitches to indulge in similar rituals). Control among pitchers was prized: in this game, which went ten innings, there was a total of two walks and one wild pitch.

Another element contributing to the speed of the game was the ritualistic practice of having the next batter bunt when a man reached first base with less than two out. In the game the teams combined for three successful sacrifice bunts, and four more unsuccessful attempts that produced force-outs. Although both teams expected the opponent to bunt in certain situations, and defended against it, a batter had the option of faking a sacrifice bunt and slapping the ball past a charging infielder. Given this possibility, fielders could not play too close to the plate even when pitchers batted (early twentieth-century pitchers were often skilled hitters), so the sacrifice remained a viable strategic option. It also sped up the game by producing, in most cases, an automatic out for the team at bat.

An additional factor contributed to the briskness of the pace. In the deadball era hitters worked at perfecting the art of slapping the ball, directing it on the ground and in all directions. Fielders wore small gloves with comparatively little webbing, making the snagging of ground balls and line drives more difficult than in today's game. Thus if batters hit the ball on the ground, spread their hits to all fields, and ran hard, they forced the fielders to secure ground balls and throw them out. Major league baseball, in 1914, was still a game in which balls were not replaced very often and could be discolored or scuffed by the pitchers at will. This meant that there was a reduced incentive for batters to try to hit the ball long distances. A ball will not carry very far after it has been spat upon, scuffed, rolled in the dirt, and hit a good many times, and uppercut swings were more likely to produce fly balls and pop-ups than grounders.

The deadness of the ball, especially as the game progressed, affected the offensive and defensive strategies of the game, and these too had an impact on the game's pace. Pitchers were able to keep their opponents from scoring many runs, which meant they could remain in the game longer. Fewer pitching changes meant less time spent in that process and fewer visits to the mound by managers or players. The dominance of pitchers also meant that scoring runs was very important, which helped to make sacrifice bunts so commonplace. This was even more significant because the deadball era's emphasis on hitting balls sharply on the ground made double plays more likely. Sacrifice bunts thus were valuable not only for advancing a runner but for keeping an inning alive. Further, the batting styles of the deadball era, oriented toward producing line drives rather than high fly balls, also helped to speed up games, because an inside-the-park home run takes less time than one hit into the stands. The latter home run, uncommon in the large ballparks of the era, produces a slow trot around the basepaths and the necessity of replacing the baseball; in the case of the former the batter and fielders are moving as quickly as they possibly can.

Of the nine games played in the major leagues on this particular Saturday, the longest took two hours and fifteen minutes, the shortest went one hour and forty-three minutes, and only three of the games were over two hours. The Braves-Giants game, which lasted ten innings, took one hour and fifty-two minutes.

That game amounted to a minor classic of the deadball era. For eight innings neither team seriously threatened to score. In the last of the seventh inning an incident occurred that serves to mark a contrast between baseball's past and present. With one out and George Burns on first base for the Giants, Fred Snodgrass hit a hard line drive down the third base line. The Braves' third baseman, Red Smith, leaped in the air and made a backhanded catch, landed on his feet, and whipped a throw to first to double up Burns. A huge roar of approval burst forth from the crowd, with some spectators rising from their seats, even though the play had ended the inning and prevented the Giants from mounting a serious scoring threat. It was as if the New York partisan crowd believed that accomplished play transcended partisanship. It seems unlikely that a home crowd in the 1990s, watching a tense game between its team and the chief contender in a close pennant race, would be inclined to cheer a visiting player who performed the same feat.

The game remained scoreless through the Braves' half of the ninth inning. In the bottom of the ninth, with the score still 0–0 and Lefty Tyler and Christy Mathewson still the pitchers, the Giants appeared poised to win. After one out, Mathewson batted for himself (another contrast to today's game) and worked Tyler for a walk after fouling off two pitches. Tyler next gave up a single to Bob Bescher, sending Mathewson to second. Larry Doyle then grounded to the left of Boston second baseman Johnny Evers, whose only play was to first, sending Mathewson to third and Bescher to second with two out. Tyler then pitched carefully to George Burns, eventually walking him. This brought up Fred Snodgrass, and the crowd noisily rose to its feet in anticipation. But Snodgrass grounded routinely to shortstop Rabbit Maranville, who threw to Evers to force Burns at second for the final out.

In the tenth the Braves struck. With one out, Smith singled between short and third, bringing up catcher Hank Gowdy. Gowdy had hit Mathewson well that day, with two previous hits, including a triple that came with two out and no one on in the fourth. On Mathewson's second pitch Gowdy lined a drive into left center, and Bescher was unable to cut it off. He chased it down in the vast outfield of the Polo Grounds, but by the time he had thrown it back to the infield Smith had scored the first run of the game and Gowdy was on third base.

Mathewson's first pitch to Tyler sailed over the catcher's head and Gowdy scored. Mathewson recovered to strike out Tyler and get Josh Devore to ground out, but Boston had taken the lead and now threatened to sweep the series.

Having gone ahead, the Braves displayed some nerves. Art Fletcher led off for the Giants in the bottom of the tenth and hit a routine grounder in the direction of Maranville, but Smith cut in front, lunged for the ball, and dropped it, putting Fletcher on first. Fred Merkle was the next batter, and he singled to right, sending Fletcher to third.

This brought up John ("Chief") Meyers, who had replaced Larry

McLean as the Giants' catcher. The second pitch from Tyler plunked Meyers in the ribs, loading the bases for the Giants with none out. McGraw sent in a pinch runner for Meyers, reserve outfielder Dave Robertson, whose presence was announced to the spectators.

Unfortunately for the Giants, the tail end of their batting order was coming up. The eighth-place hitter, third baseman Milton Stock, popped up to Smith at third base. Mathewson was next, and the Giants pinch-hit for him, sending up John ("Red") Murray, a reserve outfielder. Murray struck out, taking a called third strike. This left leadoff batter Bob Bescher as the Giants' last hope, and Tyler got him to hit a slow ground ball to Evers, who threw him out at first to end the game. The outcome brought the Braves within three and a half games of the Giants and served notice that Boston was truly a pennant contender.

On reflection, the ambience of the game played between the Braves and Giants on August 15, 1914, was inseparable from the ambience of the ballpark in which it was played. The new Polo Grounds was intended to be a "palace," a monument to civic pride, but it was also a ball field that was configured to baseball as played in the deadball era, and whose configuration reinforced that style of play. The horseshoe shape of the Polo Grounds made grandstand viewing attractive, since the shortness of the foul lines allowed more people to sit close to most of the action. At the same time it produced a huge, vast outfield, meaning that fielders had to cover more space and triples of the sort that Gowdy hit would be more common. Home runs in the stands were obviously no part of the design. The foul line distances were absurdly short by modern standards, and most of the outfield distances absurdly long. But they were unremarkable for a time in which few fair balls were hit into the stands at all.

In some ways the Polo Grounds in 1914 was reminiscent of a vast city park, such as Hyde Park in London, Golden Gate Park in San Francisco, or Stanley Park in Vancouver, where sports contests were played in a limited but at the same time open space, and people gathered to watch them as part of a summer outing. But in other ways the Polo Grounds was more like a modern baseball stadium. Its spatial effect was vastness, but enclosed vastness: a huge, flowing outfield eventually confined; a massive, ornate grandstand looming around part of a grassy oval.

The ambience inside the Polo Grounds complemented the architectural effect it created. It appeared on the upper Manhattan landscape as a huge amphitheater; a building among bluffs, a river, and meadows; the terminus of an elevated train network; a symbol of the growth and presence of a city in the countryside. It served to extend the skyline of New York, even though it was nestled in bluffs. Its capacity to draw comparatively huge crowds of people to upper Manhattan on a Saturday afternoon in August reinforced the unmistakable fact that the ecology of Manhattan Island had been transformed by the existence of the people, trains, noise, and congestion, the sights and sounds of a growing early twentieth-century New York City. The Polo Grounds appears, from this perspective, as a civic landmark, like the structures built in connection with the Chicago Exposition of 1893.

But the Polo Grounds, at this point in its history, does not appear as a completely "urban" structure. It also appears as a kind of modified "grounds": a place where people watched sporting games in a picnic-like atmosphere. It did not house sculpture or inventions or paintings or the projected technological achievements of the immediate future: it housed athletes playing baseball. It was so obviously massive, so resolutely free from the dangers of disintegration or eradication, that it surely seemed a "permanent" fixture of New York. But it did not symbolize the dark, cloistered, dangerous, industrial features of early twentieth-century life; it symbolized the bright, expansive, reassuring, open-air features of that world.

◆

The Polo Grounds of 1914 remained essentially unchanged for the next several years, even though major league baseball itself was to go through significant changes, which included the collapse of a fledgling third major league, the Federal League; the "Black Sox" gambling scandal of 1919–20; the outlawing of the spitball and other "doctored" pitches; the legalizing of Sunday baseball in New York; and the emergence of Babe Ruth and the in-the-stands home run as defining elements of the game. Ruth became a national celebrity, in fact, with the Polo Grounds as his home field: the Highlanders left Hilltop Park, became the Giants' tenants, changed their name to the Yankees, and acquired Ruth from the Boston Red Sox after the 1919 season. The sensation created by Ruth and his home-run-hitting ability, plus the advent of Sunday baseball after 1919, created pressure on even the comparatively large seating capacity of the Polo Grounds. Both the Yankees' and Giants' owners responded to that pressure in revealing ways.

In 1915 Tillinghast Huston and Jacob Ruppert, after purchasing the

Yankees from Farrell and Devery, announced that they were going to build a new ballpark for the club in Queens.[30] Their choice of location was based on considerations that paralleled those of Ebbets: the borough of Queens was expanding, trolley car and subway lines were in place to connect it to Manhattan, the population of the New York area was growing, and Manhattan Island was consequently becoming less available as a place of residency. Reaction to the announcement, however, was not encouraging. Both *The Sporting News* and New York baseball writers criticized the proposed location on two grounds. First, they expressed concern about the economic feasibility of building an additional "permanent" park in the New York area in the uncertain economic times produced by World War I and the emergence of the Federal League. Second, they argued that in locating a ballpark other than in Manhattan the Yankees would be disengaging themselves from New York and would lose their civic identity. The Bronx and Queens, according to this argument, were, like Brooklyn, separate cities from New York: tourists and area fans would no longer associate the Yankees with that metropolis. The civic pride taken by Brooklyn residents in the building of Ebbets Field served to reinforce this argument.[31]

The arguments prevailed: Huston and Ruppert remained tenants of John Brush and the Giants. But as World War I ended, the Federal League collapsed, and the American economy showed signs of returning to its prewar vigor, the Yankees' owners again began to consider building their own park. Their eventual decision to do so was made easier by the owners of the Giants.

By the end of the 1920 season, Sunday baseball, the spectacular presence of Ruth (who hit fifty-four home runs that year), and the booming postwar economy combined to make Huston and Ruppert realize they might well have the most valuable franchise in all of baseball. In addition, John Brush, in worsening health, had sold the Giants to Horace Stoneham, who in his first year as an owner relied heavily on McGraw for advice on all aspects of the operation. McGraw resented the Yankees' success and believed that if they were evicted from the Polo Grounds they would lose their identity.[32] By May 1920 Huston and Ruppert knew that they would be evicted from the Polo Grounds after the 1921 season. In an editorial, the *New York Times* questioned the economic sense of the eviction, echoing earlier arguments.[33]

Eventually all the major league owners became involved in the matter, and Stoneham was persuaded to allow the Yankees to remain in the Polo Grounds as tenants through the 1922 season, while they secured a site for and built a new park. Huston and Ruppert began to canvass the New York metropolitan area for sites. They considered, and rejected, several sites in Manhattan and one in Long Island City. At the end of January 1921, they announced that they had retained the Osborn Engineering Company of Cleveland, who had rebuilt the Polo Grounds, and that they would be building a park at 163rd Street and Amsterdam Avenue in Manhattan. A week later, however, they closed on the purchase of a ten-acre lot in the extreme western portion of the borough of the Bronx, just across the Harlem River from the Polo Grounds. Unbeknownst to almost everyone, Huston and Ruppert had acquired an option to purchase the lot a year earlier from the estate of William W. Astor, who had been renting it as a lumberyard. Despite being outside Manhattan, it was by 1920s standards an ideal site, lacking the hard granite bedding of most of upper Manhattan and being convenient to mass transit lines.[34]

As Yankee Stadium took shape, its construction revealed that it was to symbolize the culmination, and at the same time the transformation, of the early twentieth-century "permanent" ballpark. In making construction decisions Huston and Ruppert tried to balance the considerations their predecessor ballpark builders had balanced, and at the same time to add some elements that they thought were new but important.

Like their predecessors, Huston and Ruppert felt that mass transit access to the park was a crucial consideration, as was a location near an expanding or at least promising sector of urban real estate. The west Bronx location suited them perfectly in those respects. Not only was it at an important junction of mass transit lines, it was adjacent to the developing "Grand Concourse" thoroughfare of the Bronx, which was projected as an affluent, sophisticated, beauteous strip, modeled on the broad, fashionable, thronging streets of Europe.

Huston and Ruppert did not choose, however, to locate Yankee Stadium in a neighborhood, in the manner of Ebbets Field, Shibe Park, and many of the other early concrete and steel ballparks. Instead they planned to build a truly massive, monumentlike structure, a stadium rather than a ball field, a place adaptable to other large-crowd events such as boxing matches, football games, and political rallies. To do that they needed more space, and they even delayed beginning construction until securing a special use permit from the New York City zoning board to allow them to encroach upon 158th Street and Cromwell Avenues in the west Bronx.[35] In addition, they borrowed from the techniques of early twentieth-century football stadium construction, exemplified in structures such as the Yale Bowl in New Haven and the University of Pennsylvania's Franklin Field in Philadelphia. Those football stadiums were largely concrete-based amphitheaters, built into hillsides by use of the "cut and fill" technique, in which the playing surface was sunk in a hollow of a hillside and the earth of the hillside used to reinforce support for sloping concrete stands. This eliminated the necessity for a great many steel columns, and provided natural sight lines for spectators.

Baseball, of course, could not easily be adapted to a amphitheater, but it was possible for the builders of Yankee Stadium to use the natural hillsides of the Astor estate site as support for the grandstand portion. After cutting and filling the hillsides to produce a section of an amphitheater, they then mixed crushed stone and poured concrete with the filled earth, producing a version of reinforced "floor slab." Next they sunk steel columns into the slab. The slab itself supported the lower deck of the grandstand; the columns the upper decks. Through this technique Huston, Ruppert, and their architect, Bernard Green of Osborn Engineering, were able to construct a triple-decked facility, with the three decks intended eventually to extend around the entire field.

Moreover, Green and his Osborn colleagues were able to modify the usual double-decking technique, in which the upper deck was set back from the lower deck, supported by pillars, and not significantly sloped. They employed a cantilever technique, borrowed from football, which permitted more sharply sloping second and third decks. Most innovative of all was the creation of a mezzanine deck, partially cantilevered to provide good views, and supported by its own steel horizontal beams, which were attached to the columns that supported the upper deck and its roof. This meant that a great many more spectators were able to be seated where they could watch the action around the infield.

Because of construction costs, the triple decking was instituted on a piecemeal basis, so that initially it extended only around the infield, as in the earlier ballparks. By 1937, however, three decks circled the foul and fair territory in left and right field. At this point it became apparent that any additional triple decking would have a serious effect on the amount of light coming into the park, so the centerfield area was left open.

Massive triple decking of this scale had never before been attempted. The Yankees had chosen to abandon proximity to a local street in order to increase seating capacity, to make a more substantial architectural statement, and to respond to their belief that with Babe Ruth, and his incredible batting prowess, the in-the-stands home run would become an established feature of major league baseball. With Ruth, a left-handed hitter, in mind, Huston and Ruppert made the distance down the right field foul line, and into much of right field proper, comparatively short. They also placed seats in fair territory in the outfield and provided for a low fence. At the same time they designed the left field foul line distance to be quite short, but then had the left field dimensions sharply lengthen, producing very lengthy left center field and center field areas, reminiscent of the Polo Grounds.

The result of these decisions was that in some respects Yankee Stadium was not a particularly spectator-friendly ballpark, at least when compared with many of its predecessors. Many seats were quite far from the batter and the pitcher. Many seats had obstructed views. Moreover, the angles of sunlight created by the towering stands and the late afternoon sunshine produced shadows on the field and glaring sunshine in some portions of the stands. Finally, the Yankees had chosen to protect player privacy as opposed to fan proximity to the athletes: the clubhouse was in center field, as in the Polo Grounds, but passages led from the dugouts to the clubhouse, allowing the players to go to their dressing rooms at the conclusion of the game without having to mingle with spectators on the field.

At the same time the builders of Yankee Stadium added an innovation that arguably revolutionized the participation of baseball fans in major league baseball. In right center field they constructed a huge electric scoreboard, supported by steel girders. On the scoreboard appeared the usual information given in hand-operated scoreboards: the lineups for both teams, along with the players' positions in the field and in the batting order, the inning-by-inning line score of the game, and the cumulative totals of runs, hits, and errors. In addition, however, the Yankee Stadium scoreboard provided a list of all other games in progress in major league baseball that day, complete with inning-by-inning line scores, cumulative runs and hits, and the present pitchers for both teams, their numbers keyed to numbers on the scorecards. The scoreboard was large enough to be seen by every spectator in the park, at least when Yankee Stadium opened, and was operated by electricity, its white numbers flashing out of a black background.

The Yankee Stadium scoreboard was a symbol that the Yankee management wanted spectators to be truly involved in major league baseball. Not only would they be able to know the identities of all the players participating in the game they were watching, but the progress of other games around the leagues. They would be able to see their game in the context of pennant races, the fortunes of other teams, the fortunes of other pitchers. They would not have to strain to hear lineups announced from a megaphone. And, six years later, they would be able to match the numbers on the scoreboard with numbers that were not on their scorecards, but on the backs of players' uniforms. The Yankees would be the first major league team to institute this custom.[36]

Another decision made by Huston and Ruppert reveals how much Yankee Stadium, despite its innovations, was a structure that can be firmly associated with the first twentieth-century "permanent" ballparks. Despite the vast acreage of the site Huston and Ruppert had selected for the ballpark, despite their conscious decision not to place the park in the confines of an urban neighborhood, and despite their obvious desire to see their new structure as a stadium, a massive monument to the future, Huston and Ruppert provided very limited parking for automobiles on the site. They apparently felt that most people who came to Yankee Stadium would come on mass transit or on foot. Even though the automobile had been mass-produced in America for a decade before Yankee Stadium opened, and even though social commentators were beginning to speak of its ubiquity and dominance in American civilization, Huston and Ruppert implicitly decided that there was no compelling need to undertake the additional costs of providing automobile access to, or extensive automobile parking around, their wondrous new structure. In this respect they were at one with John Brush and Charles Ebbets and Ben Shibe and the builders of every other early twentieth-century ballpark. But those people had built or rebuilt between 1908 and 1915; the Yankees had built in the early 1920s.

Yankee Stadium, pictured in 1928, five years after it opened. Notice the triple decks, which extended well into the outfield. The elevated train runs beyond the bleachers, and the automobile parking appears limited, although a few cars are parked on a makeshift lot north of the stadium. The large electric scoreboard is visible at the top row of the bleachers in centerfield. (National Baseball Library and Archive, Cooperstown, N.Y.)

Yankee Stadium can thus serve as an emblem of the transformation of major league baseball from a "deadball" to a "liveball" game, from a game played in parks to a game played in stadiums. But, as with every aspect of baseball in its early and mid-twentieth-century history, the transformation was partial and incomplete. In many respects—acreage, earth and concrete slab foundations, triple-decking, projected capacity, fan information, cost, expected use, expected profit, fan seating—Yankee Stadium was a revolutionary facility, unlike any previous park, self-consciously built on the basis of state-of-the-art construction techniques and designed for the sort of offensive baseball that Babe Ruth personified. But in other important respects—the irregularity of its dimensions, the absence of ample parking, its proximity to mass transit lines, its decorated friezes and lobbies, its obstructed seats, its steel girders, its centerfield clubhouse—Yankee Stadium was no different from Shibe Park.

◆

To say that the first permanent steel and concrete ballparks reflected the way early twentieth-century baseball was played, or early twentieth-century conceptions of urban land use, or even early twentieth-century styles and tastes in architecture and engineering is, at a general level, not to say anything particularly startling. But when one goes beyond the truism that baseball reflects the culture and the time in which it is played to particularize the details of that reflection, one does not always find the obvious.

Why did the first generation of "permanent" ballparks have such vast outfields? Why did they have such comparatively limited seating capacity? Why were most of them packed into relatively dense city lots, making it difficult, in later years, for their owners to expand seats except by moving in outfield fences? Why did the owners of the parks devote so much comparative time and attention to elaborate ornamental decorations of the grandstand portions, and so little time to making the outfield walls decorative? Why, by the time Yankee Stadium was built in 1923, had not a single major league ballpark provided extensive automobile parking?

Why did the owners and builders of the first "permanent" ballparks assume, in positioning the angles of their fields, that all of the games played in their parks would start between 3:00 and 4:30 P.M.? Why did no owner consider installing lights, or playing games at night, even though night baseball had been first tried in 1880 and would have been technologically feasible in any of the first "permanent" ballparks? Why were the Polo Grounds and Yankee Stadium unusual among the early ballparks in providing mainly covered seating around the entire park? Why did the builders of new parks quickly consider providing enhanced comforts for fans, in the form of limited valet parking and spacious rest rooms, but not consider, until much later, installing tunnels so that ballplayers could pass from their dugouts to the clubhouse without treading on the field?

Such questions take us directly to the sensibility of the first generation of twentieth-century baseball owners. They had a fixed conception of the game of baseball, a game in which they did not expect balls to be hit over fences and into outfield stands, in which they did not anticipate regular crowds of over 10,000. They thought of the construction of a new ballpark as a civic exercise, a way of permanently associating a ballclub with a city. They wanted their parks to be in the heart of cities, easy to reach through public transportation, even if this meant locating them on crowded city lots. They wanted their parks to be impressive civic monuments, decorated in the classical motifs of public buildings.

When they noticed that the game had changed, with in-the-stands home runs becoming more prominent, they modified the design of their ballparks to reflect that. But at the same time they still thought of a ballpark as being nestled in a city, not an autonomous sports arena. Yankee Stadium was near elevated tracks and the burgeoning Grand Concourse section of the Bronx; it did not need its own parking facilities. Nor did they take player comforts as seriously as fan comforts. Games started late in the afternoon to accommodate working hours, and the huge decks of Yankee Stadium could hold more spectators. The fact that these accommodations made it harder for players to see the ball in the angles of afternoon sunlight was not deemed important. At the same time night baseball, as we shall see, was not even considered for the major leagues for ten years after Yankee Stadium opened, even though playing games at night would have enabled far more people to attend. The night was an alien time for the game of baseball, early owners believed. That assumption was part of their sensibility.

The builders of the first generation of "permanent" ballparks believed that in constructing their new facilities they were building for eternity, that their structures would be an enduring part of the city in which they were located. Associated with that belief was an inability to conceive that as major league baseball endured, it might fundamentally change. Fifteen years after Shibe Park opened the construction of Yankee Stadium signified that baseball had changed dramatically, but the builders of Yankee Stadium were still unable to imagine a future that would include night games and games broadcast on the radio, and they would resist those changes. Nor could they imagine that Yankee Stadium would be the last major league ballpark built with private funds. The next, Cleveland's Municipal Stadium, built in the hope of hosting the 1932 Olympic Games, established a pattern in which cities now openly compete to attract major league sports franchises by funding stadiums.

It is arguable that the generation which produced the original steel and concrete major league ballparks—Shibe Park, Forbes Field, League Park, Comiskey Park, Griffith Stadium, Redland Field, Navin Field, Ebbets Field, Fenway Park, Sportsman's Park, Wrigley Field, the Polo Grounds, Braves Field, and Yankee Stadium—established the sensibility that was to affect major league baseball for a full fifty years of its twentieth-century history. All of the original steel and concrete parks were still operative at the close of the Second World War.[37] Moreover, the original cities in which major league baseball was played in 1903 were still the major league cities at the opening of the 1953 season. The association between baseball's "permanent" steel and concrete parks and its original franchise cities had contributed to its timeless quality, to the point where, even in the face of massive demographic changes in America over a fifty-year interval, major league owners strenuously resisted any franchise realignments.

The experience of ballpark construction between 1908 and 1923 was to foster an implicit conviction among those closest to the game of major league baseball that the sport had become "permanently" established and linked to the identity of certain American cities. So it was to remain, the builders imagined, in the future. The ideals and aspirations of the first generation of ballpark builders came to be seen as permanently attached to the game of baseball in America. This was to result, over time, in the belief that baseball took strength from its past, and that its past practices should be zealously retained. A peculiarly archaic conception of the game thus took root early in its history. This conception lay at the heart of the image of baseball as America's national pastime.

2

The Enterprise, 1903–1923

ON APRIL 23, 1902, the Baltimore Orioles of the newly formed American League opened their season against the Philadelphia Athletics. An overflow crowd of 12,276 attended the game at Baltimore's Oriole Park, witnessing the first contest in which two legendary managers, John McGraw of the Orioles and Connie Mack of the Athletics, opposed one another. For most of the game, however, the home crowd was disappointed. The Athletics jumped ahead early and eventually won 8–1. The result augured a disastrous year for baseball in the city of Baltimore, which was to lose its manager to the New York Giants of the National League in the middle of the season, and by the end of the season to lose the team itself when the franchise was sold, moved to New York, and in 1903 renamed the Highlanders.

At the end of the seventh inning of the Orioles' 1902 home opener, however, an incident occurred that would surely have lifted the spirits of the Baltimore fans, had they been aware of its implications, which most of them were very likely not. As the Athletics returned to their dugout after the Orioles had been retired in the seventh, they were met by a process server commissioned by the Supreme Court of Pennsylvania. The process server presented three of the Athletics' players, Bill Bernard, Charles ("Chick") Fraser, and Napoleon ("Nap") Lajoie, with copies of an injunction granted to the Philadelphia Phillies of the National League, which prevented Bernard, Fraser, and Lajoie from playing baseball for the Philadelphia Athletics. The injunction had been based on the fact that all three players had signed contracts with the

Phillies to play in the 1900 season, and those contracts had contained clauses reserving the rights of the Phillies to employ the players on similar terms for future seasons.

The three players' legal difficulties had begun after the close of the 1900 season, when they breached ("jumped") their contracts with the Phillies to sign more lucrative contracts with Connie Mack's Athletics, who were seeking a competitive edge against the more established National League entry in Philadelphia. Contract jumping was particularly common in the first years of the twentieth century, as the former Western League, under the direction of the ambitious ex-newspaperman Byron Bancroft ("Ban") Johnson, sought recognition as a competitor to the National League at the major league level, luring National League players in the process. For the first three years of the twentieth century, team rosters, player salaries, and contractual obligations in major league baseball were in a state of turmoil, reflected in the actions of Bernard, Fraser, and Lajoie.

The early owners of major league baseball franchises initially seemed to have reacted to contract jumping with a certain degree of fatalism, or at least had not often sought remedies in the courts. Part of their tacit acceptance of the situation may have stemmed from a sense of the legal and practical vulnerability of their position. First, their contracts with their players were personal service contracts: courts declined to force human beings to perform personal services for their employers once they had given evidence of no longer wanting to do so. Involuntary servitude came to mind, as well as the practical difficulty of having an unhappy ballplayer playing for a team he had tried to leave.

Second, even if the owners had sought only to prevent jumping players from performing for any other team, the contracts they had entered into with their players were not necessarily ones that a court of equity, sitting to grant injunctive relief, would enforce. An old maxim of equity jurisprudence was that one seeking an equitable remedy, such as an injunction, must come into court with "clean hands," that is with a conscionable basis for the remedy. Another legal maxim, this one from contract law itself, was that for a contract to be valid, and thus the basis for equitable relief, "mutuality" had to exist between the contracting parties, that is, the contract had to impose obligations, and confer rights, on both of the parties who made it.

On both grounds the early owners of major league baseball franchises were vulnerable. With only a few rare exceptions, they had issued standard form contracts to their players which contained two provisions that appeared to be remarkably one-sided. One was a provision reserving the services of the contracting player for the succeeding year, typically on terms to be determined by the parties. This "reserve clause," as it came to be known, had originated in the late nineteenth century, as owners sought to provide themselves some security against frequent contract jumping by designating a small number of particularly valuable players whose services they desired for the following year. By 1900, however, the reserve clause had widened and hardened into an industrywide practice. All major league teams issued player contracts that included reserve clauses, and the effect of the clauses was that players were prevented from signing with any other team until the owners of their team had declined to offer them a contract for the year. By a tacit understanding among baseball clubs, no other teams would bid for their services: their options were to sign on the terms offered by their present club or not to play.

The reserve clause itself smacked of one-sidedness, since it typically did not even bind an owner to offer a player the same salary he had made in the previous year. But it was the coupling of the reserve clause with the "ten-day clause," another standard provision in major league baseball contracts, that most acutely raised the spectres of unconscionability and lack of mutuality. The ten-day clause allowed a team to dismiss a player on ten days notice if it concluded that the player's services were no longer required. No reasons needed to be given; the only requirement was ten days notice. Of course a dismissed player became a free agent, and as such had the option of selling his services to another team, but in practice the ten-day clause was not invoked except in case of physical or emotional inability to perform, and in such cases few other teams could be expected to bid for the dismissed player.

On the one hand, then, the owners of major league baseball teams could expect to retain the services of their players on a year-to-year basis. So long as they chose not to trade the players, and continued formally to offer them contracts, they could keep them on the team for whatever price they chose, taking into account the value of the player and the assumption that unhappiness over remuneration might be expected to affect player performance. On the other hand, a player had no ability to increase his compensation by offering his services to competitor franchises in the league. He was bound to accept the terms offered to him by an owner each year, although he could seek to negotiate his salary, based on the criteria of performance and projected happiness, and he might even, in unusual cases, secure a contract that extended for more than one year. Not only, however, was his compensation significantly dependent on the attitude of his owner, his job security was as well. He could be traded at will or fired on ten days notice; in either case he had no redress.

Given the relative power of owners and players created by the standard early twentieth-century baseball contracts, it is not surprising that many owners might not have wanted to expose their contract disputes with players to the scrutiny of courts. One owner, however, was sufficiently incensed by contract jumping that he decided to take his chances. This was Colonel John I. Rogers, a politically connected Pennsylvania lawyer, who along with sporting goods magnate Alfred J. Reach had acquired the Phillies of the National League in 1883. Rogers handled the salary negotiations for the Phillies, and he was known for being shrewd and careful about money. He was also well aware of the efforts of American League teams to recruit his players, especially the Cleveland Broncos, in which Ban Johnson had a continuing interest, and the Philadelphia Athletics, whose original owner, Ben Shibe, was a business partner and in-law of Alfred Reach.[1]

Between the 1900 and 1902 seasons Rogers lost five of his best players to American League clubs. In addition to Bernard, Fraser, and Lajoie, all of whom were enticed to the Athletics, they included Ed Delahanty and Elmer Flick, the former jumping to the Washington Senators and the latter to the Athletics, who eventually traded Flick to Cleveland.[2] These were not minor losses. Bernard won twenty games for the Athletics in 1901 and Fraser won seventeen; Lajoie's .422 batting average was best in the American League. Delahanty was one of the superstars of the deadball era, and he succeeded Lajoie as American League batting champion in 1902.[3] Flick was an excellent outfielder and an effective hitter and base stealer who was to become a fixture in Cleveland.

Of all the losses, however, that of Lajoie may have been the most galling for Rogers. Lajoie was a future Hall of Famer, a gifted, graceful infielder as well as a superb hitter. In addition, he was a natural leader, captain of the 1901–2 Athletics and of the 1902–5 Cleveland Broncos, and playing manager of the Broncos from 1906 through 1909. Tommy

Napoleon Lajoie, defendant in *Philadelphia Ball Club v. Lajoie*, pictured in 1909, still playing for the Cleveland Indians. (National Baseball Library and Archive, Cooperstown, N.Y.)

Leach, who played for the Pittsburgh Pirates from 1898 to 1918 and encountered Lajoie as an opponent during the 1900 season, said that "every play [Lajoie] made was executed so gracefully that it looked like it was the easiest thing in the world." Leach added that Lajoie "was a pleasure to play against . . . always laughing and joking. Even when the son of a gun was blocking you off the base, he was smiling and kidding with you. You just *had* to like the guy."[4]

In addition, Rogers must have been especially irritated by the circumstances of Lajoie's departure from the Phillies. In 1900, Lajoie had signed a three-year contract with Rogers for $2,400 a year. After the 1900 season he learned, first, that Connie Mack, on behalf of Ben Shibe's Athletics, was prepared to offer him $3,000 a year to sign with them, and, second, that Ed Delahanty, Lajoie's teammate with the Phillies, was making $3,000 a year. Rogers was also aware of both of these facts, but when Lajoie, in a meeting with Rogers in the spring of 1901, asked that his salary be raised to a level matching Delahanty's, Rogers refused. Lajoie then jumped to the Athletics along with Bernard and Fraser, proceeded to have the best offensive year of his entire baseball career, and played a significant part in the emergence of the Athletics as the more successful of the two Philadelphia major league franchises.

In the spring of 1901 Rogers, who controlled 51 percent of the Phillies' franchise, sued Lajoie, Bernard, and Fraser on behalf of the Phillies, seeking to prevent the players from playing for the Athletics for the duration of their present contracts with the Phillies. Despite the vulnerability of the standard baseball contract, Rogers believed that he could obtain an injunction against the players. He was particularly motivated to enjoin Lajoie, because his legal case was strongest against that player and because he accurately perceived that Lajoie's defection to the Athletics had done the Phillies the most damage.

Rogers's case against Lajoie and the others was brought, in the form of a bill in equity for an injunction, before Judge Robert Ralston of the Court of Common Pleas, Philadelphia County, in March 1901. Rogers recited that he had given Lajoie written notice of his intention to renew his contract for 1901 prior to October 15, 1900, as the contract provided; that he had subsequently renewed Lajoie's contract; and that "in the meantime [Lajoie] [and Bernard and Fraser] had signed contract[s] with the Philadelphia American League Base Ball Club."[5]

Judge Ralston set forth the pertinent provisions of Lajoie's contract with the Phillies, which was substantially similar to those of Bernard and Fraser except that Lajoie's salary was higher and the contract extended over a term of three years. The first of those provisions stated, in relevant part, that if Lajoie left the service of the Phillies at any time during the term of his employment, or performed services for any other club, he could be expelled from the Phillies. Alternatively, if the

Phillies franchise chose, "it may institute and prosecute proceedings in any court of . . . equity . . . to enjoin [Lajoie] . . . from performing services for any other person or organization" during the period of his contract.

The second material provision, according to Judge Ralston, was one allowing the Phillies to terminate Lajoie's contract on "ten days written notice of [their] intention to end . . . all its liabilities and obligations" under the contract. Lajoie was entitled, under this provision, to be paid his full salary for those ten days, whether the Phillies required him to play baseball for them or not. To this "ten-day clause" provision Judge Ralston added a third significant provision, the "reserve clause" of Lajoie's contract. That clause gave the Phillies "the option or right to renew this contract with all its terms, provisions, and conditions for another period of six months, beginning April 15, 1901, and for a similar period in two successive years thereafter." The Phillies were required to give Lajoie written notice of their intention to renew their option on his services "prior to the 15th day of October of the current year of this contract and of the current year of and renewal thereof."

The last provision of Lajoie's contract that Judge Ralston found significant read in part as follows: "In consideration of the faithful performance of the conditions, covenants, undertakings and promises herein by [Lajoie], inclusive of the concession of the options of release and renewals prescribed in the [previous] paragraphs [of the contract], the [Phillies ballclub] . . . hereby agrees to pay to [Lajoie] for his services for [the 1901 baseball season] the sum of $2400."[6] The clause in this paragraph that read "inclusive of the concession of the options of release and renewals" was arguably important because it could be read as a signal that Lajoie, when he signed the contract, was fully aware of the advantageous position of his employers, and had nonetheless elected to go forward with the bargain. That decision on his part could be seen as evidence that "mutuality" of bargaining position really did exist between ballplayers and their clubs.

Judge Ralston, however, did not agree with that reading of the "inclusive of the concession" clause of Lajoie's contract, and dismissed the Phillies' bill for injunctive relief. His decision was based on three grounds. First, he noted that in order to secure the quite drastic remedy of an injunction that would prevent a person from performing services for anyone other than his former employer, the employer needed to show that the loss of his employee's services would cause "irreparable" harm. Ralston, despite finding that Lajoie was "an expert baseball player in any position," and that "his withdrawal from the team would weaken it, . . . and would probably make a difference in the size of the audiences attending the game," concluded that the loss of Lajoie was, in the end, simply the loss of one very good player among nine on-field players in a team game. Lajoie's place on the roster could be filled: the consequences of his loss were too speculative to make that loss "irreparable."

Second, Judge Ralston's opinion referred to two established principles of the law of personal service contracts. The first was that the breach of a contract for personal services would never result in the remedy of specific performance, whereby the contract jumper was forced to play for his former ballclub. The second was associated with the first. It was that the remedy of injunctive relief for a breach—which in the *Lajoie* case might have the effect of forcing Napoleon Lajoie to play for the Phillies or no one—was limited to instances where the personal services provided to an employer were "unique" or "extraordinary," making the employer's loss irreparable. The latter principle had first been laid down in an English case involving an opera singer whose particular musical talents were thought to distinguish her from all other practitioners of her art.[7] Judge Ralston concluded that Lajoie's services to the Phillies were not "unique, extraordinary, and of such a character as to render it impossible to replace him," another way of finding that his loss was not irreparable.

Finally, Ralston concluded that when all the pertinent provisions of the contract between the Phillies and Lajoie were taken together, the contract lacked mutuality and was thus unenforceable in a court of equity. He paid particular attention to the ten-day clause, suggesting that the one-sidedness of that clause was not overcome by the "inclusive of the concession" clause. He maintained that a contract could hardly be characterized as a mutually binding undertaking if one party was bound to perform services for the other year after year, and the other could terminate its obligation to pay for those services, for any reason, on ten days notice. Ralston denied Rogers's bill for injunctive relief.

Rogers promptly appealed, securing an expedited hearing before the seven-judge Pennsylvania Supreme Court in January 1902. By April that court had handed down its decision, unanimously reversing

Ralston and granting Rogers an injunction against Lajoie, Bernard, and Fraser. Between January and April the Phillies, to protect themselves, had renewed the three players' contracts for the 1902 baseball season.

Despite the fact that all three players were named as defendants in the Phillies' suit, and the injunction papers were eventually served on all of them, the Pennsylvania Supreme Court treated the case as if Lajoie solely were involved. This was undoubtedly strategic. If any of the players' services were "unique and extraordinary," they were those of a regular member of a team's starting lineup who had captained the team, hit .422 to lead the league in batting, also led the league in hits and doubles, and was acknowledged to be the premier defensive second baseman in major league baseball. Moreover, if any of the players involved were vulnerable to the argument that he had voluntarily and knowingly accepted the one-sidedness of the contract, it was Lajoie, who had, in the face of the reserve and ten-day clauses, and notwithstanding his great abilities, signed for three years. Justice William P. Potter's opinion for the Pennsylvania Supreme Court was to emphasize those features of Lajoie's situation.

Potter first took up the "uniqueness" of Lajoie's services, and the related issue of the irreparableness of the damage to the Phillies from losing Lajoie to the Athletics. He disagreed with Judge Ralston's assessment of Lajoie's value. As Potter put it, Lajoie

> has been for several years in the service of the [Phillies], and has been re-engaged from season to season at a constantly increasing salary. . . . In addition to those features which render his services of peculiar and special value to the plaintiff, and not easily replaced, Lajoie is well known, and has great reputation among the patrons of the sport, for ability in the position which he filled, and was thus a most attractive drawing card for the public. He may not be the sun in the baseball firmament, but is certainly a bright particular star.[8]

One might quarrel with Justice Potter's description. The Phillies had not constantly increased Lajoie's salary; their 1900 contract with him had given them the option of paying him the same salary for the 1900, 1901, and 1902 seasons. Lajoie was undoubtedly a "most attractive drawing card," but other such players existed in major league baseball, and, given the nature of the game and the aging process, one could not predict with any assurance that a "drawing card" for one year would continue to be in the future. Nonetheless Potter had made much of

Lajoie's "star" status. He concluded that Lajoie's services were "of such a unique character, . . . and so difficult of substitution, that their loss will produce irreparable injury, in the legal significance of that term," to the Phillies.

Potter then turned to the question of whether the contract between Lajoie and the Phillies was so one-sided as to be lacking in mutuality. He obviously considered this a more troublesome issue, since he devoted most of the rest of his opinion to it, and at times his language appears strained. He first noted that the whole issue of mutuality might be irrelevant because partial performance of the contract had taken place. Lajoie had signed the contract before the 1900 season; he had played that season for the Phillies; he had been paid in full. "It might well be questioned," Potter wrote, "whether the court would not be justified in giving effect to [the contract] by injunction, without regard to the mutuality or nonmutuality in the original contract." This was because the Phillies had "so far performed [their] part of the contract in entire good faith" by paying Lajoie, and in Potter's view "it would be inequitable to permit [Lajoie] to withdraw from the agreement at this late day."[9]

Justice Potter was not on very firm ground in making this "part performance" argument. To be sure, Lajoie had signed a contract that gave the Phillies the option not to raise his salary for three years. But in a market in which the employers of baseball players reserved an option to renew player contracts every year, the only negotiable issue facing players and owners at the close of a baseball season was the player's salary for the next year. Moreover, that issue was likely to be the only one on which a player had any leverage. If a player had had a very good year, as Lajoie had in 1900 (he had played in 102 games for the Phillies, hitting .337), he might expect that his club, unless they had fared poorly financially, would reward him with a salary increase in order to "keep him happy." Thus Lajoie's signing for three years could have been taken as a tacit admission by both parties that Lajoie was good enough to be paid a comparatively high price for two more years, and that if Lajoie performed spectacularly well, the Phillies could always renew his contract at an even higher figure.

Moreover, Lajoie's "part performance," despite the "inclusive of concessions" clause, said little about the mutuality of the contract. No player in the major leagues then had the option of playing with a contract that did not include the reserve and ten-day clauses; no other contracts existed. A player could refuse to sign a contract, but then he would not be able to play baseball at the major league level. His only options, on receiving a contract offer that his owners declined to modify, were to sign, leave the game, or jump to another club and take his chances. In this context part performance was hardly an admission that a player accepted all the draconian terms of his contract. It was an admission of his quite limited bargaining power.

Justice Potter, of course, rejected this analysis. On the contrary, he found that even if the fact of Lajoie's partial performance were placed to one side, the contract between Lajoie and the Phillies met the legal requirements of mutuality. His analysis of the mutuality issue was primarily impressionistic. He denied that "mutuality of remedy requires that each party should have precisely the same remedy." He referred to "the peculiar nature of the services demanded by the business" of major league baseball. And he announced that "freedom of contract covers a wide range of obligation and duty as between the parties, and it may not be impaired, so long as the bounds of reasonableness and fairness are not transgressed." Employing those criteria of "reasonableness" and "fairness," he concluded that the provisions of Lajoie's contract were reasonable, that no evidence of "any attempt at overreaching or unfairness" by the Phillies had been shown, and that "substantial justice between the parties" required that Lajoie and the other players should be restrained from playing for any other baseball club during the term of their contracts with the Phillies.

Lajoie, Bernard, and Fraser were thus removed from the Philadelphia Athletics' roster after the opening game of the 1902 season in Baltimore. Their careers, however, were far from over. Ban Johnson quickly arranged for Lajoie and Bernard to be traded to Cleveland, where they were to remain for several years. Fraser jumped back to the Phillies, where he stayed through the 1904 season, then moving on to the Boston Red Sox and eventually finishing his career with the Chicago White Sox. For the remainder of the 1902 season, Bernard and Lajoie did not accompany their Cleveland teammates to Philadelphia, so as to avoid the Pennsylvania courts' jurisdiction over them. Beginning in 1903, the National Agreement, entered into by the owners of National and American League franchises, was to put a temporary end to player recruitment and contract jumping.

If the result of the *Lajoie* case was somewhat anticlimactic, the legal and economic underpinnings of Justice Potter's opinion for the Pennsylvania Supreme Court were of far greater moment. The *Lajoie* case signified that the enterprise of major league baseball, in the early years of its history, would be regarded as Potter had characterized it: a business with a "peculiar nature and circumstances." It was to be regarded not as a conventional business, with conventional production and distribution techniques, conventional entrepreneurial practices, and conventional labor relations, even for its times. It was to be thought of, by those directly engaged in it and those vicariously affected by it, as an enterprise at once more light-hearted, more trivial, and also more engaging, more culturally significant, than other American enterprises. It was to be thought of as a "game," a "sport," an entertainment, but also as a deadly serious, highly affecting, and vital activity. It was never thought of, even by those who adopted mercenary attitudes toward it, simply as a means of making money. Making money in a business enterprise has been highly valued in America, and was highly valued in the first fifty years of the National and American Leagues' joint existence. But the enterprise of major league baseball was "peculiar" in that, at some level, it was valued even more highly than making money. It was not simply a business, or a sport, or a means of getting rich; it was the national pastime.

◆

Justice Potter's opinion in the *Lajoie* case had implicitly involved, but not explicitly addressed, the set of questions that appeared to make the enterprise of major league baseball so "peculiar." How could the courts, the participants in the enterprise, and the public tolerate a business whose labor force seemed to operate so much at the mercy of their employers? How could a player such as Nap Lajoie, one of the most distinguished professional athletes of his day, perform at the highest level of his skills, for the entertainment of large crowds, with full awareness that he had virtually no control over the conditions or terms of his employment? How could a nation in which a collective suspicion of cartels, trusts, and monopolies had surfaced by the time of the *Lajoie* decision tolerate an industry in which all the owners of major league baseball teams tacitly agreed not to intervene in the relations between their competitors and their "reserved" players? Why did the players, faced with standard-form contracts containing reserve and ten-day clauses and with no opportunity to offer their services on the open market, decline, or fail, to organize themselves in a union or association? How could any court conceivably take the position taken by the Pennsylvania Supreme Court in *Lajoie*, that contracts such as that between Lajoie and his teammates and the Phillies were reasonable, fair, and not unconscionable? And why, when Colonel Rogers secured the injunction against Lajoie and the others, did the executives of major league baseball respond by simply trading the players, thereby removing them from the reach of the injunctions and in effect allowing them to jump their contracts after all?

What, in short, were the roots of the "peculiarity" of the enterprise of major league baseball in America? That question requires an extended answer, of which this chapter is a beginning. But there is a shorter form of the answer, or at least a starting place from which to address the question. That starting place is a consideration of what American major league baseball, from an entrepreneurial perspective, is fundamentally about. American professional baseball, played for money, is at bottom an exhibition of two highly competent athletic teams, playing a "game" or a "sport," for the vicarious satisfaction of spectators who are willing to pay for the opportunity to observe the spectacle. Moreover, the audience is an American one, bringing with it certain indigenous cultural attitudes about competition, spectator involvement, and the game of baseball itself.

In the early years of the twentieth century, three indigenous cultural attitudes seem to have been especially important in shaping the entrepreneurial character of American major league baseball. Those attitudes were translated, by persons interested in exhibiting games for a profit, into collective assumptions about the audiences for those games. The assumptions were that the audiences for baseball games wanted close competition among rival clubs, as distinguished from a particularly outstanding performance by one club; that a significant portion of their vicarious satisfaction in watching games would come from their role as "home town" residents of the city with which a particular team was affiliated; and that their "home town" affiliation with a team was likely to be enhanced if the identity of the players on that team remained relatively constant.

Few of the early owners of major league baseball franchises seemed to have been inclined toward putting their thoughts on paper. Moreover, assiduous efforts on the part of subsequent students of those owners' lives and careers have not revealed much direct evidence that they held, in their roles as baseball entrepreneurs, the assumptions I have attributed to them. But there is very strong indirect evidence that those men, together with the baseball executives with whom they joined to organize major league baseball after 1903, structured the enterprise of baseball, in its first twenty years, in a fashion consistent with those assumptions. That evidence can be found in the "rules" of what later came to be called "baseball law": the central purposes of the major provisions of the National Agreement of 1903 and the implementation of that agreement over the next two decades. It can also be found in the way in which baseball, as a legal and economic entity, was treated in the courts.

The immediate background to the National Agreement, in which the National and American Leagues established themselves as major league enterprises, in which other minor leagues were created and classified, and in which a set of governing rules for organized baseball in America was promulgated, was the baseball "wars" of the late nineteenth and early twentieth centuries, in which the Western/American League had come into existence and sought to establish itself as a genuine rival to the National. The *Lajoie* case typified the era of the interleague wars: it was a period of fluctuating player salaries, active recruitment by the newer league of the players held by the older league's franchises, and persistent efforts on the part of Ban Johnson and his associates to establish competitive American League franchises in some National League cities.

The *Lajoie* case also raised the possibility of one logical, but unfortunate, culmination of the interleague wars: recourse to the courts by unhappy owners of players who had been enticed away from their clubs, and a defiant response on the part of the recruiters. Was every contract jumper to be hauled into equity court and prevented from playing for his new team? Would an injunction issued by one state court be enforced in another state, as Colonel Rogers contemplated the Pennsylvania injunction against Lajoie being enforced in a court in Ohio? Would a bidding war for talented players emerge between the leagues, with players jumping back and forth, perhaps on a monthly basis, as their salaries escalated? Was injunctive relief against contract jumpers really a practical solution, given the vulnerability of the owners' legal position and the difficulties in enforcing an injunction in every city in the leagues? Would the reserve and ten-day clauses themselves eventually be outlawed by a court? And what about the agreements by owners within the same league not to interfere with each others' "reserved" players? Didn't that amount to a collective effort to restrain competition, in violation of the Sherman Anti-Trust Act? The more baseball owners contemplated this aspect of the interleague wars—the scrutiny of the internal workings of their enterprise by the courts—the more they may have felt it was time for peace.

In any event, peace, when it came, was accompanied by a determined effort on the part of the executives of the enterprise of major league baseball to write, and to enforce privately, their own version of law. At the cornerstone of their new edifice were three rules of "baseball law," each of which can be matched up with the collective assumptions about the entrepreneurial dimensions of baseball in America noted earlier. So fundamental were these three rules, so enduring in their persistence over time, and so unique in their legal and economic implications, that they can be said to have defined the sport for the first fifty years of its twentieth-century existence.

The first rule was that the reserve clause practice, originally limited to a select number of players, would become a universal feature of major league contracts, and would be enforced by an understanding that no club would seek to hire the disgruntled players of another. Over the next fifty years the ten-day clause would gradually disappear, the fringe benefits accorded players by their clubs would increase, and the general standard of living enjoyed by major leaguers would reach one of relative comfort, especially in the context of American professional athletics at large. The reserve clause and the practice of "blacklisting" uncooperative reserved players, however, would be rigidly and universally applied. Since the reserve clause was not only applied to all major league players but was enforced by all major league teams, it meant that a player dissatisfied with the terms of his employment had only three options: to accept those terms, to quit major league baseball, or to try to convince his employer that in his case dissatisfaction would result in diminished performance that would adversely affect his club.

It is obvious how the owner-architects of the enterprise of major league baseball benefited from universal enforcement of the reserve clause. Less obvious, especially to a modern observer, is how the players saw themselves as benefiting as well. It is clear, however, that to an extent the players did. They did not, after 1903, regularly jump clubs or otherwise seek to test the legality of their contracts,[10] nor did they

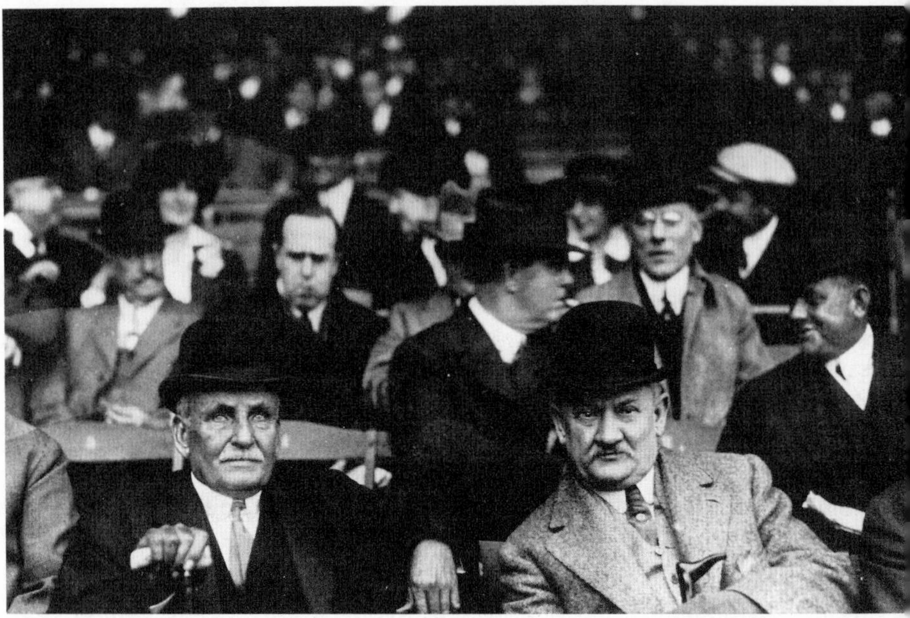

Ben Shibe (left) and Garry Herrmann, two of the original owners of the National League franchises at the time of the National Agreement of 1903, pictured in Shibe Park in the early 1920s. (National Baseball Library and Archive, Cooperstown, N.Y.)

resort to any form of collective bargaining, or, for that matter, to any established form of union organization. Two sporadic efforts at player solidarity, the Protective Association of Professional Baseball Players and the Professional Baseball Players Fraternity, emerged between 1903 and the First World War. But in that period only one strike involving major league players, that by the Detroit Tigers on Saturday, May 18, 1912, occurred. That action, protesting Ty Cobb's having been peremptorily suspended for ten days for assaulting a heckling fan, lasted only forty-eight hours, the players returning after being threatened by Ban Johnson with expulsion from major league baseball.[11]

Various reasons have been advanced by commentators for the failure of player associations or unions to take root in major league baseball in the fifty years after 1903, including claims that the sorts of individuals who choose to become professional ballplayers are too "independent," too uneducated, or too serendipitous in their temperaments to become attracted to collectivist labor organizations. Such claims appear less cogent in light of the current state of the major leagues, where millionaire professional athletes seem to have no difficulty identifying with a players' association that openly characterizes itself as protecting the collective interests of "laborers" in the baseball market. One is inclined to surmise, in fact, that an instinctive antipathy toward industrial collectivism in general or unionization in particular had little to do with the insignificant status of player organizations in major league baseball's early years. Instead two other factors emerge: the major league owners' determined resistance to any such organizations, and the players' own belief (conscious or unconscious) that the reserve clause, and the structure of team competition and fan support that it engendered, provided a kind of economic security for players so long as their skills remained intact.

Put another way, the ballplayers who tacitly agreed to submit themselves to what one judge, in the course of interpreting a reserve clause in a player contract, called a "species of quasi peonage,"[12] may have done so because they believed that the alternative—free movement of players from club to club in response to ongoing bidding—would eventually destroy both competitive balance and fan loyalty among major league clubs. They may also have believed, fatalistically, that they were poor working stiffs who had no real hope of exercising any economic power over rich, plutocratic owners in a world in which they pictured plutocrats as invariably oppressing stiffs. The frequent appearance, in the early twentieth century, of players commenting that an owner "played square" when a player's salary was being cut hints at such fatalism. If that resigned attitude was widespread, however, it may well have been accompanied by a hard-headed appraisal of the costs, to the economic security of the players, of a world of continuous contract jumping.

The ubiquitous reserve rule thus smoothly dovetailed with the two other fundamental rules of baseball as an enterprise. These rules were the territorial autonomy of established major league franchises and the structuring of Organized Baseball as a "buyers' monopoly," or a monopsony. The reserve clause, territoriality, and the monopsonistic buying and selling of players' services were each interrelated rules, but at the same time they had separable legal and economic implications.

We have seen that the reserve clause had been based on the assumption that if baseball was to flourish as a business enterprise, fan support was dependent upon close competition among teams, which meant a competitive balance among the player rosters of league franchises. Competitive balance, in the early twentieth century, did not mean what is now called "parity" in professional sports franchises. If parity was ever contemplated in baseball, it quickly broke down. Some teams, such as the New York Yankees, New York Giants, Brooklyn Dodgers, Philadelphia Athletics, Detroit Tigers, and St. Louis Cardinals, regularly finished high in the standings, and other teams, such as the Philadelphia Phillies, St. Louis Browns, Washington Senators, and Boston Red Sox, rarely did so. But if parity never existed, neither did abysmal gaps between the level of play of the stronger and weaker teams in a league.

The reserve clause rule, in fact, ensured that rich and successful teams could not simply outbid less fortunate teams for players on major league rosters. Team improvement could only come from the ingenious purchasing and development of younger players, effective trades, or, perhaps, judicious use of existing players by a particularly gifted manager or general manager. This was especially true in the years covered by this chapter. Beginning in the 1920s the minor leagues and the "farm system" played an increasingly important role in team improvement, but in the years from 1903 to 1923 team competition, on the whole, remained keen, balanced, and varied, testifying to the effectiveness of the reserve clause as a stabilizing device.

Close competition was assumed to nurture fan support, but seeing a keenly contested game is one thing, and seeing such a game in which one has a partisan interest is arguably quite another, at least doubling the level of vicarious fan involvement. How had partisanship entered major league baseball? Those who structured the enterprise in the early twentieth century proceeded as if they knew the answer to that question. Partisanship was tied to local affiliation, to sense of place, to regional and civic pride. It was a manifestation of the persistence of a "village mentality" among even peripatetic Americans. Most of all, it was the partisanship of a rooted sense of belonging to an early twentieth-century American city. It was no accident that the first generation of steel and concrete ballparks was associated with the "City Beautiful" movement in growing American cities around World War I. Major league baseball was part of a city resident's commitment to the locally distinctive, but at the same time nationally ambitious, growing urban space in which he or she lived.[13]

In assuming that the prospective fans of a franchise would care more about its destiny because it was associated with their city, the owners of early baseball clubs were concluding that among the benefits of their possession of the franchise was an important reservoir of civic and territorial goodwill. It followed from this conclusion that the owners desired something like a monopoly on that goodwill, and would be zealous in protecting their territory from competitors. The baseball wars of the turn of the century provided ample illustration of the validity of those behavioral hypotheses. So did the owners' response to the emergence of the Federal League between 1914 and 1916. In both instances an aspiring rival league, the Western/American or the Federal, began by establishing franchises in cities without major league teams, and then sought to expand from this base by invading the territory of existing major league clubs. In both instances the more solvent and comparatively successful of the invading rivals were able to negotiate a peace agreement in which they were made part of the major league enterprise.

Thus, just as Ban Johnson was able to parlay the American League's invasion of New York, Philadelphia, Boston, Chicago, and St. Louis into the designation of those franchises as "major league" under the auspices of the 1903 National Agreement, three wealthy Federal League owners, Charles Weeghman in Chicago, Phil Ball in St. Louis, and Albert Sinclair, who sought to move into New York from his temporary base in Newark, negotiated their way into the ranks of major league owners in 1916, Weeghman and Sinclair purchasing the Chicago Cubs and Ball the St. Louis Browns. In that same "peace treaty" between the major league owners and the Federal League, the owners of Federal League teams in Brooklyn and Pittsburgh received cash settlements for abandoning their franchises. The Federal League owners in Baltimore, Buffalo, and Kansas City, however, whose franchises were less solvent and had been less successful, were paid nothing. They only obtained the right to sell players from their rosters to major league clubs without those players being blacklisted.[14]

The Federal League "war," like the earlier wars, demonstrated the close relationship between territoriality and the reserve clause rule; it also demonstrated the connection between both of those rules and the efforts on the part of major league owners to establish a buyer's monopoly in the services of players. When the Federal League was launched, its franchises immediately began bidding for the services of players on major league rosters, such as Hal Chase, who jumped from the Chicago White Sox to the Buffalo Buf-Feds. Despite the strong informal pressures against contract jumping, several players could not resist the lure of strikingly higher salaries, and joined Federal League teams. Moreover, it became apparent that the owners' legal vulnerabilities, which the *Lajoie* case had not fully effaced, would surface again in challenges to Federal League contracts.

When the White Sox sought to enjoin Chase from playing ball for the Buf-Feds, Chase's lawyers attacked the mutuality of his contract with the White Sox and the "monopolistic" practices of the owners in blacklisting players who refused to honor standard baseball contracts. They went even further, arguing that all major league baseball contracts were invalid because the practice of standard-form reserve clause contracts, enforced through tacit "blacklisting" sanctions, amounted to a combination or conspiracy on the part of the owners to restrain competition in interstate commerce in violation of the Sherman Anti-Trust Act, in this instance the commerce of baseball games whose performance required players and teams to cross state lines.[15] This last argument, which Judge Herbert P. Bissell rejected in the White Sox's suit against Chase, was to be picked up by the disgruntled Baltimore Federal League franchise and eventually to produce the most significant legal decision in the early history of baseball.

The reserve clause rule, coupled with blacklisting practices, thus protected the integrity of team rosters, insuring continuity of personnel. At the same time continuity of personnel reinforced territorial goodwill by ensuring a nucleus of visible players which fans from a city could identify as "their team." The territoriality rule preserved that goodwill and reinforced that fan identification by making it very difficult for a competing franchise, with a competing list of prospective local heroes, to enter into the consciousness of the baseball fans of a city. As a result, the territoriality rule and the reserve clause rule, operating in a self-reinforcing fashion, made it easier for owners to control the price of players' services. The players' best chance of increasing their salaries, as the two early twentieth-century baseball wars demonstrated, was through contract jumping to higher bidders. The structure of the enterprise of major league baseball necessitated that the only potential high bidders in the market for player services would be outside "invaders" such as the Federal League teams, invaders who were zealously resisted or bought off by the established owners.

By 1914, the year the *Chase* case was decided and the Federal League was launched, it was apparent to anyone knowledgeable about the enterprise of major league baseball that the three fundamental rules of that enterprise were designed to create and to preserve a territory-based monopsony whose ultimate purpose, paradoxically, was to maintain keen competition among an established group of major league clubs. If there had been any doubt about the rules' primary purpose, it was dispelled by the response of major league baseball to the Federal League challenge.

The 1916 settlement to the Federal League war was noteworthy in one additional respect. The varied treatment of Federal League rival franchises by the existing owners had, of course, reflected the comparative financial weight and associated market power of the separate rivals, as Sinclair, Weeghman, and Ball were ushered into the major league fraternity, and other Federal League owners excluded. But at the same time the established franchise owners rigidly reaffirmed the existing territorial structure of the enterprise. Baltimore had had no major league team since 1903, and Baltimore continued to be excluded. Pittsburgh had been a one-team city in the years after the merger of the National and American Leagues; it continued to be, as did Brooklyn. Kansas City had never had a major league franchise; it too was excluded in the Federal League settlement. Albert Sinclair was permitted to be one of the buyers of the Chicago Cubs, but not to bring a fourth team into the New York City area. The only teams sold to Federal League owners were in cities that already had two teams. In short, the geographic map of the major leagues looked exactly the same after the Federal settlement as it had before.

The territorial rule of the enterprise of baseball, as the twentieth century evolved, thus came to take on a quality of being frozen in time. Everybody in the inner circles of the game understood the importance of territoriality and the identification of teams with civic and regional fan loyalty. But what was meant by "territory"—that is, the conception of the appropriate geographic centers for major league baseball—became equated with the original territorial configuration of teams at the time of the 1903 National Agreement. St. Louis was to have two teams, and Detroit one, even though the population growth of Detroit far outdistanced that of St. Louis in the fifty years after 1903. Large urban centers in the traditional geographic sectors (the northeast and midwest) in which baseball had been played at the major league level, such as Indianapolis, Milwaukee, Baltimore, Buffalo, and Kansas City, were never to house major league franchises in those years, even though several of the franchises in established cities, notably the

Albert Goodwill Spalding, relentless publicist for "America's National Game," pictured shortly before his death in 1915. (National Baseball Library and Archive, Cooperstown, N.Y.)

Browns, Phillies, and Washington Senators, had quite dismal attendance for some years of that time span. Most significantly, perhaps, other sectors of the American nation rapidly expanded their population, so that cities such as Miami, Atlanta, Dallas, Houston, Denver, Minneapolis/St. Paul, and especially Los Angeles and San Francisco became major metropolises, outdistancing several of the existing cities in population. By the Second World War Los Angeles, with no major league baseball team, had 688,229 more people than St. Louis, which had two franchises.[16]

The frozen quality of the territoriality principle was not, of course, as myopic as it might first appear. The geographic distribution of major league franchises produced a relatively compact transportation network, stretching from Boston west only to St. Louis and south only to Washington. In a time when trains were the standard mode of long-distance travel in America, and in which clubs rarely visited rival cities for more than four days at a time, the 1903 territorial structure of baseball had its own efficiencies. But rigid territoriality in early twentieth-century baseball began to create strains as the automobile, the airplane, and the radio began to change the meaning of what a locality or a region meant in American life.

In merging their beliefs about the issues that moved their prospective customers with their assumptions about how they could best maximize profits and satisfaction from the "peculiar" business of baseball, the owners of clubs in the two decades after 1903 had behaved in what, in retrospect, might appear to be a singularly practical, self-serving, and inspired fashion. They had established an enterprise in which they could control player salaries, assure a general continuity of team personnel, provide "exhibitions" of closely matched baseball teams of a high level of skill, promote civic and regional pride, and keep rivals out of their market. They had fashioned the legal and economic rules of their enterprise with no interference from governmental bodies and little interference from the courts. Their employees appeared satisfied to labor under conditions of employment fashioned and controlled, in almost all respects, by their employers. Best of all, they had used the principles of the reserve clause and territoriality to foster deep associations between American cities and their ballclubs. As twentieth-century urban centers had grown and developed, their baseball teams had become part of their identity. As early as 1911 Albert Spalding had claimed, without any sense of irony, that baseball was "America's National Game; that it has . . . unbounded public favor."[17]

◆

In the years between 1914 and 1922 the enterprise that had been created by the National Agreement and nurtured by its fundamental "rules" confronted a lengthy lawsuit that placed its continuing existence, at least in its self-fashioned form, in jeopardy. The case began as an outgrowth of the Federal League war and peace settlement, and slowly worked its way up to the Supreme Court of the United States. As the arguments in that case were constructed and refined, it seemed as if the entire legal structure of the enterprise of major league baseball might be exposed, found to be unlawful or unconstitutional, and discarded, so that the enterprise created in 1903 would need to be fundamentally revamped.

Such an outcome did not occur. The Supreme Court of the United States, in a unanimous opinion written by Justice Oliver Wendell Holmes, let all of the fundamental rules of "baseball law" stand, and did so by characterizing those rules in a fashion that, to an interested lay person at the time, might well have seemed to resemble otherworldly legal gobbledygook. Indeed with hindsight the decision appears strikingly out of touch with its subject matter, treating baseball as an amateurish "game" when it was clearly a highly professionalized business. But hindsight in this instance is misleading. The most telling feature of major league baseball's first appearance in the Supreme Court of the United States was the very "naturalness" and conventionality of Justice Holmes's legal conclusions, once one takes into account the jurisprudential and economic assumptions of the time and the resultant image of baseball as an enterprise.

The orthodoxy of the Court's decision in *Federal Baseball Club of Baltimore, Inc. v. National League of Professional Baseball Clubs, et al.*[18] is all the more striking because the decision, viewed as an effort to characterize the actual legal and economic character of major league baseball in 1922, was remarkably myopic, almost willfully ignorant of the nature of the enterprise. One is confronted in *Federal Baseball* with a vivid juxtaposition of abstract legal and economic concepts and the enterprise to which they are being applied. The concepts, and their associated assumptions, produce a characterization of the enterprise that seems naive. But the characterization also seems to make a kind of historical sense: to fit with the image of American professional baseball extant at the time. In the end the *Federal Baseball* decision demonstrates how treacherous it was—and is—to think of baseball as solely a "business."

In the Federal League peace settlement of 1916 the Baltimore franchise had been ignored. The owners of that franchise had apparently not been present when negotiations began between the Federal League and representatives of the major leagues, and when they learned of the coming peace, they objected to its terms, offering to buy one of the existing major league franchises instead. They were summarily rebuffed in this offer, with the owners of some established teams ridiculing their aspiring "major league" status, and were eventually offered only $50,000 for disbanding their club. They rejected that overture, and when they realized that their erstwhile Federal League competitors had disbanded, they sold their ballpark to the Baltimore entry in the International League, raised $50,000 to finance legal expenses, and, in March 1916, a month after the Federal League settlement was made official, sued Organized Baseball in federal court for treble damages under the Sherman Anti-Trust Act.[19]

Their suit actually named the National League, the American League, John K. Tener, president of the National League, Ban Johnson, president of the American League, and August (Garry) Herrmann, owner of the Cincinnati Reds and chairman of the National Commission, as defendants.* The attorneys for the Balt-Feds franchise set forth the terms of the 1903 National Agreement and made three arguments. First, they claimed that major league baseball was engaged in interstate commerce. Second, they charged that major league baseball, through the National Agreement, had attempted to monopolize, and did monopolize, a portion of that commerce. They cited the uniform reserve clause in player contracts and the "ineligible list" (blacklisting) practices for contract violators, arguing that these devices gave the owners of major league baseball franchises a monopoly in the services of highly skilled baseball players. Third, they maintained that major league baseball had conspired to destroy, and had destroyed, the Federal League by depriving them of skilled players, with the purpose of retaining and perfecting their monopoly of professional baseball.

The original suit filed in March 1916 was withdrawn in June 1917, as both sides expected to be able to reach an out-of-court settlement. But negotiations broke down, and in September 1917, the Baltimore owners refiled in Judge Wendell P. Stafford's federal district court in the District of Columbia. A trial was delayed until 1919, when Judge Stafford decided for the Balt-Feds on their first two arguments, finding that the giving of exhibitions of baseball games did constitute "trade or commerce" within the meaning of the Sherman Act, and that Organized Baseball had monopolized a portion of that commerce. He left

* Between 1903 and the creation of the baseball commissioner's office in 1921, the National Commission, composed of the presidents of the two major leagues and an owner of one of the clubs as chairman, was Organized Baseball's official governing body.

the question of whether the Balt-Feds had been damaged by the monopoly of interstate commerce to the jury, and the jury found that they had, awarding them damages of $80,000, which were trebled under the provisions of the Sherman Act. Judge Stafford entered judgment for the owners of the Balt-Feds for $240,000. Organized Baseball promptly appealed to the U.S. Court of Appeals for the District of Columbia Circuit.

On December 6, 1920, Chief Justice Constantine J. Smyth of the District of Columbia Circuit handed down an opinion reversing the trial court. The Balt-Feds had chosen to make antitrust arguments the centerpiece of their litigation. This was partly a matter of necessity, because they themselves had not been involved with any direct contractual dealings with Organized Baseball and therefore could not get at the reserve clause through the doctrine of mutuality, as Lajoie's lawyers had sought to do. Their goal was to tie the reserve clause and blacklisting practices to the antitrust laws by demonstrating that their effect was to allow the established major league franchises to monopolize the market for skilled baseball players. The monopsonistic effects of the reserve clause had been noted by the court that declined to enjoin Hal Chase from jumping from the White Sox to the Buffalo Federal League franchise. The Balt-Feds sought to build on that argument.

It was one thing, however, to establish that the reserve clause and associated practices made players' contracts invalid for lack of mutuality, or even to demonstrate that a concerted scheme to universalize standard-form reserve clause contracts for major league players amounted to a common law monopoly, as the judge had found in Chase's case. Those findings benefited players, not potential competitors in the market for player services. For those competitors to demonstrate that they had been damaged, they needed to show that the practices amounted to conspiracies or combinations having a tendency to monopolize interstate trade or commerce. That was the operative language of the Sherman Anti-Trust Act, and that was the basis of federal court jurisdiction in the *Federal Baseball* case. Unless the Balt-Feds could show that major league baseball was a form of interstate trade or commerce, they would not be able to show an antitrust violation. And only by showing an antitrust violation—a conspiracy by Organized Baseball to monopolize player services in major league baseball—could they show that they had been damaged. The loss they needed to establish was the loss of an opportunity to compete with the major league franchises for players.

Part of the difficulty commentators have had with the *Federal Baseball* case is unraveling exactly what the Supreme Court of the United States eventually decided in it. In order to clarify that question, it is first necessary to consider Chief Justice Smyth's Court of Appeals opinion in some detail. But before that task is undertaken, a problem that has haunted the *Federal Baseball* case, and most discussions of major league baseball's apparent "immunity" from federal antitrust laws, needs to be addressed: the apparently one-sided nature of the antitrust issues. Since it has been clear to most students of the rules of early baseball that a primary purpose of those rules was to create a buyer's monopoly in player service contracts, why weren't the rules immediately seen as a concerted effort to fix the prices of baseball salaries? In addition, since baseball teams regularly crossed state lines and baseball clubs represented cities in different states, why did this not constitute an obvious violation of the Sherman Anti-Trust Act?

It might appear, as a commonsensical proposition, that baseball games were articles in interstate trade or commerce. The players rode on trains that crossed state lines in traveling to their games. The players were affiliated with teams that bore the names of different cities, from different states. The major league franchises were corporations that did not earn their revenues solely from the exhibition of games in their home locality. They also divided the revenues from the games their teams played on the road with the home teams; they received income from sources other than the games themselves, such as concession sales, the rental of their ballparks, and advertising on scorecards and ballpark fences; they housed their players in hotels and fed their players in restaurants across the country. The results of baseball games in one locality were telegraphed to countless other locations. From this point of view, Chief Justice Smyth's conclusion, for the Court of Appeals, that "[a] game of baseball is not susceptible of being transferred," ignored the essence of the enterprise.

But like many commonsensical propositions, the logic of treating baseball games as objects in interstate commerce had the capacity to prove too much. If a tomato, grown in a backyard and sold by a child at a curbside stand, was taken by the buyer on a train to another state, did it become an article in interstate commerce? If so, Congress could regulate the sale of backyard tomatoes by homeowners, and if two children decided to fix the price of backyard tomatoes along a dead-end street on which their houses were located, they were potential violators of the Sherman Act. The act's language was so sweeping, and its scope so broad, that if it were literally applied nearly any two-person transaction that tended to restrain free trade, or retard free competition, would fall within its purview. In an earlier opinion construing the Sherman Act, Justice Holmes had noted that it could not be treated as revising the common law of restraint of trade, which did not seek to restrict all legal combinations. He put the example of two stage drivers, once competitors, who formed a partnership to drive passengers across a state line. If "the restraint on the freedom of members of a combination caused by their entering into a partnership is a restraint of trade," he warned, "every such combination, as well the small as the great, is within the Act."[20]

There was another difficulty with the commonsensical conclusion that major league baseball games amounted to interstate trade or commerce. This difficulty was not so much logical as it was historical. The concepts of "trade" and "commerce," by the 1920s, had not fully detached themselves from their nineteenth-century origins and become the pliable terms of art they would become in American jurisprudence after the New Deal. They continued to have specific, and limiting, associations. "Trade" was associated with the buying and selling of products of a discrete type or class, such as the spice trade, or trading in sugar or household necessities. It could include the buying and selling of currency or speculating in currencies or their equivalent, such as trading in gold or commodities futures, but it typically was not associated with the buying and selling of personal services. One did not trade in opera singers or jugglers or servants. In America there had once been a trade in slaves, but that was because slaves were legally considered property as well as persons.

"Commerce" had comparable historical associations. It referred to "traffic" in goods as distinguished from the goods themselves, and also as distinguished from the manufacture or production of the goods. In an influential early construction of the Commerce Clause of the Constitution, Chief Justice John Marshall had expanded the meaning of commerce to include "intercourse" as well as "traffic," but his purpose was only to bring within congressional regulatory power such activities as steamboats operating on interstate waterways: he continued to associate commerce with the distributional as distinguished from the productive spheres of the American economy. Agriculture, mining, farming, and shipbuilding remained activities that were not included within the term.

As the Sherman Anti-Trust Act, with its emphasis on prohibiting restraints of "trade" or "commerce" undertaken in combination, became the subject of judicial interpretation in the late nineteenth century, the courts engrafted onto their readings of the act the older restricted meanings of commerce. In general, if a group of firms charged with combining or conspiring to restrain trade or commerce under the Act could show that their business was local, or that it involved manufacture as distinguished from commerce, or involved "personal effort, not related to production," it could escape liability under the act.[21] This was true even where the business transported products across state lines, if that transportation was "incidental" to rather than the "essence" of the business.

Given these established historical associations of the terms "trade" and "commerce," and the intuitions driving those associations, the exhibition of baseball games for profit, even if the exhibitions took place in more than one state, did not easily fit within the coverage of the Sherman Anti-Trust Act. Indeed they raised the possibility that the act might reach nearly every economic activity carried on in America. Chief Justice Smyth, in reversing the trial court's decision in *Federal Baseball*, mentioned two examples of the Sherman Act's prospective reach if baseball exhibitions were deemed interstate trade or commerce. Under the same reasoning, he declared, a firm of lawyers, based in one city, would be within the act if one of its members crossed state lines to argue a case, or the Chautauqua Lecture Bureau, which dispatched knowledgeable persons around the nation to give lectures on various subjects, would be within the act if it sent a lecturer out of the state where it was located.[22]

One might respond to Chief Justice Smyth's examples by pointing out that he had confused two distinguishable associations of the phrase "interstate trade and commerce," associations having to do with the geographic coverage of that phrase and associations having to do with its activity coverage. The examples did not help in establishing the "local" nature of practicing law or lecturing; in fact the examples demonstrated that those professions were not confined by geography. The very existence of an organization such as the Chautauqua Bureau testified to the advantages gained by lecturing across state lines. The examples helped, rather, in reestablishing the old association of "trade" or "commerce" as traffic in goods rather than personal services. Lawyers and lecturers were valued for their "personal efforts," not for the commodities they brought when they crossed state lines.

When the *Federal Baseball* case came up to the Supreme Court, it became apparent that the multiple associations of interstate "trade" and "commerce" had not been clearly disentangled. Nor had the relationships among the separate legal issues in the case. In the trial court the Balt-Feds had argued three distinct issues, and won on each of them: that the franchises which composed Organized Baseball engaged in interstate commerce; that their concerted efforts to institute the reserve clause and blacklisting practices had constituted a "monopoly" of such commerce within the meaning of the Sherman Act; and that their monopoly had damaged the Balt-Feds by depriving them of the opportunity to sign high-caliber baseball players. The first two of these issues were jurisdictional. If no effort to monopolize interstate trade or commerce was shown, the fact that the Balt-Feds might have been damaged by Organized Baseball's tactics became irrelevant, because their suit was solely based on a Sherman Act violation. Since the Balt-Feds won on the two jurisdictional issues at the trial court, however, the question of whether they had actually been damaged was properly passed on by the jury.

When Chief Justice Smyth reversed the trial court, he did not find it necessary to address the question of whether the "monopolistic" practices had actually damaged the Balt-Feds, because he concluded that they were not practices in interstate commerce. He meant that conclusion in two senses: first, that putting on exhibitions of baseball for profit was not itself interstate trade or commerce; second, that putting on baseball exhibitions did not illegally restrain anyone else's movement in interstate commerce. As discussed, his opinion devoted most of its attention to arguing on behalf of the first part of that conclusion. He then went on, however, to argue that the reserve clause practices were reasonable efforts on the part of the major league clubs to preserve a competitive balance among teams and player rosters, and therefore related "directly to the conservation of personnel of the clubs, and did not affect the movement of the [Balt-Feds] in interstate commerce." Whatever effect the reserve clause practices had, Smyth concluded, "was incidental, and therefore did not offend against the [Sherman Act]."[23]

Smyth's last argument was, quite simply, incoherent. The reserve clause and associated practices had played no part in determining the "interstate" character of baseball. Whether baseball was or was not found to be an "interstate" activity depended on whether one emphasized the fact that a precondition to the playing of most major league games was that at least one of the teams crossed state lines to do so, or whether one used various devices to deemphasize that fact, rendering it "incidental." The rules the major league franchises had created to govern contracts between players and owners were simply not germane to that analysis.

If all the major league franchises had been deemed not to have engaged in interstate trade or commerce, it followed that the Federal League franchises had not engaged in it either. It was inconceivable that Organized Baseball, whose operations had been found not to involve interstate trade or commerce, could have interfered with the "interstate trade or commerce" of a rival organization whose operations were precisely the same as those of Organized Baseball. Smyth's entire argument about the function of the reserve clause practices was beside the point.

Of course Smyth's argument was designed for another rhetorical purpose, to suggest that the reserve clause practices, which he took pains to defend, were justifiable in themselves. "If the reserve clause did not exist," Smyth said, "the highly skillful players would be absorbed by the more wealthy clubs, and thus some clubs in the league would so far outstrip others in playing ability that the contests between the superior and inferior clubs would be uninteresting, and the public would refuse to patronize them." Because of the reserve clause, he noted, "the clubs in the National and American Leagues are more evenly balanced, the contests between them are made more attractive to the patrons of the game, and the success of the clubs more certain."[24]

It is important to disentangle the various arguments advanced in Smyth's opinion, because Smyth's decision was affirmed by the Supreme Court of the United States, and Justice Holmes, in his unanimous opinion for the Court, said that "the decision of the Court of Appeals went to the root of the case" and "we are of opinion that the Court of Appeals was right."[25]

Let us recapitulate the various arguments Smyth had offered as grounds for his decision. As his opinion unfolded, he had said that baseball was "local" in character; that the game of baseball "effects no exchange of things according to the meaning of 'trade and commerce'"; that the transportation of players across state lines was merely "incident" to the main purpose of the game, putting on "local" exhibitions; that baseball was "not trade or commerce," but "sport"; that baseball exhibitions involved personal services, like the putting on of operas or plays, and was thus as "far removed as possible from the commonly accepted meaning of trade and commerce"; and that Organized Baseball's creation of the reserve clause practices, designed to conserve the existing club rosters of franchises, had no effect on interstate trade and commerce.

Some of these arguments, such as the statement that baseball was "local" rather than "interstate," or that it was "sport" rather than "trade or commerce," seem merely assertive or conclusory. Other arguments, that baseball games lacked the quality of an exchange of goods, or that baseball exhibitions more resembled entertainments such as theater or opera performances, appear better grounded, in that they tracked closely the historical meaning of the terms "trade" and "commerce" in American law. Finally, the significance of Smyth's argument that the reserve clause practices were defensible, given the need for balanced competition within the major leagues, was entirely dependent on whether major league baseball games were found to be "interstate trade and commerce" or not. If so, the practices obviously interfered with interstate trade and commerce because they made it very difficult for the Federal League to obtain players; if not, any Sherman Act suit of the kind filed by the Balt-Feds would fail.

Of all the arguments Smyth advanced, Holmes made use of only two. He admitted that the organization of major league baseball "requires constantly repeated travelling on the part of the clubs, which is provided for, controlled, and disciplined by the [National and American Leagues]." But he said that this did not mean that major league baseball was therefore "commerce among the States"; on this point, he concluded, "the Court of Appeals was right."[26]

Right in what sense? Holmes then went on to indicate which of Smyth's arguments the Supreme Court was endorsing. "The business is giving exhibitions of baseball," he maintained, "which are purely state affairs." The fact that "in order to attain . . . great popularity" for those exhibitions "competitions must be arranged between clubs from different cities and States," and the fact that "in order to give the exhibitions the Leagues must induce free persons to cross state lines and must arrange and pay for their doing so" were "not enough to change the character of the business." The transportation across state lines was "a mere incident, not the essential thing."[27]

But what was "the essential thing" about major league baseball? Here Holmes began to get slightly vague. He spoke of "the exhibition," although "made for money," as not something that would "be called trade or commerce in the commonly accepted use of those words." He elaborated upon the last point, saying that "personal effort, not related to production, is not a subject of commerce." He added that an activity "which in its consummation is not commerce does not become commerce among the States because the transportation that we have mentioned takes place." He then mentioned Smyth's two illustrations of a firm of lawyers and the Chautauqua Lecture Bureau. In sum, the "essential thing" about baseball was that it was a "local" activity and that it was a display of personal effort, not related to production. It was not "trade or commerce" at all.

Going back to the only paragraph in Holmes's opinion in which he attempted to provide any reasoning in support of his conclusion, and looking carefully at that reasoning, one finds an ambiguity at its most central point. That point lies where Holmes sought to move on from his discussion of the difference between a baseball exhibition, which he had previously labeled a "purely state affair," and interstate transportation to and from that exhibition, which he described as "a mere incident, not the essential thing." He then fashioned a sentence, apparently designed to reinforce that distinction, which suggested that "the exhibition" (the "essential thing") would not be called trade or commerce as those terms were commonly understood.

Thus in the critical paragraph of his *Federal Baseball* opinion, Holmes made the following arguments in succession. Baseball exhibitions were purely local in character, notwithstanding the fact that in order to put them on effectively the players participating in them were transported across state lines. The transport was merely "incidental" to the exhibition. The exhibition, in fact, could not be called "trade or commerce" at all, because it involved exhibiting players performing feats of skill, and "personal effort, not related to production," was not within the legal definition of "commerce." Since baseball exhibitions were not "commerce" at all, they could not become interstate commerce just because the players exhibited were brought across state lines for the exhibition. Baseball players crossing state lines to participate in an exhibition of their talents no more engaged in interstate commerce than did lawyers or Chautauqua lecturers who crossed state lines to practice law or lecture.

No wonder commentators have had difficulty unearthing the basis of the Supreme Court's opinion in the *Federal Baseball* case. The opinion was a vintage example of Justice Holmes's penchant for using vivid phrases to get him over awkward logical difficulties, and should have given pause to those students of the case who have claimed, incorrectly, that "Holmes was a pretty good ballplayer in his early years." In fact Holmes, who was extraordinarily wide-ranging in his interests, never played any organized sports and paid no attention to professional athletics.[28] It is very probable that when he wrote the opinion in *Federal Baseball* he had never seen a major league game.

Looked at as a legal document from the 1920s, *Federal Baseball* was not an aberration: Holmes's insistence that baseball games were "local" and not "trade or commerce" was jurisprudentially orthodox. Looked at from almost any other perspective, the *Federal Baseball* decision was extraordinary.

First of all, in none of the courts in which the case was heard was a simple, practical distinction made: the alleged conspiracy by Organized Baseball to monopolize interstate commerce was not just intended to monopolize the exhibition of games for profit, it was intended to monopolize the market in talented player services, and thereby to stabilize the cost of player salaries and the personnel of club rosters. Those who constructed the National Agreement were not primarily interested in keeping potential rivals from coming into major league baseball. They were primarily interested in preventing constant contract jumping, salary wars, and the depletion of rosters by ambitious competitors. They did not want to be the exclusive agents for exhibiting professional baseball games; on the contrary, they anticipated that they would benefit from the growth of minor leagues whose franchises would coexist with theirs and furnish a source of players.

So the Balt-Feds, in their suit, were not complaining about being kept out of the baseball business. They had, in fact, been in the baseball business for the last three years, competing with Organized Baseball. They were complaining about the fact that the reserve system and blacklisting practices had made it very difficult for them to induce quality players from the major league rosters. They were arguing that by binding players to existing clubs, and by blacklisting those who sought to disregard their unconscionable contracts, Organized Baseball was monopolizing the relatively limited supply of talented players. They were seeking to establish this monopoly for an overriding reason: to maintain balanced competition, thereby hopefully increasing their revenues, and to hold down player salaries, thereby hopefully decreasing their costs.

Put in this fashion, could anyone but a person steeped in the niceties of late nineteenth- and early twentieth-century jurisprudence believe that the framers of the National Agreement viewed their enterprise as not engaging in trade and commerce? They were in the business of operating baseball franchises for a profit. They believed profits were tied to the fundamental variables of gate receipts and player salaries. They had concluded that gate receipts would be increased if teams were associated with one city but traveled to other cities to play games. They were prepared to include in their expenses the costs of transporting and housing players while the teams traveled. Had they believed that gate receipts would have been just as good if a team stayed in a locality all year, playing other teams from that locality, they would surely have chosen to forgo the out-of-pocket and emotional costs of transporting teams around the leagues. They obviously believed the contrary: that playing "visiting teams" from other cities boosted attendance.

Given these practices, how could anyone conclude, whatever the legal nomenclature, that major league baseball teams were not engaged in interstate commerce? How could anyone fairly characterize baseball games as "purely State" or "local" affairs? And how could anyone doubt that when the framers of the National Agreement established their three fundamental rules—the reserve clause, territoriality, and monopsonistic buying practices—that they were combining to interfere with free competition in interstate commerce? Their entire agreement had been predicated on doing just that.

◆

The dissonance between the legal arguments and conclusions in the *Federal Baseball* case and this practical reading of the rules of the enterprise of major league baseball in the early twentieth century thus needs to be explained. Could it be that contemporaries were not able to cut through the legal concepts to see what was actually going on in baseball? Although hindsight is often associated with clarity, that explanation must be rejected. Not only did the opponents of Organized

Baseball see the effect of the National Agreement on player salaries and potentially competitive franchises clearly enough, so did those within the enterprise. Only a few lawyers and judges, more familiar with the sophistic dimensions of legal concepts than with the workings of the game, were prepared to insist that major league baseball was not only not interstate commerce, it was not commerce at all.

At this point Chief Justice Smyth's assertion that baseball was "sport, not trade" looms larger than it did when it was offered as a legal argument. Although offered as a legal argument, it was not one at all. Smyth offered no authoritative support for the proposition that "sport" and "trade" were mutually exclusive legal categories, and none would have been forthcoming. Smyth's characterization of baseball as "sport," like the characterization of baseball owners as "sportsmen" and the persistent belief that baseball was not just a "business," but a "game," were cryptic efforts to capture the cultural resonance of baseball, its extra dimensions.

When a new factory moved to an American city in the early twentieth century, and began producing and distributing products that appealed to the residents, the factory might have made quite an impact. The residents might have bought its products in great numbers, talked about them with their neighbors, exhibited some pride in the success of the factory, supplied workers for the factory to employ, and contributed to the wealth of the factory owners. But however successful the factory, and whatever its importance, over time, to the economy of the city, its presence could never approximate the excitement, the civic pride, the sense of diverse residents being brought together in a common cause that would be generated by that same city's baseball team in the late stages of a pennant race. Nor could the pleasure a city resident found from purchasing or using one of the factory's products remotely approach the level of vicarious satisfaction found from watching the city's baseball team win an important game.

Buying a product was not, for most early twentieth-century residents of cities, an activity whose outcome was uncertain, that replicated the outdoor amusement of youth, and that provided an opportunity to engage, vicariously, in athletic competition. Watching a baseball game was all those things. It was easy to think of buying a product as part of one's "business." It was much harder to think of watching a baseball game in the same manner. Indeed, it was much harder to think of baseball, even at the major league level, even for high stakes, as a "business." When one watched it, or followed the progress of the daily games in the newspaper, or noticed the pennant races unfolding, or observed the box scores and charted the progress of one's favorite players, it appeared much more as a "sport." It did seem more exalted, and at the same time more ephemeral and impressionistic, than "commerce."

Thus the astonishing inability of the Supreme Court of the United States to grasp the practical meaning of Organized Baseball's governing "rules" (and, one might add, the determination of Congress to let such myopia endure by retaining baseball's exemption from the antitrust laws) ends up being explicable as one more example of the "peculiar" status of baseball as an American enterprise. Those closest to baseball, and most directly affected by its decisions, knew full well that it was a business, and a buyers' monopoly at that. But they also knew that the American public resisted such a labeling: to them, baseball was primarily a "sport," an object of vicarious emotion, a symbol of civic identity. And for all their knowledge about the nature of the enterprise, those closest to baseball believed in the other dimensions of its identity as well. At the same time that they counted gate receipts, or their wages, and considered the price of uniforms and the cost of meals on the road, baseball owners and players reminded themselves that there were things about their profession that made it more than a business, that made it resemble a child's game, played for the pure joy of outdoor activity and competition.

3

The Rise of the Commissioner: Gambling, the Black Sox, and the Creation of Baseball Heroes

BASEBALL had begun its professional life as a working-class sport. Its first teams that played for money had been composed of "roughnecks," many of Irish or German as well as British ancestry, lacking education, mainly products of the working-class neighborhoods springing up in late nineteenth-century American cities. To A. G. Spalding, three unfortunate public perceptions about the sport had surfaced during its infancy: that it attracted rowdy fans and was thus not necessarily an inviting spectator sport; that its players were prone to drinking; and that it was linked to gambling and gamblers.[1]

A mission of Spalding and the other entrepreneurs of early twentieth-century baseball was to alter those perceptions; to make the sport wholesome. By 1911 he claimed that they had succeeded. "The elimination of the betting evil," he announced, "was the cornerstone of the success of Base Ball as an exhibition game. . . . No betting, no Sunday playing, no liquor sold on the grounds! It was a revolution in the world of professional sport. Base Ball is the only game which suits the mighty populace and yet is wholly free from ties to bind it to the gambling and the liquor-selling element."[2]

The late nineteenth century had been a period of gentry withdrawal from politics, in place at least by the Grant administration and causally related to the emergence of urban political bosses and machines. By the 1890s gentry activism had begun to reemerge, and "gentlemanly" reformers as diverse as E. L. Godkin and Theodore Roosevelt had begun to participate in national politics. One of the motivating factors behind late nineteenth-century gentry reform politics was the perception of its participants that the American political arena, especially in its urban centers, had become corrupt, venal, and bereft of traditional class-based standards of honesty and probity.[3]

The goals of the first generation of owners who built steel and concrete ballparks were testimony to the fact that the game of baseball was likewise affected by the gentrification of American culture in the first two decades of the twentieth century. As we have seen, prominent among those goals had been the upgrading of the experience of watching baseball games from a potentially rowdy, dangerous, transient one to one that was safe, wholesome, civic-minded, and uplifting: a communion with fresh air and sunshine within a grand permanent structure in which a whole city could take pride. Put starkly, the first generation of twentieth-century owner-builders was interested in establishing their sport as the personification of middle-class values, which, at the time, were synonymous with morality, respectability, and civic-mindedness.

Gambling, traffic in liquors, and rowdiness had been identified by apologists such as Spalding as not compatible with the early twentieth-century aspirations of baseball, and the presence of private police and the absence of liquor sales in the new ballparks were evidence of the owners' conscious efforts to create a wholesome atmosphere. Gambling, however, posed a more complicated problem. Gambling on professional sports was not illegal, and baseball, with its relatively slow pace and systematic amassing of statistical information, was a fertile field for betting. Baseball clubs could announce that betting was forbidden within their ballparks, and ostensibly take steps to banish violators. That was easier said than done, however, as discerning what constituted a bet was not easy, and the clubs ran the risk of offending their patrons with overzealous surveillance.

A more fundamental problem was the large amount of gambling on baseball that did not require attendance at ballparks at all. This took place through baseball pools, in which prospective bettors were given choices among teams or players, and wagered that their choice would surpass competitors in the number of runs scored, hits made or games won, during a given time period. The pool, which amounted to an informed lottery, required only a central place of operation and an operator who, for a commission, oversaw the processing and distribution of the bets. Despite the advantages of pools from the operator's point of view, operators were often corrupt, claiming to winners that mythical other winners existed, deducting their alleged winnings, and intimidating those who sought to press their inquiries any further.[4] Operations such as pools widely expanded the amount of gambling on baseball and posed a major difficulty for those interested in upgrading the game's image.

In 1919, in an afterword to an authorized biography, Charles Comiskey rhapsodized about the wholesomeness of his sport. "Baseball," he wrote, "is the greatest sport in the world. It is the cleanest. . . . Formerly sport was not regarded as a proper calling for young men. It is beginning to assume its rightful place in society. To me baseball is as honorable as any other business. . . . It has to be or it could not last a season out. Crookedness and baseball do not mix."[5]

During the same year that Comiskey was writing these words, his own White Sox players were in the process of demonstrating how closely linked baseball and gambling still were.

◆

In a 1911 indictment of the connection between gambling and baseball Spalding had not minced words in describing how an active interest on the part of gamblers in the outcomes of games could foster an interest on the part of some players in corrupting the games themselves. "Betting on the result of games," Spalding noted, "naturally begot collusion between those who bet their money and some of those who played the game. Per consequence, it was soon discovered that unprincipled players, under pretense of accident or inability to make points at critical stages, were 'throwing' games."[6]

Despite identifying a ready connection between gambling and player corruption in baseball, Spalding nonetheless insisted that the existence of corrupt players was a stage in baseball's past. Singling out the expulsion of four players of the Louisville team in the National League in 1877 for "crookedness" in consorting with gamblers to throw games, Spalding asserted that a "great victory . . . over gambling and the gamblers" had "eradicate[d] the evil" of player cheating "from that day to this." By 1901, he claimed, the National League "had made players to so regard their interests that not one of them cared or dared to be seen with a gambler." By 1911, the year his history of baseball appeared, "the press of the country was united in its conviction that the game was clean; that gambling had been kicked out."[7]

The claims of Spalding and Comiskey appear as inflated rhetoric, given the fact that betting on baseball games continued at a brisk pace during the first two decades of the twentieth century. But the rhetoric was not disingenuous. It was a testament to the importance those within the inner circles of Organized Baseball attached to an image of their sport as wholesome and incorruptible. What, then, was to be done by those at the center of baseball's establishment when evidence of a continuing connection between active gambler interest and player corruption surfaced? The answer, for several years, was nothing; at least nothing that would call public attention to the possibility that crookedness and baseball might mix.

In 1904 John W. Taylor, then a pitcher for the St. Louis Cardinals, was accused by the president of the Chicago Cubs, James Hart, of not giving his best in the 1903 series between Taylor's former team, the Cubs, and the White Sox for the championship of Chicago. Hart, in the course of charges before the National Commission, claimed that Taylor had told him that he had been paid $500 to lose games in the city series. The matter was investigated, but the National Commission, not having any direct evidence and concerned that the charges would be taken as emanating from the Cubs' pique over losing the series, dismissed the case against Taylor. A few months later Taylor was again accused of throwing a game to the Pittsburgh Pirates in July 1904, but all that was established was that Taylor had been drunk the night before the game, and he was let off with a $300 fine. Taylor continued to pitch in the National League for four more years.[8]

Near the end of the 1908 season rumors about fixed games surfaced again. This time they centered on the New York Giants, in the throes of a close pennant race with the Pirates and the Cubs for the National League pennant. Among the rumors were that the Giants' manager, John McGraw, had attempted to bribe players on the Boston Braves and Philadelphia Phillies, who had games against the Giants at the end of the season, to allow the Giants to win; that Joe Kelly, the manager of Boston and a former teammate of McGraw's, had persuaded his club not to give its best against the Giants; and that one of the umpires of the playoff game between the Giants and the Cubs for the pennant,

Bill Klem, had been offered a bribe by the Giants' team physician. An investigation was launched by the National Commission, but no action was taken, apparently because of a concern that penalties against alleged offenders might trigger libel suits.[9]

In 1910 another controversy arose as a result of suspicious behavior on the part of St. Louis Brown players during a game between the Browns and the Cleveland Indians on the last day of the season. Before the season the Chalmers Motor Company had announced that it would give an automobile to the winner of the batting championships in both leagues. Going into the final day, Ty Cobb of the Detroit Tigers held a close lead over Napoleon Lajoie of the Indians for the American League batting title. Cobb did not play in the Tigers' last two games, but Lajoie, playing in a doubleheader against the Browns, got eight hits in nine times at bat to pass Cobb. Of Lajoie's hits, only one was unambiguous: six were bunt singles and the seventh an infield grounder to the Browns' shortstop, who failed to throw to first in time. Lajoie was not a fast runner, but the Browns' third baseman continued to play back on the outfield grass, and then justified his actions out of a fear that Lajoie might hit him with a line drive.

The Sporting News, describing the game as a "disgraceful proceeding," pointed out that Cobb was particularly unpopular among other players in the league. The American League investigated and eventually cleared the Browns' manager, Jack O'Connor, and a Browns' scout, Harry Howell (who had allegedly offered the official scorer a bribe to treat Lajoie favorably), of any complicity, but both were fired. Cobb was awarded the batting championship, allegedly on the basis of recalibrated statistics, but Lajoie received a car as well. The award for batting champion was abolished, and replaced by a most valuable player award, to be selected by a committee of baseball writers representing each of the major league cities.

The pattern demonstrated by these incidents was an unsettling one. It suggested that in the years between the formation of Organized Baseball in 1903 and the 1919 World Series there was frequent interest in enticing major league players to throw games, or at least the outcomes of plays within a game, and some evidence that players could do so. At the same time the incidents suggested that if no one came forward with documented evidence of cheating, the National Commission would be deterred from taking any firm action against suspected players for fear of lawsuits. Since it was unlikely that anyone involved in a baseball fix would volunteer incriminating information, and evidence of poor play on the field was not in itself sufficient to incriminate, the incidents actually served to encourage cheating.

Of those who profited from the difficulties in discovering and punishing "crooked" ballplayers, no one was more successful, or conspicuous, than Hal Chase, the first baseman of the New York Highlanders, Chicago White Sox, Cincinnati Reds, and New York Giants from 1905 to 1919. During his days with the Highlanders Chase acquired the reputation of an extremely talented but self-centered player, who intrigued against his manager and was regularly accused of not always giving his best in games. In 1910 Chase was accused by Highlander manager George Stallings of throwing games, but American League president Ban Johnson acquitted him, and eventually Chase succeeded Stallings as manager. He was not a success, and in 1913 he was replaced by Frank Chance.

During the 1913 season Fred Lieb, in the early years of his lengthy career as a baseball writer, was told by Chance that Chase was throwing games. Heywood Broun of the *New York Tribune* was also a participant in the conversation, and Broun wrote an article the next day to the effect that Chance believed Chase wasn't playing up to his ability. Highlander president Frank Farrell immediately protested to Broun, but two days after Broun's story appeared Chase was traded to the Chicago White Sox for two undistinguished players. Lieb, in reflecting on the incident many years later, said, "What struck me . . . was that the American League must have known the Chase record and the suspicions underlying what Chance had told Broun and me. But instead of disciplining Chase or calling for an investigation, they let Farrell trade him to a club that was much higher in the standings."[10]

In 1914 Chase jumped to the Federal League, precipitating the case in which a judge invalidated the standard reserve clause on the grounds it lacked mutuality. The incident underscored that Chase was a shrewd, mercenary individual, not disinclined to challenge rules if he thought he could profit by doing so. A year later the Federal League collapsed, and the Cincinnati Reds purchased Chase's services. Chase led the National League in hitting in 1916, but he clashed with Christy Mathewson, the Reds' manager, and on August 7, 1918, Mathewson suspended Chase for "indifferent play and insubordination," his actions allegedly based on Chase's attempting to bribe players on his own team to throw games.

Chase sued the Reds for back pay, and in January 1919 National League president John Heydler heard testimony from several players that Chase had attempted to corrupt them. Mathewson, now overseas with the army, was not present at the meeting, and Chase was officially cleared on February 5. Heydler declared that although Chase's "loose talk" had precipitated "many rumors," and Chase had acted "in a foolish and careless manner," there was no hard evidence of his fixing games. Chase was traded to the Giants, who paid his claims against the Reds. To make matters complete, Mathewson returned from abroad to join the Giants' coaching staff and declared that he had only accused Chase of uneven play.

In August 1919, however, Chase's machinations eventually caught up with him. Heydler received a signed affidavit from Jim Costello, a Boston gambler, that on July 25, 1918, Chase had agreed to throw the game that day between the Reds and the Boston Braves, and had placed a bet on the Braves for $500 with him. A copy of Chase's certified check was enclosed with the affidavit. Apparently Chase and another player, Lee Magee, guaranteed that the Cincinnati starting pitcher, Pete Schneider, had been corrupted, and gave Costello checks as security. Schneider did not start the game, however, and the Reds won. Magee then stopped payment on his check to Costello, which eventually prompted Costello to approach Heydler.

Despite Chase's complicity, he was not formally suspended from the Giants, although he was removed from most of the remainder of their 1919 games, the public explanation being that he had sprained his wrist. After the 1919 season he was issued a contract from the Giants, but for a trifling amount, and he quit major league baseball, never to return. That October, while playing semi-pro ball in California, he reportedly made about $40,000 betting on the Reds against the Chicago White Sox in the World Series.[11]

Chase's litany demonstrated how comparatively powerless Organized Baseball's hierarchy was to prevent unscrupulous players from attempting to fix games for profit. First, cheating was difficult to detect: Chase's technique, according to those who were convinced of his duplicity, was to use his considerable grace as a first baseman to convert safe throws into wild ones by timing his arrival to first base so as to just miss a throw. Second, no one involved in a fixing attempt usually had any incentive to come forward, whether it succeeded or not: the action by Costello that implicated Chase in the July 25, 1918, incident was an atypical example of a gambler vindictively exposing a player who had welshed on his payment. Finally, and most important, the members of Organized Baseball's high command wanted to conceal from the public any evidence tending to suggest that the game in which they had so much invested was corrupt. Their treatment of Chase was characteristic. Even though his "crookedness" had been widely known within baseball circles from at least 1908 on, and even though by 1919 baseball executives had direct evidence that he had bet on games in which he played, he was never publicly expelled or suspended. Evidence of his corruption was responded to by his being traded to another team, by false declarations of injuries, and by low salary offers designed to get him to quit the major leagues.

Thus by the close of the 1919 season three consequences of the close relationship between gambling and major league baseball had become established features of the game. One was that players were made regular offers to fix games for profit, and several, over the years, responded affirmatively to those offers. A second was that player corruption was difficult to detect, and Organized Baseball appeared extremely reluctant to discipline even players whose corruption was quite obvious. A third was that the public statements issued by baseball owners and officials, and the general attributions of the game's straight and clean image, revealed how sensitive the question of player corruption was regarded by those at the heart of the enterprise. It was as if those in baseball's official circles were embarked upon a self-contradictory strategy: repeated public insistence that the game was incorruptible and repeated efforts to conceal evidence of its corruption. The incompatibility of these two goals was to become apparent in the Black Sox scandal.

◆

The Black Sox episode, in which eight members of the 1919 Chicago White Sox allegedly agreed to lose the World Series to the Cincinnati Reds in exchange for payments from gamblers, is one of the elemental stories of American sports. There have been other sports gambling scandals, including one, the point-shaving episodes in college basketball in the 1950s, that resulted in comparable penalties for the offenders, who were banned from the sport for life. Numerous athletes have been barred from their sports for gambling-related offenses, ranging from criminal conduct to poor judgment in their choice of betting subjects. There has, however, been nothing like the Black Sox episode in its centrality. The revelation of the scandal forced the owners of major league franchises to create the office of baseball commissioner, who would be charged with overseeing their own conduct as well as that of the players. In theory, the owners relinquished a considerable amount of their power and autonomy in the act of creating a commissioner. They did so even though they had been the victims, not the perpetrators, of the scandal.

Much has been written on the Black Sox scandal, and because of the persistent digging of some of those writers, the curtain of silence that those intimately involved with the episode erected after it broke has been penetrated. The following account, based on the anonymous revelations of participants, is now widely accepted.[12] The scandal originated in the resentments by a clique of White Sox players of owner Charles Comiskey, and came to fruition because none of those players felt that, on balance, winning the World Series was worth more than making money. The corrupt process began with players approaching gamblers and inviting payoffs for losing games, and was nearly botched when the gamblers charged with delivering those payoffs to the players lost that money on their own unsuccessful bets. The loss of the Series was eventually achieved through a death threat to Chicago's starting pitcher in the decisive eighth game of the best-of-nine series. The facts and details of the fix were covered up by a variety of people, including Comiskey, for nearly a year after it occurred. The Black Sox scandal was, in its details, a small, sordid tale of greed and chicanery, not unlike a corrupt bidding process for a municipal utility contract or a stuffed ballot box in a closely contested election.

But because the Black Sox affair linked gambling with baseball, at a time when the aspiration of major league baseball was to be seen as, in the words of Charles Comiskey himself, "the most honest pastime in the world,"[13] the scandal had ramifications that far exceeded its prosaic details. It occurred at a moment when the aspirations of baseball to become an American cultural icon and the realities of baseball as a business and a sport were thrown into an awkward juxtaposition, so that those with a direct stake in the enterprise of baseball were faced with two choices. They could either lower the game's aspirations, thereby implicitly reducing baseball to the status of boxing or horse racing, two other professional sports with close connections with the gambling industry, or they could seek to reaffirm baseball's image as "the most honest pastime in the world" by prescribing a stringent moral code for the sport.

The process of dissociating baseball from gambling transformed the Black Sox episode from a not particularly remarkable example of early twentieth-century corruption to a piece of baseball lore, a story that seemed almost incomprehensible in retrospect. Yet in the context of baseball's early history, the Black Sox affair was only a slightly exaggerated version of a routine dimension of the sport, that of players deliberately trying to lose games in order to obtain shares of the money gambled on them. Baseball and gambling had come to be closely linked in the first decades of the twentieth century, and that linkage posed a growing threat to the self-image of baseball. The Black Sox episode brought that threat out into the open.

Given the penuriousness of Comiskey, the cliquishness and poor chemistry of the White Sox, and the established connections between baseball players and gamblers, the creation of a fixed World Series in 1919 was not a particularly surprising development for the time, however inexplicable it may have appeared later. More surprising was the length of time it took for the fix to be made public, and the gap between the intuitions of those who were closely connected to the 1919 Series, or close observers of it, and the intuitions of the general public.

The fix involved eight players on the White Sox: Arnold ("Chick") Gandil, Eddie Cicotte, Charles ("Swede") Risberg, Claude ("Lefty") Williams, George ("Buck") Weaver, Oscar ("Happy") Felsch, Fred McMullin, and Joseph Jefferson ("Shoeless Joe") Jackson.[14] The duplicity, and the direct contributions of the eight "Black Sox" to the fix, varied. Gandil and Cicotte, by some accounts, initiated the fix themselves by approaching gamblers, and both contributed some inept plays. Risberg and Williams also gave evidence of not playing their best in spots. Although both Felsch and Jackson later admitted involvement in the fix, their performances in the Series were generally flawless. McMullin was a utility infielder who did not play in the Series at all. Weaver, who persistently and vociferously maintained that he had not participated in the fix, had a very good Series.

Many among those directly affected by the results of the Series, such as Comiskey, White Sox manager Kid Gleason, and several White Sox players who had not participated in the fix, were strongly suspicious that certain members of the Sox had not given their full efforts in the

The 1919 "Black Sox" from Chicago. Manager Kid Gleason is in the back row, first on the left. The eight players eventually banned from baseball for associating with gamblers before the World Series are Swede Risberg, back row, fifth from left; Fred McMullin, back row, sixth from left; Joe Jackson, back row, second from right; Happy Felsch, second row, third from right; Chick Gandil, second row, second from right; Buck Weaver, second row, first on right; Eddie Cicotte, first row, third from left; and Lefty Williams, first row, second from right. Ray Schalk is in the second row, first on left, and Eddie Collins is in the first row, first on left. (National Baseball Library and Archive, Cooperstown, N.Y.)

Series. This same impression was shared by members of the Chicago press corps, such as Ring Lardner and Hugh Fullerton, and others working for out-of-town newspapers covering the Series, such as Fred Lieb and Christy Mathewson. There were ample reasons for their suspicions. The regular-season records of the two clubs suggested that the White Sox would be heavy favorites to win the Series, but shortly before the Series opened a great deal of money was bet on the Reds, considerably lowering the odds. Fullerton and Mathewson, in observing the games, had noticed some plays by White Sox players, notably Cicotte, Risberg, and Gandil, that suggested a lack of effort. Cicotte and Williams, two very reliable pitchers all season, had had sudden lapses in the Series. Williams, in particular, had been chronically wild in places, even though he was known for his good control.

In the immediate aftermath of the Series, rumors circulated that it had not been "played square." Hugh Fullerton was in Charles Comiskey's office after the last game when manager Kid Gleason stated to Comiskey that some of the White Sox players had been corrupted. Comiskey then declared that, if the charges were proven, there were seven men who would never play for the White Sox again. The next day Fullerton wrote a column in which he hinted of a fix and denied it at the same time. "Almost everything went backward," Fullerton said. "So much so that an evil-minded person might believe the stories that have been circulated during the Series. The fact is, this Series was lost in the first game, and lost through overconfidence. Forget the suspicious and evil-minded yarns that may be circulated." At the same time he added, "Yesterday's game also means the disruption of the Chicago White Sox ballclub. There are seven men on the team who will not be there when the gong sounds next Spring."[15] He referred to all the Black Sox save Weaver.

On October 11 the *New York Times* reported that Charles Comiskey was offering $20,000 "for a single clue to lead to evidence that any of his players had deliberately attempted to throw any of the world series games to the Cincinnati Reds." "I believe my boys fought the battles of the recent world series on the level, as they have always done," Comiskey was quoted as saying, "and I would be the first to want information to the contrary."[16] That announcement by Comiskey was the first step in a strategy, designed by Comiskey's attorney Alfred Austrian, to control the course of the Black Sox scandal. The strategy, in general terms, was for Comiskey to appear to be leading an investigation into rumors of a fix while at the same time covering it up.

Comiskey's motives in pursuing that strategy were clear enough. He had nothing to gain from the exposure of a conspiracy to fix the World Series. The seven players that he suspected were the heart of his ballclub: if they were revealed to have thrown games, he was already on record as having said they would never again play for him. By leading the investigation, he was free to disregard incriminating evidence if he doubted it could be proved. Over the winter of 1919–20, a few ballplayers and gamblers came to him with rumors. Although the information made it all the more certain that a fix had taken place, none of it was likely to hold up in court, and Comiskey declined to pay any money for it.

At the same time Comiskey withheld World Series paychecks for the seven players he suspected, and hired a private detective to investigate their financial affairs. Only one, Gandil, was reported as having suddenly spent large amounts of money. By November Comiskey mailed out the World Series checks. Meanwhile Hugh Fullerton was still obsessed with the fix and wrote a series of articles outlining the close contacts between gambling and major league baseball. His own paper, the *Herald-Examiner*, declined to print the articles, expressing a fear of libel suits. Other Chicago papers also declined, and Fullerton eventually published his findings in the *New York World* on December 15, 1919. He stopped short in his articles of claiming that the Series had been fixed, suggesting only that there had been numerous accusations of tampering, syndication, and bribery in baseball, and that the major league owners had done nothing to investigate or to refute such charges. Fullerton's articles prompted Comiskey to announce that his investigation had "discovered nothing to indicate any member of my team double-crossing me or the public last Fall."[17]

The reaction to Fullerton's articles demonstrated the strong investment those who closely followed baseball, but had not been directly affected by the fix, had in denying the possibility of its existence. Fullerton was excoriated by *Baseball Magazine*, a Boston-based periodical that regarded itself as a kind of house organ of baseball's establishment. *Baseball Magazine* claimed that Fullerton had picked the White Sox to win the Series and, when his prognostication failed, attempted to concoct the preposterous story of a fix. Conceding that gamblers were strongly interested in the outcome of baseball games, *Baseball Magazine* nonetheless found it incredible that baseball players themselves could be corrupted. That attitude was representative of followers of baseball at the time. On October 16 *The Sporting News*, in its first issue announcing the results of the World Series, reported Comiskey's $20,000 offer for information about a fix and commented:

> President Charles A. Comiskey of the White Sox has made a proposition that ought to mean pretty soft picking—if the peddlers of scandal can make good. Because a lot of dirty, long-nosed, thick-lipped and strong-smelling gamblers butted into the World Series—an American event by

> the way—and some of said gamblers got crossed, stories were peddled that there was something wrong with the games that were played. Some of the Chicago players laid down for a price, said the scandal-mongers. Comiskey has met that by offering $20,000 for any sort of a clue that will bear out such a charge. He might as well have offered a million, for there will be no takers, because there is no such evidence, except in the mucky minds of the stinkers who—because they are crooked—think all the rest of the world can't play straight.[18]

The reactions of *Baseball Magazine* and *The Sporting News* suggested that the greatest obstacle to the Black Sox scandal becoming more than a collection of rumors was the fact that baseball fans in America simply didn't want to believe that those who participated in the game could be crooked. As the scandal unfolded, there emerged alongside public interest in its details a comparable interest in denying that it could have ever happened. Even when three of the White Sox players confessed their involvement to a grand jury, and details of their confessions were reported in the newspapers, a jury was subsequently able to acquit all of the players of any crimes. The same grand jury before which the players had been originally indicted, in its final, November 6, 1920, report to the judge, Charles MacDonald, who impaneled it, had this to say about the game that had been corrupted in the 1919 Series:

> The jury is impressed with the fact that baseball is an index to our national genius and character. The American principle of merit and fair play must prevail, and it is all important that the game be clean, from the most humble player to the highest dignitary. Baseball enthusiasm and its hold upon the public interest must ultimately stand or fall upon this count. Baseball is more than a national game; it is an American institution, having its place prominently and significantly in the life of the people. In the deplorable absence of military training in this country, baseball and other games having 'team play' spirit would be entirely lacking if it were relegated to the position to which horse racing and boxing have fallen. The national game promotes respect for proper authority, self-confidence, fairmindedness, quick judgment and self-control.[19]

From December 1919, when Fullerton's articles appeared, until well into the 1920 baseball season, the fix seemed to have disappeared from public view. All of the corrupt White Sox had returned for the 1920 season save Gandil, and most of them had received salary increases.

Jackson had signed a three-year contract for $9,000 a year, believing, wrongly, that it contained no ten-day clause. Weaver had signed for three years at $7,500 a year. Eventually, two days before the season opened, Risberg signed. Cicotte and Felsch were also back on the roster. The White Sox continued to play good baseball: as August began they were locked in a three-way pennant race with the Indians and the Yankees. Incredibly, some of the corrupt players continued to throw games, here and there, during the season. In late August the White Sox faced an important series against the Boston Red Sox, a weak club, and lost all three games. After the series White Sox second baseman Eddie Collins met with Comiskey and told him that he believed that several Sox players had thrown the games. Comiskey took no action.

Eventually rumors of the past and present fixing of games found their way to the overall baseball press corps. One reporter, James Cruisenberry of the *Chicago Tribune*, became outraged about the situation and wrote of the consistent, uncensored participation of big-time gamblers in baseball. When Cruisenberry became privy to hard information about the 1919 fix, however, he found that he couldn't print it because of the fear of libel suits. In July 1920, White Sox manager Kid Gleason tipped off Cruisenberry and Ring Lardner that Abe Attell, a former boxer who was one of the gamblers, was in a New York bar talking openly about his role in the fix. Cruisenberry and Lardner, whom Attell did not know, went to the bar and for their benefit Gleason asked Attell questions about the operation. Attell named his former boss, Arnold Rothstein of New York, as the principal financier of the fix.

Thrilled with the scoop, Cruisenberry prepared to write an article revealing the Series fix. He was told by his editor, Harvey Woodruff, that it was a waste of time. Attell, as well as Rothstein, would simply deny the story and possibly sue for libel. The public was not prepared to believe the story without hard evidence. It did not seem as if that evidence would ever come to light.

Then an apparently trivial episode, involving the alleged fixing of a meaningless game, eventually resulted in the Black Sox scandal being made public. On August 31, 1920, the Chicago Cubs, then in fifth place in the National League, were scheduled to play the Philadelphia Phillies, occupying eighth place. Unaccountably, large amounts of money were bet on the Phillies in Detroit. William Veeck, president of the Chicago Cubs, was informed about the situation, and he quietly offered Cubs pitcher Grover Cleveland Alexander a $500 bonus if he would win the game. In any case the Phillies lost. Veeck decided to launch an investigation modeled on that of Comiskey's into the 1919 World Series: one whose progress and nature he could control.

In the meantime, however, an anonymous letter was sent to the *Chicago Herald-Examiner*'s sports desk. It said that hotel lobbies in Detroit had been "crowded with gamblers wanting to bet any amount of money" on the Phillies-Cubs game, and that "conditions were so openly rotten that I was prompted to write as I do." This was the lead Cruisenberry and Hugh Fullerton had been looking for: on September 4 the *Herald-Examiner* ran a story titled, "$50,000 Bet on the Cubs and Phillies Sure-Thing Game." Now convinced that he could no longer control his own investigation, Veeck decided that the matter was for a Chicago grand jury, and on September 7 Judge MacDonald, with the support of American League president Ban Johnson, impaneled one. The grand jury's mandate, at that time, was limited to the Cubs-Phillies game.

Cruisenberry believed that the convening of the grand jury would give him an opportunity to revive the incidents of the 1919 Series. He arranged for a well-known Chicago businessman, Fred M. Loomis, to cooperate with him in writing a letter to the press demanding a grand jury investigation into gambling in baseball, including the 1919 Series. Cruisenberry wrote the letter for Loomis's signature, and the letter was printed on September 19 in the *Chicago Tribune*. As a result of the letter, the scope of the grand jury investigation was widened to include events in 1919.

On September 23 and 24, New York Giants pitcher John ("Rube") Benton was summoned before the grand jury to corroborate a story that Hal Chase, his teammate on the Giants, had offered him money to throw a game to the Cubs. Benton denied accepting the bribe, and claimed to have won the game, but admitted that the incident was not the only time he and Chase had had a conversation about the fixing of games. A week before the 1919 Series, Benton said, he heard from Chase that the World Series was to be thrown, and that the White Sox would lose the first two games. At the same time, while in another player's room in the Hotel Ansonia in New York, Benton had seen that player receive a telegram informing him that the Sox would lose. Chase, Benton said, had won over $40,000 betting on the Reds.

Charles Comiskey (left) and Chicago Cubs' owner William L. Veeck as they waited to testify before a Chicago grand jury investigating the "fixing" of ball games, September 23, 1920. Shortly thereafter Eddie Cicotte confessed his participation in corrupt 1919 World Series games, and the "Black Sox" scandal broke. (National Baseball Library and Archive, Cooperstown, N.Y.)

When asked which White Sox players were involved, Benton said that a betting commissioner from Cincinnati had told him that Gandil, Cicotte, Williams, and Felsch were among the corrupt players. He suggested that the grand jury call in Cicotte and ask him for details. Benton's testimony floated out of the grand jury investigation and reached the ears of the White Sox players. Ray Schalk, one of the "Clean Sox," gave a statement to the press that he was going to "tell all I know" to the grand jury. Meanwhile Cicotte, in the course of his traveling with the White Sox, had discovered that he was being tailed by a private detective in the employ of Ban Johnson. He began to feel as if things were closing in.

So did the newspapers. On September 23 the *Chicago Tribune* had reported that Charles ("Buck") Herzog, then an infielder for the Cubs, had told the grand jury that five White Sox players had thrown the 1919 Series to the Reds. No names were mentioned in the article, but two days later the *New York Times*, in a story on the grand jury's investigations, reported that "a boxer" had approached gamblers to raise money to fix the Series, and had stated that five White Sox players were cooperating. In the same article the *Times* noted that Charles Comiskey had withheld Series checks from eight of his players, and named the eight participants in the scandal.[20]

Matters then came with a rush. On September 28 the grand jury indicted all eight players, and Comiskey issued a statement suspending all but Gandil, who was already under suspension for failing to report for the 1920 season. In a formal notice to the suspended players, Comiskey stated that if they were guilty of any wrongdoing, he would try to see that they were permanently banned from baseball, but if they were innocent they would be reinstated. On hearing the news of their indictment Cicotte, and then Jackson, were persuaded to make statements before the grand jury. They were not represented by counsel, and they both signed statements waiving immunity from prosecution, not grasping what they were signing.

Excerpts from Cicotte's and Jackson's confessions were widely quoted in the newspapers. Cicotte described how he had initially resisted involving himself in the fix, how he had held out for $10,000 in cash, payable in advance, and how he had received that sum the night before the opening game. He described how "I wasn't putting a thing on the ball" in the first game against the Reds, and how he had "deliberately cut off a throw from the outfield which might have prevented a run" in the fourth game. "I never did anything I regretted as much in my life," he said. "I've played a crooked game and I have lost, and I'm here to tell the whole truth."[21]

Jackson's statement, as reported, was less clear, as was his motivation for making it. He said that when Judge MacDonald had approached him, he claimed that he was an honest man, but when MacDonald responded, "I know you are not," he "figured somebody had squawked," and decided to "tell him what I know." He took pains to stress to MacDonald that he had asked for $20,000 and had only received $5,000, and that was why he was cooperating, and then reported that MacDonald had said to him that if he had received the entire $20,000 he would not have come in to testify. "I don't think the judge likes me," Jackson was quoted as saying. "I never got the [extra] $15,000 that was coming to me."

Jackson's actual description of the fix and his involvement in it, as reported in the press, was cryptic. He stated that he had been tempted to participate by Gandil and Risberg, and that when he had not received the amount he had been promised he threatened to talk about the fix. Others responded by calling him a "poor simp" and claiming that there were participants who had been promised more, and received less, than he. His resentment at this treatment, he insisted, was "why I went down and told Judge MacDonald and the Grand Jury what I knew about the frame-up."[22] Nowhere did Jackson indicate what he had done to participate in the fix. He had led the White Sox in batting in the Series, had hit a home run, and had made no errors in the field. The *New York Times* reported that "according to the officials . . . . Jackson testified that throughout the series he either struck out or hit easy balls when hits would mean runs," but there is no evidence of his doing so.

On September 29, two additional Black Sox were reported as having "confessed." Lefty Williams gave a statement to the grand jury that was of interest because he identified a meeting in the Warner Hotel in Chicago in which gamblers had met with all of the fixers except Jackson, and offered $5,000 to each player for throwing the Series. Other than that, Williams's testimony was unremarkable, although it demonstrated that the ballplayers involved in the fix had an incredibly small amount of information about how much money they were getting, what they were expected to do, and even whether the fix was still taking place. For a group of co-conspirators, they had very little to do with one another.

The incredibly amateurish and informal nature of the fix was further revealed in Happy Felsch's confession, which was not made before the grand jury, but to a newspaperman, Harry Reutlinger of the *Chicago American*. Felsch's conversation with Reutlinger was reported in several papers, including the *New York Times*:

> I got into the deal when I found out the others were in it anyhow—I'd have been $5000 out if I'd stayed out. Not that that's any excuse. It happened that I didn't have any chances to throw any of the games. Whether

> I would have carried out my part in the deal if I had the chance I don't know. The coin looked good to us—I suppose I would have done the same as the rest. . . .
>
> We've sold ourselves and our jobs—the only jobs we know anything about. We've gotten in return only a few dollars—while a lot of gamblers have gotten rich. Looks like the joke's on us, don't it?[23]

The Black Sox scandal appeared to be just getting off the ground when Cicotte, Jackson, Williams, and Felsch confessed, but actually it had reached its emotional peak, and most of the rest of the story was anticlimactic. The gamblers—eventually identified as New York racing entrepreneur and financier Arnold Rothstein, his associate Nathanial ("Nat") Evans, William ("Sport") Sullivan, a bookie from Boston, and Abe Attell—scrambled to avoid being indicted by the grand jury. Rothstein, assisted by his lawyer William Fallon, voluntarily made an appearance before the grand jury, denied any involvement in the fix, and identified Attell as the ringleader. At the same time Fallon arranged a meeting with Alfred Austrian, Comiskey's attorney, at which he made it clear that Comiskey, and Organized Baseball, had nothing to gain from a vigorous investigation into the fix and the links between baseball and gambling. Out of that meeting developed the strategy of having the players' confessions before the grand jury disappear from the office of Illinois state's attorney Maclay Hoyne, an event that eventually resulted in the Black Sox players being found innocent of any criminal charges.

Rothstein, through Fallon, had convinced Comiskey that it was in his best interest to have his players found innocent, reinstated, and back on his roster. At the same time he convinced Sullivan and Attell that they could escape indictment by the grand jury by the simple expedient of leaving the country. He would pay their expenses. Sullivan cooperated, but Attell, after spending some time in Montreal, tired of the exile and returned to New York, where he was promptly arrested. Fallon then argued that the person arrested under the name Abe Attell was not the person who had conspired to fix the 1919 Series. In connection with that argument Fallon bribed a gambler who had previously told the grand jury that Attell had bet with him on the Series to recount his testimony. Without any proof that Attell had actually participated in the fix, the grand jury was powerless to indict him. As for Nat Evans, he had been known only by an alias, Rachael Brown, and no one could find Brown.

With all the primary fixers absent, the State of Illinois moved to indict the Black Sox players on conspiracy charges on February 14, 1921. The arraignment hearing was a farce. There were no other participants other than the players before the court, and when the prosecution attempted to read excerpts from the players' confessions, defense attorneys objected, claiming that the players had never signed confessions. Pressed to introduce the actual documents, the prosecution had to admit that they were no longer in the state's attorney's files, and Judge William Dever ordered that the entire indictment be dismissed as insufficiently based. He gave leave to the State of Illinois to prepare new indictments. The ballplayers, amazed at these developments, were also impressed with the high-priced lawyers that had been enlisted in their defense. They wondered who was paying for their services. It turned out to be Charles Comiskey.

It was no surprise, then, after the state of Illinois eventually indicted the Black Sox on conspiracy charges, that on the evening of August 2, 1921, a jury rendered a verdict acquitting all of the players. It now appeared as if Comiskey's and Austrian's strategy had worked. The ballplayers had been found innocent, and were thus free to return to the White Sox. The Comiskey-led investigation had managed to delay the scandal's becoming public long enough for all the major fixers to evade indictment, and Comiskey's financing of the players' defense seemed to have been a good business judgment.

◆

At this point a new figure entered the Black Sox scandal, and the mythology of the episode as being aberrational, even inexplicable, began. Judge Kenesaw Mountain Landis, who in the wake of the scandal had been appointed as the first baseball commissioner, took the first in a series of actions that were to establish him as a law unto himself within the regime of Organized Baseball, and the symbol of a morally incorruptible sport. Despite being hired by the owners, Landis signified by his action that not all his decisions would necessarily be in the owners' interest. He read a statement to the press that concluded as follows: "Regardless of the verdict of juries, no player who throws a ball game, no player that undertakes or promises to throw a ball game, no player that sits in conference with a bunch of crooked players and gamblers where the ways and means of throwing a game are discussed and does not promptly tell his club about it, will ever play professional baseball."[24]

Landis's statement made it clear that all eight Black Sox would be banned from baseball for life. Included were Weaver, who had apparently never agreed to participate in the fix but knew about it and did not report it; Jackson, who had not attended any meetings with gamblers; and McMullin and Felsch, who had not had any opportunities to throw games. Comiskey's strategy had been shot to pieces. His team was not to be a pennant contender for the rest of his lifetime.

A few sidelights of the scandal remained. Buck Weaver appealed to Landis for reinstatement, but he was denied on the grounds that he could have come forward with information about the proposed fix. He sued Comiskey for the balance of the three-year contract he had signed in 1920 and eventually received a settlement in 1924. He continued to seek reinstatement throughout the tenures of Landis and his successors as commissioner, Albert B. ("Happy") Chandler and Ford Frick; he died in 1956, still banned from baseball.

Joe Jackson, at loose ends without the opportunity to play baseball, attempted to latch on with various semi-pro teams. He continued to play sporadically at the semi-pro level until the 1930s, when Greenville, South Carolina, where Jackson had been living, was offered a minor league franchise and sought to name Jackson player-manager. Landis refused. In the intervening years Jackson had won a jury verdict in a suit for back pay against Comiskey, but the judge had set it aside on the grounds that Jackson had committed perjury, his confession before the Chicago grand jury having mysteriously reappeared during the suit. Like Weaver, he settled out of court. Over the years Jackson's memory of the Black Sox scandal changed: he now had become an innocent victim. There was talk of a campaign to clear his name, but he died in 1951 before it could be launched.

The man who had dramatically intervened in the Black Sox scandal, to transform it from a carefully managed farce to a morality play, was in many respects a fortuitous participant in the drama. He had not been named baseball commissioner because of the Black Sox affair, but because of internal discord among those who ran the game. He was not a former baseball player or an executive, but a federal judge, a position he continued to hold for approximately a year after being named commissioner. He was a baseball fan, but he was first and foremost a patriot, an uncompromising moralist who inevitably saw his decisions as contributing to the uplifting of America's youth, and a man entirely comfortable with exercising power arbitrarily, in accordance with his intuitions. In naming him commissioner the owners of major league baseball found that they would have to deal in the future with a person with the self-image and autocracy of a czar, but at the same time they could have appointed no more visible personification of militant old-fashioned morality.

Kenesaw Mountain Landis, named for the site of a Georgia Civil War battle where his father had lost a leg, grew up in Indiana, first dropping out of high school but eventually taking an interest in law, going to Union Law School in Chicago (he never attended college), and passing the bar.[25] He became involved in Progressive Republican politics in Illinois, managing the campaign of Governor Frank Lowden. Through Lowden he made contacts in the national Republican party, including Theodore Roosevelt, who nominated him for a federal judgeship in 1905. Two years later he received national attention after imposing a $29 million fine on the Standard Oil Corporation for allegedly accepting rebates from one of its carriers, the Chicago and Alton Railroad, in violation of federal law. The Supreme Court overturned Landis's verdict.

Perhaps because the Standard Oil case and his affiliation with Progressive elements in the Republican party had earned him the reputation of a foe of big business, Landis was selected by the Federal League to preside over its 1915 antitrust action against Organized Baseball. That did not turn out to be a wise choice. Landis may have been a colleague of "trust busters," but he was a regular patron of the Chicago Cubs, and shortly after the trial opened he declared, "Both sides must understand that any blows at the thing called baseball would be regarded by this court as a blow to a national institution."[26] He then contrived to hold back his decision in the case for the entire year of 1915, at which point the lawsuit was dropped as part of the settlement between Organized Baseball and the Federal League.

By 1917 Landis was reported to be tiring of the bench and distressed with the comparatively low salary, $7,500 a year. The prospect of serving in World War I revived his spirits, but he was overage and had to remain content with bellicose outbursts, such as urging that the Kaiser be extradited to Chicago to face trial for murdering a Chicago native who was a passenger on the *Lusitania* in 1916. On May 1, 1919, Landis was on a list of prominent citizens, including Justice Holmes, who were sent bombs in the mail by an anarchist group. One reporter who regularly covered his court described Landis as "an irascible, short-tempered, tyrannical despot," whose courtroom manner was "more arbitrary than the behavior of any jurist I have ever seen before or since."[27]

As Landis chafed in his judgeship, internal dissension was surfacing within Organized Baseball's executive circles. Between 1915 and 1920 a series of squabbles over the disputed ownership of players, including star outfielder George Sisler and pitchers Scott Perry, Jack Quinn, and Carl Mays, caused certain owners to resent the decisions of baseball's three-man National Commission. The commission awarded Sisler to the St. Louis Browns rather than the Pittsburgh Pirates, causing Pirates owner Barney Dreyfuss to become estranged from Chairman Garry Herrmann, whom he felt had been swayed by Johnson. It then awarded Perry to the Boston Braves in a dispute with the Philadelphia Athletics, but the Athletics secured an injunction against the order. Dreyfuss again attacked Herrmann, who had voted for the Braves, for failure to recommend an injunction in the Sisler case.

Meanwhile Johnson began to alienate elements in his own league, led by Charles Comiskey, for awarding Jack Quinn to the Yankees in a dispute with the White Sox and for suspending Carl Mays of the Red Sox, even though his owner had declined to do so, after Mays walked out of a game in Boston and said that he would never play for the Red Sox again. The Red Sox traded Mays to the Yankees, in defiance of Johnson, and eventually the Yankees secured an injunction against Johnson and the American League, and Mays won eight games for them in the 1920 season. Johnson responded, after the season ended, by holding up the Yankees' third place purse, claiming that the games Mays had won for them were tainted. By now open feuding had developed within the ranks of American League owners, pitting Boston, New York, and Chicago against the other five clubs, who continued to support Johnson.

The Mays affair brought to a head Ban Johnson's control of the National Commission, whose chairman, Herrmann, had resigned under pressure in January 1920. Herrmann's ineffectual performance, and the growing divisions within the ranks of franchise owners, resulted in the owners' concluding that Herrmann's successor should come from outside baseball circles. Johnson, however, consistently opposed any candidate who surfaced, and by September 1920, the officialdom of

Organized Baseball, ostensibly represented by a two-man National Commission, was in chaos. Then the Black Sox scandal broke.

The news of the scandal convinced baseball's owners that they needed to replace the current National Commission with outsiders in order to give the impression that Organized Baseball was cleaning itself up. A plan originally conceived in 1919 by Albert Lasker, a Chicago advertising executive, of replacing the National Commission with a three-man board drawn from outside baseball was revived. When Johnson continued to resist the plan and line up owners loyal to him in opposition to it, the insurrectionist American League owners joined forces with the National League and announced that they were creating a new major league, the National-American League, with John Heydler as president. They also implemented the Lasker plan, creating a three-man governing board for baseball. They named a chairman of that board: Judge Kenesaw Mountain Landis.

Landis's emergence as a candidate for the new governing board was the product of support from Heydler. As early as January 1920, *The Sporting News* ran an article by Oscar Reichow, a former Chicago baseball writer who was the business manager of the minor league Hollywood Stars, boosting Landis to replace Herrmann as head of the National Commission and quoting Heydler.[28] Johnson, however, who did not have a high opinion of Landis as a judge, resisted. Eventually the threat of a new league forced Johnson's supporters to withdraw their opposition to the Lasker plan, and eventually to Landis. In a series of meetings after the World Series of 1920, culminating in a joint meeting of the American and National Leagues on November 12, Johnson was forced to ratify the creation of a baseball commissioner and the choice of Landis. The commissioner's salary was fixed at $50,000 a year; Landis agreed to take $42,500 and remain a federal judge.

The original intention had been to make Landis the chairman of a three-man board, but over the winter of 1920 the composition of the commissioner's office was altered so that the league presidents would serve as advisers to the commissioner and there would be no other outside officials. The change was designed to be an overture to Johnson, but it suited Landis's autocratic style. Once he formally assumed the position of commissioner on January 12, 1921, he declined to consult his "advisers," making policy decisions for Organized Baseball in the same manner that he made decisions as a federal judge: on his own.

Judge Kenesaw Mountain Landis throws out the first ball at the Polo Grounds, opening the 1922 World Series between the Giants and the Yankees. At the time, Landis had been commissioner of baseball for almost two years. He was to remain in office until his death in 1944 at the age of seventy-eight. (National Baseball Library and Archive, Cooperstown, N.Y.)

At the time of Landis's formal assumption of the position of baseball commissioner, *The Sporting News* quoted "his plans for the government of the game." Landis emphasized, the paper noted, "the big reason for his [becoming commissioner], which is to clean out the crookedness and the gambling responsible for it and keep the sport above reproach." "The Judge made it plain," the article continued, that "he would have no mercy on any man in baseball, be he magnate or player, whose conduct was not strictly honest. They must avoid even the appearance of evil or feel the iron hand of his power to throw them out of any part of the game." The article concluded by stating, "The Judge will be absolute ruler of the game."[29]

The emphasis of that article on Landis at the moment of his assuming office set the tone for his entire career as commissioner, which stretched until his death in November 1944 at the age of seventy-eight, a week after baseball's owners had elected him to another seven-year term. During his twenty-three years as commissioner Landis consistently attempted to keep baseball "above reproach," and he consistently demonstrated that he was "absolute ruler of the game." Even though he gave up his judgeship a year after becoming commissioner, he continued to run the commissioner's office the way he had run his federal courtroom, as a device for fashioning policies out of his intuitive likes and dislikes.

A brief recapitulation of some of Landis's major decisions as commissioner will give a sense of his autocratic style and the impressionistic nature of his decision making. Most celebrated of those, of course, was his banning the eight Black Sox from the game for life, even though they had been acquitted of any wrongdoing by a jury. Landis's categorical exclusion of the Sox players was particularly revealing in light of his disinclination to assist Ban Johnson in the latter's efforts to dig up incriminating information for the prosecution of the Black Sox affair. Landis apparently did not want to associate his office with an endeavor that Johnson had initiated, did not think that the conspiracy charges had much chance of success in court, and had already resolved to ban the indicted players, regardless of the jury's verdict.[30] His decision to ban the players, announced on the heels of their acquittal, underscored the independence of his office and its identification with the proposition that even the appearance of evil would be rooted out of baseball.

The first decision Landis made as commissioner did not involve the

Black Sox and was on its face much less earthshaking. Nonetheless it was a harbinger of the cast of his regime. In 1920 the owner of the New York Giants, Horace Stoneham, and the Giants' manager, John McGraw, had purchased Oriental Park, a race track in Havana, Cuba, along with the Jockey Club, a casino on the track's premises. The purchase was not illegal, but Landis disapproved of it. He believed that horse racing was a corrupt sport, and that the gamblers who had fixed the 1919 Series based their operations on race tracks. (This was correct in the case of Arnold Rothstein, who owned a profitable casino in Saratoga, New York.) Landis insisted that Stoneham and McGraw divest themselves of the Havana properties, even though they had purchased them as private individuals, McGraw owning property in Cuba and vacationing there in the winters. After forcing Stoneham and McGraw to disengage themselves from horse racing, Landis continued to look critically upon any association of baseball with racing. In the 1930s singer Bing Crosby attempted to purchase ownership in a major league team, but Landis regularly prevented it, believing that Crosby was too actively involved with the horse racing industry.[31]

The most publicized of Landis's decisions involved players whose questionable conduct or associations raised the possibility of their being banned from baseball. In a series of rulings, Landis barred some players and exonerated others, and his decisions, at first blush, appeared inconsistent to the point of being arbitrary. He continued to resist Buck Weaver's regular pleas for reinstatement, despite Weaver's demonstration that he had only been guilty of knowing about the Black Sox fix and not revealing that knowledge; but he allowed the Cincinnati Reds to purchase pitcher Rube Benton's contract from a minor league team even though Benton, who admitted to the Chicago grand jury that he had heard that the 1919 Series was going to be fixed, was designated an "undesirable" player by the National League after the 1920 season and dropped from the New York Giants' roster.

Landis also banned three members of the Giants, coach Cozy Dolan, utility infielder Jimmy O'Connell, and pitcher Phil Douglas, for allegedly inviting members of other teams to throw games. O'Connell, purportedly on Dolan's behalf, approached Philadelphia Phillies infielder Heinie Sand before a game against the Giants and said that "it would be worth $500" if Sand "laid down" that day. Douglas, in a fit of pique after John McGraw had given him a tongue lashing, wrote a letter to St. Louis Cardinal player Leslie Mann offering to "go home for the rest of the season" if the Cardinals "would make it worth his while." O'Connell admitted to approaching Sand but said that, as a junior member of the Giants, he was just doing what Dolan had told him, and that others on the Giants knew about the offer. Douglas said that he was drunk at the time he wrote the letter. Landis threw Dolan, O'Connell, and Douglas out of baseball for life.

At the same time Landis acquitted Ty Cobb and Tris Speaker, the player-managers of the Detroit Tigers and Cleveland Indians, respectively, of wrongdoing after Hubert ("Dutch") Leonard had accused them of conspiring to fix a game between the Tigers and Indians at the end of the 1926 season, and then attempting to place bets on the game. Leonard's charges came in letters he wrote to Ban Johnson after the 1926 season, outlining the arrangement, whereby Speaker's Cleveland team, which already had second place clinched, would lose to Cobb's Detroit team, which was fighting for third place and a share of the World Series profits. Leonard also produced two letters to him from Cobb and Joe Wood, another member of the Indians, that referred to Wood's having bet on the game and Cobb's attempting to do so. Ban Johnson immediately brought pressure on Cobb and Speaker to resign from baseball (Joe Wood had already retired to become baseball coach at Yale), and so after the 1926 season both players quietly "retired."

Landis launched an investigation of the incident and asked Leonard to come to Chicago to confront Cobb and Speaker. Leonard declined. Cobb admitted acting as a go-between for Wood in placing bets but denied that he had made any bets himself or participated in fixing a game. Speaker denied any involvement in the matter at all. Landis eventually concluded that Leonard's charges were unreliable and possibly the result of his holding grudges against Speaker, who had dismissed him from the Cleveland club at the end of the 1925 season, and Cobb, who had declined to purchase him for Detroit. He did not treat Cobb's acting as a go-between for Wood as grounds for dismissing him from baseball, and he did not pass on Wood's case since Wood had already left the game. Ban Johnson had accompanied the announcement of Cobb's and Speaker's retirement with a statement that they "would never play in the American League again"; Landis pointedly allowed Cobb and Speaker to negotiate with any American League club for their services, and they both signed contracts with the Philadelphia Athletics.

In two other cases Landis banned players for life even though the players involved had not engaged in any formal wrongdoing. The players were Benny Kauff, a former Giant pitcher who had been accused, but not convicted, of throwing games during the 1919 season and had remained with the Giants in 1920, and Ray Fischer, a pitcher with the Cincinnati Reds who had signed a contract including a salary cut for the 1921 season but then subsequently left the Reds to coach baseball at Michigan. Kauff, after being dropped from the Giants after the 1920 season, signed with Toronto and then attempted to rejoin the Giants for the 1922 season. Meanwhile he was charged with having stolen a car in 1919, and Landis placed him on the temporarily ineligible list while his trial was pending; Kauff was eventually acquitted. In Fischer's case, when the Reds offered to take him back, restoring his pay cut, he asked as part of the negotiations that he be placed on the Reds' voluntarily retired list, in exchange for joining the Reds after Michigan's season ended. This angered Garry Herrmann, who placed Fischer on the permanently ineligible list. Fischer then applied to Landis for a clarification of his status.

Landis, after reading the transcript of Kauff's trial, banned him for life, and also banned Fischer for life for jumping his contract with the Reds. He concluded that Kauff's acquittal had been "a miscarriage of justice," and that his continued involvement with baseball would dishonor the game. He also found that to allow Fischer to use his position at Michigan, which he had obtained after jumping from the Reds, as a bargaining chip to reenter baseball on more favorable terms would encourage other players to jump into the coaching ranks as part of their salary bargaining.

The Kauff and Fischer decisions appeared particularly severe. Kauff had never been shown to have thrown games, and he had been acquitted of car theft. Landis seemed to have substituted his intuition that Kauff was a dishonorable character for the judgment of two juries. Fischer had simply sought additional employment options after being dissatisfied with the terms of his contract with the Reds, and although he had violated that contract, the Reds had agreed to take him back on more favorable terms. Their placing him on the permanently retired list, when all he had done was attempt to negotiate with them, seemed simply punitive. But Landis allowed them to impose that punishment.

The above decisions would seem to confirm the charges that Landis was idiosyncratic and arbitrary in his decision making. But there is another explanation of the decisions that gives them a kind of consistency, if not necessarily a principled basis. In cases in which Landis was the sole decision maker—those involving Weaver, Kauff, Dolan, O'Connell, Douglas, and Fischer—he was inclined to be severe in his judgments and to stress the appearance of improper conduct as much as its formal existence. He believed that people who supported the corruption of baseball by not disclosing potential fixes of games, or by acting as go-betweens in attempted fixes, or by offering to be bribed, or simply by being dishonest persons, should be forcibly removed from the game. If he drew this conclusion about a participant in major league baseball, he would remove him regardless of what others had concluded.

Landis also believed in protecting the fundamental rules under which the enterprise of baseball was structured. He supported the reserve clause, blacklisting, and territoriality. As a consequence he opposed any efforts to undermine those rules or to move in the direction of increased player bargaining power. Actions such as those Ray Fischer took, jumping a major league contract to coach at the college level and then attempting to return on more favorable terms, encouraged contract jumping and undermined the reserve system. College coaching jobs were as much part of the market for baseball players as rival teams or leagues. Landis did not want increased player leverage.

But Benton, like Weaver, had known of a prospective fix and not passed on that information to officials, and Cobb, like O'Connell, had been a go-between in a profit-making scheme involving prospective player collusion. The different treatment of Benton's and Cobb's cases appeared to flow from the fact that someone other than Landis had attempted to discipline the players before the matter reached Landis. Benton had been declared ineligible by John Heydler, Cobb and Speaker by Ban Johnson. Landis wanted to make it clear that he made decisions on his own authority. Cobb may also have benefited from the fact that at the time of his alleged conversation with Speaker and Wood it was not illegal for players to bet on their own teams, and Detroit was intended to win the game. Nonetheless Cobb, if Leonard's account was to be believed, had knowledge of a prospective fix that he declined to pass on. And of course Buck Weaver and Rube Benton were in exactly the same situation except that the fixers were Weaver's teammates. But in Weaver's and Kauff's cases, the previous decision maker, a jury, had acquitted them of wrongdoing: Landis thus had the additional incentive of wanting to make it clear that he reserved his own judgments on matters concerning baseball, morality, and corruption.

◆

In deciding that after 1921 they would be governed by a commissioner, baseball's owners were in effect deciding that the policies of Organized Baseball would be in accord with the beliefs and inclinations of Kenesaw Mountain Landis. There were a few exceptions to the autocratic rule of Landis over the next twenty-four years, but not very many. The most conspicuous one involved baseball's reaction to the development by some major league clubs, led by the St. Louis Cardinals under their general manager Branch Rickey, of working agreements with, and eventually ownership of, clubs in several minor leagues. This so-called farm system, structured primarily for the purpose of developing players for the major league clubs, was sufficiently successful that it enabled the Cardinals, a small-market team from the 1920s on, not only to compete successfully with their more affluent competitors but to control, by the late 1930s, a vast amount of the talented players in the minor leagues.

Landis was an inveterate opponent of the farm system. Its structure, which combined major and minor league clubs in a large corporate pyramid, and served in some cases to retard the opportunities of players in the minor leagues to reach the majors, offended his Progressive sensibility. He saw it as encroaching upon the independence of the minor league franchises, trapping promising players in the minors, and rewarding corporate ruthlessness on the part of major league clubs, who brought up promising farmhands in the middle of the season without regard to the effects of their departure on the minor league franchises for whom they were playing. Landis also believed that in the minor leagues, where smaller cities and local franchises relished their mutual associations, American baseball lay in its purest form. He raged when organizations such as the Cardinals simply moved a minor league franchise from one city to another because the new location offered them a more lucrative arrangement.

But Landis had little success persuading or cajoling baseball's owners to dismantle the farm system. Without major league ownership of minor league franchises, many close to the game believed, the minors would not have survived the Depression, and farm systems continued to grow in the thirties and forties, with the Detroit Tigers, New York Yankees, Brooklyn Dodgers, Chicago Cubs, and New York Giants, all comparatively wealthy organizations, expanding their operations and finding that their major league clubs were improved in the process. The most Landis could do about the farm system was to make an occasional exposure of blatant tampering with or covering up of minor league prospects, where he would "free" assorted minor leaguers with a flourish, enabling them to sell their contracts to the highest bidder. The farm system eventually declined as the costs of major league clubs owning minor league franchises outright escalated after World War II, but all clubs continue to have working agreements with minor league teams today.

The farm system was an isolated instance, however, of Landis's ideological assumptions running at variance with the perceived needs of baseball owners and the latter prevailing. In three major areas, Landis revealed how much his consciousness was rooted in the years in which he had been a Progressive Republican and first became a federal judge, and how much that consciousness was congenial to baseball's inner circle over the years of Landis's tenure, making Organized Baseball an institution strikingly frozen in time.

The first area has already been discussed: baseball's legal and economic "rules." In the three decades of Landis's tenure, the demographic landscape of America and its labor relations changed dramatically. Yet baseball's franchise map, reserve clause practices, territoriality rules, and blacklisting sanctions were still intact the year Landis died, and Landis and the owners had resisted every effort, either within the game or from outside, to change them. The second area involved Organized Baseball's response to African-American players, to be detailed in the next chapter.

The third area involved Landis's reaction to night baseball. Here again his views seemed frozen in time and impervious to the cultural changes that had occurred during his tenure as commissioner. When Landis took office in 1921 the technology existed to stage baseball games at night, and, as we shall see in a subsequent chapter, exhibition night games had been played in several cities, including Cincinnati.

Landis resisted every attempt on the part of major league owners to expand night baseball. Since night games were first staged in the National League, that league led the way in their expansion, with the exception of the New York Giants, who refused to play against Cincinnati when the Reds inaugurated night baseball. By the 1940s, however, the American League had become enamored with night baseball, with franchises such as Washington, St. Louis, and Philadelphia seeking to expand the existing limit of seven night games per club. In a 1942 vote, the National League affirmed the seven-game limit and the American League voted to allow teams to decide for themselves. Landis resolved the issue by endorsing the National League's position. The next year, encouraged by a letter from President Franklin Roosevelt to Landis urging that night baseball be extended so that more workers in the war effort could attend games, the major leagues voted to increase the number of night games to fourteen per club, and some owners sought permission to exceed those figures. Landis voted for an absolute limit of fourteen games.[32]

◆

In the long tenure of Kenesaw Mountain Landis baseball solidified itself and set upon two decades that were free from internal strife and external scrutiny by the courts. The face of the game, at the major league level, maintained a surface continuity, with franchises remaining constant and schedules taking on a familiar rhythm. Nonetheless the game of baseball was changing, and in addition baseball was not invulnerable to changes in the larger culture.

The deadball was eliminated in the 1920s, when club owners decided to forbid trick pitches and replace discolored or damaged balls with new ones. A few spitballers were allowed to continue to throw their specialty if they could demonstrate that their careers depended upon it, but all the other techniques by which pitchers defaced the baseball or added foreign substances to it were banned. The decision to end trick pitches signified the recognition among owners that in-the-stands home runs were a particularly attractive feature of the game to fans. As demand for seats at baseball games increased during the affluent 1920s, owners realized that the configuration of their steel and concrete ballparks often did not permit expansion of seating capacity except by adding seats in fair territory in the outfield, thus reducing outfield distances. This made in-the-stands home runs easier to hit, and the elimination of trick pitches and damaged baseballs further emphasized the home run.

Baseball changed accordingly. Between 1903 and 1919 major league hitters, collectively, averaged about .250. Between 1920 and 1930 they averaged over .280. For the earlier time period about three players a season drove in more than a hundred runs; for the latter period about fourteen players did. Pitchers' yearly earned run averages for the 1903–1919 period clustered around 2.80; between 1920 and 1930 the average ERA was about 4.00. Between 1912 and 1930 the number of stolen bases in the major leagues dropped by more than half. In 1920 Babe Ruth, who hit fifty-four home runs, outdistanced every other American league *team*. In the 1930 season major league hitters produced 1,565 home runs. And in that same season National League hitters combined for an *average* of .303. Major league baseball had evolved from a game oriented around pitching and defense to one oriented around hitting.

Unfortunately the extraordinary offensive accomplishments of the 1930 season were not reflected in fan attendance. Baseball proved to be as susceptible as any other enterprise to the Depression. The 1930s, in fact, witnessed the first significant financial problems for major league franchises since the first decade of the twentieth century. Some clubs in two-team cities or in small markets, such as the St. Louis Browns, the Boston Braves, the Philadelphia Phillies, and the Cincinnati Reds, found themselves in what amounted to a chronically depressed condition in the early years of that decade. They were consistently outbid for promising minor league players and their records were poor, while their ballparks began to deteriorate and their attendance dropped. For the first time since the National Agreement the original map of major league franchises began to show some signs of age.

In light of these developments it was no coincidence that at the height of the Great Depression, Organized Baseball created two events whose purpose was to raise revenue, to cement the image of baseball as America's national game, and to underscore the connection of the current sport with its early twentieth-century past. Those events were the mid-season All-Star Game, first played on July 6, 1933, in Comiskey Park in Chicago, and the Baseball Hall of Fame, located in Cooperstown, New York, the purported birthplace of baseball in America. The first election of players to the Hall of Fame took place in 1935, with five players being selected, and the first induction ceremony followed four years later, additional players having been named in the interval.

Taken together, the All-Star Game and the Hall of Fame were efforts to reestablish the investment of Americans in the game of baseball. By elevating the status of certain players to stars, and eventually to Hall of Famers, the events emphasized the heroic dimensions of playing major league baseball and the continuity of the game over time.

In the first election of players to the Hall of Fame in 1935, two criteria controlled the selection process, one explicit and one implicit. The first criterion limited eligible players to those who had begun their careers around the turn of the century, close to the time that the National Agreement was signed. This amounted to a recognition by those in the inner circles of baseball that their sport's history had begun around 1903, when the current franchise map had been created and the fundamental rules of the enterprise laid down. Nineteenth-century professional baseball amounted to prehistory: it was a different game.

The second criterion was implicitly reflected by the choice of the five players selected to constitute the first class of Hall of Famers. All of those players, including Babe Ruth, had begun their careers in the deadball era, and all of them, including Ruth, had been deadball stars. Of them, in fact, only Ruth had produced career accomplishments that reflected the transformation of baseball from a defensive-oriented to an offensive-oriented sport. The other original inductees, Honus Wagner, Christy Mathewson, Walter Johnson, and Ty Cobb, had become conspicuous successes by adapting their talents to the requirements of the deadball game. In celebrating those players the Hall of Fame voters, sportswriters who covered major league baseball, were implicitly celebrating an earlier phase of the game, now made the source of legends.

Cobb was first on the list of initial Hall of Famers, receiving 222 of the 226 votes cast (75 percent of the total votes was required for election). He was followed by Ruth and Wagner, who each received 215 votes, Mathewson, who received 205, and Johnson, who received 189. The quintet's service stretched from 1897, when Wagner joined the Louisville club, then in the National League, to 1935, when Ruth retired from the Braves in the middle of the season. Cobb played twenty-four years in the major leagues, Ruth twenty-two, Wagner and Johnson twenty-one, and Mathewson seventeen. When Wagner entered baseball, the ballparks were all wooden; when Ruth retired, there had been a night game in the majors. Between them Cobb and Wagner hit 229 home runs; Ruth had passed that number by 1922, his third season as a full-time outfielder.

Other great players, as well as the celebrated managers Connie Mack and John McGraw, were recognized at the first Hall of Fame induction ceremony in 1939. Napoleon Lajoie, Tris Speaker, Cy Young, George Sisler, Eddie Collins, Willie Keeler, and Grover Cleveland Alexander had been elected to the Hall by that date. None of those players, however, made it on the first ballot. This was despite the fact that Keeler, Speaker, Sisler, and Lajoie had higher career batting averages than Wagner. Collins had hit .333 in twenty-five seasons, the longest tenure of any of the inductees. Alexander had pitched more innings and won as many games as Mathewson. Young had appeared in more games, won more games, pitched more innings, and pitched more complete games than any pitcher in baseball history. What, then, distinguished Cobb, Ruth, Wagner, Mathewson, and Johnson from the rest?

It was apparent that the selection of the five original Hall of Famers was not based entirely on statistical accomplishments. Cobb's and Ruth's statistics, to be sure, were overwhelming, but in the cases of the others intangibles were at play, and intangibles affected Cobb's and Ruth's selection as well. There was something special about each of the ballplayers who inaugurated the Hall of Fame: each of them embodied something that a group of baseball writers in 1935 particularly prized in American baseball players. Each of the original Hall of Famers was, in his own fashion, a nonpareil. Wagner can be celebrated for his versatility, Mathewson for his intelligence, charisma, and mastery of the strike zone, Johnson for his ability to combine blazing speed and pinpoint control, Cobb for his offensive prowess, and Ruth for his incomparable slugging. Each was, in addition, a singular personality: Wagner the embodiment of a team player; Mathewson the gentlemanly purist; Johnson the archetype of consistency and humility; Cobb the intimidator; Ruth the superhuman.

In voting for that quintet of players in 1935 the baseball writers were expressing two themes about the game and its history. One was that a type of player who was disappearing from the game should be celebrated. It is hard to imagine Mathewson or Johnson winning anything like their number of games in the 1930s and successive decades; it is equally hard to conceive of Cobb, or any other player, approaching Cobb's lifetime average, let alone using his slap-and-slash batting style. Wagner, Mathewson, Cobb, and Johnson were players who had played a different game, a game that had been lost over time and was being recaptured in the Hall of Fame itself. Ruth had grown to stardom playing that lost game, but in the process he had transformed baseball to a game that still exists, emphasizing slugging and the dramatic home run. In 1933, when the All-Star Game was first played, Ruth was still active, one of the last links to the deadball era. The fact that he had helped make baseball so different a sport from that played in his early career was a good reason to remember and to celebrate the earlier version. The fact that baseball was going through its first economic downturn since its early history was another reason to emphasize its history.

The creation of the All-Star Game in 1933 was comparably motivated by a concern to link baseball's past and present. The idea of a mid-season exhibition game featuring stars from both leagues was conceived by Arch Ward, sports editor of the *Chicago Tribune*, who first approached American League president Will Harridge with a proposal on April 20, 1933.[33] Among the selling points that Ward presented to support his proposal were that baseball "needed an opportunity to show that it was not in a state of decadence"; that the timing of the game would coincide with Chicago's Century of Progress Exposition, which was to be held that summer; that "the fans of the nation would be invited to help pick the all-star teams"; that all the profits of the game would go to the Baseball Players' Charity Fund, whose purpose was to give financial aid to destitute former players; and that the *Tribune* would guarantee all expenses if the games were rained out. Harridge was enthusiastic about the proposal and submitted it to a meeting of American League owners on May 9, where it was unanimously approved.

Three of Ward's selling points demonstrated the close connection he made between a revival of baseball's economic health and a renewed interest in its heroic past. An All-Star Game, featuring the major leagues' best players, would demonstrate that baseball was not in "a state of decadence." The process of selecting teams would stimulate the interest of fans in their own clubs and potentially result in increased attendance for regular season games. And the tying of All-Star Game proceeds to a pension plan for retired players explicitly identified the game as a means by which former players could be thanked for their contributions to the game and its history.

The *Tribune* eventually invited fifty-five other newspapers to help generate fan ballots, and awarded cash prizes for the fans coming closest to picking the starting lineups, including the pitchers for both staffs in the order they would be chosen to work (three pitchers were expected to participate for each league). Between May 19, when the *Tribune* first announced the game would be played, and July, the paper ran a series of articles stating that All-Star votes were "pouring in," and that the response of fans was "overwhelming." The attention the game received demonstrated to the *Tribune* that "baseball leaders have no reason to fear that the sport is fading."[34]

The pension fund created by All-Star Game receipts marked the first systematic effort on the part of Organized Baseball to pay attention to the welfare of players from its past. Prior to the 1930s no significant pension fund for ballplayers existed, which resulted in most players having to join the general work force after they could no longer play baseball. Given the educational level of some ballplayers, this resulted in an occasional former player being unable to find work and becoming destitute. The number of such former players increased in the 1930s, and in some cases, such as Honus Wagner, whose sporting goods store in Pittsburgh went bankrupt, the plight of a former player became a subject of public attention. It was noteworthy that the first steps to enhance the Baseball Players' Charity Fund came from a newspaper rather than a baseball executive.

Once the reluctant National League was persuaded to reschedule some games to accommodate the proposed July 6 date for the All-Star Game, Organized Baseball embraced the project, and the game has become an annual event. The first game attracted a standing-room-only crowd of 49,000 to Comiskey Park and featured a home run by Ruth in a 4–1 American League victory. The *Tribune* reported that over 500,000 votes had been cast for the team rosters, that fans from forty-six states attended the game, that it had been broadcast on two Chicago radio stations, and that the game had grossed $56,378.50, of which $46,506 was earmarked for the players' pension fund. So positive had been the experience, the *Tribune* noted, that "nearly every city in the major leagues wants to promote a similar contest next season."[35] For Arch Ward the contest confirmed the fact that baseball was "truly America's game."[36]

Two years after the first All-Star Game was staged, Stephen Clark, a resident of Cooperstown, New York, learned that an old baseball had been found near Fly Creek in Cooperstown. Clark, the grandson of Edward Clark, who had prospered mightily as the lawyer for Isaac

Singer, the inventor of the sewing machine, managed Clark family assets and was involved in historical and civic affairs in the Cooperstown area. Clark family money had supported a community gymnasium, a farmers' museum, a folk art museum, and a regional medical center. On learning about the discovery of the old baseball, Edward Clark concluded that it might be appropriate to collect and exhibit some baseball memorabilia.

The connection between Cooperstown and the history of baseball in America had been established by a commission chaired by Abraham G. Mills, a former baseball player who was president of the National League from 1882 to 1885. The connection was spurious and the place of Cooperstown in the history of baseball contrived. The idea of a commission's authoritatively declaring the origins of baseball came from none other than Albert G. Spalding and was part of his single-minded mission to establish baseball as America's national game. Part of that mission involved demonstrating that the origins of baseball were indigenous to America, and that the game was not derivative of the English game of rounders.

The rounders theory of baseball's origins had been proposed by Henry Chadwick, a journalist who was born in England and moved to New York at the age of twelve in 1836. Chadwick, who invented the box score and the concept of a batting average, was the editor of the first baseball guides and a close friend of Spalding's. In 1905 Chadwick, at Spalding's request, began a book on "the origins and history of baseball," and Spalding confronted the rounders theory. Spalding and Chadwick then engaged in a debate about the origins of baseball in the 1905 edition of their jointly published *Spalding's Official Baseball Guide.*[37] As an outgrowth of that debate, Spalding urged that a commission be created to explore the subject, and he hoped to conclude definitively that baseball was an indigenous American sport. In order to ensure that outcome, he proposed his old friend Abraham Mills to chair the commission.[38]

The Mills Commission's investigations were virtually nonexistent. The commission began with the premise that the first organized playing of baseball was undertaken by the Knickerbocker Club of New York under the direction of Alexander Cartwright in 1845. It then drew upon the reminiscences of a Cooperstown resident to trace an apparent connection between Cooperstown and the Knickerbocker Club. Finally, it investigated the possibility that a member of the Knickerbocker Club had lived in Cooperstown, and although that connection was never established, the commission concluded that baseball had originated in that hamlet.

In 1907 Abner Graves, then a resident of Colorado, wrote Spalding a letter in which he asserted that he had grown up in Cooperstown and was on one occasion playing marbles with a schoolmate, Abner Doubleday, when Doubleday proposed they play another game. Doubleday, according to Graves, then drew a diagram in the shape of a baseball diamond, established positions for various players, and explained how the game was played. The diagram had not been preserved, but Doubleday had gone on to be an officer in the Union Army during the Civil War, rising to the rank of major general. He was thus an ideal candidate to be the inventor of American baseball, and Graves's letter suggested that Doubleday had dreamed up the game himself.[39]

In the course of its investigations the Mills Commission had interviewed former members of the Knickerbocker Club, and one had testified that in 1845 one of his fellow members, a "Mr. Wadsworth," had presented a diagram of a baseball field, which they then followed in playing the game. The commission then sought to establish a connection between that diagram and the one that Graves remembered Doubleday as having drawn in Cooperstown in 1839. In a 1907 letter to the Collector of Customs for New York City, Mills inquired whether Wadsworth, known to be a former employee of that office, had ever been a resident of Cooperstown. His hope, Mills said in the letter, was that "a connecting link between Doubleday at Cooperstown and the beginning of the game in New York could be established."[40]

The link between Wadsworth and Doubleday was never documented, but ten days after making the inquiry the Mills Commission issued a report in which it concluded that baseball had been invented in Cooperstown by Abner Doubleday. *Spalding's Baseball Guide* announced the commission's findings in March 1908, and in *America's National Game*, published three years later, Spalding referred to the commission's "long, thorough, painstaking investigation of all available facts" that had resulted in its "important decision."[41] Henry Chadwick took his defeat with good humor, writing Mills in March 1908 that the Mills Commission report was "a masterly piece of special pleading which lets my old friend Albert escape a bad defeat." He added that the debate over baseball's origins was "a joke between Albert and myself."[42]

With the Mills Commission's report having established Cooperstown as the birthplace of baseball, the finding of an old ball in the Cooperstown area stimulated the interest of Edward Clark and one of his employees, Alexander Cleland. Together they assembled some additional baseball memorabilia from the area and exhibited them in the village library. Cleland, aware that in 1939 the centennial of Abner Doubleday's "invention" of baseball would be taking place, then suggested to members of Organized Baseball's inner circle that an all-time all-star team be created in connection with that event. Ford Frick, a former journalist who was then president of the National League, decided to take Cleland's proposal one step further. He proposed to Edward Clark the creation of a permanent baseball Hall of Fame, to be housed in Cooperstown. Clark agreed to help finance the construction of a Hall of Fame museum.

In 1935 Organized Baseball launched the Hall of Fame project by directing the secretary of the American League Service Bureau, Henry P. Edwards, to poll the members of the Baseball Writers Association of America to select the first members of the Hall of Fame. A crowd of 10,000 persons jammed Cooperstown for the first induction ceremony in 1939, doubling the population of the village. Since then the Hall of Fame has remained, a celebration of baseball's past and a testament to Spalding's determination to dissociate baseball from anything English.

◆

Kenesaw Mountain Landis was a prominent figure at the Hall of Fame dedication. At seventy-three, in his eighteenth year as baseball commissioner, he rode in a car leading the procession down Main Street to the grounds of the National Museum and Hall of Fame. He gave the chief address at the dedication ceremony, confirming that Cooperstown was the "birthplace" of baseball in America and announcing that the museum belonged "to all America, to lovers of good sportsmanship, healthy bodies, clean minds." Those, Landis believed, were "the principles of baseball." Five years later Landis himself was elected to the Hall of Fame.[43]

In binding themselves to the idiosyncratic presence of Judge Landis the owners of major league baseball got, in effect, more than they bargained for. After their unsuccessful effort to cover up the Black Sox scandal failed, and they confronted the cozy relationship between baseball and gambling that the scandal revealed, they determined to restore their position as an incorruptible moral enterprise by dissociating themselves from gamblers and associating themselves with an uncompromising moral zealot. This they successfully did, and when Landis died in 1944 there had not been the slightest whisper of a gambling or fixing scandal in baseball for nearly two decades. Moreover, when Landis died baseball had clearly restored its position as a sport that deserved to be thought the ideal of youth, a sport that was clean and wholesome. As commissioner, Landis had made sure that baseball did not disappoint the kids of America.

But in securing the services of Landis baseball had acquired more than a symbol of morality. It had acquired an impulsive, opinionated despot whose operative principles were the preservation of his autocratic powers and the implementation of his often whimsical judgments. It had also acquired a person whose value system was set in place at the time he assumed the office of commissioner, and gave no evidence of changing for the next two decades, despite some significant changes in the cultural context in which baseball was set. The result was that Landis's idealized image of baseball, the image that drove his policies and lay at the foundation of many of his decisions, was an increasingly anachronistic one.

But that image suited a sport whose legal and economic structure had been fashioned in 1903 and remained essentially intact in 1944, the year of Landis's death, and whose self-fashioned identity had largely been a product of the Progressive Era. Baseball was synonymous with the reserve clause, with a fixed franchise map and the territoriality principle, with games in the daytime, and with all-white teams. Landis strenuously attempted to maintain those defining features even as the demographics and labor economics of America changed. He also labored to make a reality the previously dubious claim of baseball as a "clean," wholesome sport, free from the influence of gambling and corruption. Despite his idiosyncrasies as an executive, he succeeded in both tasks, helping nurture the peculiarly anachronistic, peculiarly evocative character of baseball in America.

4

The Negro Leagues

BETWEEN 1903 and 1923, baseball was firmly established in America. In each of the major league cities new concrete and steel ballparks were built, "permanent" features of the city landscape. The organizing legal and economic principles of the enterprise—the reserve clause, blacklisting of contract jumpers, and territoriality—were in place, creating a monopsonistic industry that had nonetheless been held to be outside the scope of federal antitrust laws. The close connections between baseball and gambling had been exposed, and largely severed, by the Black Sox scandal and the installation of Kenesaw Mountain Landis as baseball commissioner. Years of prosperity were in the immediate future, and in that future baseball would become even more popular and even more closely associated to some inner core of American civilization.

Yet Organized Baseball, as it rose to cultural prominence in the twenty years after its formal modern organization, was singularly incomplete in one respect. It was an enterprise not open to blacks.* In their tireless pursuit of new players for their rosters, the major league clubs did not scout black players. No black players could be found on minor league teams. No black player between 1903 and 1923, or for at least twenty years thereafter, had any prospect of playing in Organized Baseball.

No stated policy or written rule existed that barred blacks from participating in Organized Baseball. It was nonetheless apparent that no

* The term "African American" does not capture the nature of racial discrimination in Organized Baseball from 1903 to 1946. Players with black skin were barred from baseball, whether they were African Americans, Cubans, or Latin Americans.

blacks could participate. Prior to the advent of the twentieth century, as baseball became a professional sport, a small number of black players appeared on team rosters. By 1900 that was no longer the case. As in the rest of American life, a period of experimentation with interracial activities, initiated after the Civil War, had been replaced by a period of increasingly rigid racial segregation. It was apparent to prospective black ballplayers that if they wanted to play baseball they would have to form all-black teams that played in all-black leagues. The Negro Leagues were a product of this situation.

It is very probable that the black ballplayers who joined all-black teams in the early and middle years of the twentieth century did not do so by choice, in the sense of preferring to play baseball in a segregated setting. Presumably they would have preferred to play within the structure of Organized Baseball, with white players, making more money, enjoying far greater stability of employment, and playing and traveling under far more comfortable conditions. They did not have that option, and they wanted to play baseball, so they joined Negro League clubs.

In so doing they entered a world that was in many respects the antithesis of Organized Baseball, in which all the economic elements that white baseball's hierarchy had fought to contain were set loose. Had those in the center of Organized Baseball's officialdom looked closely at the Negro Leagues that shadowed the major leagues from 1903 through the 1940s, they would have been horrified. Everything that they and their predecessors had sought to strip from the enterprise was present in the Negro Leagues. Franchises were only loosely attached to cities; teams barnstormed. Players jumped contracts at will, shifting rosters in mid-season. No sanctions existed for transgressors: if a player had left a club in the middle of one year, he would be willingly taken back if he sought to return, providing his playing skills had not diminished. Racketeers and gamblers not only associated with teams, they owned them. All the dangerous "trick" plays and practices, from sliding with spikes high to pitching spitballs and emery balls, were present in the Negro Leagues. But those close to the center of Organized Baseball were probably unaware of these features of Negro baseball in America. That game, to them and to most white Americans, was largely invisible.

In retrospect, young black ballplayers who were barred from Organized Baseball and entered the Negro Leagues might be expected to have felt a bitterness at the arbitrariness of their situation, especially when contrasted with their contemporary counterparts, who have access to the vast salaries that accompany stardom in today's game. The recollections of former Negro League players suggest otherwise. Participation in the major leagues was not an option for them; most did not agonize over its loss. The opportunity to play Negro League baseball was, for them, an enticing prospect. As young men growing up in a racially segregated society, one driven by the premise of black inferiority, their occupational prospects were extremely limited. Playing baseball for money offered at least a temporary respite from the apparently inexorable future of low-paying, low-status jobs available to male blacks for the first fifty years of the twentieth century.

◆

In the years before World War I, when Organized Baseball was becoming an important part of the urban landscape of America, most blacks lived in the south. The great migrations of black families, in which they took their worldly possessions and headed for Chicago, Detroit, Philadelphia, and other northern cities, were just beginning. Segregation, while legally enforced, had not yet assumed its most rigid phase, in which the very prospect of contact between the black and white races seemed to invite some sort of social contamination. The guiding assumptions of a racially segregated society were in place, but the logic of segregation had not yet been taken to absurd lengths. The south was noticeably disadvantaged economically as compared with other regions of the nation, but the general prosperity of the first two decades of the twentieth century had reached it as well.

In this world male blacks could expect some regular, if seasonal and unpromising, employment. They could work as farm laborers or at other menial jobs. They could become unskilled workers—stockhands or delivery "boys"—in some stores. They could be waiters and sometimes cooks. The south did not have a strong tradition of organized labor, so blacks were not excluded from working for railroads or shippers or other enterprises that had become unionized in the north. In short, the same tasks that black males had performed in a slaveholding society—menial labor and domestic service—were available to them in the "free" early twentieth-century south.

Alongside these prospects, baseball offered not only adventure but comparative wealth. Black baseball players did not earn anything like their white counterparts, and could not expect that their income would be stable. But they could clear $50 to $250 a month, depending on their status, and they could play baseball all year. When the North American weather turned too cold for baseball, the Negro League teams barnstormed to Cuba, Puerto Rico, the Dominican Republic, and Mexico. A salary of $250 a month, for twelve months, was much more than most male blacks could expect to earn in the twentieth-century south. In addition, playing baseball was not a low-status job calculated to engender drudgery and boredom. It was fun, and the players were treated as celebrities. No wonder that a constant theme of the reminiscences of Negro League ballplayers was how privileged they felt to be able to play baseball, how fortunate they considered themselves to have been given the requisite athletic talent to escape, at least for a time, the humdrum prospects of their contemporaries.[1]

Through the 1930s, then, most Negro League ballplayers came from the south. But most Negro League teams were based in the north, often in cities that had white major league teams. When the Negro National League was first organized in 1920, the cities represented were Chicago, Dayton, Detroit, Indianapolis, Kansas City, and St. Louis. Between 1920 and 1930 Cincinnati, Pittsburgh, Cleveland, Brooklyn, Washington, and Philadelphia also entered teams. The only southern cities with Negro League clubs in this period were Memphis, Nashville, and Birmingham.

The affiliations of clubs with cities were somewhat deceptive; as noted, Negro League teams played many of their games on the road, often in "neutral" cities and towns. But there were strong reasons for the clubs to favor an association with northern cities. First, those cities had existing ballparks, and Negro League teams, for the most part, could not afford to build their own. They thus played games in parks they rented from white major league clubs or in parks that those clubs had abandoned. Second, the economic base of northern cities was far stronger than that of southern cities in the twenties and thirties. Even though more blacks lived in the south, the black population of northern cities was constantly growing after World War I, and those blacks that lived in the north were comparatively better off than their southern counterparts. Further, in some cities, such as Kansas City and Indianapolis, that did not have major league teams, white fans as well as blacks frequented the games.[2]

Finally, the owners of Negro League teams had to have reached a certain level of affluence. The vast majority of them were black: for years J. L. Wilkinson of the Kansas City Monarchs was the only white owner in Negro League baseball. The odds were overwhelming, in early twentieth-century America, that if a black man had made enough money to own a Negro League baseball team he lived in a northern city. The odds were also good, especially after the onset of the Depression, that if a black man could afford to own a Negro League team, he had made his money in the numbers rackets.

In 1920 Andrew ("Rube") Foster, a former player, orchestrated the formation of the National Negro League. Foster had first played baseball in 1902 and had become a player-manager by 1910, centering himself on a team known as the Chicago American Giants. At that time New York and Chicago had the largest black populations of American cities, and a number of black barnstorming franchises sprung up in those locations. By 1920 Foster, convinced that black ballplayers had no prospect of playing in the major leagues and wanting to prevent white booking agents from reaping profits from games played by black teams, proposed the creation of two leagues, patterned on the model of Organized Baseball. Not enough interest was generated for two leagues, but a single eight-team league came into being, and was to remain extant for the next decade.

Foster's principles for the Negro National League's formation were comparable to those that had guided the founders of Organized Baseball. He felt that the keys to the NNL's economic success, and to profits for its owners, would be stability and competitive balance among its teams. To this end he proposed that no club be allowed to enter the league until it had secured a ballpark as a home base; that trades and assignments be made among the teams so that competition could be maintained; and that the owners of the teams make their own scheduling arrangements and take a percentage of their gate receipts. The last suggestion was made with the goal of bypassing booking agents.

Foster was named president of the NNL and paid no salary, but he took 5 percent of the receipts from all league games. Some of his financial records from the 1923 season have survived and suggest that he had made the NNL into a profitable enterprise. That year the NNL fielded eight teams, two of which, the Toledo Tigers and the Milwaukee Bears, did not complete the season. Attendance for the entire season (with most teams playing between fifty-five and seventy-five

Adrian ("Cap") Anson (left) and Andrew ("Rube") Foster, pictured together, ironically, in the 1920s. Anson, a Hall of Fame first baseman and manager for the Chicago White Sox from 1876 to 1897, was an outspoken advocate of excluding blacks from Organized Baseball; Foster was an early black barnstorming star and founder of the Negro National League in 1920. (National Baseball Library and Archive, Cooperstown, N.Y.)

games) was 402,436, an average of about 1,650 spectators per contest. That figure might seem incredibly low, but major league teams averaged less than 10,000 spectators per game at the same time. The NNL's total gate receipts were $197,218. Players' salaries were $101,000. Rail fares for all the teams amounted to $25,212; meals and streetcar fares $9,136. Baseballs cost $7,965 and umpires $7,448 (the NNL made a practice of hiring black umpires, paying them about $25 a game, far less than their white counterparts). Other expenses, including advertising, totaled $11,664. The NNL thus netted a profit of $34,793, split among the club owners, and Foster made about $9,861. If one assumes that the club owners earned about $5,000, and Foster nearly $10,000, these were certainly adequate sums for businessmen of any kind in 1923 and quite high incomes for black businessmen.

Despite Foster's acumen, continued prosperity, and the growth of black populations in northern cities, factors mitigated against the NNL and its counterpart, the Eastern Colored League (which came into being in 1923 and lasted until 1928), from becoming significant financial successes.[3] One major problem was the Negro League clubs' dependence on the major league clubs, minor league clubs, or cities from which they rented ballparks. They had to schedule their games at the convenience of those clubs or cities, when white teams were not playing. As a result their schedules tended to be sporadic and irregular: a feature of Negro League standings was that the teams invariably played an uneven number of games. The scheduling seems to have taken place as the season progressed, making advance publicity for the games difficult.

A second problem was that imbalance among the teams persisted despite Foster's efforts to maintain parity. Invariably certain teams—Foster's Chicago American Giants and Wilkinson's Kansas City Monarchs in the NNL and the Hilldale (Philadelphia) and Bacharach (New York) clubs in the ECL—led the leagues and dominated the gate receipts. Weaker clubs regularly folded, sometimes in the middle of a season. Examples of such teams were the Pittsburgh Keystones, the Cleveland Browns, the Washington Potomacs, and the Newark Stars, all of which survived for only one season or less. Standings demonstrated the gaps between the teams. In 1924, for example, the Kansas City Monarchs of the NNL had a record of 55 wins and 22 losses; the Cleveland Browns a record of 15 and 34. In the ECL the Hilldale club had a record of 47 and 22; the Washington Potomacs were 21 and 37.[4]

In addition, the Negro Leagues occupied what might be called an ambivalent status in the black community, at least if their reception in the black press is any guide. Every major city in the north, during the early twentieth century, had a least one paper oriented toward the black community. Examples were the *New York Amsterdam News*, the *Philadelphia Tribune*, the *Pittsburgh Courier*, and the *Chicago Defender*. These papers usually did not cover major league baseball, and did report on the Negro Leagues. Their coverage of those leagues, however, tended to be concentrated at the beginning of the season, and then to diminish. Part of the reason appears to be that the papers either could not afford to send reporters to cover their local clubs' away games or declined to do so; in addition, the teams were sporadic in their reporting of games. Scorebooks were not a regular feature of the Negro

Leagues, so box scores were impossible to compile unless a reporter attended the contests. When scores were kept, the scorekeeper often used nicknames or only the last names of players, and spellings varied.

Thus blacks in urban areas, if they read both "black" or "white" newspapers, received detailed information about the local major league baseball clubs during the course of a season, but only sporadic information about the Negro League teams. Information about a ballclub in the newspapers can form the basis of an attachment to that club: one can arguably root more avidly, and certainly more knowledgeably, about a team or a player if one knows a club's place in the standings or a player's batting average. Press coverage made this sort of rooting possible for blacks as well as whites, but mainly with respect to white teams. Blacks were usually not given the opportunity to be comparably knowledgeable fans of the Negro League teams. Sometimes they were not given any information about the teams at all.

The experience of Kansas City in the 1920s provides an example. In that decade Kansas City had two teams, the American Association Blues and the Negro National League Monarchs. The Blues were an indifferent club and the Monarchs a perennial power. Although Kansas City was a segregated community, both black and white fans attended the games, sitting apart at Blues games and together at Negro League games. Two Kansas City papers, the *Star* and the *Call*, the latter oriented toward the black community, covered baseball games.

Although the *Star* reported on some of the Monarchs' games, occasionally including box scores, it gave no information on the Negro National League, referring to it as a "booking agency." It reported in detail on the Blues' games. The *Call*, in contrast, attempted to report extensively on both Kansas City clubs' home games, sending a scorekeeper to each. But it did not send a correspondent to the Monarchs' road games, and consequently its coverage of the NNL's season was sporadic. At the same time, because of information supplied by the American Association, its coverage of the Blues' season was quite detailed.

The impression fostered by this coverage was clear enough. The Negro National League was a second-class operation, the progress of its season uncertain, its statistical base cloudy, many of its operations obscure. It was not even treated by the principal "white" newspaper as a league at all. On the other hand the American Association, despite being a minor league, appeared, in comparison, stable, organized, and professional. The message seemed to be that fan association and identification with the Negro Leagues, or with the Monarchs, was a somewhat treacherous undertaking: one could not be sure that the object of one's affections would survive. On the other hand identification with the Kansas City Blues could be taken for granted as a feature of living in Kansas City.

In 1974 Art Rust Jr., longtime correspondent for the *Amsterdam News*, published a series of profiles of former Negro League baseball players. In the preface to that book Rust described his experiences growing up in New York, in the shadow of the Polo Grounds, as a young black baseball fan. At the time of Rust's youth, the late thirties and forties, New York, in addition to the Giants and Yankees, had a Negro National League club, the New York Black Yankees. Rust's father, a native of Jamaica, had for some reason attached his loyalty to the St. Louis Cardinals, and his son continued that affection. At the same time he took an interest in Negro League games. Rust described his consciousness about baseball and race at the time:

> I remember my general impression when I attended the Negro National League games at Yankee Stadium and the Polo Grounds. It was more like a carnival: blacks eating chicken, drinking heavily, women over-dressed, everybody raunchy as hell. . .
>
> July 1941. I'm in my room listening to the All-Star game from Briggs Stadium in Detroit. I'm happy right now. I'm a National League fan, and they're ahead. . . . Then, all of a sudden, in the bottom of the ninth, up steps Red Soxer Ted Williams, who smashes one over the top of the roof in right field off Cub right-hander Claude Passeau. I remember sitting there in tears and my mother laughing at me and saying, "What the hell are you getting so upset over the white man's game for anyway?"
>
> At Yankee Stadium, in 1939, while leaning over the bleacher wall in right field with other youngsters seeking autographs, Washington Senators player Taft Wright called me "black son of a bitch" when I put my scorecard in front of his face.
>
> At the Polo Grounds I was called "black bastard" by St. Louis Cardinals left-hander Clyde Shoun when I was trying to get his autograph. My head was rubbed for good luck by St. Louis Cardinal right-hander Fiddler Bill McGee as he walked out of the clubhouse past the bleachers.
>
> In 1939 I had one hell of a baseball scrapbook, filled to the brim with pictures of lily-white baseball players. I remember how proudly I carried

> it under my arm to the Polo Grounds. . . . I had photos of every St. Louis Cardinal player from 1939 to 1942. I'll never forget Enos "Country" Slaughter signing a picture for me and walking down Eighth Avenue muttering, "How did that little nigger get all those pictures?"[5]

In Rust's recollections one can see the mixed messages about baseball and race that he and his contemporaries received. Baseball had major leagues, the ones the papers covered, the ones whose games were broadcast on the radio. Those leagues were for white ballplayers only. Baseball also had Negro Leagues, with black fans, drinking and eating heavily in the stands, "everybody raunchy as hell." Young Art Rust wanted to be a ballplayer, but not a Negro League ballplayer. The Negro Leagues were just not first-class: "typical Negro League behavior" was fans getting overdressed and acting raunchy.

Art Rust Jr. may have been an unusual member of the young black community at the time of the Negro Leagues. One is tempted to conclude, however, that his reactions to the message he received about baseball and race were widespread among his contemporaries. Surely there was a logic to them. When one professional baseball league, which bars blacks from participating, is regularly publicized, when its players are elevated to the status of childhood idols, and when another league, composed of outcasts from the "major" league, is underpublicized and apparently followed only by blacks, when its games are irregularly scheduled, sometimes canceled, and played at the whims of the white leagues' schedules, the unmistakable message is that one league, the black league, is inferior to the other. And when the "superior" league reinforces its status by barring black players from participating because of the color of their skin, the message is widened: the white league is superior because the white race is.

The publicizing of the Negro Leagues was thus of a piece with their creation. They were tacitly publicized in a way that confirmed their "inferiority" to the white major leagues, and this confirmation provided additional justification for the retention of a color barrier for major league baseball. The Negro Leagues were, in a sense, what one who was nurtured on the legitimacy of racial separation expected: disorganized, with inferior playing facilities, without continuity or integrity of schedules or rosters, patronized by "raunchy" fans. They were a testament to what could happen to the game of major league baseball if blacks were included within it. When Negro League teams rented major league ballparks for games, the owners of the parks often insisted that the black ballplayers not use the showers at the ballpark. To do so would purportedly contaminate the showers. Since the Negro League clubs had no alternative, they accepted the terms. In so doing they confirmed the stereotyping.

◆

Despite all the burdens under which Negro League baseball labored, it became an expanding and somewhat profitable enterprise in the late thirties and forties. The Depression had an effect on major league baseball, lowering player salaries, and barnstorming increased among major league players, who sometimes joined teams that occasionally played against black barnstorming clubs. This served to publicize the black clubs and their players. As the United States became involved in War World II, defense industries provided additional employment for blacks, who had more money to spend on entertainment.

In addition, in the early thirties a different, more affluent group of owners entered Negro League baseball, led by Cumberland Posey and Gus Greenlee.[6] Posey was an unusual figure in the world of the early Negro Leagues. His father, a former riverboat engineer, was the general manager of a coal company who could afford to send his children to college. His mother was herself a college graduate. He had light-colored skin and blue eyes. In 1909 he matriculated at Penn State, planning to study chemistry, but it quickly became apparent that his principal interest was athletics. By 1913 he had left college to play semi-pro baseball and basketball with black teams, the baseball team being the Homestead Grays, a team organized by steel mills in the Pittsburgh area. In 1917 Posey became manager of the Grays. He was to remain as manager and part owner of the Grays through the 1940s.

Perhaps because of the Grays' semi-pro origins, Posey was wedded to barnstorming rather than to league play. The Grays played around the Pittsburgh area, facing white as well as black semi-pro teams, entering into an arrangement with the Pittsburgh Pirates that allowed them to use Forbes Field for home games, although they were barred from the locker rooms. Posey would insist on 75 percent of the gate receipts. In October 1926, the Grays challenged a team of major league all-stars, winning three out of four games. The series was repeated the next two years, with the major leaguers winning four straight in 1927 and the Grays two straight in 1928. As the Grays traveled around, Posey was constantly alert for new players. He raided teams from the Negro Leagues, securing players such as the star Oscar Charleston, who was then on the Hilldale club, and Josh Gibson, then an unknown nineteen-year-old but later the Negro Leagues' dominant catcher. One player on the Grays called Posey "the shrewdest owner that I played for," particularly adept at "billing, booking ball games, getting good attractions, [and] getting good gate guarantees."[7] Posey was not, however, very good at managing money, and after 1922 he relied on the financial support of black businessman Charlie Walker.

As the Depression widened in the 1930s, barnstorming became less profitable, and the Grays considered joining the Negro National League. By that time another Pittsburgh entry had emerged, the Pittsburgh Crawfords, owned by Gus Greenlee, a fight promoter who had entered the numbers business in the early thirties and needed a reputable business to front for his numbers profits. Greenlee launched the Crawfords, in fact, by raiding players from the Grays, including Charleston and Gibson. He also acquired Leroy ("Satchel") Paige in 1932 from the Cleveland Stars, who went bankrupt that year. Although the Grays successfully challenged the Crawfords to a Pittsburgh city series in September 1932, winning three games out of four, it was clear that the Crawfords had cut into their territory.

Finally, in 1935, Posey took on as a business partner Rufus ("Sonnyman") Jackson, a Pittsburgh racketeer, and entered the NNL. This move signaled the pattern of Negro League franchise ownership in the thirties and forties: the franchises were controlled by persons active in the numbers racket. The numbers game, now openly and legally administered in the form of state lotteries, was illegal at the time. It was also the most reliable business for black entrepreneurs in the Depression. Greenlee, who had begun his career as a highjacker during the Prohibition years, was able to launch a successful restaurant and night club, the Crawford Grille, with his numbers profits. He was interested in adding an additional legitimate business in order to avoid possible prosecution for racketeering and income tax avoidance. Most of the profits from numbers games came in the form of cash, which was not reported. Greenlee wanted a means of accounting for his assets. A Negro League baseball team, even if it lost money, was an ideal vehicle.

In 1933 Greenlee revived the Negro National League, which had disbanded after Rube Foster's death in 1930. Two years later, with Jackson's support, Posey joined the league. The Homestead Grays were still intact when major league baseball admitted its first black player in 1947. Between 1933 and 1947, in fact, Negro League baseball enjoyed its period of greatest visibility and financial success. The major reason, ironically, was that its franchises could afford to lose money, since most of them were controlled by entrepreneurs in the numbers business. In 1937, for example, the Crawfords, the Grays, the New York Black Yankees, the Washington Elite Giants, the Philadelphia Stars, and the Newark Eagles were owned by numbers operators.[8]

In 1933 Gus Greenlee launched another project that was to become an important source of profit for, and perhaps the single most vivid symbol of, the Negro Leagues. This was the All-Star Game, played most years in Comiskey Park in Chicago. The game featured an "East" versus a "West" team, the teams initially being created, arbitrarily, out of the Negro National League, and after 1937 representing the Negro National and Negro American Leagues. After its first game, which drew 8,000 spectators, the All-Star Game became an astonishingly successful venture. Attendance at games between 1935 and 1950, when the game was disbanded, ranged between 19,000 and 51,723 spectators. One year two games were played, drawing a total of 61,474 fans. In 1948, when four black players were playing in the major leagues, the game drew 42,000.[9]

The success of the All-Star Game reflected the economics and sociology of black communities in America in the thirties and forties. A "World Series" between Negro League teams had been played, sporadically, since 1924, but it had never been a financial success. The reason was simple: most black fans could not afford to go to consecutive games. Recognizing this fact, Rube Foster made the Series a traveling operation in 1926, playing games at Atlantic City, Baltimore, Philadelphia, and Chicago. By 1929 no Negro League World Series was played, and it was not revived until 1942, when it was again played on a traveling basis, a pattern that continued until 1948. Attendance for these World Series games was sufficiently poor that in 1926 one player was quoted in the *Chicago Defender* as saying, "We could have made more in two games barnstorming than we'll get out of the whole series."[10]

The stature of the Negro League World Series was undermined by

The East All-Stars, pictured before the 1937 East-West Negro Leagues All-Star Game. Standing, left to right, are Barney Morris, pitcher; Pepper Bassett, catcher; Andy Porter, pitcher; Mule Suttles, first base and outfield; Bill Wright, right field; Buzz Mackey, catcher; Barney Brown, pitcher; Jake Dunn, outfield; Buck Leonard, first base; and Bill Holland, pitcher. Kneeling, left to right, are Ray Dandridge, third base; Fats Jenkins, left field; Willie Wells, shortstop; Chester Williams, second base; Jerry Benjamin, centerfield; and Leon Day, pitcher. Notice the centerfield bleachers already filled with fans. The East won the game, 7–2. (National Baseball Library and Archive, Cooperstown, N.Y.)

its timing, which often came after the major league season had ended and white clubs were available as barnstorming opponents, as well as the lack of franchise identity and the movement of Series games from city to city. In contrast, an All-Star Game, supposedly featuring the top players in the league, taking place in the middle of the season, and being held in a major league ballpark in Chicago, one of the centers of Negro baseball, seemed designed to elicit attendance. But another element contributed to the success of the All-Star Game. It became a social event in the black community: a place where aspiring socialites could confirm their place in society by their attendance.

The *Pittsburgh Courier*, Greenlee's hometown black newspaper, was a major force in getting the East-West game started. The major leagues had staged their first All-Star Game at Comiskey Park in Chicago in July 1933, and Greenlee resolved to play the first Negro Leagues All-Star Game at the same site. Beginning in late July 1933, the *Courier* began a steady barrage of publicity for what it called "a big colored classic."[11] Adopting the same format as the major leagues for selecting players, it announced that fans could receive coupons from "leading colored weeklies" and mail in their choices.[12]

On August 19 the *Courier* declared that the prospect of an East-West game was "sweeping the country like wildfire!" It then expressly identified the idea of a Negro League All-Star Game with the goal of publicizing the Negro Leagues in the white community. "Baseball, most cosmopolitan of all sports," the *Courier* maintained, "is looking at a 'fading' colored line. For years there has been agitation about added color in the big leagues. Fans have been wanting to see new color, and they've wanted that color to be dark." The *Courier* then listed a number of exploits by black ballplayers that demonstrated their ability to compete with whites. "Cannonball" Dick Reddy had "stood big league hitters on their heads with a display of speed." White sportswriters had compared Oscar Charleston with Tris Speaker. Catcher Bruce Petwig had thrown out Ty Cobb stealing three times in one game. Johnny Beckwith had been the first player, "black or white," to hit a home run over the left field fence in Cincinnati's Redland Field. These exploits demonstrated that the forthcoming East-West game would be "baseball 'deluxe.'"[13]

As the game approached the *Courier* reported that "encouraging comments continue to come" from white big league owners "attesting to the calibre of Negro ballplayers." It quoted Pittsburgh Pirates president William Benswanger as saying, "I have seen any number of your games and was impressed with the ability of some of the players." Some, in Benswanger's judgment, were "worthy of the highest in baseball." The *Courier* concluded that "Benswanger's words of praise will probably re-open the eternal question about whether or not Negro baseball super-stars are of big league calibre." In the same issue the *Courier* announced that "[once] again league owners and sporting editors of leading dailies have joined the parade of well-wishers and boosters of the East-West baseball classic." Officials of the Boston

Braves, New York Giants, and Pirates were recorded as "commend[ing] the game to the fans." The *Courier* took the occasion to label the East-West game "the greatest ever promoted by Negroes."[14]

After the first game, played on September 10 in Comiskey Park with the West defeating the East 11–7, the *Courier* devoted a column to praising Gus Greenlee. "A fighter who gives his best when the road is toughest," it declared, Greenlee was "a MAN in every sense of the word, whose statement is better than a gilt-edged bond," and who was "respected and liked by owners and ball players alike." Greenlee had persevered even when few other Negro League owners had supported him, "when Chicago went 'cold' to the idea," when "insiders propaganda went the rounds in the Eastern newspapers" to the effect that the game was merely a contest between the Chicago American Giants and the Pittsburgh Crawfords. Greenlee "had rolled his big Lincoln over the Allegheny Mountains to obtain the signature of probably every ballplayer whose name was being voted on." Thanks to the cooperation of other black newspapers, such as the *Kansas City Call* and the *New York Age*, and to Chicago radio station WEN, which had interviewed Oscar Charleston and West starting pitcher Willie Foster before the game, as well as to the "wonderful" support of "Chicago society," which "rubbed elbows with the good fan," Greenlee had made the game "an event which will never die."[15]

The next year, under better weather conditions, attendance at the game rose from approximately 8,000 to "more than 25,000," the *Courier* reported. The crowd included "countless celebrities, city and state officials. . . , bevies of pretty girls," and "nearly 5,000 white fans," which prompted the newspaper to call the second East-West game "a new day in negro baseball." The white fans, it announced, "forgot the color line before the great goal of sports." Their favorable comments on the game "branded [it] as a remarkable exhibition of baseball and on a par with anything ever seen in the major leagues."[16]

In 1937 the *Courier* reported that attendance at the East-West game had grown from 8,000 in 1933 to 21,000 in 1936.[17] Part of the reason for increased attendance had been the paper's self-conscious description of the All-Star Game as a spectacle frequented by "society." A year earlier the *Defender* had announced that the game would be reported on its society page, stating that Satchel Paige had been selected for one of the teams and adding that "without Satchel the ball game would be well worth attending as all of the major Race players compose the opposing teams, and with Satchel present, baseball takes on the aspect of a social affair."[18] In another edition the *Defender* described the All-Star Game as "a highlight in the affairs of the elite." "The East-West baseball game," it added, "has been popularized to a fine social point. Social registerites take a greater interest in the game now than ever before. Rest assured that society will be represented at Comiskey." The *Defender* printed a list headed, "Socialites to Attend East-West Ball Game."[19]

The All-Star Game was one of the major sources of profit for Negro League entrepreneurs in the thirties and forties. That profit, however, was not widely dispersed. The game had been originally financed by Greenlee and two other owners, Robert Cole of the Chicago American Giants and Tom Wilson of the Nashville (later Washington) Elite Giants. Between 1933 and 1935 Greenlee, Cole, and Wilson simply divided up the profits. After 1935, when it became clear that the game was going to be a financial success, half the profits were put into an emergency fund that would protect owners against prolonged rainouts or players in case owners defaulted on their salaries. In 1938, all the teams in the Negro Leagues began to share in the profits. Greenlee still managed to take 10 percent of all the gate receipts, and white booking agent Abe Saperstein (the founder of the Harlem Globetrotters basketball team), who handled publicity for the game, took another 5 percent. The owners of Comiskey Park also took another 25 percent for leasing their facility. Nonetheless there was still money to go around, and black newspapers claimed that three-fourths of the profits ended up in the black community.[20]

Until the 1940s players received nothing for participating in the game. Led by Satchel Paige they began agitating for compensation, and eventually, in 1942, they received $50 plus expenses. Paige held out for a percentage of the gate receipts, claiming, perhaps accurately, that he was responsible for an additional one-third of the crowd. In 1943 Paige received $800 for three innings of pitching, and that same year the East players received $200 and the West players $100 plus expenses. By 1945 players were receiving $100 plus expenses, managers and coaches $300, and owners $3,500 from the profits. The game had become the most profitable event in Negro League baseball.[21]

By the 1940s Negro League teams were well established and relatively profitable. Buck Leonard, who played for the Homestead Grays for seventeen years, reported that he made $500 a month plus 75 cents eating expenses in 1941; that his pay was doubled to $1,000 a month in 1942; and that by 1944 he was up to $1,100 a month, or $4,500 a season, which ran from May 1 to October 1. Leonard also said that in the war years the Grays averaged about 20,000 fans a night, and in Washington they outdrew the Senators. (Cumberland Posey had the Grays play a number of games in Washington in the 1940s, particularly on Sundays, since Pennsylvania continued to have a law preventing the playing of Sunday baseball.) Leonard singled out John Morrissey, the Senators' ticket manager, as being very helpful to the Grays and to their Negro League opponents by handling publicity, printing tickets, arranging police protection, and compiling revenue statements at the end of games.[22]

Leonard also mentioned another reason why Negro League baseball was to survive the Depression and become relatively solvent during the Second World War. On Tuesdays and Thursdays in Washington, Leonard noted, the Grays would play night games. As Leonard remembered,

> We used to play ball in Griffith Stadium by the football lights! Griffith Stadium had no lights then for baseball. I remember one night we were playing, it was kind of foggy, drizzling rain. The ball would go up and you *just could* see it. You couldn't get a good jump on a good line drive. Or get a good jump on a ground ball. A high fly would go up higher than the lights, go up in the dark. You're standing there waiting for it to come down.[23]

Night baseball had its origins in two places, the white minor leagues and the Negro Leagues. In 1929 J. L. Wilkinson, who had first tried a night game under gaslights in Iowa in 1920, hired Giant Manufacturing of Omaha to build the Kansas City Monarchs a portable lighting system. The system cost nearly $100,000 to build, and Wilkinson had to take on a limited partner, Thomas Baird, to finance it. It arrived in time for the 1930 season. It consisted of telescoping poles, which could be raised to a height of forty-five to fifty feet. Two poles, raised parallel to one another about five feet apart, supported six floodlights, themselves about four feet across. The poles were fastened to the beds of trucks, and raised by a derrick. Each truck bearing the poles and lights was placed along the outfield foul lines, protected by a six-foot canvas fence that stretched the circumference of the outfield. Another truck with poles and lights was parked behind home plate, or if the ballpark

Josh Gibson, the legendary Negro Leagues catcher, scores for the Homestead Grays against the Newark Eagles in a 1942 game at Griffith Stadium in Washington. Notice the relatively sparse crowd, apparently composed entirely of black spectators. (National Baseball Library and Archive, Cooperstown, N.Y.)

had a grandstand roof behind home plate, floodlights were attached to the roof.

The entire system was powered by a generator, set up in distant center field, with wires running from it to the poles. The generator, which had a 250-horsepower motor and was as large as a car, ran continuously throughout games, making a great deal of noise. It used up fifteen gallons of gasoline every hour. The system took about two hours to assemble before each game, and some time to be dissembled and packed on to trucks after it had been used. The Monarchs traveled with a revamped bus on which the generator was stationed, three trucks with poles and lights, and cars for the players.

A portable lighting system perfectly complemented the barnstorming tendencies of Negro League teams. Between 1931 and 1937 the Monarchs did not join the Negro National League, choosing to barnstorm. Before inaugurating their season, in fact, they leased their lighting system to the House of David barnstorming team, a largely white but regularly integrated club. The Monarchs and the House of David had the same booking agent, and the Monarchs would hold off starting their own season until they had made a sufficient income from the rental arrangement. Some years they traveled with the House of David, the traveling teams playing games against each other as well as local teams. The key to the Monarchs' success was their lighting system. It enabled them to play nearly every day in small towns. In 1934 the Monarchs played a barnstorming series against the "Dean All-Stars," a white team of major and minor leagues featuring Jerome ("Dizzy") Dean and his brother Paul ("Daffy") Dean. The teams averaged between 14,000 and 20,000 fans a game, at about 75 cents a ticket. The Deans later claimed that they earned about $14,000 for four games against the Monarchs.[24]

Playing under the lights required a few adjustments. The generator, as Leonard suggested, tended to sputter, causing the lights to dim, sometimes in the middle of a play. Outfielders could trip over the wires from the generator to the poles, or run into the poles themselves. An actual limit was placed on the number of bases a runner could take if a high fly was hit into the darkness, since once a ball got above the lights on the poles, as Leonard said, players had to wait for it to come down before they could see it. Despite these problems, portable lights had the distinct advantage of allowing baseball to be offered at night at a time when many Americans could not afford to take off from work to watch a baseball game. By 1933 Gus Greenlee, who had built his own field for the Pittsburgh Crawfords, installed lights in it. Several white minor league teams did as well. The possibility of night baseball in the major leagues became a subject for debate, and in 1935 the first major league night game was played. The Monarchs' portable lighting system had allowed them to weather the Depression, and by 1937 they were able to enter the newly created Negro American League, which they would dominate for the next decade. Negro League baseball prospered with them: between 1942 and 1946 the income of franchise owners was estimated at about $25,000 a year.[25]

◆

The relative success of Negro League baseball hastened its demise. Observers from Organized Baseball had noted the crowds at the All-Star Games, the growing black populations in major league cities, and the rising pool of talent among black ballplayers. But those were not sufficient conditions for the integration of the major leagues and the attendant death of the Negro Leagues. In order for that to take place, a change in racial consciousness was necessary.

As late as 1943 it was evident that older attitudes about black ballplayers still prevailed within baseball's inner circles. That year Bill Veeck, the son of the former owner of the Chicago Cubs, attempted to buy the floundering Philadelphia Phillies. Working through connections with the Negro Leagues, such as *Courier* sportswriter Wendell Smith and Abe Saperstein, Veeck planned to raid black baseball to stock his new team. Rumors circulated about Veeck's strategy, and after he had arranged to finalize the purchase of the Phillies with their owner, Jerry Nugent, he informed Commissioner Landis of his plans. The next day Veeck learned that Nugent had sold the Phillies to the National League, who subsequently sold them, at a lower price, to William Cox, whose business practices were sufficiently disreputable that he was soon forced out of baseball.[26]

The incident caused Veeck and others to conclude that there would be no possibility of black players entering Organized Baseball as long as Landis remained commissioner. Landis, for his part, publicly insisted that the major leagues had no policy excluding blacks, and regularly maintained that there were no players in the Negro Leagues capable of making major league rosters. The patent absurdity of this argument was demonstrated as soon as baseball became integrated in 1947, and in any case the argument did not explain why black players were not on *any* rosters in Organized Baseball, especially at a time when some minor leagues came close to disbanding because of the wartime depletion of the supply of players. A one-armed white player, Pete Gray, made it to the major leagues during the Second World War, but no black players did.

Despite Landis's resistance, a change in attitudes began to emerge in the 1940s. World War II introduced America to conspicuously racist enemies and dramatized the gap between democratic ideals and racism at home. The great black migrations to northern cities continued, and the increased success of the Negro Leagues during the war reflected the increased earning power of blacks. Americans began to reexamine their racial attitudes, and the eventual integration of major league baseball reflected a reformulation of race consciousness that would eventually stretch to the most intimate and fundamental sectors of American life, such as marriage and the education of school children. The first steps of that reformulation were necessary before Jackie Robinson could have entered the major leagues. It was those steps that made some old arguments on behalf of segregation in baseball no longer reflexively accepted. One argument was that southern ballplayers would not tolerate any departure from it; another was that southern regions, where many major league teams trained, would not countenance its removal; a third was that ballplayers from the Negro Leagues lacked the talent, or the experience, to hold up to the rigors of a major league schedule.

None of the arguments carried much weight in themselves. White and black players had barnstormed with one another for years, playing on the same teams in Cuba and elsewhere in Latin America. Only a handful of major leaguers, such as Ty Cobb or Rogers Hornsby, were virulent, outspoken racists. Most ballplayers were far more interested in playing baseball for money than in contemplating the intellectual justifications for racial segregation or integration.

As for training in the south, the Brooklyn Dodgers treated that issue very cautiously in 1946 and 1947, when they introduced Jackie Robinson to their Montreal and Brooklyn rosters, choosing to train in Havana, Cuba, in the spring of 1947, Robinson's first year. Between 1947 and the early 1960s black ballplayers continued to encounter some resistance to their staying in "all-white" hotels or eating in all-white restaurants in some southern states, and the major league teams chose not to make an issue of that resistance, resulting in some humiliating and bewildering experiences for black ballplayers, particularly those who had not grown up in the south. Nonetheless there is no evidence that white fans stayed away from spring training games because major league teams had blacks training with them, or that training camp cities sought to abrogate their affiliation with a major league club. Birmingham, Alabama, was one of the centers of "massive resistance" to court-ordered desegregation after the Supreme Court's decision in *Brown v. Board of Education*. But in early 1954, before the *Brown* decision was handed down, the Birmingham City Council repealed the city's ban on interracial sporting competition in order to allow the Dodgers to play a spring training game there.

The fact of the matter was that southern spring training locations, and individual white ballplayers, had so clear an economic incentive to accommodate themselves to blacks in the major leagues that only the most fanatical racists would have chosen to make an issue of it. The reserve clause was still in effect when Jackie Robinson became a Brooklyn Dodger. White ballplayers who did not want to play with Robinson, or against him, always had the option of leaving their club. But no other major league club would hire them. Spring training cities always had the option of discouraging the Dodgers or other clubs who were among the first to invite blacks to spring training from using their city as a base. They would simply lose the considerable revenue that a long-term attachment with a major league club produced. Another city would doubtless be happy to accommodate the team.

As for the relative lack of talent or lack of experience of Negro League ballplayers, most persons making that argument simply had no basis for their claims. In 1946 Organized Baseball created a steering committee to consider a number of issues of interest and concern, including player pension plans, competition from the emergent Mexican League, and rule changes. Among the issues was the "race question." The committee's discussion of blacks in baseball, drafted by Brooklyn Dodgers general manager Larry MacPhail, included an argument that signing a few blacks would be a futile gesture because the black pool of talent was inadequate. The argument rested on the assumption that a "major league baseball player must have something besides great natural ability." Major league players, MacPhail asserted, "must [also] possess the technique, the coordination, the competitive attitude and the discipline, which is usually acquired only after years of training in the minor leagues." Since no blacks had been in the minors, MacPhail noted, they could not have received such "discipline," and the Negro Leagues had not emphasized fundamentals. Hence few black players would be able to meet the demands of Organized Baseball.

The first part of MacPhail's argument, that blacks lacked "discipline" because it was acquired in the minor leagues and blacks had been excluded from them, was simply a piece of sophistry. The second part, however, had been echoed by black ballplayers themselves and by close observers of the Negro Leagues. MacPhail's discussion quoted extensively from Sam Lacy, sportswriter for the *Baltimore Afro-American,* who had been a consistent advocate of integration of the major leagues. Lacy believed that the Negro Leagues had not given proper attention to the fundamentals of baseball, and on one occasion had written that "we haven't a single man in the ranks of colored baseball who could step into the major league uniform and disport himself after the fashion of a big leaguer." MacPhail reprinted this passage in his report and added, "Mr. Lacy's opinions are shared by almost everyone, Negro and White, competent to appraise the qualifications of Negro players."[27]

Lacy's observation that the Negro League teams did not emphasize fundamentals was confirmed by players. In his autobiography Roy Campanella, who moved from the Baltimore Elite Giants to the Brooklyn Dodgers after integration, contrasted the spring training routines in the two leagues: "*Play* yourself into shape! That was the only way the Negro leagues got on the ball. Man, we didn't just sop up sun and orange juice and run laps and play 'pepper' and listen to theory on the 'pickoff play' those first few days after reaching camp. No sir—regular exhibition games with the hat being passed."[28] Buck Leonard made similar comments to John Holway: "There was nobody to tell me how to hit. . . , like in the major leagues, where they got coaches that take you out in the morning and give you extra batting practice. . . . We had to play until we learned it. Now that was what we used to call inside baseball. We weren't taught that; we weren't taught the fundamentals."[29]

However accurate the view that Negro League players lacked the grounding in fundamentals of their white minor league counterparts, it hardly formed a solid basis for excluding them from the major leagues. Babe Ruth had had no "grounding" when he joined the Red Sox: his batting style and swing were the opposite of orthodoxy for the time. Although proper technique is an important part of the execution of some of the subtle plays of baseball—holding runners on base, executing pickoffs, rundowns, relays, double plays, and the like—much of baseball consists of elemental contests between pitchers and hitters. One can teach hitting or pitching only up to a point. The truly gifted player will surface: his skills are to an important extent natural. The "fundamentals" argument was a makeweight: the real question was how deep the pool of talent in the Negro Leagues ran.

On that issue, former Negro League players suggested that the general level of ability in the leagues was varied, with some players the equal of major leaguers, some decidedly not, and the collective level of teams approximating the high minor leagues. William J. ("Judy") Johnson, who played between 1921 and 1938, told John Holway that "you could have picked enough players then to put a team in each major league—a whole colored team in each league—and they would have been the same calibre as the other big-league teams." But "we had men in some positions who weren't major league calibre. . . . There were a couple of positions where men would have to be replaced."[30]

Buck Leonard was more specific: "We didn't have star men at every position. We didn't have—as the majors did—two good catchers and six or seven good pitchers and good infielders and outfielders. We had about four good pitchers and about two or three mediocre pitchers. . . . I would say we would have been a good Triple-A team for this reason—we didn't have the replacements that the major league teams have."[31]

The comments suggested that when major league baseball resolved to accept black players in the late 1940s, only a few of the Negro League players would be tapped, and this turned out to be the case. But the process under which black ballplayers were initiated into the major leagues was such that probably far fewer eligible players, if raw talent had been the only ground of eligibility, were chosen than were available. The extremely selective nature of Organized Baseball's racial integration was a product of several factors, including race consciousness.

The economics of integration, for example, was affected by racial attitudes. Although those within Organized Baseball who considered the prospect of adding black players to rosters were motivated in part by the growing profitability of Negro League baseball and the expanding black fan base in major league cities, they were cautious about the implications of too dramatic an outpouring of support for major league teams from the black community. Washington's black population in the 1940s was sizable, and the success of the Homestead Grays suggested a substantial black fan base. But Clark Griffith, who flirted with the idea of signing black players in the early 1940s, hesitated because he feared that white fans might boycott the games if "too many" blacks attended. There were other implications as well. Washington was a segregated city. If blacks were permitted to play with whites on the field, were they permitted to sit with whites in the stands? Such issues made some major league owners view the prospect of black fan support for their clubs as a mixed blessing.

Another complicating factor in the economics of baseball integration was the attitude of the Negro League owners. Newark Eagles owner Effa Manley symbolized the ambivalence of her peers toward the prospect of having blacks play in the major leagues. Herself exceptionally light-skinned, quite possibly with no African-American heritage, Manley was the illegitimate child of a white German woman from Philadelphia who had two black husbands and whose children were considered black. In her youth she moved to New York, lived in a black community in Harlem, but "passed" for white in her job in Manhattan. In 1932 she met and married Abe Manley, a racketeer twenty years her senior, and became co-owner of the Newark Negro National League franchise with him. At the same time she was an outspoken advocate of integration, serving as treasurer of the New Jersey NAACP and being active in the Harlem-based Citizens League for Fair Play, which pushed for the desegregation of retail store hiring.

In the 1940s Manley's Newark Eagles were a successful and profitable club, leading the league in 1946 and 1947. They were also in the New York area, currently supporting three major league teams, including Branch Rickey's Dodgers. By the 1940s the New York Yankees and Giants had fashioned agreements with the Negro League Black Yankees and Cubans that resulted in those clubs renting the Polo Grounds and Yankee Stadium. The increased attendance for Negro League contests in that decade, and the 20 percent rental fee typically received by the major league teams, meant that the Yankees and Giants could earn a good deal of money from these arrangements, as much as $50,000 a year from New York area teams alone. The Negro League Brooklyn Eagles, however, had moved to Newark in 1937: the Dodgers received nothing from their games, since the Newark park was owned by the Yankees. As the black population of Brooklyn grew, Rickey came to realize that a connection with Negro League baseball might be to his advantage.

Effa Manley, however, despite her vocal support for integration, was opposed to the major leagues becoming open to black players. Her position was shared by all the owners of Negro League franchises. Their reasons were clear enough: they all felt, accurately as it turned out, that the integration of Organized Baseball would result in the death of the Negro Leagues. A year after Jackie Robinson signed with the Dodgers, and began play in the International League, the Newark Eagles' attendance dropped from 120,000 to 57,000; by 1948 it was down to 35,000. Manley complained, and black newspapers criticized her for supporting Jim Crow.[32]

At least Manley was able to secure some compensation for players that the major leagues recruited from her club and other Negro League clubs. Branch Rickey, in signing Jackie Robinson to a three-year contract in October 1945, had paid the Kansas City Monarchs nothing. He had no legal obligation to, and the Monarchs' leverage over their players, in a league in which contract jumping was routine, was negligible. Rickey argued that the Negro Leagues were "in the zone of a racket," amounting to booking agencies rather than leagues. He also realized that Negro League owners could not protest too much or they would be treated as blocking the advancement of black players. Manley referred to the owners' position as "being squeezed between intransigent racial considerations on one hand, and cold business reasoning on the other."[33]

Nonetheless the Monarchs' owners, J. L. Wilkinson and Thomas Baird, resented Rickey's actions. Wilkinson stated, "I feel that the Brooklyn club or the Montreal club owes us some kind of consideration for Robinson," but added that "we will not protest to Commissioner [Happy] Chandler," and "I am very glad to see Jackie get this chance." Despite his public posture, Wilkinson was hurt by Rickey's actions, and Baird later said that Rickey's celebrated religiosity "runs toward the almighty dollar." When Bill Veeck of the Cleveland Indians attempted to sign Larry Doby from Manley's Eagles in 1947, Manley negotiated in the press, eventually receiving compensation, which was later fixed at a minimum of $5,000 and applied to contracts that Rickey purchased.[34]

There was, in the end, little that Negro League owners could do to prevent their rosters from being raided by major league clubs. But those clubs were not in a hurry to raid. By 1948, three years after Rickey had announced the signing of Robinson, only four blacks were playing in the major leagues: Roy Campanella and Robinson on the Dodgers and the Indians' Larry Doby and Satchel Paige, whom Bill Veeck had signed that year despite Paige's reportedly being forty-two years old. It was to be another ten years before all major league teams had at least one black player.

The reasons why the signing of Robinson did not create a flood of black players in the major leagues were complex. First, there were not a large number of players in Negro League baseball itself. In the 1940s the Negro National and Negro American Leagues had a total of twelve or thirteen teams, each of which maintained a roster of about fifteen or sixteen players. There were no black minor league teams. Some blacks played baseball on interracial semi-pro teams, and some played in

Mexico, but their numbers were not large. Thus the major leagues had a total pool of only about two hundred black players, at the most, to draw upon.

Second, of the eligible players, a number of them were not considered "draftable" by the major leagues because of their age. When the Dodgers, the Indians, and the New York Giants, the first teams to take a serious interest in Negro League rosters, began signing black players, they demonstrated a clear preference for younger players. Players such as Buck Leonard, Josh Gibson, Willie Wells, Ray Dandridge, James ("Cool Papa") Bell, Martin Dihigo, and Vic Harris, who were still active in the Negro Leagues when the stirrings of integration began, were eliminated from consideration because of their age. Only Paige was signed as an "old" player, and he was signed by Veeck, a consummate promoter, as much for his charisma and showmanship as for his pitching ability.

Beyond the factors of age and a limited pool of talent, however, was one overriding factor: concern among white major league owners that they sign the "right" kind of black player. By that designation they meant a player capable of adopting to a virtually all-white environment that would include significant public scrutiny, racial hostility, and social as well as athletic pressure. The story of Branch Rickey's submitting Jackie Robinson to an interview in his office in which he directed a variety of abusive racial insults at Robinson, to see how he would react, and then instructed Robinson that he was never to fight back at that abuse, however it irritated, has often been told. Rickey wanted the first black he signed to be capable of dealing with any amount of pressure and stress. Indeed he wanted someone whose competitive instincts would enable him to respond affirmatively to stressful conditions. In Robinson Rickey found a suitable candidate.

Robinson's signing was not greeted with rousing applause by those close to official Organized Baseball circles. *The Sporting News*, which in 1942 had suggested that black players should remain in their own leagues and had blamed "agitators" for "mak[ing] an issue of a question on which both sides prefer to be let alone," reacted by suggesting that Robinson's skills were overrated and that he would have a hard time in the white leagues. After suggesting that even Branch Rickey believed "there is not a single Negro player with major league possibilities for 1946," the paper said that Robinson "is reported to possess baseball abilities which, were he white, would make him eligible for a trial with . . . the Brooklyn Dodgers' Class B farm at Newport News." Robinson "conceivably will discover," *The Sporting News* concluded, "that as a 26-year old shortstop just off the sandlots, the waters of competition in the International League will flow far over his head."[35] Even some of Robinson's Negro League contemporaries felt there were several better players than he in the league and wondered why he had been chosen.[36]

Robinson quickly proved his critics wrong. Playing second base for the Montreal Royals against the Jersey City Giants on the opening day of the International League season, he went four for five, hit a home run, scored four runs, drove in three, stole two bases, and forced a pitcher to balk him in from third base twice. He went on to lead the league in hitting, batting .349, and in runs scored, while finishing second in stolen bases and leading second basemen in fielding percentage. The Royals won the International League pennant and defeated the American Association's Louisville Colonels in the Little World Series.

As the Dodgers prepared to bring Robinson up to the Brooklyn club for the 1947 season, some incidents over the winter revealed the extent to which the issue of blacks in major league baseball was still dominated by racial stereotyping. At the 1946 New York baseball writers' annual show, Commissioner Happy Chandler, a native of Versailles, Kentucky, was pictured as a southern "massa" and Robinson as a "darky" butler, complete with dialect. Around the same time Rickey spoke at a meeting of the Carlton Branch of the Brooklyn YMCA, a predominantly black organization whose members included a high number of professionals. The invitees for Rickey's speech were doctors, lawyers, realtors, teachers, a minister, and a judge. The invitation from the YMCA had indicated that Rickey would be addressing "the things which are on his mind as well as ours, in connection with the projection of what seems to be inevitable."[37]

Rickey took the occasion to lecture his audience on the necessity of black baseball fans behaving with propriety and moderation toward the prospect of blacks playing in the major leagues. "The biggest threat to [Robinson's] success," Rickey said, "is the Negro people themselves." He expressed concern that "you will go and form parades and welcoming committees," that "you'll strut" and "wear badges," that "you'll get drunk," "fight," and "be arrested," and "wine and dine the player until he is fat and futile." Rickey warned that "if any individual, group, or segment of Negro society" treated Robinson's integration "as a symbol of a social 'ism' or schism, a triumph of race over race," he would see that "baseball is never so abused and misrepresented again." Rickey's audience responded with "deafening applause" and established a committee to instruct members of the black community to take a low-key approach to Robinson's promotion to the big leagues. The committee, using "Don't Spoil Jackie's Chances" as a slogan, began to operate throughout the New York area in the spring of 1947, encouraging blacks not to drink liquor before attending baseball games and not to indulge in ceremonies honoring Robinson at ballparks.

The reaction of black "community leaders," as gauged by their comments in the black press, was to regard Rickey's comments as accurate rather than patronizing. One warned readers of the *Pittsburgh Courier* to "learn something about the game [of baseball] in order that we won't humiliate Jackie by our lack of knowledge." Even black sportswriters engaged in stereotypes. Dan Burley of the *Amsterdam News* cautioned his audience:

> We can get full of Sneaky Pete before we go to Ebbets Field, or we can take our Sneaky Pete and watermelons with us as we do at some of the more sociable events. [We need to avoid] transferring our Yankee Stadium routines [to Ebbets Field]. You know of the Yankee Stadium routines, don't you. They are unique, they are staged with beer and pop bottles. Knives, sometimes. Once in a while they use blackjacks for props. [Sometimes] two big, fat, ugly women get to wrestling with each other in the grandstands, sweating and cussing like sailor-trained parrots.[38]

Despite these imprecations, the black press and the black community could not conceal the great enthusiasm with which they responded to Robinson's presence in major league baseball. When Robinson appeared in his first game in Brooklyn, 14,000 black fans attended. The *Boston Chronicle*'s headline ran, "Triumph of Whole Race Seen in Jackie's Debut in Major League Ball." The *Baltimore Afro-American* covered the preseason series between the Dodgers and the Yankees, describing Robinson's every move during the games, ranging from his appearances at bat to his sitting on the bench while his teammates hit. When the Dodgers made their first road trip, black fans flocked to see him in all cities. Mike Royko, columnist for the *Chicago Daily News*, reported blacks "[coming] by the thousands, pouring off the north-bound ELS and out of their cars" at Wrigley Field. "They didn't wear baseball-game clothes," Royko noted. "They had on church clothes and funeral clothes—suits, white shirts, ties, gleaming shoes, and straw hats." When Robinson batted, "long, rolling applause" came from the black fans. Royko described "a tall, middle-aged black man . . . next to me, a smile of almost painful joy on his face, beating his palms together so hard they must have hurt."[39]

Of all the surprises accompanying Robinson's entrance into major league baseball in 1947, the greatest was undoubtedly the positive reaction it precipitated from some whites. Robinson received awards from white as well as black groups, was besieged for autographs by white fans, got volumes of complimentary mail from whites, and finished high in popular opinion polls. A Jackie Robinson Day was celebrated on September 23 of his first season with the Dodgers. He received the Rookie of the Year award, Thomas Spink of *The Sporting News* flying to Brooklyn to deliver it in person. At the end of the season Robinson had hit .297, led the league in stolen bases, and helped the Dodgers win the pennant. The Dodgers had also drawn over a million fans for the first time in their history, and National League attendance had set an all-time record. There were negative reactions as well: the St. Louis Cardinals threatened to strike rather than play against him in May, and the Philadelphia Phillies, led by their manager, Ben Chapman, subjected him to regular racial abuse. But the National League informed the Cardinals that striking players faced the possibility of dismissal from the game, and Chapman was pressured and cajoled into publicly shaking hands with Robinson. By the end of Robinson's first year it was clear that baseball had been integrated.

Robinson's success paved the way for additional former Negro Leaguers to join the major leagues. Don Newcombe, Roy Campanella, and Joe Black of the Baltimore Elite Giants followed him to the Dodgers; Doby, Paige, and Luke Easter of the Homestead Grays joined the Indians, Paige winning the 1948 Rookie of the Year award in the American League, at the age of approximately forty-two. Monte Irwin of the Newark Eagles and Hank Thompson of the Kansas City Monarchs were signed by the Giants; Sam Jethroe of the Cleveland Buckeyes was secured by the Boston Braves, becoming the National League's Rookie of the Year in 1950. Eventually, in the early 1950s, came very young players who would become stars in the major leagues: Hank Aaron of the Indianapolis Clowns, Ernie Banks of the

Monarchs, Willie Mays of the Birmingham Black Barons, and Minnie Minoso of the New York Cubans, the last named American League Rookie of the Year in 1951.

By the mid-1950s the symbiotic relationship between Organized Baseball's exclusionist practices and the Negro Leagues was underscored by two simultaneous developments: the emergence of conspicuously talented black players, such as Frank Robinson and Bob Gibson, who had chosen to sign directly with major league clubs and enter the minor leagues rather than play in the Negro Leagues, and the netting of only $5,000 in gate receipts from the 1957 East-West Negro Leagues All-Star Game in Comiskey Park. By 1957 the Negro National League had folded, and there were only four clubs left in the Negro American League. By 1960 the only all-black professional baseball team was the Indianapolis Clowns, who were entirely a barnstorming, entertainment-oriented franchise, like the Harlem Globetrotters. When the black community was at last given a choice between supporting Negro League baseball and attaching itself to major league teams with integrated rosters, it was clear what that choice was. In 1948 sportswriter Wendell Smith wrote in the *Pittsburgh Courier* that "when Negro players walked in . . . the big league doors, . . . Negro baseball walked out." Nine years later A. S. ("Doc") Young, writing in *The Sporting News*, pronounced the Negro Leagues dead and added that most blacks were "far from being sorry" at their demise.

◆

When the Negro Leagues had come within the consciousness of those within Organized Baseball, they had been seen as a reverse mirror image. If Organized Baseball was free from gambling and corruption, the Negro Leagues were run by racketeers. If Organized Baseball was premised on the roster stability of the reserve clause, the Negro Leagues were the province of contract jumpers. If Organized Baseball was structured around permanent franchise cities and regular schedules, the Negro Leagues were a kaleidoscope of changing franchises and whimsical scheduling. If Organized Baseball was a clean, wholesome, upwardly mobile sport, Negro League games were the scenes of rowdy, disorderly, vulgar behavior. By being the opposite of Organized Baseball's idealized image, the Negro Leagues served as their own justification for the exclusion of blacks from the major leagues.

They appeared to demonstrate just how "contaminated" major league baseball would become if blacks were allowed to play it.

But blacks finally were allowed to enter Organized Baseball, and the only significant result of their admission was to demonstrate how conspicuously well they could play the game. As in other areas of American life, the principal justifications for racial segregation—black inferiority and fear of "contamination"—proved to be simply myths once segregation was ended. In the end the Negro Leagues cannot be separated from the twentieth-century experience of racial segregation and integration in America. They were premised on racial inferiority, and the fans who supported them and the entrepreneurs who profited from them were, however unwittingly, reinforcing that premise. When it became clear that major league baseball needed no longer to be a white man's game, that some talented players whose skin happened to be black would be included in the major leagues, supporters of the Negro Leagues grasped what the function of those leagues had been: to underscore a purported connection between all the virtues of major league baseball and whiteness. Once those fans saw how they and their Negro League teams had been seen, and that the alleged connection had been broken, they stopped going to Negro League games.

5

The Coming of Night Baseball

IN SEPTEMBER 1880, a group of spectators gathered on a lot adjacent to the Sea Foam House Resort in Hull, Massachusetts. Other onlookers sat on the balconies of the resort. They were watching an exhibition of the versatility of Thomas Edison's new invention, the electric light bulb. Lights on poles were arranged around the corners of the lot, and a group of locals played a baseball game. There is no indication of the quality of the baseball played that night; the purpose of the exhibition was not to publicize baseball but electricity. The incident did demonstrate, however, that baseball was capable of being played under electric lights at night.

Twenty years later the popularity of baseball as a professional American sport had become firmly established, and Organized Baseball, with the major leagues its centerpiece, had come into being. The owner of the Cincinnati Reds, Garry Herrmann, staged a fund-raising event to raise money for his campaign to become the Grand Exalted Ruler of the Elks Lodges of America. The event he chose was a night exhibition baseball game, played on the evening of June 19, 1909. The location was Cincinnati's Palace of the Fans, the wooden park that was the home of the Reds prior to the construction of Redland Field. The players in the game were members of the Elks Lodges in Cincinnati and nearby Newport, Kentucky. Four thousand persons attended the event, including local sportswriters and representatives of Organized Baseball.

Press commentary on the game developed two themes. The first focused on the technical competence of the lighting and the capacity of baseball to be played at night in a manner that would not diminish the level of play for players or spectators. On that theme the comments were highly supportive. The *Cincinnati Enquirer*'s correspondent wrote, "The appearance of the field was a revelation to those who had considered the announcement of a night game of ball as in the nature of a joke." Most spectators, the *Enquirer* concluded, "felt that . . . for the first attempt it was a remarkable success," and "there is a serious future for the system." "To walk into the park out of the darkness," he noted, "one would think they were seated directly under the sun's rays, the lights having wonderful lighting power." Another correspondent, from *Sporting Life*, described the "patiently elaborated and fully-patented system" of George Cahill of Holyoke, Massachusetts, who had designed "ingenious lamps, reinforced by expert knowledge of chemistry." *Sporting Life* "venture[d] the prediction that within a very few years night base ball will be played everywhere and be a part of even major league base ball."[1]

The Sporting News also sent a correspondent to witness the spectacle. He reported, "The lights were extremely bright, and one had but little trouble in following the ball." This same theme was sounded a year later by a correspondent for the *Chicago Tribune*, who witnessed an exhibition staged at night by Chicago White Sox owner Charles Comiskey in newly constructed Comiskey Park. "The game," the correspondent observed, "was played under exactly the same conditions as a contest in broad daylight. The ball could be followed as readily as if thrown under natural light."[2]

As technological events, then, early night baseball games were clearly successful. Alongside the theme of their technological success, however, observers raised another theme, one that was to have a profound impact on the place of night baseball in the major leagues. *The Sporting News*, already the voice of Organized Baseball's establishment, sounded this theme in its report on the 1909 Cincinnati exhibition. "We had our first taste of night baseball last week," *The Sporting News* reported on June 24, 1909, "and it can't be said that anyone has gone particularly daffy over it." Although the lighting was effective, "the rays of the good, old sun were missing; the grass didn't take on the right hue, and you couldn't see the inside workings of the minds of the spectators." The game, in short, was not being played "under natural conditions."[3] The "natural" state of a baseball was in a park or field, in the daytime, in the fresh air. The nightlife of a city, with its theaters, clubs, and other adult amusements, was "urban"; baseball was an alternative to urbanized existence. Thus it was not "natural" to play baseball in urban centers at night.

Over the next two decades night baseball remained an "unnatural" alternative to the daytime version. This was even though there was a fair amount of evidence that night baseball might make good economic sense. Despite conscious efforts to portray the sport as no longer identified with its "rough" origins, it was clear that to attract large crowds a club needed to draw on a base of working-class fans. Many of these fans worked six days a week and were thus prevented from attending many games. As the laws prohibiting Sunday baseball were gradually repealed during the first two decades of the twentieth century, Sunday games came to draw the biggest crowds. The owners needed only to observe the composition of those crowds to realize that their ranks were being swelled by persons who worked six-day weeks.

Night baseball would thus expand the opportunities for working-class fans to attend games. At the same time night baseball offered a means of avoiding the problem of staging baseball games in the extreme heat of the summers. Only Cincinnati, St. Louis, and Washington, among major league cities, had consistently hot summers, but a number of minor league teams were located in the south and southwest, and night baseball seemed to make a good deal of sense in those regions. Finally, other entertainment sources had sprung up in the first two decades of the twentieth century that catered on Americans' greater mobility in the evenings. Moving pictures were the most conspicuous example: their popularity demonstrated that Americans would willingly leave their homes in the evenings in search of entertainment.

That early baseball owners were willing to temper the ideal of baseball in the sunshine for their economic advantage can be seen in the starting times of baseball games. From the first years of Organized Baseball through the Second World War, day games in most cities, with the exception of Sunday games, started at three o'clock or later. This was not, as noted, because the late afternoon was a superior time to play a baseball game: the angle of the sun made conditions more difficult than at noon. It was because of the club owners' expectation that more fans would be able to leave work in the afternoons to attend games. The late starting times were also made possible by the fact that most games, at least through the 1930s, could be played in two hours or less, so the prospect of a late afternoon game's having to be called on account of darkness was reduced. Still, the late afternoon starting time was an "artificial" deviation from ideal sunshine conditions, and no one thought to mention it.

Through the 1920s, however, a sharp distinction was retained between "day" and "night" baseball. As late as 1930, the year that discussions of night baseball first entered the popular press with any frequency, one commentator argued that "twilight" games would respond to the problem of games competing with work, but would not require lights. Apparently the commentator preferred altering the conditions of the game significantly, in order to increase attendance, to restaging games at night. The response suggested, as would be borne out in the subsequent debate about night baseball, that offering baseball at night was perceived as a radical transformation of the sport.

The prosperity of the 1920s, and the attractiveness of baseball to a widening circle of fans with the added emphasis on offense engendered by the accomplishments of Babe Ruth and others, resulted in increased attendance and profits for most clubs throughout the decade. With the stock market crash of 1929 and the ensuing Depression, however, baseball's economic prospects changed for the worse. The first impact of the change came outside of major league baseball, in the minors and the Negro Leagues, and it was in those two markets that night baseball first emerged. It was in 1930 that night baseball was first experimented with in earnest, and thus the first year when it received extensive coverage in the press. The result was a fascinating testament to the deep identification of baseball with images from its early history, and of the reluctance of those at the center of the game to alter those images.

◆

We have already seen that the peculiar economics of the Negro Leagues made them an ideal forum for experimenting with night baseball, although the economic investment in a lighting system was formidable, and doubtless discouraged many owners. As noted, throughout their existence Negro League franchises had a chronic problem of finding ballparks to house their contests. Very few owners could afford to build their own ballparks, so that the majority of teams were forced to lease major or minor league parks. The result, we have seen, was that

Negro League scheduling was haphazard, and barnstorming loomed as a potentially more profitable alternative.

In the late 1920s, as Rube Foster's health problems affected the Negro National League's financial health, more teams turned to barnstorming. J. L. Wilkinson of the Kansas City Monarchs' investment in a portable lighting system in the winter of 1929, which cost him most of his assets, was evidence of his belief that barnstorming was the most profitable option for his club, and that scheduling games for Negro teams would be far easier at night. Wilkinson's success, in the lean years of the 1930s, encouraged other Negro League club owners to consider lighting systems; we have noted that when Gus Greenlee built his own ballpark in Pittsburgh in 1933 he included lights.

The Negro Leagues were also clearly building on a working-class fan base, another reason for experimenting with night games. Few club owners in the Negro Leagues followed Wilkinson's and Greenlee's lead, however, because of the considerable start-up costs associated with a lighting system. Although Lee Keyser, the owner of a white minor league franchise, the Des Moines Demons, had been able to install lights in his park for $19,000, Wilkinson had paid over $50,000 for his portable system. Had more Negro League owners been able to raise that level of funding, it is likely that more clubs would have had portable light systems. Needless to say, Negro League clubs were not going to pay for the installation of lights in ballparks they leased from major or minor league clubs.

Keyser's decision to install lights in his park thus marked the first effort to establish night baseball on a "permanent" basis, and was treated as a major event by the baseball world. The first night game in Des Moines took place on May 2, 1930, and its later innings were broadcast nationwide on NBC radio. Commissioner Landis attended the game. Two earlier night games had been played on April 28, in Independence, Kansas, between the Class C Independence Producers and the Muskogee Chiefs, and in Enid, Oklahoma, between Wilkinson's Monarchs and a team from Phillips University. Both of those games had taken place under portable lighting systems, but the Des Moines game received much greater attention. Its "successful" staging (the *New York Times* reported that "in the opinion of many fans the contest was viewed as clearly as a game played under daylight conditions")[4] set off an extended discussion within baseball publications of the desirability of night baseball for the major leagues.

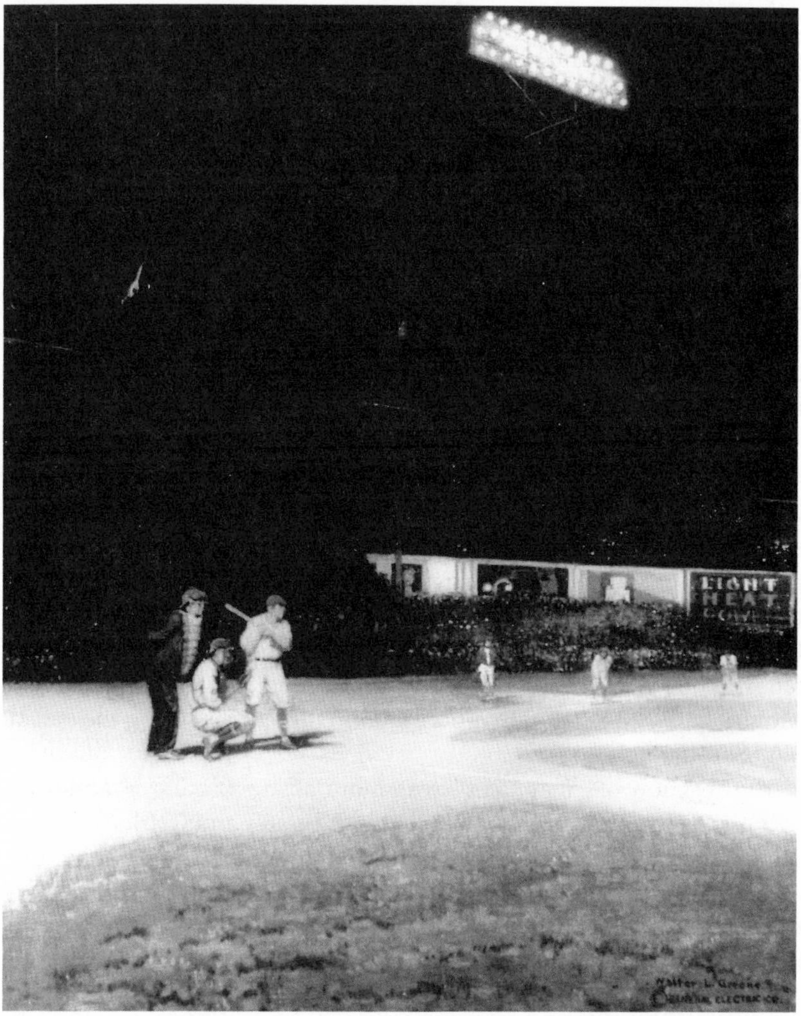

An artist's rendition of the first widely publicized night game in Organized Baseball, played on May 2, 1930, in Des Moines, Iowa. Notice that the lights are on towers stationed outside the park. (National Baseball Library and Archive, Cooperstown, N.Y.)

The first contribution to that discussion was Lawrence McAdams's "Twilight Baseball" article in *Baseball Magazine*'s July 1930 issue. Although McAdams directed most of his attention to the feasibility of twilight baseball, he pointed out that some of the arguments in favor of that game would also be true for baseball played at night. More fans could attend contests that did not conflict with their working schedules; games played after the sun went down would be more comfortable for fans; and the games would provide an evening option for young boys who otherwise might be tempted to indulge in delinquency.[5] These arguments would become staples of the ongoing debate over night baseball that surfaced in the 1930s.

Baseball Magazine devoted its October 1930 issue to a discussion of night baseball, commissioning the veteran sportswriter Frank C. Lane to report on a survey of "prominent major league magnates, managers, and players" about the prospect of playing big league games under the lights. Lane listed a number of arguments, many more negative than positive.

The players and managers, Lane reported, had expressed concern that fielding the ball would be difficult because of the grass becoming damp in the evening; that both batters and fielders would be unable to see the ball clearly at night; that the cool, damp air would adversely affect pitcher's arms; that having to pitch at night would be disruptive to pitchers' routines; and that playing baseball regularly under the lights would strain the players' eyes.[6] They did not cite any advantages of night baseball, although players interviewed after the Des Moines game had stated that they had no difficulties seeing the ball at bat or in the field.[7]

The reaction of "magnates" was more abstract. Lane interviewed owners Barney Dreyfuss of the Pittsburgh Pirates and Clark Griffith of the Washington Senators. Dreyfuss said that "the National game is a daylight game," and that "any attempt to take it from its natural surroundings, where it has always been played, is to destroy its appeal as an open game." For Dreyfuss night baseball was "not baseball at all": it "[made] a hippodrome of the game by assuming the guise of circus stuff under the lights." Dreyfuss concluded that night baseball did not have "a chance to invade the major leagues."[8]

Griffith agreed with Dreyfuss, raising an additional objection. He claimed that "high-class baseball cannot be played at night under artificial light." As a result "there is no chance of its ever becoming popular in the bigger cities, " because "people there are educated to see the best there is and will stand for only the best." It is not clear whether Griffith was suggesting, by these comments, not only that the absence of sunlight would result in inferior baseball, but that the staging of games at night would result in inferior crowds, from a social point of view. If he meant to make both suggestions, his latter argument was also endorsed by Dreyfuss, who was reluctant to cater to what he called the "cheaper element" of society for his fans.[9]

The rhetoric of Dreyfuss and Griffith juxtaposed the "natural" condition of daylight baseball against the "artificial" version created by the lights. Daylight baseball was "natural," night baseball "not baseball." "Fresh air and sunshine" were "natural"; "night air and electric lights . . . a poor substitute." The artificiality of night baseball was underscored by Dreyfuss's use of the word "hippodrome," with its associations of the make-believe atmosphere of the circus.[10] "Hippodrome" was to become part of the standard vocabulary of the night baseball debate.

Lane also presented some arguments on behalf of night baseball. Many of the persons he sampled observed that despite their misgivings, night games seemed to be established in the minor leagues. There was some evidence that night lighting actually improved batting, since it surrounded the ball instead of striking off it at various angles, as did sunlight. These positive comments were far outweighed by negative ones, but Lane concluded that "in the last analysis, it makes little difference what owners think or what players think. The public is the supreme and final judge. . . . And if the public wants night baseball, you may rest assured they will get night baseball."[11]

Beginning in 1931, night baseball became a regular topic of the baseball journals. Of those, *The Sporting News* continued to have the widest circulation and the most influence. We have seen that *The Sporting News* consistently endorsed what those within Organized Baseball regarded as the traditional values of their enterprise. These included fervent opposition to gambling, corruption, or any other manifestations of a less than fully honest sport; consistent support for the autonomy of big league franchise owners; opposition to any efforts at governmental regulation of baseball; and a decidedly skeptical attitude toward the Negro Leagues and racial integration of the majors. *The Sporting News* was comparably skeptical about night baseball. Nonetheless the paper realized that with the introduction of night baseball to the minor leagues after 1930 the issue of its potential introduction to the majors was a live one. For the rest of the decade *The Sporting News* gave consistent, if opinionated, coverage to the night baseball debate.

In July 1931, *The Sporting News* noted that the Oklahoma City minor league franchise had decided to play night games only on Monday and Friday nights for the remainder of the season. Night baseball had been introduced widely in the southwest, and many of the clubs had scheduled the majority of their games at night. The paper quoted John Holland, the Oklahoma City owner, as saying that he was "convinced that ballplayers will not develop into major league prospects under the lights." Night baseball, in his judgment, had "too many [features] that are bad for the good of the game and advancement of players." *The Sporting News* found Holland's comments "very interesting," but they were "neither surprised nor startled" by them.[12]

For the remainder of 1931 *The Sporting News* took some apparent pleasure in reprinting information suggesting that night baseball was not popular with players or not thriving in the minors. On October 15 *The Sporting News* referred to an article in *Variety* which concluded that "night baseball has run its course and the end is near." *The Sporting News* noted *Variety*'s bias, since the magazine catered to the theater trade, but reprinted a portion of the article. And on November 15 *The Sporting News* printed a column consisting of an interview with Lefty Leifeld, the manager of the St. Paul team in the American Association. Leifeld, the column pointed out, "believes that night baseball for minor league clubs is on the way out." His basis for this conclusion was his "experience" with the sole American Association team with lights, Indianapolis, "and his observance of the work of players graduating from the nocturnal loops." Leifeld believed that "baseball is a day game," and "you can't play it at night and expect the game to have the same appeal." He added that in one night game against Indianapolis two "mediocre pitchers" had struck out eight and six men respectively in the first three innings. He suggested that catchers and umpires were both bothered by the lights. *The Sporting News* added an editorial note stating that the manager of the Quincy franchise in the Three-I League had different views on night baseball, and those would appear in the next issue.[13]

By January 1933 *The Sporting News* was confident that night baseball "appears to have run its course." In an editorial it added another argument against night games: that uneven lighting systems "made a travesty of the sport" by creating different conditions in different ballparks. It was hard to see how such conditions, since they affected both teams, were any different from the discrepancies between ballparks that existed all over baseball, but *The Sporting News* asserted that the lack of uniform standards had precipitated a "unanimity of unfavorable opinion among the players about the night game." It repeated that "baseball is essentially and fundamentally a day-time game," and claimed that "there is a growing tendency to get back to the daylight brand."

Interestingly, the same editorial commented favorably on the Boston Braves' interest in introducing twilight games. "It may be," *The Sporting News* speculated, "that Boston will furnish the answer to the problem by its consideration of twilight games, staged before dark, but late enough in the afternoon to enable the majority of employed fans to attend without losing any time from work." This was a curious argument in light of the earlier emphasis by the paper on the difficulty of pitching, fielding, and even batting at night. If poorly lighted conditions were making "a travesty of the sport," it would seem that conditions at twilight, with poor sun angles and fading light, might be even worse. Indeed Lefty Leifeld's recollection that "mediocre" pitchers had amassed a large amount of strikeouts during the first three innings of a game could be explained by the fact that the game had started in twilight and the lights had not fully taken effect.[14]

Thus it would appear that *The Sporting News*'s objection to night baseball was that it was played at night, not that it offered inadequate playing conditions. The objection was premised on the belief that baseball was "essentially and fundamentally a day-time game," that night was an alien time for it. Twilight was still "day-time," however hard to play in. "Night" conjured up a whole series of unfortunate associations. *The Sporting News* concluded its editorial by noting that "the night-game fantasy is fading out."[15]

Nineteen thirty-four did not turn out to be a good year for those who believed, with the editors of *The Sporting News*, that baseball was essentially a daytime sport. *The Sporting News* attempted to get the debate started in a helpful fashion with an editorial on February 8, entitled "Is It Taps for Night Ball?," in which it reasserted that "it never seemed natural to be playing baseball after dark," and "the players never . . . accommodate[d] themselves to it." It claimed a trend in the minors away from night games, and noted that no major league clubs had introduced them and no "magnates" had indicated an interest in doing so. It speculated that with the New Deal, Americans would have "more leisure with money to spend in enjoying it." This would mean more crowds at daytime games. "It was a noble experiment," the editorial concluded about night baseball, "but like so many others it didn't live up to the expectations of its supporters."[16]

By August, however, *The Sporting News* had heard rumors that an occasional night game might be staged in the major leagues. "The suggestion has been made," an August 23 editorial began, "that the majors might well consider playing one or two games a week at night, especially on blue Mondays or whatever other slim-attendance days they may have—and even the best of clubs have such days." The Depression, in short, was still a conspicuous feature of American life, and "financial and attendance" arguments were "irrefutable" for all of major league baseball.

The Sporting News concluded that a fresh look at night baseball needed to be taken. Although it remained convinced that "night baseball is . . . unnatural, and that the game is essentially a daylight diversion," it pointed out that professional hockey had not become a major sport until it began to be played on artificial ice in arenas at night. It also noted some other manifestations of the fact that "times are changing."

First, there was a "trend toward shorter work weeks and . . . more leisure weekends, but less time for diversion during the rest of the week." This meant that "men are not going to quit their tasks during the week to go to ball games, for their jobs are too precious and the time too short." Second, there seemed to be a need for "outdoor diversion" in the evenings during the summer. Movies provided only indoor entertainment, and "the ball park would exercise a natural attraction on warm nights."

Third, adequate lighting systems cost money, but were "worth the price" because they made "the field almost as light as day" and eliminated the handicap of poor visibility in some inadequate minor league parks. "We doubt," *The Sporting News* opined, "whether it is any more of a detriment for the player to perform under the arcs than under a 100-degree sun in such cities as St. Louis, Cincinnati and Washington in the middle of the summer, or whether it is any more trying to the spectators." Finally, the practice of major league clubs of scheduling Sunday doubleheaders suggested that they were beginning to cater to the more intensive work week with greater leisure on weekends.

"The Sporting News," the editorial concluded, "is not wagering a campaign for night baseball in the majors. It simply is presenting the facts, as they stand, believing that they merit more study than hidebound prejudice has heretofore accorded them." Longstanding arguments about the "unnatural" character of night baseball might be "hidebound prejudices" after all. *The Sporting News* pronounced itself interested in "help[ing] fill the stands on days when many of them are empty."[17]

The August 1934 reversal of position by *The Sporting News* suggested that the economic concerns that had motivated the Negro Leagues and the minor leagues to experiment with night games had reached the majors. By 1934 major league attendance was in its third year of decline, and the financial condition of some clubs was becoming precarious. It was clear that most clubs could not rely on people of the "leisured class" to keep them operating at a profit. It was equally clear that in an economy in which unemployment continued to be high, those members of the working classes who held jobs were not going to jeopardize them to attend baseball games. Moreover, the working week had been reduced in hours, although jobs were scarcer to come by. In addition, in the 1930s none of baseball's prospective competitors for nighttime entertainment in the summer months had the benefit of air conditioning. Theaters and movie houses were hot and stuffy at that time of the year. Baseball parks were in the open air. Finally, as electrification spread to most homes in the 1930s, fostered by government sponsored hydroelectric projects, Americans began staying up later, and became more accustomed to going out at night.

Three weeks after the editorial, *The Sporting News* ran a column by Edgar Brands that took a quite different posture toward night games in the minor leagues from what had previously appeared in the periodical. Brands quoted "the minor league magnates" as stating that night games "have come to stay" in their leagues, and predicting that "the majors will be coming to them within a few years." "If the majors don't play one or two night games a week," Brands quoted "the boys" from the minors as saying, "they are biting off their noses to spite their faces." He reported favorably on a night game he attended in Davenport, Iowa, and suggested that for $25,000 major league clubs could install "a deluxe" lighting system. He concluded his column by noting that the Boston Braves were "contemplating the installation of lights for their last home stand this season for one or two games a week."[18]

Actually, it was the Cincinnati Reds who emerged as the pioneers of night baseball in the major leagues; the Reds' role was a product of both economics and personnel. In 1933 the Reds were drawing so poorly, and in such financial straits, that their owner was forced by the Cincinnati Central Trust bank to fire his general manager and replace him with Larry MacPhail, who had developed a reputation for promoting baseball and making money with the Louisville Colonels' minor league club. In 1931, when he introduced night baseball to Louisville, MacPhail outdrew the St. Louis Cardinals for the year by more than 30,000 fans.

MacPhail convinced Powel Crosley, a wealthy manufacturer of radios and owner of broadcasting stations, to acquire a controlling interest in the Reds. He also convinced him to introduce lights to Cincinnati, and the Reds made an application to the National League at the 1934 winter meeting to stage some night games in the 1935 season. Their principal arguments were economic. Cincinnati was the smallest city in the league in terms of its population base. The Reds had finished regularly in the second division in the 1930s, and their prospects of fielding an improved team in 1935 were not good. Their attendance in the 1934 season had been under 300,000, down from 875,000 in 1926. Most strikingly, 70 percent of the Reds' gate receipts had come from games staged on Sundays or holidays, with opening day being counted as a holiday. This meant that the Reds were averaging more than 20,000 fans on nonweekday games and less than 3,000 on weekdays.

On December 12, 1934, the National League voted to allow each of its franchises to stage up to seven night games a season. The New York Giants, Brooklyn Dodgers, and Pittsburgh Pirates voted against the proposal. Of those clubs voting for it, the Reds were the only one that resolved to install lights for the 1935 season. The St. Louis Cardinals expressed interest, but because they merely leased Sportsman's Park from the St. Louis Browns of the American League, which did not vote to allow night games, they were in no position to install their own lights. The Boston Braves and Philadelphia Phillies also supported the proposal but declined to install lights, citing financial considerations. The Chicago Cubs, who provided the fifth vote in support of the Reds, intimated they might install lights in Wrigley Field in the near future but chose not to do so for 1935. The night baseball proposal, as adopted, provided for the Reds to play night games against each of the seven other clubs in the National League unless one of those clubs objected.

In its coverage of the National League's decision to initiate night baseball, *The Sporting News* demonstrated its new posture of cautious support. An editorial on December 20, 1934, called the decision "significant" and noted the "success of after-dark games in the minors." It hoped that any lighting systems installed in the majors would be of sufficient quality, and claimed that "the attitude of officials and fans, and even some of the players has generally been favorable" to night ball "where the best equipment is installed." On the other hand, it pointed out, if a "fair test" of night baseball were provided and it failed to attract fans, "it would be established, once and for all time, that night baseball is not the ready panacea for the majors that has been claimed."[19]

Seven days after the editorial appeared, *The Sporting News* reported that the New York Giants were declining to take part in the night baseball experiment. Owner Charles Stoneham was quoted as delivering "a vehement blast against night baseball" and declaring that "his club wants nothing to do whatever with night ball." Stoneham's reasons centered on the safety of players and spectators. He felt that fastball pitchers posed serious risks to batters because their pitches might not be picked up well under the lights. This would result in the batters becoming "wary," which would eventually affect their performance in day games as well. Women, children, "and even men" sitting in the stands "could not judge [balls] coming out of the bright lights at [them]." Stoneham added that it would cost at least $40,000 to install lighting systems, and there would be additional costs of "keep[ing] those lights burning." "Besides," Stoneham concluded, "baseball is strictly a daytime sport and I will not be a party to any scheme that tries to make it anything else."[20] His conclusion revealed the strength of the assumption that night baseball was "unnatural" to major league club owners in the 1930s.

Meanwhile the Reds went about their preparations for installing lights in Crosley Field. They entered into a contract with General Electric, whose illumination laboratory was in Schenectady, New York, to build a lighting plant, using the Cincinnati Gas and Electric Company to perform the layout and the Ken Rad Lamp Works Company, based in Owensboro, Kentucky, to manufacture the bulbs. Ken Rad Lamp Works had made tubes for Powel Crosley's radio stations; at the Reds' request they made light bulbs with a higher intensity than usual. This resulted in brighter lights that did not last as long but required fewer towers to produce a satisfactory level of wattage. Eventually 616 lights were installed in Crosley Field on eight light towers, producing slightly under a million watts of light. The lighting plant cost the Reds $50,000 to build, and their additional cost for running the lights for one night came to about $250. After the first year with the lighting system, in which the Reds staged seven night games, the Crosley Field lights had paid for themselves.[21]

The Crosley Field lighting system provided additional evidence of the validity of a proposition about night baseball that had been true at least since Garry Herrmann's 1909 experiment in Cincinnati. Any problems that existed with the illumination of baseball fields at night were not inherent in the deficiencies of "artificial " electric light, but instead were a function of layout, design, or cost. If a sufficient number of light towers, of a sufficient height, were installed in a ballpark, and a sufficient number of lights were used, visibility at night games, for both players and spectators, could be made comparable to that at any day games staged in bright sunshine.

Minor league and Negro League franchises had not sunk a comparable amount of money into lighting systems, and as a result the visibility at their night games was not comparable to that achieved by the Reds. Nonetheless, we have seen, the Kansas City Monarchs and several minor league franchises played most of their games at night. This suggests that they were making a trade-off between the "unnatural" or "inferior" quality of night baseball and the profitability of night baseball as compared with the daytime alternative.

We have seen that for the Monarchs, barnstorming was more profitable than any other form of staging their games in a world in which they did not own a stadium and could not expect to gain regular access to major league ballparks during the day. A portable lighting system greatly enhanced their barnstorming opportunities and allowed them to stage games when more African-American fans could attend. In addition, for many minor league franchises located in the south and southwest, the night was a far more inviting time to play and to watch baseball during the summer. More fans could come to the games, and players and fans could avoid extreme heat. Thus the comparison between night and daytime baseball for those clubs was not a complex one: considerations of "naturalness" and optimum visibility quickly became ephemeral.

The Reds took pains to respond to the visibility consideration, drawing on MacPhail's experience with night baseball and Crosley's connections with the lighting industry. But they still confronted the "naturalness" consideration, and even after their first season of staging night games had been a demonstrable financial success, no other major league club would join them in installing lights for three years. The Reds' experiment set the stage for a conceptual reorientation of the place of night games in major league baseball, but that reorientation, given the economic difficulties of many major league clubs in the 1930s, was strikingly slow to take place.

◆

As the Reds prepared for their first night game in the 1935 season, proponents and opponents of the venture sought to publicize their views. Two additional National League teams, Brooklyn and Pittsburgh, announced that they would not play night games against the Reds in 1935. The Cubs and Cardinals continued to express support for the venture. On January 24 *The Sporting News* ran its most extensive treatment of the issue, a long article by Edgar Brands on the experience of the minor leagues with night baseball. Brands discovered that sixty-seven minor league clubs were currently staging night games, and "the forecast is freely made that they will never abandon games at night." He surveyed thirty-six parks, ranging from Class AA (then the highest minor league level) to Class D. He interviewed owners and players about their experience with lights and described the lighting systems in several parks.

Brands's article, purporting to be an objective survey, was in fact a strong endorsement of night baseball. His second paragraph revealed his point of view: "There seems to be little doubt that [night baseball] increases attendance—gains registered in the minors ranged from 'better attendance' to 'more than four times'—and, with scant dissenting opinion, it is declared that the majors will experience the same encouraging response."[22] Brands announced that his survey of the minor leagues' experience with night baseball had been made "with a view of ascertaining the real facts and presenting an impartial view" of the night game at a time when "it has passed the experimental stage so far as [the minors] are concerned."

Brands concluded: "Based on the experience of the minors, most of the objections [to night baseball] seem to be refuted." Attendance had unquestionably been increased by night games, so much so that "unless positive proof is shown to the contrary," one could predict that attendance would increase at the major league level as well. Longtime fans had accommodated themselves to it, and it had attracted a host of new fans, hitherto unable to attend games. "Much of the antipathy of the players" toward the game had receded. Most lighting systems in minor league parks were adequate, and the night games were very far from being "crude affairs," but instead resembled day games in the level of play. In short, the minors had unquestionably been advantaged by night baseball.

Brands ranged on through the minor leagues, sampling comment about the pros and cons of night ball. The results were overwhelmingly favorable:

> Compares favorably and is more spectacular than in daylight. Played better in daylight. . . . Just as good, if enough light. . . . Satisfies in every way when fans become accustomed. . . . Faster at night. . . . More satisfactory all around, as fans cannot get away in daytime. . . . No difference between two when sufficient wattage is used. . . . Ball seems to travel faster and game looks faster; crowds more cheerful and enthusiastic, probably because day's worries are over; batting lighter and pitchers have more strikeouts; press against it. . . . Some fans resent it, but new fans are made, especially among those who work and cannot go to day games and won't go on Sunday.

Brands's comments take on particular interest when the early history of night baseball in the major leagues is examined. After the Reds instituted night games in 1935 and the Dodgers followed in 1938, both decisions precipitated by Larry MacPhail, no other club followed until the 1939 season. Between 1939 and 1941 seven more clubs installed lights, but then no further installations took place until 1946. If one tracks the opposition to night baseball in the majors during that period, every one of the arguments Brands had cataloged in 1934 was advanced. That was particularly remarkable because every one of the arguments was either specious or demonstrably false. The opposition to night baseball demonstrated the power of an entrenched image of the sport.

The first night game in the major leagues took place on May 24, 1935. President Franklin Roosevelt threw a switch from the White House that illuminated the light towers on Crosley Field. National

Earl D. Payne's photograph of the first night game played in the major leagues, at Cincinnati's Crosley Field on May 24, 1935, between the Reds and the Phillies. Ethan Allen is the batter, Gilly Campbell the catcher, and Bill Klem the umpire. Billy Sullivan of the Reds is the first baseman. Notice that the light towers are erected on the grandstand roof. Payne, Al Rutterer, and Charles Young of the Cincinnati Gas and Electric Company designed the lighting layout. The moist night air made the lights hazy, a fact commented on by newspaper reporters attending the game. (Robert B. Payne)

League president Ford Frick, American League president Will Harridge, and Leslie O'Connor, secretary to Commissioner Landis, attended the game between the Reds and the Philadelphia Phillies. Judge Landis himself, who had allegedly told Larry MacPhail, "Young man, . . . not in my lifetime or yours will you ever see a game played at night in the majors," did not attend, pleading illness.[23] Among the spectators was George Wright, brother of Harry Wright, the captain of the first professional baseball club, the 1869 Cincinnati Redstockings. Legendary umpire Bill Klem was behind the plate and said afterward that he found the conditions no different from day ball.

The game had been rescheduled from the previous evening because of bad weather, and the night was cloudy and chilly. It started at 8:30 P.M., with 20,422 fans in the stands. The Reds defeated the Phillies, 2–1. *The Sporting News* pronounced the "experiment" a success, concluding that "from now on night baseball cannot be considered an experiment. It has proved its value." At the same time *The Sporting News* noted that "the night was too cool and there was too much moisture in the air," and recommended that no night games in the majors be played before June.[24]

Two weeks after the first game in Cincinnati, *The Sporting News* reviewed some objections among "some of the old-line writers" to night baseball, and concluded they were insubstantial. The first objection was that baseball contests could not be successfully staged at night at all, and this argument had been irrefutably rebutted by the Cincinnati game. "Having been convinced of this," opponents "have shifted to new objections": that adopting night games "means the disintegration of baseball . . . from a competitive contest into a circus-like exhibition" and that if the players were asked to play frequent games at night, their "physical well-being" would be "ruin[ed]."

With respect to the latter objection, *The Sporting News* produced a list of young ballplayers who had entered the major leagues having played many night games in the minors. The success of those players, *The Sporting News* argued, made them "living refutations of the charge that the nocturnal brand spoils players for the daylight game." The former objection, *The Sporting News* conceded, was based on a sound supposition: they would not contend that "baseball is anything but a daylight sport." But there was "a vast army of fans who cannot be reached in the afternoons, and . . . their support should be considered." The "ultimate fulcrum on which the future of night ball in the majors will swing" was the support of these fans. The experience in Cincinnati suggested that support would be forthcoming.

By the end of the 1935 season *The Sporting News* could hardly keep from crowing at the obvious attendance boost night baseball had given to the Reds. In seven night games the Reds had drawn 130,337 customers. In sixty-nine daylight games they had only drawn 324,256. Their total home attendance in 1934 had been 206,773, so they had more than doubled that figure. One game, with the Cardinals, had drawn over 30,000. In a September 12 editorial *The Sporting News* noted, "Other arguments against the night brand have fallen, one by one. The attendance didn't decline, interest didn't lag, players were not maimed or bruised, the pitchers didn't gain any decisive advantage over the hitters, . . . the dampness of the evening didn't affect any arms, insects didn't take control, the lights were adequate." Nonetheless it continued to maintain that "undoubtedly, a steady diet of night ball would be ruinous to the majors. . . . But one night game a week during the hot period seems to be the most desirable compromise. Thus limited, it does not turn the game into a night hippodrome."

Accordingly, *The Sporting News*, after asserting that "the only danger is that some clubs, in their newly-found enthusiasm for the nocturnal pastime, may want to overdo the experiment," advocated retaining the National League's seven-game limitation for night games "as a check upon over-exploitation of the night game by any club, and to preserve its advantages when used as an occasional feature."[25]

The logic of *The Sporting News* is hard to capture. If night baseball was clearly more profitable than the daytime version, excepting Sunday and holiday games, and if night baseball allowed many new fans to come to the ballpark, and if studies of the minor leagues had revealed no essential difference in the performance of ballplayers at night and by day, and if none of the expected discomforts of night ball, ranging from dangers to players and spectators to the appearance of insects, had come to pass during the Reds' experiment, how could *The Sporting News* conclude that "a steady diet of night ball would be ruinous to the majors"? Several minor league cities had played virtually all their games at night; the increased fan base engendered by night games, and the Reds' success at Cincinnati, suggested that night ball was intrinsically more profitable than its daytime version; no after effects in the form of player or spectator discomfort had surfaced. What was it, then, that would make a "steady diet" of night baseball "ruinous"? Apparently it was the premise that baseball was designed to be played in the day; that playing it "too much" at night would be "unnatural"; that major league baseball would become a "night hippodrome."

◆

One can only conclude that this fear that night baseball was something "unnatural" was deeply entrenched within major league baseball circles in the 1930s. For after the Reds' undoubtedly successful experiment in 1935 the other major league franchises did not act as one might have expected a group of profit-conscious entrepreneurs to act. They did not rush to install lights in their ballparks. On the contrary, not only did no other National League club follow the Reds' lead for three more years, but the American League, on the first occasion it had to take up the subject of night baseball, unconditionally banned it. The major league executives took this action in the face of information that the lights in Cincinnati had paid for themselves after two night games. They did so in the face of evidence that Cincinnati had drawn a third as many customers in seven night games as it had in sixty-seven daylight games. And they did so in the face of studies that suggested that the game of baseball was not fundamentally different at night and during the daytime.

As the 1936 season opened, the Reds continued to offer seven night games, this time against every team in the league except Pittsburgh and New York. Meanwhile the Birmingham franchise of the Southern Association spent $18,000 to install a lighting system, a price, *The Sporting News* noted, that was more than the original cost of some of the ballparks in that minor league.[26] And on July 1, 1936, a Monday night, the Reds and the Cubs drew 33,468 to Crosley Field. That was enough for *The Sporting News* to get back on the night baseball bandwagon. It reported a column written by Bill Corum of the *New York Journal* that quoted George Weiss, general manager of the Yankees' farm system, as saying that "the big league teams all would be playing night baseball within the next two or three years." "Either the moguls will install lighting systems and schedule night games," Weiss remarked, "or they can't count money, and while I have found some of them a bit dull at times, I never have found any of 'em that couldn't count."

When in a meeting in November 1936 the American League owners agreed to allow their clubs the discretion to stage night games, *The Sporting News*, while hailing the action, discovered a new basis for reconciling night contests with its conviction that baseball should be played in the daytime. The context for the American League's action was the sale of the St. Louis Browns, whose new ownership asked for the option of staging up to seven night games. The American League owners' action approving night baseball on that basis was justified as an "emergency" response to the troubled financial state of the St. Louis franchise. As *The Sporting News* put it, "Whether the moguls of Organized Ball like it or not, night ball has come to stay, probably never as a daily feature, but assuredly as an occasional spectacle during the hot months. As a means of saving poverty-stricken clubs, it has won its rights to a permanent place in the game, unless someone devises a better way of attracting crowds to once-vacant stands."[27]

In applauding the American League owners' action, *The Sporting News* cautioned them not "to overdo exploitation of night games." "Too great an emphasis on after-dark contests," the paper maintained, "might destroy the novelty upon which the value of night ball itself depends." Night baseball was presented as a "novelty" because "it is widely recognized that baseball is essentially a daylight pastime."[28]

With Connie Mack of the Philadelphia Athletics and Alva Bradley of the Cleveland Indians expressing interest in night games in 1936 and 1937, it appeared as if the American League would soon have night baseball.[29] But the project became sidetracked. The St. Louis "emergency" measure had trouble getting off the ground, as the new owner of the Browns, Don Barnes, and Sam Breadon, owner of the Cardinals, haggled over the price of installation. The St. Louis situation was complicated by the limited space around Sportsman's Park, which necessitated light towers having to be set atop the stands rather than behind them. This significantly raised the cost of the installation, since the stands on the towers needed to be set in steel and concrete, which required tearing away portions of the existing park. The average cost of a lighting system anticipated by the Browns and Cardinals was about $50,000, but the Sportsman's Park installation was expected to run about $150,000.

Given this cost, Barnes suggested that Breadon, who had been a longtime enthusiast for night ball, install the lights himself, and that the Browns rent them on nights they desired to stage games. Breadon and Barnes also got into a dispute as to which St. Louis club would host the first Sportsman's Park night game. So negotiations stalled, and the 1937 season ended without night games taking place in any city except Cincinnati. Meanwhile Alva Bradley applied to the American League for permission to hold seven night games in Cleveland, and the league owners denied him permission on the grounds that no "emergency" existed with the Indians' franchise. At the same time the American League revealed that any "emergency" permission granted clubs to install lights would be for one year only, which made the prospect of a franchise's assuming the cost of installation, with the expectation of only being able to use lights for a year, remote. Major league baseball's resistance to night ball continued.

In 1938, however, Larry MacPhail again took action while his confederates stalled. Having left Cincinnati to become general manager of the Brooklyn Dodgers that season, MacPhail immediately announced plans to hold seven night games. Light towers were installed on the roof of Ebbets Field, producing a total of 1.2 million watts, power surpassing that of any other ballpark. On June 15 the Dodgers hosted Cincinnati before 38,748 fans, the second largest crowd in their history. Johnny Vander Meer of the Reds pitched a no-hitter, his second in two starts, to add to the publicity generated by the event. By August 11 Tommy Holmes reported in *The Sporting News* that the Dodgers had drawn an astonishing 153,498 fans in the five night games they had held so far, a figure exceeding the entire home attendance of several clubs, including the St. Louis Browns.[30]

The Dodgers' 1938 experience with night baseball was striking in other respects. By August 11 they had averaged over 30,000 for their five night games; the average of their other weekday home games was about 4,000. In 1937 they had drawn around 480,000 fans; in 1938 they were to draw over 750,000, even with a sixth-place ballclub. *The Sporting News* reported on August 18 that MacPhail had already been "using the profits of his successful debut as Brooklyn's baseball boss to strengthen the Dodgers for the future," acquiring five new players with the money taken in from additional gate receipts.

By the 1939 season the American League, with some of its franchises floundering, had seen enough evidence. The Athletics, Indians, and White Sox were all given permission to install lights and each held night games that year, the Indians drawing 55,305 fans to a Municipal Stadium contest against the Detroit Tigers on June 27. Four more clubs, the Browns, Cardinals, Pirates, and Giants, added lights in 1940. The last two clubs were noteworthy because they had originally voted against the National League's discretionary policy and had vehemently opposed night baseball in the 1930s. One more franchise, the Washington Senators, added lights in 1941, leaving only six teams without them.

World War II put a moratorium on any additional construction of lights for stadiums, largely for security reasons. It was discovered that when lights from the Polo Grounds or Ebbets Field were turned on in the New York area, the locations of ships moored in New York harbor became clearly visible. The Giants and Dodgers were thus prohibited

The first night game at Ebbets Field in Brooklyn, June 15, 1938, at which Reds' pitcher Johnny Vander Meer no-hit the Dodgers, 6–0. The Dodgers were only the second major league team to install lights. Larry MacPhail was their general manager at the time, as he had been the Reds' in 1935. (National Baseball Library and Archive, Cooperstown, N.Y.)

from staging night games until the 1944 season, and it was not until 1946 that Yankee Stadium installed lights, along with Braves Field in Boston. Fenway Park followed a year later, and Briggs Stadium in Detroit in 1948.

Only the Chicago Cubs, who had ordered lights in 1941 but donated them to the war effort, resisted night baseball. The Cubs' recalcitrance was a function of two factors. First, as the nature of ballparks changed in the sixties and seventies, and night games became common, Wrigley Field, the Cubs' intimate park located in a residential neighborhood, became a symbol of an older era in baseball, and day games helped enhance that image. Second, the Cubs continued to draw very well despite playing all their home games during the day, so the necessity for lights was less acute, especially since residents of the Wrigley Field neighborhood staunchly opposed the lights, and the Cubs were not interested in lowering property values around their ballpark. Eventually, in 1988, even the Cubs scheduled a limited number of night games.

Meanwhile, as baseball has expanded to include southern and southwestern cities such as Houston, Dallas, Denver, Kansas City, and Miami, and northern cities with domed stadiums such as Montreal, Toronto, Seattle, and Minneapolis, night baseball has become the norm in many places. Many teams only play one day game a week, Sunday, and some, such as the Florida Marlins (Miami) and the Texas Rangers (outside Dallas), almost never play day games. The domed stadiums, featuring artificial turf, overhead lighting, and the absence of wind or sunlight, arguably convey far more of a "hippodrome" effect than the original night games. The experience of the immediate past, however, has demonstrated that if one is to offer baseball as an attractive spectator sport, playing in the afternoons in some locations is not compatible with spectator comforts. One may wax romantically about baseball in the sunshine, but in Miami in July, or in Seattle, Montreal, or Toronto in any summer month, sunshine is either an excess of a good thing or a scarce commodity. On the whole, midweek night games have come to be the norm in the major leagues for the same reasons that night baseball was originally a success. They are more comfortable for fans on summer nights, and they do not conflict with most people's working hours.

◆

In retrospect, the most fascinating aspect of the coming of night baseball to the major leagues was how long it took to get there, and how fiercely it was resisted. Part of the delayed entrance of night baseball to the majors may have been a result of the inability of major league owners to conceive of the vast possibilities for baseball attendance. When Yankee Stadium was built in 1923 it completely dwarfed any other stadium in the majors: only the Polo Grounds, as it expanded, and Cleveland's Municipal Stadium, not built for baseball, would rival it for the next two decades. The average size stadium held 20,000 to 30,000 fans. A crowd of 10,000 was considered large; one of 5,000 a conventional size. It was not uncommon for clubs to draw under 200,000 fans a season, playing seventy-seven home games. Part of the reason why club owners did not consider night baseball, then, was they had what in retrospect look like modest expectations for their sport as a gate attraction. They simply did not conceive a future in which clubs such as the Toronto Blue Jays or the Baltimore Orioles could sell out every home game.

In a world of comparatively modest profit expectations, where player salaries could be controlled by the reserve system and in which some owners continued to think of themselves as "sportsmen" rather than entrepreneurs, it made sense to play baseball in the day. Electric lighting on a massive scale was uncommon; baseball only required a level field and natural outdoor light; and the nature of the game allowed spectators to ring the field in patterns convenient for viewing. Night baseball seemed to introduce a variety of "artificial" hazards; there seemed no more reason to play it at night than to play it in ice or snow.

In the 1930s, however, the routine of day baseball, especially at the minor league level in cities with hot climates, revealed itself to be too costly to maintain. Costly, that is, in the sense of spectator discomfort and spectator inconvenience: in a depressed economy, a fan was unlikely to take off from a job he or she badly needed to watch a minor league baseball game outside in the heat. Thus minor league fans, and apparently Negro League fans as well, began going to games in fewer numbers. The response on the part of the Kansas City Monarchs, the Pittsburgh Crawfords, and several minor league franchises was to "experiment" with playing games at night.

Those who did experiment found, quickly, that if they could provide only a minimal level of decent lighting—enough to keep the game from truly becoming a circus—fans would come. They would come even if the Negro League teams had to change the rules to prevent fly balls lofted into the darkness from becoming home runs; even though outfielders would trip over light cables and run into poles. And as some minor leagues realized that their economic survival depended on a steady diet of night ball, they learned that many of the original hazards attributed to the game did not materialize over time. Pitchers did not have a tremendous advantage over hitters; fielders could adjust to the night conditions; fans could see the action and enjoy the game; the "night air" did not produce illnesses or sore arms. All that regular night games meant was that the players, in effect, joined the night shift. They had to adjust their biological clocks accordingly. No one ever said the night shift was more fun, but it's better than no shift at all.

Night baseball began, then, out of necessity. It began in the majors for the same reason. Had the Cincinnati franchise not been close to the limits of its financial existence in the early 1930s, faced with the combination of a mediocre ballclub, a small population base, and a depressed economy, its investors might not have been inclined to hire Larry MacPhail, who had a history of unorthodox, if profitable, tactics. Had the Reds not immediately profited from their seven night games a season—so much so that two years after the first night game in Crosley Field they had been able to restock their roster and become a pennant contender—other baseball clubs in financially precarious positions might have felt that the start-up costs of night baseball were too high. And had MacPhail not done precisely the same thing with Brooklyn in the late 1930s that he did four years earlier with the Reds—take a losing team in poor financial shape, introduce night baseball, garner astounding receipts at night games, and use the profits to buy new players and improve the team—the American League might have continued to resist night ball, and the eventual break in the wall of resistance, demonstrated by the installation of lights in seven major league parks between 1939 and 1941, might not have occurred.

Necessity was truly the progenitor of invention where night baseball was concerned. Looking back, however, one with a modern consciousness about night games wonders why the advent of night ball came only out of necessity. The logic of night baseball seems, in retrospect, compelling. Baseball is a summer game; baseball fans, on the whole, hold jobs during the weekday. Baseball is not like polo or golf, a sport identified with the leisured classes; it is also not a sport that one associates with being played indoors. Originally a "rough" sport, then purportedly transformed into a sport for ladies and gentlemen, it has remained a working person's sport, a sport that engenders local pride and fan identification among "ordinary" citizens. It became the "national pastime" in part because of its capacity to be appreciated by diverse people, to be somehow above or beyond wealth or class.

Given the nature of baseball's appeal and the time of the year when it was played, why didn't its owners think to offer it as a night spectator sport sooner? One answer may be simpler than expected: baseball had not been played at night before. As we have seen, the lateness of night baseball cannot be attributed to deficiencies in the technology of electrical engineering that were suddenly corrected, because all that the new lighting systems for ballparks did to improve visibility, was, in effect, increase the number of lights on a given light pole and put up more poles. They did not invent any vastly superior light bulbs, lighting arrangements, or electrical circuits. They simply added to what they had.

Night baseball was thus not an example of technological innovation producing attitudinal change. It was, on the contrary, an example of attitudinal changes fostering expanded uses for existing technology. When the new steel and concrete ballparks of the era between 1908 and 1923 were built, they could all have included light towers. None did. The reason was simply that no one thought of playing baseball at night.

But what of the vast fan base, not able to attend games because of their working hours, that night baseball apparently began to tap into? Why weren't the owners and general managers aware of them? One answer is that the fan base might not have been as visible to early twentieth-century owners as it appears in retrospect. Baseball was arguably a game for specialist aficionados before Babe Ruth and the in-the-stands home run made it more exciting and accessible. Owners did adjust the times of games to less than ideal hours, given the quantity of sunlight, in order to attract working people. Until the 1920s, when Sunday baseball became legalized in all eastern cities except those in Pennsylvania, club owners had little experience with attendance on nonworking days. The increased crowds that attended Sunday games, once they began to be scheduled, may have acquainted owners to the possibilities of drawing working fans to games, but, they probably reasoned, what could they do? Baseball simply wasn't played at night.

Thus the decades of inactivity, stretching through the 1920s, are relatively easy to account for. Baseball was a daytime game; it tried to accommodate itself to working fans; there were limits on its accommodative capacity; there were also limits on the owners' consciousness about fan participation. More difficult to explain, from a modern perspective, is the resistance of owners, and of mouthpieces for the attitudes of Organized Baseball such as the editors of *The Sporting News,* to night baseball once it emerged in the minors, at a time when maintaining and increasing the fan base of baseball was a necessity. The editorials of that paper reveal beyond question that even after *The Sporting News* had identified itself as a spokesman for limited night baseball, had torn apart the arguments against it, and had hailed the successes of the Reds and the Dodgers, it retained its conviction that baseball was essentially a daytime sport and warned that over-exposure of night games would turn the national pastime into a "hippodrome."

What lay behind that attitude? The ambivalence of *The Sporting News*, and of major league owners, seemed to be based on more than mere inability to accept change. It seemed to encompass a fear that if baseball were played at night the nature of the game would be altered. It seemed to stem from an association of baseball with "the daytime," the sunshine, an uncomplicated world in which shadows were natural and one could witness one's environment in an honest and clear fashion. There appeared to be something sinister, something artificial, something destabilizing about the night. It was the atmosphere of the circus, the opera, the hippodrome. It was more sophisticated, more contrived, and more dangerous than baseball merited.

Some of that sense that baseball needed to remain a day game to retain its own honesty, stability, and virtue comes through in a *Sporting News* article written by Edgar G. Brands on June 16, 1938, describing a night game on June 8 between the Reds and the Philadelphia Phillies at which Bill McKechnie, the Reds' manager, was given the award of "No. 1 Manager of 1937" by *The Sporting News*. After describing the "almost daylight conditions" created by the Crosley Field lights, and noting the 15,000 spectators, as contrasted with the "thousand or so" accustomed to seeing midweek games involving the last-place Phillies, Brands noted in passing that the Reds "have riddled the argument that night games cause more injuries and otherwise adversely affect the players," and that night games in Cincinnati "have been paying dividends" in attendance ever since the Reds initiated them. He then turned to what seemed to be his central impression of the evening:

> As for the game itself, it appears to be more spectacular and faster under the lights than under the sun. . . . Unquestionably, thrown and batted balls and the players in the field all seem faster, an optical illusion that appears to be produced by the artificial light.
>
> To step out on a field, lighted as is the Cincinnati park, brings a strange feeling of unreality, however. No sky is to be seen, just a battery of lights from various sides and corners of the field, casting their glow on a grass

> that seems much greener under their illumination. There are no shadows, as would be created by the sun, and the mass of humanity packed in the stands appears to be a huge audience waiting for some indoor spectacle, such as the municipal opera in St. Louis, a prize fight, or a horse show.[31]

Brands had been one of the writers of *The Sporting News* most interested in the development of night baseball in the minors. He had surveyed lighting systems and compared statistics, and his articles were designed to rebuff complaints about night baseball and to reassure those concerned about its development. Yet when he came to witness a game himself his first impression was that it was "unnatural." There seemed to be something illusory about the spectacle: the game "appear[ed]" faster, the ball "appear[ed]" to be hard hit, the players "seem[ed]" faster of foot. It was as if Brands could not trust his senses at night, could not be sure that what he was observing was really baseball.

More than anything else, those who resisted the coming of night baseball to the major leagues had difficulty grasping it as real. For them the reality of baseball was its uniqueness, its "natural" features. It was played in an atmosphere where lights could not make things seem greener than they were, or make players and batted balls appear to be swifter or faster. Somehow the fact that baseball had always been played in the daytime became associated with its being a sport that produced a unique product and offered spectators a unique experience. The prospect of its being played at night threatened those associations. Terms such as "hippodrome," "spectacle," and "circus" were ways that those who were apprehensive about the "reality" of night baseball signalled their concern about the prospective loss of the game's uniqueness. It was that concern, above all, that kept night baseball out of the major leagues for a far longer time than was necessary or desirable.

6

Baseball Journalists

AS THE YEARS PASSED, it became increasingly important for the owners of major league franchises to give the residents of their cities every incentive to identify with their local baseball teams. Thanks in part to the reserve clause, early twentieth-century ballclubs had become, instead of anonymous groups of professional athletes, familiar collections of personalities. Very few fans, however, had the time or resources to attend games on a regular basis, and clubs spent a good portion of their seasons away from their home city. How did the franchise retain the interest of fans during the large percentage of time when those fans could not attend games? The answer, for at least the first three decades of Organized Baseball's existence, came to be increasingly obvious. There were two principal means by which fans could keep up with the fortunes of their favorite ballclub: specialized baseball journals and the sports pages of local newspapers.

◆

By far the dominant baseball periodical of the first half of the twentieth century was *The Sporting News*, which had been founded in 1886 by Al Spink, a St. Louis promoter of sports and theatrical events.[1] Initially a paper covering racing, boxing, and the theater in addition to baseball games, by the close of the nineteenth century *The Sporting News*, now under the direction of Charles Spink, Al's younger brother, had devoted itself exclusively to baseball. As the paper struggled, a friendship surfaced between Charles Spink and Ban Johnson, then in the newspaper business in Cincinnati, and when Johnson launched his Western League and then challenged the National League after 1900, Spink strongly supported his efforts. Johnson remained in Spink's debt for the rest of his career, and when the National Agreement between the National and American Leagues came into being in 1903, Joe Flanner, then the editor of *The Sporting News*, drafted it.

The Johnson-Spink friendship marked the emergence of *The Sporting News* as more than a weekly reporting on baseball. From 1903 on the paper became what amounted to a house organ for Organized Baseball's establishment, reflecting views held within the inner circles of the enterprise. For this reason *The Sporting News*'s coverage of baseball issues, ranging from the reserve clause and the farm system to night baseball, radio, and the major leagues' color barrier, represents more than an incidental source of information about baseball. Often the response of the paper to an emerging issue exemplified Organized Baseball's "official" position. *The Sporting News* was consistently traditionalist to the point of being reactionary about most innovations in the game, although it made an effort to give a fair-minded presentation of most issues.

The Sporting News prided itself on the thoroughness and depth of its baseball coverage, and on its close connection to Organized Baseball's inner circles. That connection was underscored when the paper ran into financial difficulties in the early years of the twentieth century; during World War I it was saved from bankruptcy by the American League's underwriting the distribution of 150,000 copies to men in the armed services. *The Sporting News* revised its coverage after Taylor Spink succeeded his father as publisher on Charles Spink's death in 1914. Taylor Spink initiated the practice of having established baseball writers on major and minor league cities moonlight for *The Sporting News*, providing fresh weekly information. By the 1940s the paper had over three hundred correspondents and fifty freelancers on its payroll. Taylor Spink's close connections to Johnson and other baseball executives resulted in his consistently having access to inside information within baseball circles, and he even participated in some internecine deals, such as the signing of St. Louis Cardinals' manager Miller Huggins by the Yankees in 1917, an arrangement engineered by Ban Johnson. Eventually, *The Sporting News*'s influence was considered so great that in 1942 *The Saturday Evening Post* called Taylor Spink "Mr. Baseball": "the game's unofficial conscience, historian, watchdog and worshipper."[2]

For the four decades in which Taylor Spink was the publisher of *The Sporting News,* the paper's perspective consistently mirrored the insularity of those at the center of Organized Baseball. Although *The Sporting News* tirelessly covered even the lowest minor leagues, it never covered the Negro Leagues, acting as if they did not exist. The paper resisted integration and night baseball; it would also resist baseball broadcasts. It denied the initial rumors of the Black Sox scandal, but after the scandal broke it became a tireless crusader for cleanliness and decency in baseball, entering into a supportive, although charged, relationship with Commissioner Landis.

Despite its traditional bias, *The Sporting News* had a sense of when changes were on the verge of taking place in baseball. Its opposition to baseball on the radio did not prevent it from creating a column, "On the Airwaves," when broadcasts of games began to proliferate in the 1930s. Similarly, it changed its position on night baseball after that enterprise seemed to be catching on. Although it expressed skepticism when the Dodgers signed Jackie Robinson to a minor league contract in 1946, it covered the story extensively. In short, *The Sporting News* had its finger on Organized Baseball's pulse for the entire period of this study.

There were other specialized baseball journals, of which *Baseball Magazine* had the closest connection to Organized Baseball, but none matched the importance of *The Sporting News.* Of very great significance in the promotion of major league baseball, however, were the daily newspapers of franchise cities. Those papers had been slow to recognize the importance, to their circulation, of maintaining detailed coverage of baseball. At the time that the National Agreement was first codified, few papers had separate sports pages. Events such as heavyweight boxing championships or, after 1903, World Series games tended to be treated as front page stories; routine coverage of baseball games was confined to a few newspapers and not always grouped in a separate section. By the time that the first steel and concrete ballparks began to be erected in major league cities, however, nearly every city with a team in the big leagues had at least one paper that had an identifiable sports section.[3] In 1949 Stanley Woodward, then sports editor of the *New York Herald Tribune,* polled circulation managers, who estimated that about 25 percent of their readers bought the paper because of its sports coverage. This fact had been recognized by newspaper executives many years earlier, with the result that by the first decade of the twentieth century major league baseball franchises and the newspapers in their cities had formed a kind of alliance to generate publicity about their local ballclubs.

When separate sports sections began to evolve before World War I their pages were often dotted with advertisements. The revenue from the ads was apparently sufficient to permit each paper to hire at least one writer whose principal responsibility, at least during baseball season, was to report on the local club's games. If a city had more than one team, eventually separate reporters would be assigned to each club, but originally one writer was expected to cover both local clubs. When Fred Lieb inaugurated his sixty-six-year career as a baseball writer with the *New York Press* in 1911, he covered the Giants and the Highlanders, attending home games only. For coverage of road games the *Press* relied on the reports of writers of some of the afternoon papers, who traveled with the teams.[4]

Eventually, by the First World War, Lieb's *Press* and most newspapers began sending their baseball writers on the road with the clubs to which they were assigned. Initially the clubs paid all their expenses, and as late as the 1940s some newspapers still had not assumed all their reporters' travel costs.[5] The arrangement reflected the baseball clubs' sense that they gained considerably from having a reporter giving daily, live coverage of their road games. It also symbolized the double role of baseball journalists as both reporters and publicists for their teams. No question was more central to the profession of baseball journalists in the first five decades of the twentieth century than the question of where a particular journalist was "coming from."

◆

A series of interviews that sportswriter Jerome Holtzman conducted with senior and retired sportswriters between 1971 and 1973 serves to illustrate the tensions between the writers' dual roles of reporter and publicist. The interviews also convey a clear sense of the unwritten canons of baseball reportage in the early twentieth century, canons that implicitly defined the subjects that were appropriate and inappropriate for coverage.

Daniel M. Daniel, who covered the Dodgers and the Yankees for a variety of New York papers from 1909 until the 1960s, revealed the tension between the reporter and publicist roles in his interview with

Holtzman. Daniel recalled that when he first began covering baseball, "After the game you came back to the hotel, had your dinner, went up to your room and batted out your game story. Then you went down to the lobby, and who was in the lobby? The manager, the coaches, and a few players. I was not a gourmet. I ate in the hotel, usually. I didn't chase around. I didn't go to movies. I was pretty much addicted to the hard and fast lines of the job."[6]

Daniel's interview fashioned a sharp distinction in the profession of baseball journalist between "the hard and fast lines of the job" and what he called "going by the wayside," which he felt became the fate of many baseball writers. The distinction turned on personal abstemiousness and moderation in place of "booze" and "chas[ing] around." It was as if Daniel saw his success as a baseball writer as dependent on his not being tempted by the things that tempted the players.

There was not, however, a comparable sense in Daniel's comments that he was prepared to judge players who went "by the wayside." He was inclined to criticize writers if they deviated from "the hard and fast lines of the job," but his attitude toward the players was captured in another excerpt: "Nobody was ever afraid of me. Nobody who ever ran a ball club, general manager, president, no player. I played everybody on the level. I wasn't going around derogating people, or looking for bugs. If I saw something good I played it. I wasn't looking to run baseball down. I was eager to run baseball up."[7] It is no surprise, then, that Daniel, during the years he covered the Yankees, was "a close friend of Miller Huggins," "on fine terms with Joe McCarthy," "got along beautifully with Casey [Stengel]," was responsible for arranging the signing of Babe Ruth for $80,000 in 1930, and was the subject of a public apology from Yankee president Dan Topping for denying a story that he had been a source for Daniel—"the only time," Daniel believed, "that a club president had to eat crow."[8]

Daniel's abstemious habits may have made it easier for him to ignore ballplayers' off-the-field activities. Other writers participated in those activities, and that participation caused some professional dilemmas. A case in point was Marshall Hunt, who covered the Yankees for the *New York Daily News* in the twenties and thirties. The *Daily News*, under the direction of Joseph Patterson, was seeking to distinguish itself as a paper that paid more attention to celebrities. When Babe Ruth arrived in New York, as Hunt put it, "we recognized the Babe as a guy we could really deal with." Hunt was assigned to cover Ruth closely, to get to know him, "sometimes kidding . . . never toadying." "We covered him twelve months of the year," Hunt recalled. "I don't think he was ever aware of his role as a circulation builder."[9]

In the process of befriending Ruth, Hunt accompanied him on some of his junkets between games. Hunt described their routine during spring training when Ruth would go to Hot Springs, Arkansas: "We'd play golf every morning and then we'd get tired of the food in the hotel and I'd hire a car and we'd go out in the country looking for farmhouses that said 'Chicken Dinners.' What Babe really wanted was a good dinner and the daughter combination, and it worked that way more often than you would think."[10] "Lots of times on the road," Hunt recalled, "Babe had connections in rural places, really choice." By this he meant whorehouses. "If you liked a steak they just ripened it," Hunt said. "And everything else was excellent. . . . Sometimes the Babe would call me up and say, 'I got it fixed tonight. Don't eat in the hotel, and I'll meet you about six-thirty.' I'd meet the Babe and off we'd go. It was a little additional touch to the trips."[11]

But on at least one occasion Hunt's camaraderie with Ruth clashed with his journalistic goals. In 1923 a story surfaced in New York that Ruth had fathered a girl out of wedlock. The city editor of the *Daily News* called Hunt, who was in spring training with the Yankees in New Orleans, and asked him to interview Ruth about the paternity rumor. Hunt, attempting to take advantage of his closeness with Ruth, reminded him that although he had not asked Ruth "personal questions before," the "heat was on" from his paper. Ruth agreed to be interviewed but then became evasive. Afterward, Hunt called his paper and, as he recalled, told them, "Listen, we've got along fine with the Babe and he's done a lot of things for us. You try to get somebody else to worm this thing out in New York and not through the Babe, because we don't want to go on this personal bend that some of the other papers had tried to do."[12]

But a "personal bend" was exactly what the *Daily News* had sought from Hunt. It was as if by accompanying Ruth in search of chicken dinners and farmers' daughters, choice steaks and choice prostitutes, Hunt had ceased being a journalist and become the equivalent of a member of the ballplaying fraternity. His choice of the word "worm" in describing the *Daily News*'s efforts to follow up the Ruth paternity rumor is suggestive. The word distanced him from the underhanded tactics of the press. But he *was* a member of the press.

Other interviewees of Holtzman reinforced the sense that objectivity and distance were elusive states of being for the early baseball writers. Paul Gallico, who eventually left sportswriting to write fiction, characterized the posture of his contemporaries in the 1920s: "I was impressed by athletes, by what I was seeing and also what I was trying to do. . . . We had an overwhelming innocence in those days. We were so naive. Not only we sportswriters but the whole country."[13] Richards Vidmar, who covered baseball and wrote columns for the *New York Times* and *New York Herald Tribune* in the same period, indicated how this "innocence" in sportswriters was linked to protectiveness toward athletes: "I was always reticent about writing anything that was going to hurt somebody, and of course, I would never write anything that was told to me in confidence. . . . I just don't see where a public figure's private life is anybody's business."[14]

Another of Holtzman's interviewees was Abe Kemp, who covered baseball and racing for sixty-two years, beginning in 1907, for the *San Francisco Bulletin* and *San Francisco Examiner*. Kemp said that he had a "strange philosophy" of sportswriting: "If you can't write something nice about a ball player, don't mention his name." "I could have written some of the most scandalous stories of all time," Kemp suggested. "But I didn't. . . . If you can't pat a guy on the back when he's doing something good, why the hell destroy him because he does something bad?"[15]

A few of Holtzman's interviewees professed to be more detached from their subjects. Shirley Povich, who started with the *Washington Post* in 1922 and still writes an occasional column for that paper, spoke of being "a hero worshiper" when he first began covering the Senators and of subsequently "detaching myself from the ball players" and thus "gain[ing] independence and . . . confidence." "You say to yourself," Povich maintained, "'They're the ball players. Let them play the game. I'm a reporter.' It's a necessary separation."[16] Red Smith, the celebrated columnist, said that he would "like to be called . . . a good reporter," that he'd like "to be considered good and honest and accurate." "I've tried not to exaggerate the glory of athletes," Smith told Holtzman. "I'd rather, if I could, preserve a sense of proportion."[17] John Drebinger of the *New York Times* spoke of his sports editor's "bang[ing] into our heads . . . the basic thing . . . never show any prejudice or bias. . . . Always report objectively! . . . Above all, don't slant your stuff!"[18]

On the whole, however, most baseball journalists recognized that distancing themselves from the clubs they covered was very difficult. As Stanley Woodward, longtime sports editor for the *New York Herald Tribune*, put it, "The baseball writer's danger . . . was . . . that he would become so attached to an athletic organization and so close to its performing members that he would get out of focus on the picture he was trying to make." Woodward believed in shifting his baseball writers from club to club in New York, and recommended that editors in one-team cities shift them to other areas of sportswriting. In his experience the writers covering the Brooklyn Dodgers "always develop[ed] a great attachment for the Brooklyn ball club if long exposed to it." "We found it advisable to shift Brooklyn writers frequently," Woodward noted. "If we hadn't we would have found that we had on our hands a member of the Brooklyn ball club rather than a newspaper reporter."[19]

When one considers all the circumstances that came into play in the creation of a relationship between early twentieth-century baseball journalists and the teams they covered, one can understand how difficult it was for them to avoid being rooters for those teams. First, their single most important function, from the club's point of view, was publicizing the team to its potential fan base. If their reports from road trips were consistently negative, fans might be less inclined to pay admission to see the club when it next arrived at home. Although no publicity at all might have been worse than negative publicity—prior to the advent of radio there were no other ways other than newspaper reports for fans to stay informed about their local team's season—there was a very strong incentive on the part of club officials to encourage reporters to portray the team and its players in the best light possible. Reporters knew, then, that their negative comments on the club or its players would be resented by the people they were covering, which would make them less likely to grant them the kind of access that was helpful in writing newspaper stories.

One also has to consider the element of self-selection in a baseball journalist's choice of profession. Woodward wrote that although "all young reporters love the idea of a baseball trip," after a time many "get sick and tired of it and begin to show it." "The inured and proven baseball writer who likes his job and handles it capably over a period of years," he added, "is a comparatively rare man."[20] Those who made it their careers—such as Dan Daniel, Fred Lieb, John Drebinger, or Will

Wedge of the *New York Sun*—obviously loved the game sufficiently to put up with the deprivations of constant road travel, the mechanical routine of covering baseball games for deadlines, and the company of professional athletes, most of whom were not of a literary bent.

What did it mean for a nonplayer, whose income was not directly tied to a ballclub's performance, to make this kind of commitment to baseball? It surely meant, as a starting proposition, that the baseball journalist admired and respected the ability of certain men to play baseball at a very high level of athletic skill. A person willing to watch nearly two hundred baseball games a year, closely enough to write an account of them, is obviously someone who believes that the capacity to play the game well is an accomplishment in itself, and who, to some extent, vicariously identifies with baseball players.

Perhaps because of the writers' vicarious identification with their subjects, accounts of baseball journalists in the early and middle years of the twentieth century gave almost no sense of the extent to which major league baseball was insulated from the rest of life. The accounts, in fact, generally conveyed the opposite impression: that a baseball game was a contest of high seriousness, noble purpose, and deep emotion, with important consequences. The players, in the journalists' accounts, ceased to be limited, if gifted athletes, and became significant public figures. The narrative of the game became a drama of epic proportions, with civic ramifications. The players were not portrayed merely as young men running around on a playing field, but as heroes and villains, persons to engage with emotionally, even to emulate. And yet almost none of the journalists' readership had any real expectation of emulating the careers of professional ballplayers; nor were they given much sense of what it meant to be a professional ballplayer.

There was an additional dimension to the tension between the publicist and reporter roles of the baseball journalist. That dimension involved the cultural definition of celebrity status in the first half of the twentieth century.

The incident involving Marshall Hunt and the rumor about Babe Ruth's having fathered a child out of wedlock provides a good illustration of the ramifications of being a public figure in the years when Ruth came to prominence. Ruth was clearly a celebrity from the early 1920s on, the first professional ballplayer to achieve that status. Being a celebrity had a series of implications, but it did not have the same implications that baseball player celebrity status would have after the 1950s. The fact that Ruth was a celebrity baseball player meant, in

Hunt's time, that the public had a greater interest in him as a person than it did in virtually all of his teammates. Ruth's prodigious and revolutionary accomplishments as a player were not the only reason he had become a celebrity; some of his fame was a product of his inimitable physical appearance, accessible personality, and appealing life story. Thus when the *Daily News* attempted to "build circulation" by emphasizing the personality of Ruth and other celebrities, it was assuming the existence of a prospective readership that was interested in the personal as well as the professional lives of famous figures.

But how was that reader interest to be reflected in the coverage of the life of a celebrity baseball player? Here again Ruth was an exceptional figure. He was not only apparently larger than life as a ballplayer and as a Horatio Alger character, he was unusual among his ballplayer peers in the strength and excess of his physical and sexual urges.[21] Few persons knew this feature of Ruth better than Marshall Hunt. Moreover, Hunt knew that the newspaper for which he worked was highly interested in Ruth's sexual peccadillos, at least when they might have produced illegitimate children.

Hunt, however, was considerably ambivalent about probing Ruth on the paternity rumor, not just because of their personal friendship. As noted, he also felt that prying into the intimate affairs of a ballplayer—even a celebrity ballplayer—was a somewhat dishonorable thing to do, even for an enterprise that defined itself as gathering and disseminating news. He was not only embarrassed for himself in the incident, he was embarrassed for the *Daily News*. Yet Hunt's closeness to Ruth had been precipitated by his paper's strong interest in Ruth as a celebrity, as a person whose attractiveness to *Daily News* readers went beyond his baseball accomplishments.

Thus Hunt's account of the Ruth paternity incident demonstrates more than the tensions between vicarious identification and journalistic objectivity in baseball writers. It also demonstrates that the very definitions of reporting and publicizing the activities of major league ballplayers were shaped by cultural expectations of what the public could and should know about celebrity athletes. Although an unconfirmed report that Ruth faced a possible paternity claim may have been acceptable celebrity news in the 1920s, reports that Ruth frequented whorehouses or engaged in sexual liaisons with women in his hotel room were not. They were treated as a ballplayer's private affairs, even though the ballplayer was one of the most famous people in America.

The comparatively limited definition of "private" information that could acceptably be reported about celebrities during Ruth's career had a significant impact on the role of baseball journalists as publicists. Since baseball journalists, because they traveled with teams and spent long hours in the company of players, were the persons most likely to learn of "inappropriate" player activities, such as drinking, carousing, and fighting, their suppression of that information contributed to an image of players as upright, decent citizens. That image of players, of course, was what everyone closely involved with the enterprise of Organized Baseball wanted publicized. Thus, unwittingly or not, baseball journalists became significant figures in perpetuating one of the myths about professional baseball that is embodied in the phrase "the national pastime." Baseball players, whether heroes or villains on the field, were role models in their private lives, at least for the fans who read about them in the newspapers.

◆

Some baseball journalists came to reflect on the tensions in their professional role, and a few, such as Ring Lardner, Paul Gallico, and Damon Runyon, abandoned sportswriting entirely to become notable successes as fiction writers. Those who remained within the profession, for all their close contact with gifted athletes playing a game, were still the working employees of a newspaper, with stories to write and deadlines to meet. Their working life was both open-ended and tightly structured; it had considerable autonomy but unmistakable constraints.

The fact that major league baseball games were played almost exclusively in the daytime for the first four decades of the twentieth century made the baseball journalist's life simpler and easier. Dan Daniel, who worked first for the *New York Press*, a morning paper, and then for the *New York World-Telegram*, an afternoon paper, was a morning person. "I worked best in the morning, starting at nine o'clock," he told Holtzman. "It never mattered where I was—home, at the ball park, in the hotel, on the trains. I could write anywhere."[22] For the early part of his career Daniel had the luxury of being able to go to a daytime game, spend the early evening gathering material for his story, write it after dinner, and comfortably make his early morning deadline. Later, when he joined the *World-Telegram*, he had to go to the ballpark earlier, in order to interview players, since games started after three P.M. and few clubs permitted interviews after games. He also had to telegraph in the opening lineups, a lead paragraph, and a running account of the inning-by-inning score for the paper's early editions. He still, however, had the luxury of being able to write an account of the game for the next day's paper, which usually had a mid-morning deadline. His story completed, he was free until an hour or so before that day's game started.

The routine began to change for some journalists, however. As more newspapers came into the big city market, the tabloid paper developed, featuring brief accounts of games with pictures, large headlines, and an eye for the sensational. Tabloids such as the *Daily News* and *Daily Mirror* also moved up the deadlines for their early editions so that they could be available to theater or movie audiences.[23] This resulted in the traditional morning papers moving up their deadlines as well, which changed the process of coverage for morning paper baseball journalists. Instead of being able to dictate the box score and a lead paragraph during the game, then prepare copy at night, reporters were forced to dictate their copy as the game progressed.

Their technique was to create what was called a "running story." This consisted of a lead paragraph, written in generic fashion, which could be amended at the last minute to accommodate the eventual result of the game. That paragraph was followed by a progressive account of the game, inning by inning. Eventually, as the significance of some innings became apparent in light of the eventual result, that account was cut and shaped, and a concluding paragraph was sometimes added, along with the complete box score and line score. Then a headline was fashioned by copy editors working at the newspaper office.

When night baseball began to be played with regularity, the routine of both the morning and evening baseball writers was changed. As Stanley Woodward put it, the morning paper writer now "must [start] at the beginning of the game with his running story, writing leads covering an incomplete event, flashing final results a few minutes before an edition, then throwing it all away and starting over again just as he would if he were covering an afternoon game."[24] The evening paper writer had an even more demanding assignment. Evening papers could no longer assume that they would be first to disclose results of games: they had to treat games whose results were already

A typical press box in the 1940s, that of Ebbets Field in Brooklyn. Notice that the journalists all wore coats and ties, and most of them hats. Each had his own chair and typewriter, but shared a common desktop surface. (National Baseball Library and Archive, Cooperstown, N.Y.)

known in depth. As Woodward noted, "The reporter must carry through even if the game finishes at midnight or after. He may get his second-day story written at 3 or 4 o'clock in the morning and still be required to write running on a double-header which begins at 1:30 that afternoon."[25]

As Dan Daniel told Holtzman: "I enjoyed the fun of baseball and everything about it," he said, "until that damn night ball came in. That ruined the whole business."[26] But he was not the only one affected by the change. Clubs needed to allow reporters access to players after the games, since player reactions would be part of the detailed stories filed by the evening papers. Evening paper writers needed to work deep into the night unless they could retain enough notes from the evening before to produce an account the next morning. Morning paper writers had no hope of producing anything but "running" stories, since their deadlines came almost immediately after the conclusion of night games. They also had to decide whether to stay around after a game for interviews, which they could not of course use until later, or seek out players and club officials at some other time. One can understand why there was so little support for night baseball in the sports pages when it was first proposed.

◆

There is no question that as baseball came of age in early twentieth-century America, the profession of baseball journalism came of age as well. Major league attendance expanded for most of the two decades after 1910, and the coverage of games in the newspapers expanded as well. For a time in the years surrounding World War I and for at least ten years thereafter, newspapers themselves proliferated and made profits, spurred by a growing economy, the technological success of the telephone and telegraph, and the absence of other media competitors that could provide news on a daily or even an hourly basis. A boom in the newspaper industry created more jobs for newspaper writers, and a boom in the sports industry, led by major league baseball, meant that many of those jobs would be with sports departments. Some gifted baseball writers in this period, such as Daniel, Gallico, Lardner, Lieb, and Runyon, virtually had their pick of newspaper jobs and could command good salaries. Being a sportswriter in the 1910s and 1920s was in many respects a rewarding and satisfying job, and being a baseball writer was often the plum position in a sports department.

Baseball attendance began to decline in the 1930s as the national economy worsened, and the position of baseball journalist suffered a corresponding decline. The number of newspapers in franchise cities was reduced as advertising rates and circulation figures declined, and the market for sportswriters contracted after two decades of expansion. Nonetheless home and road coverage of major league games continued, and, as we shall see in a subsequent chapter, the emergence of radio broadcasts of baseball games did not have an adverse effect on fan attendance or on the readership of the sports pages. By the mid-1950s radio was entrenched and baseball games had begun to be televised, but the impact of the electronic media on newspaper sports coverage was slow to be felt. As late as 1953, the date of the first franchise transfers of major league clubs since 1903, every major league city still had at least two newspapers, morning and afternoon, that each employed at least one baseball journalist who traveled with his team.

It seems fair to say, then, that despite a decline in the monolithic status of newspapers as sources of general information for the public, and a decline in the economic fortunes of the newspaper industry, baseball journalists remained professional baseball's most significant publicity agents for the first five decades of the twentieth century. Moreover, baseball journalists and the clubs they covered remained in a symbiotic relationship that was not approximated in any other American professional sport. Journalistic coverage of major league games was big business for the clubs being covered and for the newspapers covering them. The access of baseball writers to players was crucially important for clubs, papers, and players. Equally important was the image of clubs and players perpetuated by baseball writers.

A newspaper writer could adversely affect a player's career, and he could also make a player into a local or even a national hero. On rare occasions a dogged maverick of a writer, such as Hugh Fullerton, could help precipitate the exposure of a scandal within the game. On more common occasions a writer could create an authorial persona for a player, such as the journalists who covered World Series games using the bylines of players. Some writers, such as Christy Walsh, Ford Frick, or Taylor Spink, became agents for players or intermediaries between players and owners.

Thus any listing of the forces that contributed to elevate baseball in America from one among several nineteenth-century recreational pursuits to the national pastime would need to include the symbiotic relationship between major league franchises and the journalists covering them. But it was not just that baseball journalists and their subjects needed each other. Nor was the significance of baseball journalism to the emergence of baseball simply a function of the absence of media competitors, or of the vicissitudes of economic growth in the baseball and newspaper industries.

The significance of baseball journalists in the emergence of baseball as the national pastime was also a function of the nature, and limits, of their coverage. Whatever journalists and players thought of one another in the fifty years after 1903, neither side could have remotely anticipated the often adversarial, stage-managed, yet sycophantic relationship that exists between professional ballplayers and the media today. All major league players are treated as celebrities by contemporary journalists; celebrity treatment means that very little information about players' lives is regarded as inappropriate for public consumption. Conversely, contemporary ballplayers are socialized not to become close to the working press, to give only structured, unrevealing interviews, and to erect shields around their private lives. Once only a superstar such as Ruth could approximate the salaries of the most sought-after baseball journalists; now no journalist remotely commands the (admittedly short-term) earning power of star players.

Contemporary baseball journalists thus regularly humanize their player subjects by revealing that they very rarely match their remarkable athletic gifts by being exceptional individuals in other respects. Baseball journalists in the period covered in this volume played quite a different role. On the whole, as Dan Daniel put it, they didn't "run baseball down," they "ran baseball up." In the process they, and their subjects, were exposed to issues that went to the nature of objectivity in their profession and to the meaning of "public" and "private" information in America. Some baseball journalists agonized over such issues; others blithely ignored them. Meanwhile baseball, from at least 1903 to 1953, welcomed the journalists and profited from their existence.

7

Baseball on the Radio

It is conventional wisdom among baseball aficionados that baseball presents itself better on radio than on television. According to this view, which I share, the game and the radio medium are good fits because of the gaps between action in baseball that can be filled in with knowledgeable talk. In contrast, television emphasizes those gaps in the action by showing an image of a baseball diamond populated by players doing nothing. Television also flattens out baseball's angles, thereby eliminating the simultaneous flights of ball and runner, or outfielder and fly ball, that make the game so dramatic for spectators. Moreover, radio is a medium which emphasizes the drama of events that cannot be seen and draws heavily on its listeners' imaginations. Much of "baseball time" is spent anticipating action that may happen and imagining the consequences of that action. A radio announcer can heighten the drama of anticipation through rhetorical imagery. Such imagery palls when the viewer can see the action itself.

Given the impressive synergy between baseball and radio, it is interesting that radio broadcasts of baseball games took a comparatively long time—twenty-five years—to become routine, nearly daily presences in every major league city. Nationwide radio was established by the early 1920s; the first baseball game was broadcast in 1921, and World Series games were aired regularly after 1923. But only a few cities—Chicago, Boston, Cleveland, St. Louis, Philadelphia, and Detroit—had stations broadcasting games in the 1920s, and coverage was limited to home games. As late as 1939 none of the New York clubs broadcast any of their games. Live away games were not broadcast at all until after World War II. Since radio broadcasts of games are like newspaper coverage in that they amount to free publicity for the clubs, and since broadcast media rights to games are now one of the major revenue sources for major league franchises, one wonders why major league baseball on the radio came so late in the history of radio broadcasting. This chapter explores that question.

◆

In the relatively short time period—the late 1920s to the early 1950s—in which baseball games were regularly, and nearly exclusively, broadcast on the radio, the impact on baseball was incalculably positive. But, as in the case of night baseball, one of the principal sets of persons financially affected by radio broadcasts, the owners of major league clubs, had considerable difficulty grasping that impact. In fact, from the coming of radio in the early 1920s, the new medium made baseball owners and those associated with Organized Baseball nervous. They responded to baseball on the radio as they had responded to baseball at night, as an alien, unsettling development.

Baseball on the radio started on August 5, 1921, when a studio announcer for station KDKA in Pittsburgh, the first station on the airways, broadcast a game between the Pirates and the Philadelphia Phillies at Forbes Field. The announcer was Harold Arlin, and the station aired the contest as an experiment in adding sports to their programming: that same year they would broadcast the first tennis match and the first college football game. The broadcast, Arlin remembered many years later, was not a great technical success: "Sometimes the transmitter worked and sometimes it didn't. Sometimes the crowd noise would drown us out and sometimes it wouldn't."[1] Arlin sat in a box seat, with his radio equipment stationed behind a screen back of home plate.

That October the World Series between the Yankees and the Giants was "broadcast," if one uses that term loosely. A newspaper reporter for the *Newark Call*, watching the game at the Polo Grounds, telephoned the results of the action to an announcer for radio station WJZ in the Westinghouse Building in Newark. The announcer, Tommy Cowan, then delivered a largely imaginative account of the games based on the bare-bones information furnished by the reporter. No crowd noise was heard. The account went out over two stations, WJZ and WBZ (the latter in Springfield, Massachusetts), which that year had combined with KDKA to create the Westinghouse Network.

In the fall of 1924 the future of radio was altered by three policies instituted by Secretary of Commerce Herbert Hoover. One permitted some "superpower" stations to experiment with frequencies of up to 50,000 watts. Another made the Commerce Department, subsequently succeeded by the Federal Radio Commission and then the Federal Communications Commission, the arbiter of radio licenses; previously stations had come into the market at will. A third allowed the Commerce Department to authorize certain stations to operate on "clear channels," free from any competition by other stations. The inevitable product of these policies was the formation, in 1926, of the National Broadcasting Company, with two networks of stations. The next year the Columbia Broadcasting System, a rival network, also came into being. The eventual result of the networks' formation was the emergence of locally based, network-affiliated stations in the prime evening hours.

The effect of these developments on major league baseball, although potentially momentous, was initially negligible, because the limited number of radio stations, and their limited number of on-air hours, made the broadcast of games on a regular basis too much of a luxury. But as early as 1922 a "network" of the informal sort was created to broadcast the World Series. Again WJZ in Newark was the center, but this time the broadcast was live. The sportswriter Grantland Rice sat in a box in the Polo Grounds, near the Yankee dugout. His voice was amplified by a three-stage amplifier, strong enough to transmit it to the WJZ studios in Newark. All the other New York city radio stations agreed to observe a silent period to further the range of the broadcast, and KDKA in Pittsburgh hoped to pick it up and transmit it further. Rice's commentary did not reach KDKA, but it was heard for a three-hundred-mile radius around the Polo Grounds.[2]

The broadcast was a technical success in that not only could Rice's voice be heard clearly, the sounds of the crowd and the game came through as well. But Rice's style as an announcer, given future patterns of radio broadcasting, was astonishing. He said nothing until a play occurred, letting the crowd noise filter over the microphone. He then briefly described what had happened in a voice that his biographer characterized as "a little flat, atonal, sometimes awkwardly modulated and unmistakably Southern."[3] The result was that listeners were confronted with long minutes of silence, followed by crowd sounds that were ambiguous, since both the Giants and Yankees, the opponents that year, played at the Polo Grounds, and fans of both were in the stands. "The broadcast officials wanted me to keep talking," Rice said afterwards, "but I didn't know what to say." One listener, however, found the broadcast "wonderfully successful." "I would hear the crowd let out a terrific roar," he said, "and it would seem ages before I knew whether it was a single or a three-bagger that had been made or whether the side had been retired. Of course it was only a matter of seconds before we got [Rice's] announcement [of what had happened], but the interest was so intense that it seemed longer."[4]

The next year the Series again featured the Yankees and Giants, this time alternating between the Polo Grounds and Yankee Stadium. A more ambitious radio network was set up, centering on New York station WEAF and extending, through telephone wires, north into Massachusetts and south as far as Washington, D.C. Rice was again assigned to the broadcast, now accompanied by Graham McNamee, in his first year with WEAF. McNamee, originally assigned to provide side comments to Rice's laconic play-by-play, replaced him after the middle of Rice's third game as the announcer. Their styles were in extreme contrast. Originally headed for a career on the stage, McNamee brought charisma and excitement to broadcasting, talking continuously to his audience. He was to be a fixture at NBC's World Series broadcasts until the mid-1930s.

With McNamee's broadcasts it became clear that baseball on the radio had the potential to attract a vast audience. A week after the 1923 Series concluded, station WEAF had received over 1,700 pieces of correspondence about McNamee.[5] Ring Lardner cracked that the games McNamee described bore no resemblance to the games he watched from the press box, but McNamee had exposed radio's quality as a medium whose listeners wanted to be stimulated by the language of its announcers and personalities.[6] And by 1926 five million homes had radios, and twenty-one million more had ordered sets.[7] It was apparent that radio was big business, and that baseball on the radio could be a potentially big draw.

In the chaotic environment of radio in the 1920s, stations in a few cities began to broadcast home games on a daily basis. The clubs whose games were broadcast seemed unclear as to how to treat the

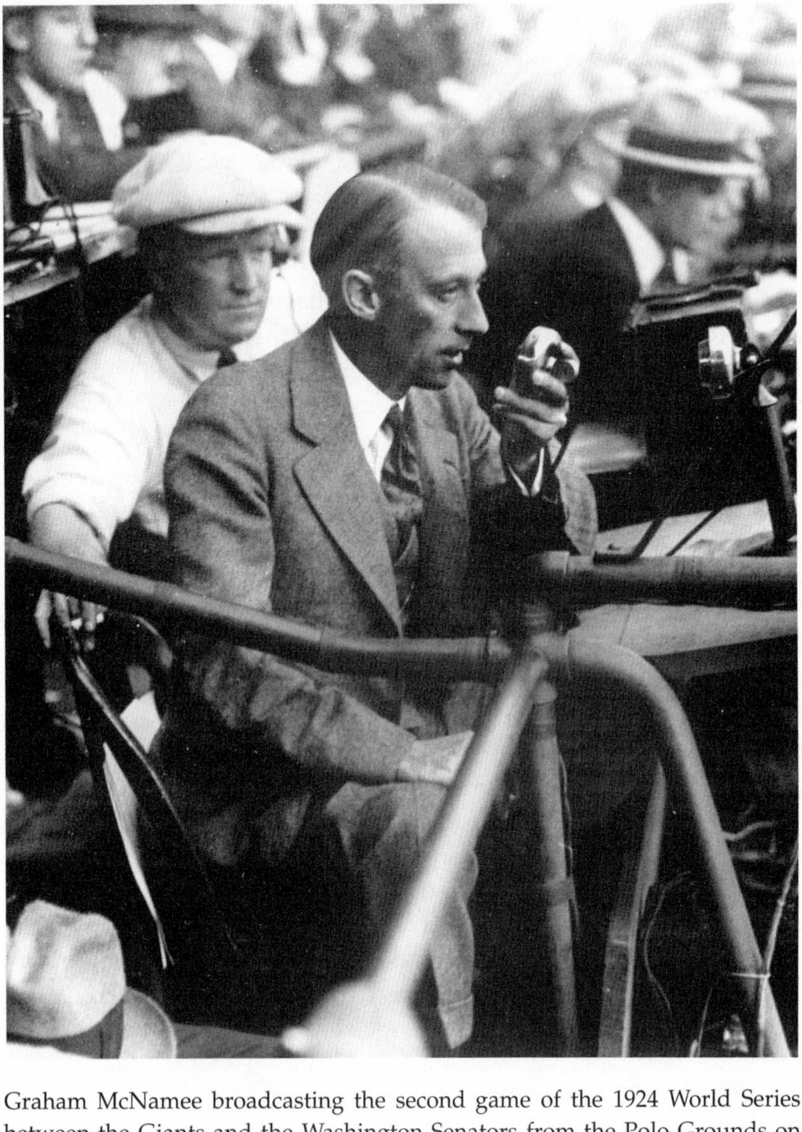

Graham McNamee broadcasting the second game of the 1924 World Series between the Giants and the Washington Senators from the Polo Grounds on October 5, 1924, over station WEAF in New York. McNamee wears no headset, although his partner, John McAvoy, has one in his left ear. (National Baseball Library and Archive, Cooperstown, N.Y.)

situation. In Chicago, the first city to have baseball broadcasts regularly, as many as five stations broadcast the Cubs' games simultaneously, two of them covering the White Sox as well. They paid the clubs nothing for rights to the games; their goal was listeners. The first station to do regular baseball broadcasts was WMAQ in Chicago, beginning on April 23, 1924. WMAQ, owned by the *Chicago Daily News* and featuring Hal Totten as their announcer, covered all the home games of the Cubs and White Sox until the Second World War.

With no restrictions on coming into the baseball market once a station had received a radio license, and no negotiations with the clubs for broadcast rights or fees, the only relevant question about broadcasting baseball for early radio entrepreneurs was their prospective audience. By the close of the 1920s, stations in Philadelphia, St. Louis, Boston, Cleveland, and Detroit were broadcasting home games. Unlike the situation in Chicago, broadcasts came over a single station, supplemented, in the case of Boston, by a network that brought games to several stations in New England. Among the early announcers were Bill Dwyer, doing the Phillies and Athletics in Philadelphia; France Laux, broadcasting the Cardinals' and Browns' games; Fred Hoey, a former sports journalist, covering the Braves and Red Sox; Tom Manning, reporting on the Indians; and Ty Tyson, whose broadcasts of Tiger games would be heard in the Detroit area until 1942. Not all the games were sponsored: the Tiger games, on Detroit station WWJ, were presented "as a public service" until 1934.[8]

Only home games were live in this period, and away games were sometimes not covered at all. In cities such as Philadelphia, St. Louis, and Boston, where the same station covered the home games of both clubs, there was no airtime for away games. But in other cities, such as Chicago, Cleveland, and Detroit, a practice of "re-creating" away games surfaced. The process of re-creation was comparatively simple. An announcer would station himself in a studio with a Western Union telegraph. At the site of the game a telegraph operator would telegraph the bare bones of the play to another operator (called a reporter), who would transcribe it for the announcer, who would then use it as the basis of a broadcast. Sometimes simulated crowd noise and devices to approximate the sound of a bat hitting a ball would accompany the announcer. If the telegraph communication failed, the announcer would have to ad-lib until it was restored.

Re-created games were still the norm until after the Second World

War. Two recollections of announcers who engaged in the re-creation process demonstrate the spectrum of presentations listeners received. One comes from Ronald ("Dutch") Reagan, who broadcast the Cubs games for station WHO in Des Moines, Iowa.[9] In a conversation with Gene Smith after he had become president, Reagan recalled that WHO was one of several stations doing Cubs games at the time, some of which had announcers at Wrigley Field. It was important, therefore, that the WHO broadcasts, which were all re-created, have an air of excitement and verisimilitude.

On one occasion Reagan was in a studio in Des Moines with a Western Union reporter who received the transmissions from Wrigley Field. When the transmission came in to the reporter, he would type up a summary of it for Reagan, and when Reagan saw him beginning to type, that would be his cue to begin describing the pitcher's windup. This time, however, the reporter's message was "The wire's gone dead." Since Reagan had already started a description of the action, he had the batter foul one off into the stands. He didn't feel that he could stop broadcasting because of the dead wire, since there were other stations whose live broadcasts could be heard in the Des Moines area, so he had the batter, Bill Jurges of the Cubs, foul pitch after pitch off, some fouls being long flies that narrowly missed being home runs, others pop-ups into the stands that caused spectators to scramble for the baseballs. Eventually the line was restored, and the telegraph operator received another message, which he handed to Reagan. It was that Jurges had popped out on the first pitch.[10]

Reagan's experience was typical of many re-created games in that stations who broadcast them did not want their readers to lose a sense that the action they heard was "live." Occasionally, however, a broadcaster declined to go along with the subterfuges of re-created baseball. In 1934 Walter ("Red") Barber left Gainesville, Florida, to broadcast the Cincinnati Reds' games over station WSAI, a 5,000-watt station. Powel Crosley, who owned WSAI and the more powerful station WLW, had taken over ownership of the Reds the preceding year. Even though he was in the radio business, Crosley was uncertain about the effect of radio broadcasts on baseball attendance, and so restricted the number of live home games that could be broadcast. He encouraged Barber, however, to do an unlimited number of road games (except in New York and Brooklyn, which refused clubs permission to broadcast any games from their parks). For the first few years of his career as a major league baseball broadcaster Barber did most of his games through re-creation.

In a 1991 radio call-in show, Barber, then eighty-three, described his approach to re-created games:

> I never put in any sound noise, except I wanted the sound of the Western Union dots and dashes heard, and the typewriter sound that the receiving operator was using heard, because I wanted the audience to know that I was doing a Western Union re-creation, that I was not seeing this game for myself. I was very strong on that point. And the audience all over the years, I think they appreciated it. . . .
>
> And when the wire went out, I'm lazy. I just said, "Well, friends, the wire's gone out. We'll fill you in on the other games, bring you up to date." And if the wire was still out, I'd say, "Well, we'll just play some easy-to-listen-to music, and when the wire comes back we'll join you again."[11]

From Reagan's and Barber's descriptions, it might appear that there was a herky-jerky quality to re-created broadcasts, with pauses in between the telegraph transmissions. But in fact the background noise of the dots and dashes was just that: the announcers talked continuously, and after a few moments one felt as if one were listening to a "live" game. Crucial to the performance were the "stories" told by announcers between pitches. "Filler" anecdotes and information, in fact, are at the heart of successful baseball broadcasting, whether re-created or live. It is through "filler" talk that an important dimension of experiencing a baseball game—the dimension when the players and those observing anticipate, attempt to prepare for, and even try to affect forthcoming action—is communicated. In those spaces of time that occur between the action of a baseball game, minds on the field and in the stands are at work, strategizing, anticipating, hoping, and worrying. A good radio announcer stimulates those minds.

In a 1936 article on Boston announcer Fred Hoey, *The Sporting News* revealed a technique Hoey and other announcers were using to make effective use of their "filler" time. Hoey and his staff had developed a "chart system" containing information on various players that could be used in connection with events in a game that brought a certain player into the limelight. "On this chart," Hoey told *The Sporting News*, "we list the name of the player, his age, height, weight, home, his record for the previous seasons including all the batting features, together with the pertinent facts of his career that might be of interest to the fans. Nothing that we announce is trusted to memory; it is all in typewritten form before us."[12] Hoey's "chart system" has been refined to the point where major league clubs now attach a full-time statistician to their baseball broadcasts, and quite precise information on players and other pertinent subjects is continually supplied to announcers.

◆

As baseball began to be broadcast on the radio, and the number of radio stations and listeners dramatically increased, the magnates of the game were forced to take note. At first they had been largely inert. Although the Chicago practice in the 1920s of multiple broadcasts, by different stations, of the same game was not duplicated in most other cities, it demonstrated the passivity of major league owners toward the new medium. Anyone with a radio license could bring equipment into a ballpark and do a live broadcast, paying nothing more than the price of admission. Anyone could buy Western Union's "Paragraph One" service and re-create the game from a studio. No one in Organized Baseball knew exactly what to make of these developments, or how to capitalize on them. For more than a decade after the Cubs and White Sox began broadcasting regular season games in 1924, baseball's officialdom struggled with the question of radio, never fully embracing the new medium or taking full economic advantage of its presence.

As with so many issues affecting baseball, *The Sporting News* reflected attitudes within established baseball circles; and as with night baseball, the paper's first response to baseball on the radio was apprehension to the point of hostility. On April 27, 1922, less than a year after KDKA had aired a game for the first time, *The Sporting News* took up "our latest problem" in an editorial. Its comments—at once reactionary and technologically prescient—are worth reproducing at some length:

> It used to be the ticker that click-clicked off the score of the game, and attendance at the ball park suffered somewhat while the gang downtown gathered about the tape in the saloon around the corner and wagered its bits or the beers on the outcome.
>
> But now what shall we do about the radio? We can't expect the W.C.T.U. and the Anti-Saloon League to legislate the wireless out of busi-

> ness. But Mr. Radio is going to butt into the business of telling the world all about the ball game without the world having to come to the ball park to find out, more than the ticker ever did.
>
> This new radio craze is already crimping attendance at anything where the feast is for the ear rather than the eye and seriously affecting spectacular entertainment because the family stays home to hear the concert or lecture or story telling in preference to going out to see the things pictured on the screen.
>
> And next we will have the whole works shot to pieces because instead of mere sounds the radio will be reproducing in every home that has a ten-dollar equipment the picture of the play. Yep, that is the possibility. When Ruth hits a homer or Sisler slides into the plate, a film will catch him in the act, wireless will carry it a thousand miles broadcast and the family sitting in the darkened living room at home will see the scene reproduced instantaneously on the wall. . . .
>
> Then what will become of baseball? Nobody will actually see Ruth and Sisler in action except the bored operators of the wireless picture producing machine who have to be out as part of their job.[13]

The excerpt from *The Sporting News* demonstrates that the early discussions of radio within Organized Baseball very probably disregarded the possibility that radio broadcasts might actually increase attendance at ballparks. The capacity of radio to reach an enormous audience of diverse persons, while acknowledged in the abstract, does not seem to have been applied to the process of attracting fans to a ball field. Radio broadcasts made baseball available to a wider class of persons, including persons who were neophytes in their knowledge of the game. Skillful announcers could teach their listeners about baseball, make them familiar with the players as personalities, and communicate a sense that watching a baseball game was an exciting and pleasurable event. Radio waves penetrated well beyond the cities with teams. And radio provided something that no other medium available at the time could provide. It allowed fans to remain at home and yet maintain a regular, "live" contact with favorite teams. No newspaper account, however vivid, could provide that immediacy.

But those within and close to the hierarchy of Organized Baseball should not be faulted for failing to grasp those advantages initially. Radio itself was a novelty in America of the twenties and early thirties; the experience of listening to the "wireless" was a source of excitement in itself. It was immediately apparent that one of the great attractions of radio was the sense of immediacy, of vicarious participation, that it produced in its listeners: witness the great success of dramatic radio programs and live concerts. It was understandable that many within baseball's officialdom feared that this remarkable new medium might be able to create in its listeners a sensation closely allied to that of watching a game in person.

Not all observers, however, reacted with the mixture of apprehension and disbelief expressed in *The Sporting News* editorial. That same year John Sheridan, a longtime and particularly literate and intelligent baseball journalist, wrote a column in the weekly that began, "The beneficial effect which radio communication, good roads and the automobile will have upon Organized Baseball does not seem to be understood by owners of baseball clubs."[14] He found that radio had "vastly increased rural interest in big league and also minor league baseball." He noticed that "every small town" in the midwest had a radio station, and "crowds gathered around the loud speaker" to find out the latest information on baseball games. The enthusiasm generated for baseball prompted "quickly organized parties" to attend baseball games in Chicago or St. Louis. The network of "good roads" that was springing up in the midwest, coupled with the wider availability of the automobile, Sheridan felt, would result in people thinking nothing of driving two hundred miles to see a game.

These developments prompted Sheridan to suggest that "baseball is entering upon a new era," in which club owners would take advantage of good roads and the radio to advertise their product and expand their fan base. Sheridan noted that at the turn of the century the territory of a baseball club was about five miles; with these new developments it would soon be "400 miles in circumference."[15] His observations turned out to be essentially correct, at least in the midwest, where radio signals carried longer distances and big league cities were spaced farther apart. The emergence of the Cubs and the St. Louis Cardinals as regional franchises in the thirties and forties drew upon states such as Iowa, Kansas, Arkansas, and Oklahoma for fans.

Nonetheless, Organized Baseball was slow to be persuaded of the value of broadcasting games on the radio. In July 1925, *The Sporting News* reported that American League president Ban Johnson had "declined to permit reports of ball games to be broadcasted from the parks of the circuit." Johnson's influence was by then declining, but *The*

Sporting News endorsed his decision, for reasons that almost precisely paralleled the negative response of baseball's officialdom to night baseball. In an editorial *The Sporting News* attacked baseball on the radio as "unnatural" and unwholesome. "Baseball," it claimed, "is more an inspiration to the brain through the eye than it is by the ear. The greatest value of baseball, next to playing it, is to look upon it. There is nothing about it which appears to appeal to wave lengths. A nation that begins to take its sport by ears will shortly adapt the white flag as its national emblem, and the dove as its national bird."[16]

The logic of the editorial associated going out to the ballpark to watch games with taking exercise and other "good, clean, honest" pursuits. If fans "could take their baseball by option over the radio," *The Sporting News* felt, "we imagine some of them in time would be too lazy to leave home or the office. We know that many thousands of human beings who should be out of doors getting oxygen, and a little reawakening mentally, would be sluggishly engaged at home or the office, with minds growing duller and duller as they placed themselves more and more under the restraint of not exerting their bodies to see live competition."

A second assumption of the editorial was that baseball was not well suited to be followed by the ear as distinguished from the eye. It likened the daily broadcasts of baseball games to the chants of a "Coney Island barker" who sought to "tell you all about the sea serpent at the top of his lungs." Descriptions of baseball "poured out in nasal tones" by radio announcers "debas[ed] . . . a perfectly good sport." Baseball was "the sport of a nation," *The Sporting News* concluded, "and it is not something [traceable] by long range through an ear trumpet, but something to see where red-blooded men give an exhibition that combines grace, strength, and mental alertness."[17]

Six years later Johnson's directive had been abandoned, with baseball club owners making their own decisions as to whether to allow broadcasts of their games, but *The Sporting News* continued to believe that baseball "isn't something to be heard, but to be seen." "Only the ear properly attuned," a December 1931 editorial asserted, "can hear at a baseball game and be properly rhapsodized." By the last statement the editorial writer was apparently seeking to distinguish between informed, knowledgeable broadcasting and other types, for he subsequently said that fans "will not care to hear" descriptions such as "a foul is hit between first and third base." The editorial also raised the possibility that the fan who "can sit with his feet on the rail of the front porch, or tip back in his office chair, and listen to what is going on" would not attend games. But it conceded that unlike "a magnificent dance," baseball was a spectacle that lent itself to being broadcast on the radio. This was a departure from the position taken six years earlier.[18]

By the early 1930s the games of teams in most big league cities were being broadcast in one form or another. Baseball's hierarchy, however, remained concerned about the effects of broadcasting on attendance, and periodic suggestions were made to the owners to ban the broadcasting of games. Astonishingly, however, none of the major league teams asked stations to pay them a fee for the right to broadcast. As late as 1933 *The Sporting News* reported that World Series games, which had been broadcast annually since 1923, were still being reported free of charge, even though Commissioner Landis's office chose the announcers and networks for the games.[19] A year earlier Cincinnati Reds' announcer Harry Hartman, citing a "rumor . . . that certain baseball higher-ups will do their utmost to abolish the broadcasting of games this coming season," wrote a list of reasons for retaining broadcasts. These included bringing access to the game "to thousands of shut-ins and cripples," stimulating new fans, bringing "thousands of women into the parks who have more chance to get away in the afternoon than have the men," and helping baseball clubs advertise.[20]

As baseball struggled with the issue of radio broadcasting in the 1930s, it continued to maintain tight controls over the broadcasts of the World Series. In 1934 Commissioner Landis negotiated a contract with the Ford Motor Company for four years at $400,000. Prior to that there had been no commercial sponsorship of the Series. A year earlier, in the course of naming announcers for that year's Series, Landis had taken the opportunity to ban announcer Ted Husing of CBS, who in the course of broadcasting the 1932 Series had referred to the umpiring as "some of the worst I've ever seen." *The Sporting News* reported that "a number of baseball writers" had protested Landis's decision to ban Husing; Harvey Boyle of the *Pittsburgh Post-Gazette* stated that "any broadcasting company . . . ought to insist that it will take no dictation from Landis, or anyone else" as to the choice of broadcasters.[21] But Landis remained firm: Husing never again broadcast a World Series game.

Nineteen thirty-four was expected to be a year in which the question of radio broadcasts of games would be authoritatively decided by Organized Baseball. The National Association of Minor Leagues, citing the apparent effect of broadcasts of major league games on attendance in minor league cities, presented a resolution at its November convention that the owners of major league franchises invoke a total ban on broadcasts or, as an alternative, a ban on broadcasts in localities with minor league clubs.[22] That year also marked the first experiment to ban broadcasts by a major league city where games had been previously aired: the St. Louis Browns and Cardinals stopped broadcasting their contests. Nothing conclusive came of either development. The major league owners took no action on radio broadcasts, tacitly deciding that they were a matter for each franchise to deal with individually, and in 1935 St. Louis resumed broadcasting. The Cardinals' attendance in 1934 had declined, despite the fact that the Cardinals had won the pennant, but the Browns' attendance had increased.[23]

By 1935 momentum seemed established on the side of broadcasts. Organized Baseball arranged for the broadcasting of the All-Star Game as well as the World Series, receiving a fee from the radio networks involved even though the broadcast was commercial-free. Increasingly clubs made arrangements with sponsors to receive fees for permission to broadcast games, and club owners realized that radio could be a source of annual income for their franchises. And the public's enthusiasm for listening to baseball on the radio was made apparent by the efforts of Tele-Flash Inc., which began sending out "bootlegged" broadcasts of the New York Giants' games to listeners in the New York area.

The Tele-Flash case came at a time when arrangements for exclusive broadcasting rights were becoming the norm for baseball broadcasting. In the place of the older freelance system, personified by Cub and White Sox broadcasts in the 1920s, clubs were increasingly moving to a practice of designating a particular radio station or network the exclusive broadcaster of their games in exchange for a corporate sponsor's fee. Some stations that had not received exclusive access were inclined to defy the clubs' ban on their broadcasts, claiming that the games were "news" and that no one could have a property right in the news.

Tele-Flash Inc., attempted to circumvent rather than to defy a ban. The Giants had forbidden any broadcasts of their games and denied stations access to the Polo Grounds. Tele-Flash stationed an observer carrying a telegraph outside the Polo Grounds, overlooking the park. The observer then transmitted accounts of the games, resembling the form of Western Union's Paragraph One service, to a receiver in a studio, who passed them on to an announcer who broadcast a re-created account. Although the American League had in 1935 added a provision to tickets sold at major league games that prevented the purchaser from unauthorized broadcasting or telegraphing of games, Tele-Flash was not affected, since their employee did not enter the park.

When the Giants sued to prevent Tele-Flash (in connection with the New York Telegraph Company, whose wires it used to telegraph the action) from broadcasting their games, a New York trial court held that the bootlegging was protected. If the Giants wanted to protect themselves, the court suggested, they needed to make their product "more exclusive." Since American League clubs already had granted Western Union the exclusive right to telegraph their games, and granted certain radio stations the exclusive right to broadcast them, it was hard to know what the court meant. *The Sporting News* speculated that it might be necessary "for the clubs to completely enclose their parks, top, bottom, and sides, and refuse departure from the park until the games are completed."[24]

In April 1936, *The Sporting News* reported that only three major league clubs, the Yankees, Giants, and Dodgers, imposed a flat ban on the broadcasting of their games. Two clubs, the Washington Senators and Pittsburgh Pirates, broadcast re-created road games only. The remaining eleven clubs had (sometimes limited) live coverage of home games, and both teams in Chicago and St. Louis, as well as those in Cleveland, Cincinnati, and Detroit, broadcast some re-created road games as well. With the exception of Cincinnati's, all the games were sponsored, the vast majority by General Mills to advertise its cereals.[25] *The Sporting News* also noted that "a survey conducted in Newark, N.J. has convinced club officials that broadcasting of games helps to swell crowds rather than reduces attendance." The survey in question concerned the International League Newark Bears, whose home and away games were broadcast on New York radio station WINS.[26]

For the rest of the 1930s, as the popularity of radio broadcasts of baseball grew, Organized Baseball came to two conclusions about its relationship with the radio medium. First, as the number of potential corporate sponsors of radio broadcasts increased, Organized Baseball recognized, once and for all, that the additional revenue to clubs from radio rights was not inconsiderable. In November 1936, *The Sporting News* reported that the American League had decided that all clubs

A fan demonstrates that listening to games on the radio was not incompatible with attending them: the Reverend Percy Kendall at a Cleveland Indians game on July 27, 1937. Rev. Kendall explained that he typically listened to the broadcast of the game he was watching, but occasionally, during the Indians' games, he switched to a Detroit station to pick up the Tigers' broadcasts. His portable radio was thirty inches high and weighed seventeen pounds. (National Baseball Library and Archive, Cooperstown, N.Y.)

should charge for the privilege of broadcasting games from their parks, and that the National League was likely to follow suit. *The Sporting News* endorsed this development. "The eagerness of broadcasting services and sponsoring advertisers to obtain these privileges," an editorial noted, "has clearly evidenced their high value. Baseball has something to sell in these play-by-play accounts, and while each club will be permitted to name its own price and to determine the extent to which it wishes to permit broadcasting from the park, none will grant free any longer a special privilege which represents so much value to the club, to radio and to the sponsor."[27]

The American League's desire to establish uniform control over radio rights was resisted by some National League clubs. In particular, William Wrigley of the Cubs had long been convinced that opening up broadcasts to an unlimited number of stations ended up increasing attendance, because more people in the Chicago area became aware of the Cubs. The Cubs also sponsored a telescoped re-created version of their away games from seven to eight in the evenings, assuming that more people would be able to listen at that hour, even if they probably already knew the score of the game. Although they agreed to sell the rights to broadcast the games, they differed from the White Sox's one-shot figure of $40,000, eventually selling the rights to six stations at figures ranging from $7,500 to $3,000 for the season.[28] When, in 1938, the American League proposed that Commissioner Landis be made the arbiter of policies involving the radio broadcasting of games, the National League, noting Landis's view that the number of stations broadcasting games in any one city should be limited, flatly refused. Again the Cubs led the opposition, with Wrigley threatening to "throw Chicago wide open to air accounts of the games."[29]

Part of the National League's opposition to Landis as an overseer of radio policy stemmed from a controversy involving a Chicago radio broadcast of a White Sox game in which a decision by umpire Charles Johnston led to a radio announcer's comment that the umpires were "incompetent." The next day, an umpire was struck on the head by a bottle thrown from the stands and had to be taken to the hospital. The American League responded at its December 1936 winter meeting by naming L. C. McEvoy, the former business manager of the St. Louis Browns, Director of Radio and charged him with listening to the broadcasts of games involving American League clubs to ascertain that broadcasters were not editorializing.[30] On March 18, 1937, *The Sporting News* ran an article by Edward Burns of the *Chicago Tribune*, entitled "A.L. Air Patrolman Must Listen to 13 Stations at Once," which poked fun at the new position. "Most fans know," Burns wrote, "that Leo Carl McEvoy has been appointed official censor, or muzzleman, of the American League. . . . We know Mr. McEvoy very well and consider him a gentleman of strong will, iron nerves, and astute judgment. If listening to 13 radio announcers simultaneously drives him crazy this summer, it will be very sad. If he doesn't go crazy, of course, he will be a standout. Or suspected of being deaf."[31]

The American League's effort to oversee the content of broadcasts was immediately controversial. *The Sporting News* quoted an article in *Variety* in May 1937, that claimed the effect of the new policy was to strip "all personality and individuality" from radio broadcasts of games. "No personalities, no individual comment, no arguments and no excitement," the *Variety* writer noted. "The instructions are specific that the baseball play-by-play spielers should do nothing that will make 'em stand out from the mob. Result is a dull sameness on all transmitters. A mere skeleton report of the game, with the only difference being a slight variation of tone quality from one announcer to the other. . . . They are evidently really afraid to be different."[32]

It is not clear that the American League's creation of a "Radio Director," charged with scrutinizing broadcasts for evidence of editorializing, ever had any effect, despite *Variety*'s claims. It was apparent, however, that from the first days of radio broadcasting the function of the broadcaster was assumed to be different from that of the sportswriter with respect to the issue of partisanship. Baseball journalists, despite journalistic canons of objectivity, were expected to be opinionated and outspoken, praising and criticizing home team players, opponents, and umpires. Radio announcers, as International League president Frank Shaughnessy put it in 1938, were "charged with presenting only an adequate picture of the game," and "the display of partisanship . . . should never overlook good work by the visiting team."[33]

It is not clear how the distinction between the expected tone for sportswriters and that for announcers originated, or why contemporaries, and many broadcasters who began their careers in the 1930s, regarded it as meaningful. One might expect that just as a journalist who regularly covered a team would tend to develop attachments to the club and its personnel, a broadcaster assigned to radio coverage would develop comparable attachments. Moreover, a broadcaster had a clear mandate from the club to encourage people to come to the park, so one would expect that along with comments minimizing the effect of harsh weather conditions one might find comments minimizing the degree of a team's bad play. Indeed there was almost no incentive for a broadcaster to be a general critic of the team he was covering. Fans liked to listen to, as well as see, clubs they found competent and interesting. Sponsors profited from larger audiences. Given all these pressures, it is remarkable that from its origins radio broadcasting had a canon of neutrality for its practitioners.

As the major leagues sought to control the revenue from and even the content of broadcasting, and coverage continued to expand in the 1930s, older apprehensions about radio persisted. Although *The Sporting News* documented the growth of radio stations covering baseball and the proliferation of corporate sponsors, it retained its traditional attitudes toward the new medium. Endorsing the American League's decision to limit the number of stations permitted to broadcast games to two per community, *The Sporting News* once again pointed out that "it is not surprising that a certain portion of the listening public is surfeited with baseball" because "after all, baseball is a game to see and not to hear, and it might be well to give the ear-drums a rest and put the optics to greater use."[34] This was even though it pointed out proudly that "more than 260 United States and Canadian stations, a record-breaking number," would be broadcasting games in 1938.[35]

That same article noted that "only the three metropolitan New York clubs . . . still bar the mike word-painters, due to a gentleman's agreement against selling broadcasting rights until 1939." Over the winter of 1938, however, Larry MacPhail left the Cincinnati Reds to become general manager of the Brooklyn Dodgers, and everyone expected that the "gentlemen's agreement" would cease with the 1939 season. MacPhail hired Red Barber of the Reds to do the Dodgers' games, signed a contract with WOR, a 50,000-watt New York station, and prepared to begin broadcasting. Meanwhile his plans became known to the Giants and Yankees, and the traveling secretary of the Giants, Eddie Brannick, reportedly told MacPhail that if he broadcast games the Giants would secure the services of a 50,000-watt station and "blast your broadcasts into the river." Red Barber remembered MacPhail's relaying the conversation with Brannick to him and adding: "By God . . . he threatened me . . . threatened to blast me into the river. . . . Listen—I don't know what announcer they've got, or what fifty-thousand-watt radio station. . . . [But] I've got you. . . . Now, young man, here are my instructions—I don't want to be blasted into the river."[36]

MacPhail's decision to begin Dodger broadcasts on the radio forced the hand of the Giant and Yankee owners, both of whom remained convinced that radio broadcasts would harm attendance, especially in New York, where the fans of one area club were notorious for their hatred of the other two. The Yankees and Giants quickly secured the services of WABC, another 50,000-watt station, to broadcast their home games. At the same time they secured sponsorship from General Mills, Procter & Gamble, and the Mobil Oil Company, and hired the man who had been doing re-created away games for the Washington Senators, Arch McDonald.

In April 1939, as the baseball season opened, *Time* Magazine ran a story on the Yankees' and Giants' decision to broadcast their games. Their decision meant, *Time* pointed out, that for the first time in history every major league team would be broadcasting its games, and each broadcast would have corporate sponsorship. General Mills was the most prominent sponsor, advertising Wheaties for fourteen of the sixteen big league teams, and Atlantic Refining Co., Socony-Vacuum, Mobil Oil, and Procter & Gamble were also involved on a regular basis. *Time* boosted McDonald, calling him the "biggest . . . and the best Wheaties announcer" in the game, and noting that, while in Washington, "he once dared obscene and unidentified telephoners to meet him somewhere and fight like men." McDonald, from Arkansas, reportedly had "a holy horror" of peach fuzz, and "once broke the jaw of a joker who rubbed some on him."[37]

Conspicuously absent in the *Time* article was any mention of the Dodgers' decision to broadcast their games as well. Red Barber, on noticing the article, called it "the ultimate insult—to be ignored," and vowed to outdistance McDonald in the New York market. "If I needed anything," Barber later wrote, "to make me completely at one with three million Brooklynites who hated and resented New York and Manhattan and the Giants and the Yankees, this complete rebuff was it." Barber responded by securing airtime on WOR for a pregame show, in which he interviewed Giants' manager Bill Terry and Dodgers' manager Leo Durocher before the two clubs met for the opening game of the season.[38] Barber's pregame show launched a custom that was to become a permanent feature of baseball broadcasts, as sponsors quickly learned that listeners, eagerly anticipating the lineups before a game or the scoring details afterward, would tolerate a fair amount of commercial interruptions.

By the 1939 season the broadcasting of games had become an established feature of major league baseball, with clubs dealing out rights, stations arranging sponsorship, and everyone allegedly profiting. The new regime was personified by a successful suit by the Pittsburgh Pirates against radio station KQV, which had attempted to circumvent the Pirates' effort to sell exclusive rights to their games by using the same bootlegging technique employed by Tele-Flash three years earlier. This time a federal court held that the Pirates had a property right in the radio broadcasting of their games and could limit broadcasting access.[39] By the 1970s the entire financial structure of Organized Baseball was affected by radio and television contracts. It is not too much to say, in fact, that the advent of television after the 1950s changed the face of baseball as an enterprise. Despite the fact that television was not a medium that showed baseball to its best advantage, the added revenue from television contracts, and the added publicity generated by television coverage, revolutionized baseball's financial structure, paving the way for vastly higher salaries and ultimately for free agency.

The impact of radio in 1939, however, was nowhere near as dramatic. But over the next decade, as radio sets continued to proliferate in the nation and television remained relatively inaccessible, the number of individuals whose primary contact with baseball was through the radio markedly increased. Much of what John Sheridan anticipated in 1922 came to pass, as radio broadcasts carried the games of teams to distant localities, stimulating new fans and boosting attendance as those fans began driving longer distances to ballparks. Eventually, after the Second World War, radio stations began to invest in live coverage of road games, and announcers began to travel with the teams they covered. This meant that a single station no longer could cover the games of two clubs, resulting in more games being carried in an urban market. As radio announcing became a more demanding profession, stations began to hire additional announcers. The result was that by the close of World War II baseball broadcasters had evolved from more or less accidental performers in experiments with a new medium to the personifications—the "voices"—of the teams they covered. They had become celebrities.

◆

For the first twenty years of baseball broadcasting, a number of memorable figures identified themselves with the radio coverage of their respective teams. As a collective body, they can be subdivided into two groups, the pioneers, who initiated their clubs' venture into radio, and a second generation, emerging in the 1930s to support or to replace their predecessors, or occasionally to initiate a reluctant club's coverage. Two other generalizations can be made about the early major league broadcasters. First, with only a handful of exceptions, they were not former players. They were knowledgeable about sports, and many of them were athletically inclined, but they were above all radio performers. That having been said, one should note that there was no deep well of experienced and talented "radio men" in the infancy of the medium. One could get a job with a radio station, as Ronald Reagan did, by having a pleasant sounding voice, an apparently likable personality, and an interest in the stage.

The second generalization that can be advanced about baseball broadcasters from the twenties through the forties is that they were much more closely identified with their teams than is the case today. Several reasons account for this phenomenon. In those years, teams remained in the same city and their rosters shifted only incrementally. Familiarity was a prized value among fans of a baseball club, and familiarity extended to the announcer. Second, multiple announcers for one club were slow to surface in the period, and when they did it was clear which announcer was the senior, prominent figure, the "voice" of the team. Third, the minimal presence of television until the 1950s (in 1947, the World Series was telecast to only four cities, Schenectady, New York, Philadelphia, and Washington)[40] meant that an announcer did not have to divide his time between different audiences or different media, or that several announcers would be identified with one club. Finally, the relative absence of television allowed radio broadcasts to remain the only way by which people not at the park could follow a game as it was taking place, so that the voices of announcers covering their teams became staples of offices, or beaches, or sidewalks during the summer months. Following the team meant listening to the voice of its radio announcer.

As radio broadcasting became established and radio broadcasters became more polished and professional in their work, they began to respond to their increased role as celebrities by adopting a stylistic identification with their community of listeners. This resulted in the emergence of distinctive regional styles of announcing. In northeastern cities, such as Boston and Philadelphia, announcers, although clearly associated with their home club, were not conspicuously partisan, following the canon of neutrality. In contrast, especially after Harry Caray succeeded France Laux in St. Louis in the 1940s, midwestern announcers began to boost their teams and, implicitly, their cities. Ty Tyson in Detroit, Rosey Rowswell in Pittsburgh, Jack Brickhouse in Chicago, Jimmy Dudley in Cleveland, and especially Bob Prince in Pittsburgh and Harry Caray in St. Louis openly rooted for their teams, praised their fans, and underscored their club's civic associations. McDonald in Washington adopted a similar posture, but elsewhere on the eastern seaboard boosterism and obvious partisanship were resisted. Red Barber in Cincinnati was an exception to the regional trends: he retained a neutral, "eastern" style.

Of the pioneer generation of broadcasters, seven figures stand out as familiar representatives of their clubs, unlike announcers such as Ted Husing or Graham McNamee, who were identified with national networks.[41] They were Hal Totten, who began with the Cubs and White Sox in 1924, covering home games of both clubs for station WMAQ in Chicago; Fred Hoey, doing the Braves' and Red Sox's games for the Colonial and then the Yankee Networks, originating in 1925 from WNAC in Boston; Tom Manning, broadcasting the Cleveland Indians' games from 1925 to 1931 for WTAM in Cleveland; Bill Dyer, who broadcast the Phillies' and Athletics' home games for WCAU in Philadelphia from 1927 on; Ty Tyson, who covered the Tigers for Detroit station WWJ, beginning in 1927; France Laux, who began reporting Cardinals' and Browns' games for KMOX in St. Louis in 1929; and Harry Hartman, who covered the Cincinnati Reds' home games from 1930 and 1934 and doubled as public address announcer for Redland Field.

The success of this first generation of announcers varied considerably. Manning lasted only until 1931, when the Indians' radio broadcasts switched to WHK and Jack Graney replaced him as announcer. Manning had begun his career as the "megaphone man" at League

Park in the days before a public address system and continued to be the club's public address announcer after leaving the radio booth. In 1956 he returned to do radio for two years. Hartman lasted only until 1934, when the Reds changed ownership and new owner Powel Crosley hired Red Barber to replace him. At the other end of the spectrum, Totten remained for twenty-one years with the Cubs and White Sox, competing with several other announcers in the Chicago area; Laux lasted eighteen years with the Cardinals and Browns; Tyson sixteen years, and then two additional ones in 1951 and 1952, for the Tigers; and Hoey fifteen years for the Braves and Red Sox.

The personalities of the pioneers were a diverse lot. Hartman was boisterous and crude, broadcasting games in his undershirt and filling his accounts with slang. Totten was understated and nondescript; Manning and Tyson emotional and animated; Laux low-key, no-frills; Dyer straightforward and bland; Hoey objective and articulate, also prone to alcoholism. They shared the common experience of broadcasters of their times: announcing the entire game; regularly doing re-created games as well; having no experience as ballplayers; being unaware, at the beginning of their careers, of the vastness of the audience they were reaching.

By the mid- and late 1930s the pioneers were joined, or supplanted, by a second group of early broadcasters, who entered into a profession at quite a different point in its history. By that point in time baseball broadcasts on the radio had ceased to be experiments in the possibilities of a new medium and become a commercially viable proposition. Even though some baseball owners remained skeptical about the effects of broadcasts on attendance, radio stations and an increasing number of corporate sponsors seemed enthusiastic about baseball as a subject of broadcasts. Corporations had discovered that the time sequence of baseball included numerous pauses between action, as well as breaks between the halves of an inning, time that could be used to plug a sponsor's product. Some baseball executives had realized that radio broadcasts, like newspapers, provided a significant amount of free advertising and publicity for a club. And knowledgeable observers of the phenomenon of baseball on the radio had begun to ascertain that a visible announcer, with a distinctive voice and style, could become a familiar link between a ballclub and his audience, a comfortable presence who entered living rooms, as it were, and made a team's fortunes part of a family's routine.

In short, by the mid-1930s baseball broadcasting was on the threshold of becoming big business, and baseball announcers were on the threshold of becoming celebrities. At the same time radio announcing was itself a more mature profession. Among the stars of this generation of broadcasters were Bob Elson, a link to the pioneer generation, who had first broadcast re-created Cubs and White Sox games in the late 1920s; Jack Graney, the first former ballplayer to become an announcer, who succeeded Tom Manning as the voice of the Cleveland Indians in 1931; McDonald, who began doing re-created away games for the Washington Senators in 1934; Harry Heilmann (another former player, who won four batting titles, hit .403 in 1923, and was elected to the Hall of Fame), doing Tigers' games on the Michigan Radio Network, which covered cities outside the Detroit area, in 1934; Rosey Rowswell, the first of the Pittsburgh Pirates' broadcasters, who began in 1936; and Byrum Saam, who moved from Minneapolis to broadcast the Philadelphia Phillies' and Athletics' home games, starting in 1938.

As radio established itself as a fixture of the enterprise of major league baseball, this group was joined by others in the late 1930s and 1940s, some of whose careers extended nearly to the present. Waite Hoyt, a former Yankee pitcher, began doing Cincinnati Reds games in 1941 and was still active in the early 1980s. Jack Brickhouse, who joined the Chicago Cubs as Elson's assistant in 1940, remained with the Cubs until 1982. Jimmy Dudley, who started with the Indians in 1947, was still active in the mid-1970s. This generation of broadcasters also produced Jim Britt, who called the home games of the Boston Braves and Red Sox from 1939 to 1953; and Bert Wilson, who covered the Cubs from 1943 to 1956.

The same generation also numbered some personalities who became national figures. These included Prince, who started with the Pittsburgh Pirates in 1948 and remained until 1975, and in 1976 joined the national telecast of ABC's "Monday Night Baseball"; and Russ Hodges, who got his start doing re-creations of Cubs and White Sox games for Chicago station WIND in the early 1930s, moved to Washington to re-create Senators games with McDonald between 1938 and 1945, the next year joined the Yankees as Mel Allen's sidekick, and in 1949 became the Giants' lead announcer. Hodges's call of Bobby Thomson's dramatic home run for the Giants against the Dodgers in their 1951 National League playoff remains one of the most famous moments in the history of radio broadcasting.

Finally, four other members of this generation are still active: Caray, who first broadcast St. Louis Cardinals games in 1944 and is currently with the Chicago Cubs; Ernie Harwell, who began broadcasting Brooklyn Dodger games in 1948, moved to the New York Giants in 1950, the Baltimore Orioles in 1954, and the Detroit Tigers in 1960, where he remained until being fired in 1990, then returned for two more years in 1992, and now freelances; Chuck Thompson, who began with the Phillies and Athletics in 1946, went to the Orioles for a year in 1955, then to the Senators from 1957 through 1961, and then back to the Orioles, where he has remained, despite efforts to retire; and Vin Scully, who joined the Brooklyn Dodgers in 1950, followed them to Los Angeles in 1957, and has continued as the Dodgers' voice. Scully, who added network television to his coverage in the 1960s and still regularly broadcasts World Series and All-Star games, would be cited by most observers of baseball broadcasting as the consummate announcer of his time.

Together, this collection of personalities helped fix a permanent allegiance between baseball and the radio medium and made themselves regional and in some cases national celebrities. But in 1978, when the Baseball Hall of Fame elected its first members from the broadcast industry, none of them was chosen. Two other men were picked, both southerners, both of whom had made their reputations broadcasting in the New York area, and both of whom had been fired, within two years of each other, by the management of the New York Yankees. They were Red Barber and Mel Allen. Strikingly different in their temperaments, approaches, and on-air personalities, Barber and Allen demonstrated that no one formula was necessary for successful baseball broadcasting.

◆

Walter Lanier Barber was born in Columbus, Mississippi, in 1908, but his father, a railroad engineer, moved his family to Sanford, Florida, in 1918 and Barber grew up in that state, eventually graduating from the University of Florida in 1930. That same year he began working as an announcer for WRUF, the university's campus radio station, doing news, sports, interviews, and country music shows. In 1934 he decided to advance his career by securing a job with one of the 50,000-watt stations in the southeast or midwest, and interviewed at stations in Atlanta, Charlotte, Cincinnati, Louisville, and Chicago.[42] None of the interviews was immediately successful, but one of the stations had been WLW in Cincinnati, owned by Powel Crosley, and when Crosley acquired a controlling interest in the Reds in 1934 his general manager, Larry MacPhail, convinced him to broadcast the Reds' games on the radio. Crosley owned WLW and 5,000-watt WSAI, and, as noted, concluded that the baseball broadcasts should be on the latter station, whose coverage was clearly local. Someone from WLW remembered interviewing Barber, and he was given an offer to broadcast Reds games on WSAI for twenty-five dollars a week. When Barber accepted the job he had never broadcast—or even seen—a major league baseball game.

Despite his lack of experience, Barber was an instant success. Part of that success can be traced to his meticulous preparation. He kept score of every game, producing a record of previous events that could be summarized at intervals. He initiated a practice of bringing a three-minute egg timer into the radio booth to remind him to give the score repeatedly for new listeners. He read the newspapers thoroughly every day, not just the sports pages, so that if necessary he could fill up unanticipated delays with observations on current events. He pioneered the pregame and postgame shows, interviewing players. He learned to anticipate whether a fly ball would be caught or carry over an outfielder's head by watching the course of the outfielder as he sought to catch it, not the flight of the ball itself.

Barber's preparation was an index of his perfectionist temperament. His performance in the radio booth, apparently relaxed and casual, conveyed the impression that he was a complete professional. He believed in the canon of neutrality and never openly rooted for the club for whom he broadcast. Although his language was colorful, it was precise. If he made a mistake, such as misidentifying a player, he acknowledged it on the air. Just as he refused to simulate crowd noise or cheering when doing a re-created game, he declined to cover up technical problems that interfered with a broadcast. If the attendance on a given day was sparse, he reported that, even if it suggested lack of fan support for the home club. If the Reds or the Dodgers or the Yankees were being beaten soundly, or playing sloppy baseball, he commented on that fact. If the crowd was roaring after a particularly spectacular play, he kept quiet and let the sound fill the microphone. With an occasional exception, his cadence, and the pitch of his delivery, remained constant whatever the situation. When Bobby Thomson hit his celebrated home run in 1951, Barber, calling the game on Dodger radio, simply said, "Swung on and belted deep out to left field. It is—a home run!,"[43] and then gave over the microphone to the crowd.

Barber's perfectionism, along with an attitude of intellectual aloofness and a tendency—especially after a bleeding ulcer in 1948 and the loss of much of his stomach in 1960—to eschew bars and restaurants when traveling, caused some of his contemporaries to view him as a remote, distant figure. Others felt even more negatively: Tom Gallery, the director of sports for NBC in the 1950s, referred to Barber as a "Psalm-singing, sanctimonious son of a bitch."[44] Those who worked closely with him, such as Jim Woods and Vin Scully, saw him with a combination of respect and fear. "He was my teacher," Scully said, "and my father. It wasn't so much that he taught me how to broadcast. It was an *attitude*. Do your homework. Be prepared. Be accurate. He was a stickler for that. He was very much a taskmaster."[45] When Barber, after retiring as a baseball announcer, began a Friday morning conversational segment with Bob Edwards of National Public Radio, he asked that a network producer call him the preceding Thursday at 10 A.M. to discuss possible topics. One morning the producer called at 10:20 instead of 10; he received, Edwards recalled, "a lecture on responsibility."[46]

The other part of Barber's success was captured in an interview late in his life with Bob Costas on Costas's syndicated radio show, "Coast to Coast." Barber discussed the state of baseball broadcasting when he came to the Reds in 1934: "When I began broadcasting at Cincinnati . . . , I think there were three commercials for nine innings. So it meant you were on the air all afternoon. You had opportunity. You had room on the air to tell stories. . . . We had, you might say, air room to be a personality."[47] The ability to tell good stories, in between the action of a baseball game, is arguably what distinguishes nonpareil broadcasters from merely competent ones. The three greatest announcers I have encountered, Barber, Scully, and Jon Miller (currently with the Baltimore Orioles and ESPN), possess that ability. Barber's stories, like those of Scully and Miller, were invariably on point: they were the product of assiduous preparation. Sometimes they were anecdotes about the player at bat or the pitcher; sometimes they were extended, unhurried descriptions of one phase or another of the atmosphere of the game. The stories could be telescoped to fit one plate appearance, or expanded to cover an entire inning. Sometimes they virtually displaced Barber's narrative of the action, with the result of pitches being added almost incidentally. They were never allowed, however, to displace important action.

Barber's stories were told in a discernibly southern accent and cadence, filled with a distinctive language of his own. That language was colloquial, but never imprecise; creative rather than clichéd. In his book *Fridays with Red*, Bob Edwards gave a list of "Barberisms," examples of that language. Baseball arguments were "rhubarbs," and Ebbets Field, where the proximity of the players to the fans and Leo Durocher's combative temperament precipitated numerous audible confrontations, was "the rhubarb patch." Marty Marion, the graceful St. Louis Cardinals' shortstop, was described as "movin' easy as a bank of fog." A ground ball tapped to the pitcher was a "come back little Sheba." A ball on a wet day, or spinning off the end of a bat, could be "slicker than oiled okra" to an infielder. A close, low-scoring game was "tighter than a new pair of shoes on a rainy day," and a high scoring game was "a ring-tailed, double-jointed doozy." Perhaps Barber's most celebrated phrase was "sittin' in the catbird seat," which he used when one team was in a particularly advantageous position, or just to describe the pleasurable sensations he experienced broadcasting from Ebbets Field on a warm, sunny day. The phrase, which Barber first heard from a winner at a poker game, is obscure in its connotations, perhaps referring to the tendency of catbirds to drive away other birds from nests. It was clear from Barber's usage that it signified the state of mind that emanates from being in a conspicuously comfortable position and knowing it.[48]

Barber's narrative skills are evident in this description of Ebbets Field in Brooklyn, advanced for a nationwide audience in the 1950s:

> For those of you who haven't seen Ebbets Field, it's a double-decked stadium, and the double-decking begins at right field's corner. In other words, there is no stand at back of right field. That's the famous fence or wall, the right-field wall. But the stands go all the way around in a rough U. Campanella fouls this one back. In back of right field is Bedford Avenue. Curveball, outside, ball two. That's one of the big thoroughfares, it's about a six-lane street in Brooklyn. But that's a forty-foot high right-field wall. If you want to be exact, thirty-nine and a half feet—nineteen and a half feet of concrete and then twenty feet of wire panels. Pitch low, outside, ball three. The field is in wonderful shape, the ballpark looking just as pretty as a brand-new bug. Got a lot of baseball going today.[49]

When something significant happened in a game that Barber was broadcasting, however, the action became the story. Here is Barber's famous call, in the sixth game of the 1947 World Series between the

Dodgers and the Yankees, of Al Gionfriddo's catch of a Joe DiMaggio drive to deepest left center in Yankee Stadium, preventing two runs from scoring:

> Joe DiMaggio up, holding that club down at the end. Big fellow sets. Hatten pitches. A curveball, high outside, for ball one. So the Dodgers are ahead, 8–5. And the crowd well knows that with one swing of the bat this fellow is capable of making it a brand-new game again. Joe leans in. He is one for three today. Six hits so far in the series. Outfield deep around toward left. The infield overshifted. Here's the pitch. Swung on. Belted. It's a long one! Deep into left-center. Back goes Gionfriddo, back, back, back, back, back, back. He makes a one-handed catch against the bullpen. Oh, doctor![50]

Not everyone appreciated Barber's unique combination of precision and lyricism. In 1950 Walter O'Malley maneuvered Branch Rickey out and himself in as president of the Dodgers, and he made it clear on assuming that role that he was not favorably disposed to employees he identified with Rickey. He saw Barber, wrongly, as such an employee, and their relationship was not close. In 1953 the advertising manager of the Gillette Safety Razor Company, who had exclusive rights to the World Series broadcasts, told Barber, shortly before the Series opened, that he had been chosen to be one of the broadcasters. Gillette's fee was two hundred dollars a game, non-negotiable. Barber decided that the Gillette executive, Craig Smith, was being peremptory, and said that his fee should be negotiated through his agent. Smith replied that Barber could take two hundred dollars a game or leave it. Barber responded by declining to broadcast the Series. Outraged, Barber sought out O'Malley, who told Barber that the matter was Barber's problem and that if he didn't want to broadcast, O'Malley would nominate Vin Scully. Scully eventually did broadcast the Series after clearing it with Barber. Bob Edwards later said that the episode "made Red Barber extremely angry until the day he died."[51] The next year he accepted an offer from the New York Yankees to broadcast for them, not as the lead announcer. The fact that he was willing to leave Brooklyn, switch leagues, and become identified with one of the Dodgers' great rivals demonstrates the depth of his estrangement.

Barber's interval in Yankee Stadium was something of a letdown after his glorious years with the Dodgers. He had health problems, including an unsuccessful ear operation in 1954, in which he lost the hearing in his right ear; his stomach operation in 1960; and phlebitis and a mild heart attack in 1964. The Yankees expanded their broadcast team, hiring Jerry Coleman, Phil Rizzuto, and Joe Garagiola, all ex-players, a species of broadcaster of which Barber was discernibly skeptical. The presence of as many as four announcers meant that each would alternate between radio and television, and Barber, although he had broadcast the first televised game for the Dodgers on August 26, 1939, did not care for the broadcaster's role in television. "The radio announcer," he once said to Bob Edwards, "is the supreme—the complete artist. . . . You paint the picture. . . . And that is satisfying to the human ego. But in television, instead of being the supreme artist, you become the servant of the monitor screen."[52] When doing telecasts of Yankee games he would often simply observe as television cameras covered action on the field, keeping his comments to a minimum. The result was to deprive viewers of his marvelous capacity for language.

Late in his career with the Dodgers, Barber had clashed with O'Malley over the issue of reporting attendance at home games. Barber wanted simply to announce the attendance and comment if he thought the crowd was sparse; O'Malley felt that if television cameras panned empty seats, viewers would be less inclined to attend games. The issues, for Barber, were honesty and objectivity: he saw himself simply as a reporter of events, neither a shill for the Dodgers nor a manipulator of the public. Several years later another version of the same issue led to Barber's being fired by the Yankees and leaving major league baseball broadcasting.

In the mid-1960s the Yankees, after a remarkable stretch of success over more than two decades, began to deteriorate at every level. Their ownership changed: the CBS network acquired a controlling interest and eventually, in 1966, the entire club. Mel Allen, the Yankees' long-time lead announcer, was suddenly dismissed in 1964. The Ballantine brewery, a perennial sponsor of the Yankees, suddenly began losing money in the 1960s and eventually ended their sponsorship. The team collapsed, finishing last in 1966. At the end of that season, on September 23, 1966, only 413 fans showed up for a game at Yankee Stadium. Barber thought the attendance was a more important story than the meaningless game the Yankees were playing, and attempted to get television cameras to pan around the stands, showing them nearly empty. His requests were refused: CBS had ordered the TV director to show as little of the stands as possible.

Four days later Barber met with Michael Burke, a CBS official who had replaced Dan Topping as president of the Yankees when Topping sold his interest in the club. Burke told Barber that his contract was not going to be renewed for the 1967 season. Barber immediately held a press conference announcing that he had been fired. He was not going to depart from his reportorial role even when the subject was himself.

◆

Barber survived his firing to live for twenty-seven more years in semi-retirement in Tallahassee, Florida. His health dramatically improved, he kept in touch with broadcasting through his NPR spot, and he never regretted his departure from major league baseball broadcasting.[53] In contrast, the other initial inductee of the broadcast wing of the Hall of Fame took his comparably premature and bizarre firing much harder, and for a long period existed in a kind of uncomprehending exile. The parallel episodes said much about the differences between Red Barber and Mel Allen.

Melvin Allen Israel was the son of Russian Jewish immigrants, Julius and Anna Israel, who were the proprietors of a women's clothing store in Johns, Alabama, near Birmingham, when he was born in 1913.[54] He was a precocious child, graduating from high school at fifteen, the University of Alabama at twenty, and its law school at twenty-three. While in college and law school he worked for Birmingham radio station WBRC, a result of his having been the manager and public address announcer of the football team as an undergraduate. He had no plans to continue in radio after passing the Alabama bar exam in 1936, but he took a vacation to New York and on a whim interviewed with Ted Husing at CBS, who had heard him broadcast an Alabama football game. The interview resulted in CBS's hiring him as a sports and special events announcer.

Like many of his peers, Allen was "in the right place at the right time," as he recalled in an interview with Curt Smith. In 1939 the Giants and Yankees, prodded by the Dodgers, began broadcasting their home games for the first time. In an unusual arrangement, CBS signed a two-year contract with the clubs but broadcast the games over the American Broadcasting Company's outlet in New York, the 50,000-watt station WABC. CBS wanted Arch McDonald from Washington to do the games, so they planned to send Allen there to replace McDonald on the Senators' broadcasts. But in the meantime Clark Griffith, the owner of the Senators, had decided to hire Hall-of-Fame pitcher Walter Johnson as a broadcaster, so Allen returned to his old special events job. By the end of the 1939 season it was apparent that the new arrangement wasn't working out. Walter Johnson was not a success as an announcer, and McDonald's rustic style did not appeal to New York listeners, so McDonald returned to Washington to replace Johnson.

In the meantime the announcer CBS had hired to assist McDonald on Giant and Yankee broadcasts had proven inept, and Allen had been told to fill in for him. When McDonald left, Allen became the lead announcer of the Giants and Yankees by default. He was twenty-six at the time, in his first season of baseball broadcasting. Then in 1942 he went into the army; when he returned for the 1946 season, Giant owner Horace Stoneham offered him his job back. But in 1945 Larry MacPhail bought the Yankees along with Dan Topping and Del Webb, and MacPhail, always an innovator, resolved to expand the Yankees' radio coverage. For the first time, MacPhail decided, a major league baseball team would send an announcer on the road to broadcast games live: the Yankees would air all their games, severing their affiliation with the Giants and broadcasting on a new station, WINS.

MacPhail offered Red Barber the opportunity to be the Yankees' lead broadcaster, but Branch Rickey matched MacPhail's offer, and Barber decided to remain with Brooklyn. MacPhail then turned to Allen, who felt himself obligated to Stoneham. But Stoneham had not yet secured a radio station for the Giants, and he told Allen that under the circumstances Allen could consider himself a free agent. Allen signed with the Yankees, and remained with them for the next nineteen years.[55]

In that period Allen profited from the Yankees' regular success. After the early experiments with multiple broadcasts of the World Series, Gillette signed a contract with Organized Baseball to secure exclusive rights to a single broadcast. At that time Commissioner Landis ruled that the announcers for the Series would be the announcers for the participating clubs. The arrangement, which was extended from radio to television in 1951, meant that every time the Yankees were in the World Series Mel Allen's voice would be carried across the country. Between 1947 and 1964 the Yankees were in the World Series fifteen times. Allen broadcast all but the last of those contests.

There was more to Allen's success than Yankee triumphs, of course.

But his appeal is not easily extracted from analysis of his broadcasts. Unlike Barber, whose colloquialisms enhanced his language, Allen's style was to fashion on a series of clichéd phrases—"going, going, gone!" for home runs, "around comes the right [or left] arm, here comes the pitch" for nearly every delivery, "How about that!" for any striking development in the action—and make them the basis of a broadcast narrative that was, on analysis, surprisingly straightforward, even prosaic.

That Allen's descriptions were largely flat and unembellished was concealed by the emotional tone of his voice. He was the stylistic antithesis of Barber, swept up in the emotion of a game, his pitch starting at a moderately high level of intensity and going upward. He was also a compulsive nicknamer of players and shiller for sponsors. Joe DiMaggio was "Joltin' Joe" or "The Yankee Clipper." Tommy Henrich was "Old Reliable." Ed Lopat was "Steady Eddie." Phil Rizzuto was "The Scooter." Lou Gehrig was "Larrupin' Lou." A home run was a "Ballantine Blast" or a "White Owl Wallop," the latter for a cigar sponsor. Those who worked with Allen said he was the best they ever encountered on skillfully working in sponsor plugs to his narrative of the game.

It appears that the secret of Allen's appeal was that his emotion came across as genuine, as if it were that of a small boy thrilled with the feats of baseball heroes he was witnessing. Allen was corny, and garrulous, and had a tendency to overdramatize, but he was a skilled professional, with a good eye for detail, a remarkable memory, and a thorough knowledge of baseball. Some of his best-known moments have a comedic quality, such as the time during a television broadcast of a 1968 game between the Minnesota Twins and the Cleveland Indians, after he had been fired from the Yankees, when he recited from memory the first thirty-seven lines of Longfellow's "Song of Hiawatha." The performance was prompted by a reference to the numerous lakes in Minnesota.[56] The episode reveals Allen's intellectual abilities, but it also demonstrates his inability to adopt to the medium of television, which requires less talk of its broadcasters. When he began announcing the World Series on television regularly in the 1950s he did not change his style, and in 1958 received a telegram before the second game of the Series telling him to "shut up."[57]

Excerpts from Allen's broadcasts cannot capture his appeal in the manner of Barber's. Here is Allen, for example, describing Enos

("Country") Slaughter's dash for home with what ended up being the winning run in the eighth inning of the seventh game of the 1946 World Series. With two out, Slaughter scored all the way from first on a double by Harry Walker as Johnny Pesky, the Red Sox shortstop, unaccountably held the ball in short left field for a moment before releasing his relay throw. Allen commented as follows:

> Enos Slaughter is on first base with two away. Harry Walker at bat. Bob Klinger on the mound. He takes the stretch. Here's the pitch . . . there goes Slaughter. The ball is swung on—there's a line drive going into left-center field—it's in there for a base hit! Culberson fumbles the ball momentarily and Slaughter charges around second, heads for third. Pesky goes into short left field to take the relay from Culberson. . . . And here comes Enos Slaughter rounding third, he's going to try for home! Here comes the throw and it is not in time! Slaughter scores![58]

The account is completely straightforward, with Allen efficiently conveying most of the crucial information. We can feel the emotion build as Slaughter "charges around second" and then "round[s] third, heading for home." "Slaughter scores!" enables Allen to end on a crescendo. But he has omitted entirely Pesky's holding the ball in the outfield. Without that fact Slaughter's dash appears unremarkable.

Nonetheless as an exercise in building drama, the excerpt is effective, especially if one imagines Allen's voice rising on "it's in there for a base hit!," falling on "heads for third," remaining at that level through "take the relay from Culberson," rising again with "And here come Enos Slaughter," and reaching its peak with "Slaughter scores." If one can imagine the same passage being delivered by an announcer with a notoriously flat cadence—Bob Elson or, to choose a current example, Herb Score of the Cleveland Indians—it would not be memorable. Allen's delivery somehow made it such.

Despite Allen's intelligence, intellectual precision was never his goal as an announcer. He sought instead a kind of middlebrow emotional resonance, to capture the feeling of being at the park and being thrilled once more. That Allen was able to maintain this resonance after so many years of regular exposure as a national broadcast personality suggests that he was not an ordinary broadcaster. His ingenuous, even gullible personality and his single-minded devotion to baseball and broadcasting (he never married and, unlike Barber, had no other consuming interests or hobbies) contributed to his capacity to convince his listeners that his reactions were spontaneous and genuine. And in the period of his greatest success, 1939 through the 1950s, the fact that he was often cornball, clichéd, garrulous, and occasionally partisan did not detract from his reputation. He looked at baseball with wide-eyed admiration, and that was the way much of his audience implicitly wanted it to be looked at.

In the early 1960s, as changes took place in the ownership of the Yankees, Allen's situation suddenly became precarious. The principal owner of the Yankees, Dan Topping, had never been a great fan of Allen's (announcer Jim Woods once told Curt Smith that Topping and Walter O'Malley, in the course of a drinking bout at Toots Shor's restaurant in 1953, agreed to trade Allen and Barber, both of whom rankled their owners);[59] and by 1964 the Yankees' principal sponsor, Ballantine Beer, had suffered financial reverses. Ballantine had earlier become convinced that bringing in former ballplayers as radio and television announcers would stimulate listener interest. Their first move along those lines was to insist that the third Yankee announcer, Jim Woods, be replaced with Phil Rizzuto when Rizzuto ended his baseball career in 1956. Then, in 1963, Ballantine demanded that former Yankee infielder Jerry Coleman be added to the broadcast team, which meant teaming Rizzuto and Coleman with Allen and Barber. Barber was even asked to take a pay cut to accommodate Coleman, but he refused.[60] And when Allen went into Dan Topping's office in September 1964 to discuss a renewal of his contract, he was told that he would not be hired for the following year. Topping, according to Allen, implied that Ballantine Beer had been behind the decision, but the Yankees did not even nominate Allen to broadcast the 1964 World Series. "The Yankees never even held a press conference to announce my leaving," Allen remembered. "They just let it leak out. So there were all sorts of lies spread around. . . . They said I was a lush or that I beat my relatives or that I'd had a breakdown or that I was taking so many medicines for my voice that I turned numb."[61]

"When Topping dropped the bomb," Allen said, "I was stunned." Red Barber remembered Allen's coming to Yankee Stadium the next day: "When I got to the booth about fifteen minutes before air time Mel was already there. He was sitting in his place. He was staring across the ball field. He didn't speak. I don't think he knew where he was. He was numb. . . . He was the saddest-looking man I have ever seen. He was in a nightmare. He was desolate, stricken."[62] The difference between Allen's and Barber's firings was marked. Barber regarded the matter as one of principle, the Yankee ownership asking him to compromise his professionalism and acting vindictively when he would not. Allen was simply overwhelmed, incredulous that the Yankees would have any reason to fire him. In fact both the Yankees and CBS believed, wrongly as it turned out, that baseball's future was in television and that Allen would not wear well as a television announcer. They may have been correct about the latter, but the next two decades would demonstrate that radio, not television, was the medium better suited to convey baseball to a wide audience.

Besieged by rumors, Allen, at fifty-one, found himself essentially out of broadcasting for the next fifteen years. Then, in the late 1970s, he reemerged with a successful television show, "This Week in Baseball," that perfectly suited his talents. It was a series of highlighted summaries of the National and American League games of the past week, with Allen's voice providing the narration to brilliant catches, home runs, impressive pitching performances, and even occasional humorous baserunning or fielding blunders. It was a show frankly designed to boost baseball and to attract potential fans, and Allen's unqualified enthusiasm perfectly complemented the package of highlights. By 1978 Allen had been sufficiently rehabilitated to join Barber in the Hall of Fame.

◆

The plethora of announcer styles—ranging from Barber or the erudite Jim Britt to the comical partisan Rosey Rowswell, and including Vin Scully and Ernie Harwell in Barber's tradition, and Bob Prince and Harry Caray in Allen's—demonstrated that successful baseball announcers can be detached intellectuals or cornball boosters, so long as they allow the radio medium to do what it does very well: enhance the drama, and at the same time the leisurely pace, of a game whose subtleties and complexities are often missed by television cameras but can be captured in lyrical prose or simply in sheer excitement.

No clearer proof of the stunning impact of radio on baseball, both as a source of revenue and as a means for promoting and advertising the game, can be found than in the short history of Gordon McLendon's Liberty Broadcasting System, which operated from 1949 to 1953. McLendon's network, which at its peak included over 450 stations, was based on a simple premise: in areas where the live broadcasts of major league teams could not be heard, there was a large potential audience of fans who would listen to re-created games. Taking advantage of population growth and increased FCC licensing of radio stations after the Second World War, McLendon simply used the techniques that re-created radio had always employed. He paid Western Union a fee for wires from ballparks, set up himself or another announcer in a studio, and charged stations outside the range of major league broadcasts a fee to do games. In 1949 his costs were $27.50 for the Western Union service, and his income was $10 per game from each of three hundred stations. His re-creations, unlike those of Barber, were complete with sound effects. For many listeners they were what baseball sounded like on the radio.

Organized Baseball, concerned about the effect of the Liberty Broadcast System on the minors and local big league broadcasts, invoked the territorial rule to bar Liberty stations from seventy-five miles of major league ballparks. McLendon responded by concentrating on the south and west, areas of growing population without major league clubs. The Mutual Broadcasting System, seeing the success of Liberty, decided to work with Organized Baseball in forming a nationwide network of live broadcasts, centered on the "Game of the Day," which would be authorized in advance. A version of Mutual Broadcasting's experiment still survives on the CBS Radio Network; by 1953 Liberty was defunct.

Liberty was defeated by a series of agreements, engineered by Commissioner Ford Frick, that barred anyone but authorized stations from the use of both radio facilities and telegraph lines. McLendon sued major league baseball for illegal interference with the free flow of commerce, but a federal judge dismissed the suit, agreeing with the major leagues that if the agreements were reasonable Liberty had no claim for which relief could be granted. The loss of Western Union privileges in ballparks meant that Liberty had to turn to other sports, and the network quickly collapsed.

Only twenty years earlier the owners of ballclubs had permitted any licensed station to come into their parks and broadcast their games. It was not until the mid-1930s before a majority of National League owners had become convinced that limiting the number of authorized stations would be beneficial to them, and it was not until 1938 before a club successfully sued to protect its radio rights. It was not until 1939 before the New York teams had broadcast baseball at all. It was not until 1946 before any team aired its road games live. But by 1949 all the major league owners had realized the advertising and revenue bonanza they had in radio rights to their games. If anyone doubted the appeal of baseball on the radio to the American public, McLendon's venture had confirmed it. Baseball broadcasting rights had now become as important to major league owners as their exclusive rights to players on their roster. Indeed by the 1960s radio and television rights had become the principal means of revenue for many clubs.

In a sense everything that sharply distinguishes the current enterprise of major league baseball from that of the first half of the twentieth century—radio and television contracts, the collapse of the reserve system and free agency, the increased importance of sports agents and lawyers in baseball labor negotiations, the emergence of the players' union as a significant force, the transfer of teams from one city to another and the expansion of teams into new markets—can be said to follow from the recognition by Organized Baseball, after the Second World War, that electronic media coverage of baseball significantly enhanced the game's appeal. But this chapter has shown that such a recognition was quite late in surfacing. Just as most persons intimately involved with major league baseball thought it "unnatural" to play games at night, and were slow to realize the economic benefits of evening baseball, those same persons were slow to bless the marriage of baseball and radio, a marriage that has turned out to be more far-reaching and profitable than even the pioneer generation of baseball broadcasters could have conceived.

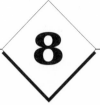

8

Ethnicity and Baseball: Hank Greenberg and Joe DiMaggio

IN DECEMBER 1923, *The Sporting News*, in commenting on reports that some baseball players were members of the rejuvenated Ku Klux Klan, decided to reaffirm its position on the role of ethnicity in Organized Baseball. "In a democratic, catholic, real American game like baseball," *The Sporting News* maintained, "there has been no distinction raised except tacit understanding that a player of Ethiopian descent is ineligible. . . . No player of any other 'race' has been barred. . . . The Mick, the Sheeny, the Wop, the Dutch and the Chink, the Cuban, the Indian, the Jap or the so-called Anglo-Saxon—his 'nationality' is never a matter of moment if he can pitch, hit, or field."[1]

The editorial captured the role of ethnicity in major league baseball in the first three decades of the twentieth century. The ethnic origins of players were, at one level, deemed relevant, and commentators freely engaged in ethnic stereotyping. At another level, however, the ethnic backgrounds and attributed ethnic characteristics of players were treated as paling in significance alongside their baseball talents—their ability to "pitch, hit, or field." Moreover, with one important exception, the ethnic diversity of baseball was not only noted, it was welcomed, being a testament to the "democratic," "catholic," and "real American" character of the game. Only in the case of black players was race or ethnicity a disqualifying characteristic for playing major league baseball.

The conventional attitude toward ethnicity expressed by *The Sporting News* editorial was founded on what would seem to be a massive internal contradiction. If in the "democratic" American game of baseball, ethnicity (or race) was ultimately irrelevant, being subsumed in "baseball-related" characteristics, why comment on it at all? And why, in the case of black players, make it a basis for excluding someone from the pool of persons eligible to play in the major leagues? The logic of subsuming ethnicity in "ethnic-blind" criteria, such as the ability to run, throw, or field, would seem to lead to the elimination of ethnic-oriented discourse in the game. And yet the ethnic origins, and stereotyped ethnic characteristics, of players were frequent topics for conversation among those who wrote about baseball from the early 1900s through the Second World War.

If one reflects on the role of ethnicity in early twentieth-century baseball, it soon becomes evident that the ethnic and racial characteristics of players were treated, by those discussing them, within the context of the "melting pot" theory of ethnicity in America. For believers in the melting pot, it was as significant that America had the capacity to contain members of diverse ethnic groups as it was that the distinctive characteristics of those groups would ultimately disappear with time.

It is important to understand that in melting pot theory, the question of what ethnic ingredients were being added to the brew of American civilization was as important as the capacity of the mixture to absorb those ingredients. The case of blacks demonstrated those dual preoccupations. Early twentieth-century stereotypes of black Americans treated them as only assimilable into mainstream American civilization in a limited fashion: as an underclass of dependent or despised persons. The stereotypes of childishness, laziness, profligacy, crudity, and intemperance that were associated with being a black person in early twentieth-century America suggested that African-Americans could never fully be integrated into mainstream American culture. In terms of melting pot theory, certain inherently "black" characteristics could never be melted down. It was consistent with those beliefs to treat American blacks as a despicable or a pitiable caste, whose extended acculturation would only contaminate the brew of American civilization. It was also consistent with those beliefs to exclude black ballplayers from Organized Baseball.

In examining the rhetoric of early twentieth-century commentators on ethnicity in baseball, one can readily observe the assumptions of melting pot theory shaping the commentary. In particular, the ethnic origins of two groups of players were treated as highly relevant, and potentially even a basis for exclusion, for the first three decades of the twentieth century. Then, in the 1940s, the ethnic origins of those groups came to be treated as much less relevant, to the point where they were rarely mentioned in discussions of individual players belonging to the groups. The groups were Jews and Italians, and the careers of two Hall of Fame players from the thirties and forties, Hank Greenberg and Joe DiMaggio, illustrate shifting attitudes toward the role of stereotyped Jewish and Italian characteristics as relevant criteria for evaluating the performance of a major league baseball player.

Several reasons account for the particular treatment of Jewish and Italian ballplayers. First, two ethnic groups, Irish and Germans, had contributed a sufficiently large number of individuals to the pool of early twentieth-century baseball players that even those commentators who fastened on the ethnic backgrounds of players were hardly in a position to argue that the ethnic origins of those groups, and associated stereotypes, were sufficient to exclude them from the game. Thus the "Irishness" and "Germanness" of players was regularly remarked upon in early twentieth-century commentary, but, instead of being data for exclusionist arguments, became data for arguments that stressed the "democratic" and "catholic" nature of America's national game.

In addition to the rare Native American, invariably referred to as "Chief," Spanish and Latino players entered the major leagues to some degree, especially after the 1920s, and their ethnicity was usually commented upon. Discussions of those players tended to center on the fact that until the 1940s most of them were either Americans with Spanish ancestry or Cubans. Americans with Spanish surnames were treated as unremarkable ethnics, like Irish, Germans, or Scandinavians. The ethnicity of players from Cuba attracted more attention, for two reasons. Cuba, from World War I on, was the leading center of baseball in the western hemisphere outside of the United States, producing a number of talented players. In addition, Cuba was a multiracial society, many of whose inhabitants were of mixed racial origins, and Organized Baseball made a determined effort to distinguish "white," "eligible"

Cuban players from "black," ineligible ones. Thus the race of a Cuban player tended to receive more attention than any stereotyped "ethnic" characteristics attributed to him.

Other than Irish, Germans, and Scandinavians, the ethnic groups contributing the largest number of potential players to Organized Baseball's pool were Jews and Italians. Commentators had difficulty specifying the status of Jews with precision. There was no Jewish national state at the time, and the majority of commentators treated Jewishness as a racial characteristic, identifying it with physical as well as intellectual or social attributes. They had no difficulty recognizing Jewishness as a relevant characteristic of a ballplayer, and they had no difficulty in associating Jewishness with a host of stereotypes. The same was true of the status of being Italian. From the time the first ballplayers of Italian origins entered the major leagues their ethnicity was commented upon, and commentators resorted to a bundle of stereotypes in their discussions.

There were two other dimensions of being Jewish or Italian, however, that distinguished players in those groups from other ethnics. One was the growth of Jewish and Italian communities within major league cities in the twentieth century, and the associated emergence of baseball, within those communities, as an attraction for prospective players and fans. By the 1930s the Jewish and Italian base of fans within several major league cities was large enough for baseball club owners to take seriously. The other dimension was the shifting status of Jews and Italians as American immigrant groups during the thirties and forties. As ethnic and racial consciousness became explicitly integrated into national policymaking in Europe, with the result that Jews were increasingly placed at risk in the 1930s and Italy became increasingly identified as a member of the forces putting Jews at risk and as a potential enemy of the United States, the status of American Jews and Italians became more charged.

Ultimately the experience of the Second World War, especially the publicizing of atrocities associated with ethnic and racial stereotyping, helped transform commentary about the role of ethnicity in baseball. From a period in the earliest years of the twentieth century, when the ethnic origins of a player were invariably regarded as relevant and often as the basis for stereotyped judgments, commentary passed to a period after World War II in which the ethnicity of Jewish and Italian players, the last two significant groups to be treated as "remarkable" ethnics, had come to be seen as further evidence of the democratic, catholic, melting pot character of the national game of baseball.

The change, however, had not been brought about solely by an altered international situation. The rise of Hank Greenberg and Joe DiMaggio to superstar status also implicitly forced a reconsideration of some stereotypes attributed to baseball-playing Jews and Italians. Greenberg and DiMaggio came to be seen as more than exceptionally gifted players: they were "American" role models, whose behavior apparently embodied model characteristics for ballplayers of that era. They appeared as humble, hard-working, patriotic individuals who took their ethnic heritages seriously but did not exhibit stereotyped ethnic characteristics. They were seen as ballplayers first, Jews or Italians second. They were, in short, not only star players but confirmations of the melting pot theory of ethnicity in America.

◆

An early example of ethnic stereotyping can be found in coverage of the 1908 season, which produced a close National League pennant race among the Giants, Pirates, and Cubs and included the memorable game of September 23, in which the famous blunder by Giants' first baseman Fred Merkle, who failed to touch second base as the winning run scored, contributed to the Cubs and Giants being tied for the pennant at the season's end. G. H. Fleming's account of the 1908 National League race, *The Unforgettable Season,* is based on newspaper accounts, principally from New York, Chicago, and Pittsburgh papers.

One theme emerging from Fleming's book is a tacit division between "unremarkable" and "remarkable" ethnic identities for players. Several of the ballplayers described in the accounts were of Irish ancestry, such as "Turkey" Mike Donlan, Roger Bresnahan, or Giants' manager John McGraw, but that fact was not remarked upon by any of the writers. That some players were of German ancestry was commented upon but not made the basis of any generalizations. Thus Honus Wagner was variously termed "the doughty German," "the big Teuton," or "the Flying Dutchman,"[2] but no qualities were attributed to him because of his ethnicity. The treatment of German players can be seen in a September 26, 1908, article by William F. Kirk of the *New York American,* in which Kirk made much of the fact that Cincinnati had a significant German population, calling the Cincinnati Reds "the Gingery

Germans from Zinzinnati," and noting that "Messrs. Hoblitzel, Ganzel, Lobert, Schlei, Beecher et al." were "worthy Teutons all."[3] Nothing followed for Kirk from that fact.

The less numerous players of Italian origin received a slightly different treatment. One such player commented upon in Fleming's accounts was Ed Abbaticchio, an infielder for the Pirates. The treatment was notable only because Abbaticchio was variously referred to as "Abby" or "Battey," an indication that reporters found his name uncongenially long or difficult, and chose to refashion it for their readers.[4] It is also possible that Abbaticchio participated in that process, since early Italians in the major leagues often changed their names, the best example being Ping Bodie, who played for the Philadelphia Athletics and Yankees from 1917 to the late 1920s. Bodie, the first of a series of Italian major leaguers to come from the San Francisco area, had been born Francisco Stefano Pizzolo.[5] At another point the *New York World* referred to Abbaticchio as "the son of Caesar."[6]

The treatment of players believed to be Jewish in 1908 was also self-conscious. A case in point was Charley ("Buck") Herzog, a rookie for the Giants that season, who quit the team in late May after McGraw had insulted him, but rejoined the club about a month later.[7] Herzog was a utility infielder who came to be a valuable asset to the Giants as the season progressed, stealing bases, hitting for a commendable average, and playing well in the field. On Thursday, September 17, Joe Vila, writing in *The Sporting News*, reported, "The long-nosed rooters are crazy whenever young Herzog does anything noteworthy. Cries of 'Herzog! Herzog! Goot poy, Herzog!' go up regularly, and there would be no let-up even if a million ham sandwiches suddenly fell among these believers in percentages and bargains."[8]

Later in the same month Gym Bagley of the *New York Evening Mail* noted that he had "received many letters asking me about Charley Herzog's nationality and what Sunday school he plays." Bagley said that he had "answered one in which I replied that Herzog's forbears were his personal property and no one's business save his own." But Herzog, Bagley added,

> himself wishes it known that he is a Dutchman. So many fans wished him a happy new year Saturday [the date of Rosh Hashanah, the Jewish New Year] it made him tired. "They've got me wrong," said Herzy to me after the game. "I'm as Dutch as sauerkraut, that's all. . . . You see, when I was a kid I fell off a cliff and broke my nose. It was never set properly, and

> that's what makes it stick out so now." Herzy's nose does stick out a bit, that's a fact. When he slides into a base he must turn on his side. Otherwise he'd be so high off the ground he might as well try to make the bag standing.[9]

The comments on Herzog are revealing. Bagley attributes the supposition that Herzog is Jewish to the fact that he has a broken nose that "sticks out" quite far. Jewish fans are thus assumed to support Jewish players, but the bulk of the descriptions are directed to reinforcing stereotypes. Later in the season Joe Vila would refer to Jewish fans of the Giants as "the long-nosed rooters who have made the Polo Grounds this summer look like the market place in Jerusalem."[10]

From 1908 through the 1920s this attitude toward ethnicity in baseball continued in the press. *The Sporting News* was typical of other papers in its consciousness of ethnicity and its association of ethnic diversity in baseball with the "democratic" character of American society. It also tracked the attitudes of its contemporaries in finding some ethnic backgrounds (Irish and German) unremarkable and others (Jewish, Italian, and Native American) the occasion for stereotyped comment.

The clearest evidence of the view that ethnic diversity in baseball reflected the democratic orientation of America came in a December 6, 1923, editorial. Reacting to "stories of discord on clubs today because of [religious] prejudices," and citing the case of a Philadelphia Athletics' pitcher, Robert Hasty, who was a member of the Ku Klux Klan, *The Sporting News* reaffirmed its commitment to ethnic tolerance, at least for whites. "It is a pity," the editorial began,

> that in a democratic, catholic, real American game like baseball—we call it our "national" game—there ever could arise that hideous monster of racial or religious prejudice. . . .
>
> When one scans a box score or a reserve list and notes from what pools of our polyglot population baseball players are drawn, it is amazing that any question ever should be raised as to a man's antecedents, or the particular form of his worship of the one Great God. . . . It matters not what branch of mankind the player sprang from, with the fan, if he can deliver the goods.[11]

The position expressed in this editorial was consistent with that taken two years earlier by *The Sporting News* in a comment on charges made by the *Dearborn Independent*, a paper owned by the automobile magnate Henry Ford, that Jews were responsible for the damage done to baseball by the 1919 Black Sox scandal. *The Sporting News*, in criticizing the *Independent*'s position, attempted to dissociate itself from blatant ethnic stereotyping, while retaining a consciousness of ethnic identity. The *Independent* had charged that other papers declined to emphasize the evidence of Jewish financial involvement in efforts to corrupt professional sports because they had been "muzzled," presumably by powerful Jews. *The Sporting News* responded: "The Sporting News is not muzzled, and . . . has not neglected to call attention at various times to the fact that the men accused of financing crooked ballplaying are largely Jews. In doing that, however, it has not taken the position that because a bunch of crooks who are Jews have besmirched the good name of baseball, all Jews necessarily are crooked."

The Sporting News suggested that "the Jew as Jew—and as an American—" could counter Ford's charges "by denouncing and ostracizing the crook and the cheat who happens to be a Jew, and by so living his life and adhering to high principles in sport and business that he can point to the crooked member of his 'race' as a remarkable exception." Then, the editorial concluded, "the buck will be passed from the Jew to the Irish, or it may be the Dutch or the Dago."[12] Six months after commenting on Ford's charges *The Sporting News* reprinted a column by Walter Trumbull in the *New York Herald* in which Trumbull asserted that "one reason that baseball really is a national game is that at some time or other it has contained all the elements . . . which go to make up a nation." As evidence Trumbull pointed out that "Lajoie represents French ancestry, Wagner the German, Bodie the Italian, Olsen the Swedish, Coveleskie the Polish, Konetchy the Bohemian, Cobb the English, Gonzales the Spanish and the Irish are more plentiful than sod in the old country. And all of them represent America."[13]

At the same time that it was exhibiting its complicated and potentially contradictory attitude toward ethnicity in baseball, *The Sporting News*, throughout the 1920s, was continuing to find some ethnic associations more interesting than others. Comments such as those of Trumbull, listing French, German, Irish, and English ancestry in a collection of diverse "nationalities" within baseball, were clearly in service of arguments for democracy and the national character of the game, since, on the whole, nothing was made throughout the 1920s of the fact that various players were French, German, Irish, or English. On the other hand, a *Sporting News* column in 1922 pictured Washington Senators pitcher Albert Youngblood as a "Heap Big Injun," noting that "they call them all 'heap Big Injuns' when red men break into baseball."[14]

Most of the self-conscious commentary on ethnic origins in *The Sporting News* in the 1920s, however, was directed toward Jewish and Italian players. In September 1923 the paper announced that the New York Giants had found "that $100,000 Jew," having purchased the contract of Moses Solomon from the Hutchinson, Kansas, franchise in the Southwestern League. "In Moses," *The Sporting News* reported, the Giants had "just the sort of hero McGraw has wished for." The article also noted that Solomon "has verdicts in several fist fights to his credit, having found it necessary to fight his way through because of reflections on his ancestry as a Jew."[15]

The interest in Solomon reflected an assumption that a successful Jewish ballplayer on the Giants would encourage the large number of Jews who resided near the Polo Grounds to attend games. In 1926 F. C. Lane of *Baseball Magazine* wrote an article entitled "Why Not More Jewish Ballplayers?," in which he quoted Eddie Reulbach, one of the few Jews to play in the majors before the First World War, decrying the small number of Jewish players in Organized Baseball. "If I were a magnate in Greater New York at least," Reulbach told Lane, "I would send scouts all over the United States and Canada in an effort to locate some hook-nosed youngster who could bat and field. Then I would ballyhoo him in all the papers. The Jewish people are great spenders and they could be made excellent fans. You could sell out your boxes and your reserved seats any time in Greater New York."[16] It is interesting that even though Reulbach was Jewish, Lane quoted him as engaging in the stereotyped characterization "hook-nosed" to describe Jewish ballplayers.

Moses Solomon did not become the Giants' equivalent of Babe Ruth. He played in only two games in the majors, both at the end of the 1923 season, getting three hits in eight at-bats. That performance would have seemed adequate to merit another year with the Giants, but Solomon got in a dispute with John McGraw when the Giants' manager asked him to remain with the club during the World Series, even though he was ineligible, without pay. Solomon refused and joined a professional football team in Ohio. McGraw made it clear that if Solomon left the Giants, he would not be asked to return, and he was not.[17]

Five years after Solomon's brief appearance on the Giants another Jewish ballplayer was heralded as a potential drawing card at the Polo

Grounds. This was Andy Cohen, who first played for the Giants in 1926, appearing in thirty-two games, but was given the chance to become a regular in 1928. Cohen, who had grown up in El Paso and attended the University of Alabama, was far from a "local boy," but was nonetheless characterized by the newspaper *American Hebrew*, on his first appearance for the Giants in June 1926, as "a pleasant faced youth of twenty with rugged features of an unmistakably Jewish cast." The characterization was typical of Jewish-oriented newspapers at the time, who simultaneously asserted that "the Jew is thoroughly Americanized" and reflected stereotyped attitudes about the appearance and behavior of Jews.[18]

After being sent down to Buffalo of the International League in 1927, where he hit .355 and made the All-Star team, Cohen returned to the Giants in 1928, expected to replace Rogers Hornsby, who had been traded to the Boston Braves, at second base. Starting most of the year, Cohen had a decent season, batting .274 in 129 games and earning a raise from $7,500 to $11,500. The reaction of New York fans to Cohen, however, far exceeded his performance. After opening day of the 1928 season, when Cohen scored two runs and drove in two in a Giants' victory over the Braves, the crowd rushed onto the field and carried him around on their shoulders. A *New York Times* account compared Cohen's reception to that of Babe Ruth or Walter Johnson. The *American Hebrew* predicted that he would become "the greatest Jew in organized baseball."[19]

Cohen followed up his 1928 season with another solid year in 1929, hitting .294 in 101 games. *The Sporting News* predicted that "the young Jewish boy" would continue with the Giants because "he can hit, field, and run" and "has dash and courage." Besides, the paper suggested, "McGraw, the master baseballman, is sweet on Andy."[20] More important than Cohen's accomplishments on the field, several sources indicated, was his box office appeal. "If Mr. Cohen will stand up [under pressure]," columnist Westbrook Pegler wrote, "the Giants will have the offset of [Yankee co-owner] Jake Ruppert's Babe Ruth."[21]

The reasons Pegler advanced for Cohen's appeal are of interest. Pegler asserted:

> The tailor shops, the meat markets, the groceries, dry goods stores—almost all the places of business [in the area] bear such names as Levkowitz, Levy, Levitch, Myer, Mandlebaum, Katz, Jacobs, and Schanz. In the tall

> apartment buildings, which stand in solid rows for miles, the names on the door bells are Jewish by a vast plurality. . . . [In seeking to tap into the prospective Jewish fan base, the Giants] desired a Jewish ball player, preferably an infielder, because an infielder plays closer to the customers. [With a successful Jewish player] the Giant firm could do business in the Jewish trade alone.[22]

The electric reaction Cohen produced from the Polo Grounds crowds tempted entrepreneurs to take advantage of his popularity by booking him as a vaudeville entertainer in the off-season. In the winters of 1928 and 1929 Cohen and the Giants' starting catcher, Frank ("Shanty") Hogan, formed an act, called "Cohen and Hogan" in New York and "Hogan and Cohen" elsewhere, in which they sang baseball-oriented parodies of popular songs. "Everywhere [Cohen] went among his own people," Harry Glantz of the Los Angeles *B'nai B'rith Messenger* wrote after Cohen's first winter as a Giant, "he was feted and ballyhooed to the skies." Glantz asked both the Giants and "the Yids" to stop "the ballyhoo" and "let Cohen earn his spurs on his ball-playing ability."[23]

Later in life Cohen gave an interview to the American Jewish Committee in which he expressed ambivalence about the "ballyhoo" that surrounded his years with the Giants. He said that "being a Jew made me stand out a lot more." This, at times, made him feel as if "I was somebody important," and what he was doing "was something special." Jewish youngsters asked for seats behind second base so that they could be close to him, not realizing the practical difficulties with their requests. A Jewish paper, the *Daily Forward*, would explain to its readers that there was no Giants' game today because "Andy must be sick." At the same time the attention sometimes made him "tr[y] too hard to live up to my reputation," and the resultant nervousness led to "some bad moments on the field." He was also not pleased with some of the commentary from the non-Jewish press, which caricatured his nose and eyebrows and said that "he made the mistake of thinking that three strikes were the symbol of his race instead of three balls." After the 1929 season he was sent back to the minor leagues.[24]

As Solomon and Cohen were making their debuts with the Giants in the 1920s, a few ballplayers of Italian descent also began to enter the majors. Ed Abbaticchio and Ping Bodie, both journeymen players, had previously been on major league rosters, but in 1926 the San Francisco Italian community sent to the majors the first of its notable residents,

Tony Lazzeri, whose contract was purchased by the Yankees from Salt Lake City in the Pacific Coast League. In the 1925 season Lazzeri hit .380 with thirty-five home runs and stole thirty bases for Salt Lake City, and in August of that year the Yankees announced that they would be bringing him to spring training.

Along with the conventional *Sporting News* language describing a prospective major leaguer ("He is reputed to have one of the best throwing arms the scouts have looked upon in years, and is rapidly approaching the finished product in fielding"), there was some indication of Lazzeri's ethnic identity. *The Sporting News* spelled his name wrong, a mistake news accounts would consistently make with Italian players in the late 1920s and thirties. In one article Lazzeri was referred to as "La Zerre," and in a second as "La Zerre, Lizziera, Laseri, and Lisiera," with the correct spelling thought to be "Li Zerri." He was also described as a "bronze Italian," "endowed with a splendid physique."[25]

By the 1931 season *The Sporting News* was prepared to maintain that "the Italians have found baseball and they like it." Its column began: "Once it was the boast of every Irish gentleman in the United States that while baseball might be the National Game of this country, it was the sons of Erin who knew best how to play it." But now "the Irish are being challenged right under their noses." Two "young men of Italian forbears," Tony Cuccinello of the Cincinnati Reds and Oscar Melillo of the St. Louis Browns, were leading their respective leagues in the number of fielding chances successfully accepted in a nine-inning game, each with fourteen. In addition, *The Sporting News* pointed out, "[Frank] Crosetti of the Pacific Coast League has been transferred to the New York Americans for 1932," and "[Ernie] Lombardi is making a fine hit as a catcher for Brooklyn." As for Tony Lazzeri, he was "an acknowledged star," and *The Sporting News* had learned how to spell his name.

As in the case of Jewish players, *The Sporting News* found economic ramifications in the emergence of Italians on major league rosters. "Little by little," the column concluded, "[Italians] are making their way into the foreground. In those cities in which there is a large Italian population, there are many boy teams made up of sons of the United States whose parents were born in sunny Italy." The appearance of Italian players in the big leagues would doubtless stimulate fan interest within Italian communities. "The Irish would better beware," *The*

Sporting News suggested. "They will be challenged to prove their racial superiority one of these days." Then the column ended on a note that reflected the ambivalence of commentators toward the ethnic dimensions of baseball. "There are still Smiths and Browns playing," the editorial concluded, "and there always will be. They represent Uncle Sam."[26]

Two years later in 1933 *The Sporting News* decided to emphasize the ameliorist rather than the exclusionist dimensions of ethnicity. In an editorial commenting on information recently released by Henry P. Edwards, the director of the American League Service Bureau, the paper pointed out that players of Irish ancestry were still the predominant ethnic group among major league ballplayers. Of two hundred players, managers, and coaches listed on American League rosters in the 1933 season, thirty-four "ha[d] Irish blood in them," eighteen were "full-blooded Germans," six "ha[d] Indian blood," four were of Italian ancestry, two were French, two were Dutch, and there was one representative each from Luxembourg, Czechoslovakia, Lithuania, Spain, Portugal, and Switzerland. There were also forty-seven players who were "at least half Scotch." The message to be drawn from these statistics was clear enough to *The Sporting News*. "So many polysyllabic names" suggested "what a melting pot the United States has become." Just as "America is the melting pot of all the world," so "is baseball, its national pastime."[27]

Throughout the 1930s ballplayers of Italian descent continued to arrive at the major league level, and *The Sporting News* almost invariably commented on a player's ancestry when discussing him. Thus Oscar Melillo of the Browns, after handling 148 chances without an error in 1932, was described as "the small Italian," and "the fine Italian hand at second."[28] Ernie Lombardi, in an article discussing his hitting prowess and his unique interlocking grip, was called "the big Italian."[29] Ernie Orsatti of the St. Louis Cardinals, in an article discussing his former career as a stunt man in the movies, was referred to as a "colorful wop" who enjoyed "home-cooked spaghetti dinners."[30] When rookie Dolph Camilli joined the Chicago Cubs in 1933 he was described as coming from "North Beach, the same picturesque Italian colony of [San Francisco] which contributed Tony Lazzeri and Babe Pinelli to the major leagues."[31] Tony Cuccinello was characterized as "[a]nother of those plucky Italian lads who have been playing [an] important part in [the] national game during [the] past decade."[32] When Phil

Cavarretta joined the Cubs at the age of eighteen in 1935, *The Sporting News* pointed out that he "was born in an Italian neighborhood near North Avenue, Chicago," was "obliged to forgo spaghetti, ravioli, and other rich dishes . . . due to misery of the stomach," had his name misspelled "more . . . than that of any player in the big time," and, "needless to say, [was] highly popular among members of the Chicago Italian colony."[33]

When Henry Edwards published another listing of the ethnic backgrounds of American Leaguers in 1937, he listed four players as having Jewish ancestry. These were Moe Berg and Al Schacht of the Boston Red Sox, Milton Galatzer of the Cleveland Indians, and Hank Greenberg of the Detroit Tigers.[34] Although there were allegedly enough Italian players in the major leagues to name all-star teams in 1934 and 1935, the number of Jewish players remained quite small. In 1935 Fred Lieb wrote an article in *The Sporting News* detailing the exploits of Jewish major league players, and concluded that there had not yet been "a real outstanding Jewish ball player." At the same time Lieb's article suggested that there might soon be one. The article was prompted by the exploits of Hank Greenberg, and those exploits, like those of Joe DiMaggio, were to prove significant enough to cause commentators, in Greenberg's case, to not so much ignore ethnicity as revise stereotypes.

In the article Lieb indicated that he had previously given some consideration to the question of why Jewish ballplayers had not yet achieved success as major league ballplayers. "It was my theory," he wrote, "that the Jew did not possess the background of sport which was the heritage of the Irish. For centuries, the Jew, in his individual business, had to fight against heavy odds for his success. It sharpened his wit and made him quick with his hands. Therefore, he became an individualist in the sport, and skillful boxer and ring strategist, but he did not have the background to stand out in a sport which is so essentially a team game as baseball."[35]

One wonders whether Lieb was advancing his "theory" with his tongue in his cheek, since it was grounded on ludicrous assumptions (the business experience of Jews made them quicker with their hands?). But in any event he conceded that "in the past few years [the theory] has been knocked into a cocked hat." The reason was the emergence of Hank Greenberg and "lesser Jewish lights," such as "Hank Danning, Buddy Myer, Moe Berg, Milt Galatzer and Phil Weintraub." The "New York Jewish fans," according to Lieb, were "no longer asking why there are no good Jewish ballplayers," but "express[ing] their indignation that Lou Gehrig, rather than their own Hank Greenberg, was picked as the American League's All-Star first baseman."

Lieb's article was accompanied by the first effort to assemble "a first class all-Jewish team," picked from the past and present major leagues. It included Andy Cohen, playing third base, Moe Berg, and Al Schacht as a coach. Jimmy Reese, who died in 1994 at the age of ninety-two, after serving seventy-eight years in major league baseball as a batboy, player, and coach, was listed as a utility infielder. Johnny Kling, a star catcher for the Cubs from 1900 to 1911, was, alongside Greenberg, the most credentialed of the players, but Kling in fact was a Lutheran; it was his wife who was Jewish.[36]

The Lieb article heralded the arrival of Hank Greenberg as a genuine star. Before its appearance most *Sporting News* articles on Jewish players had focused on the interest among New York clubs in signing a player who could attract Jewish fans to the ballparks. Thus in 1932 Harry Brundidge wrote of the consternation John McGraw undoubtedly felt in witnessing the success of James Julius Levey, who had showed up for a tryout with the Giants, only to be rejected because he had no equipment, and had subsequently become the regular shortstop of the St. Louis Browns.[37] Levey was considered, in that year, "one of few Jewish lads making good in [the] big show." Similarly Phil Weintraub's being farmed out to Nashville by the Giants just before the opening of the 1934 season was described as "particularly distressing to the Jewish population of Manhattan." The article on Weintraub elaborated: "That Weintraub boy was the Hebrew star New York has been waiting for. He was to do for the Giants what Moses Solomon, Andy Cohen and others could not do for John McGraw, who was always hunting for a Jewish star—and never finding one to his liking. You can hear the 'oi gewalts' even to this day as the batting average of that boy Weintraub reaches his well-wishers in Manhattan."[38] McGraw had died in early 1934, and in August Weintraub was called up to the Giants. *The Sporting News* reported, "Fate decreed that John McGraw, after his years of searching for a Jewish star, should die before one came along to make a place for himself with the Giants."[39]

Thus by the mid-1930s it was still the case that the arrival of a player of Jewish or Italian extraction in the majors would invariably be accompanied by comments about his ethnic orientation and speculation about whether his presence would attract fans of that "race" to the ballpark. As late as October 1935, *The Sporting News* ran an article on the Yankees' efforts to sign Washington second baseman Buddy Myer because they believed "that the big army of Jewish fans in this tremendous Metropolitan area would be lured into the park by a Jewish star."[40] But very soon the orientation of the press was to undergo a subtle change as Greenberg and DiMaggio entered the majors and established themselves as dominant players and potential Hall of Famers. Their ethnic identity, initially paramount in accounts of their exploits, eventually became overwhelmed by their athletic accomplishments. By the time of their retirements from baseball—Greenberg in the late 1940s and DiMaggio in the early 1950s—both were seen primarily as great players. At the same time Jewish and Italian ethnic status had passed from the realm of the remarked-upon to that of the unremarkable.

◆

The role of Greenberg and DiMaggio in contributing to the transformation of ethnic consciousness in baseball commentary was not accidental, and cannot be explained solely by reference to their success as players. Crucial in the transformation was the fact that Greenberg and DiMaggio became baseball stars at the same time that the implications of being Jewish and being Italian took on added significance, with the rise of ideologically racist totalitarian governments in Italy and Germany, the subsequent estrangement of the United States from those governments, and the coming of World War II. As Italy gradually became an enemy of America in the late thirties and forties, and the genocidal policies of the Nazis toward Jews began to cause anxiety and consternation for American Jews, it became increasingly important for ethnic Americans to demonstrate that they believed in the melting pot theory of ethnicity in America. The best proof of a belief in the melting pot was strident patriotism, as when Italian Americans joined forces against Italy and Jews joined non-Jews in combating Hitler. Along with their baseball accomplishments, Greenberg and DiMaggio were seen as conspicuous patriots.

In 1986 Hank Greenberg was dying of cancer of the kidney. His son Stephen approached the journalist Ira Berkow, who had written a biography of sportswriter Red Smith and ghostwritten baseball player Rod Carew's autobiography. Greenberg had produced a long manuscript of his life, his son told Berkow, and the family was interested in having Berkow shape it for publication. Berkow initially declined but subsequently agreed. By the time he resolved to participate in the project Hank Greenberg was in the last stages of his illness. He died in September 1986, at the age of 75, never having talked with Berkow about the manuscript. When Berkow began to work with what Greenberg had produced, he resolved to leave most of it intact, arranging it chronologically and interspersing it with comments. The result was a window into the consciousness of one of the most reflective and analytical baseball stars of his time.[41]

One of the surprises of Greenberg's autobiography is the evolution of his consciousness of being Jewish. When Greenberg was growing up in the Bronx and developing an interest in baseball despite the skepticism of his parents, he had no particular awareness of the consequences of being Jewish, or of ethnic prejudice. As he put it, "I never thought about anti-Semitism then. . . . I was never aware of the business and social barriers to Jews that existed in this country in the 1920s and 1930s. There was never any talk of anti-Semitism in my neighborhood."[42] Greenberg's father owned a textile plant in Manhattan, and the Greenbergs lived "a fairly middle-class life" in a Jewish settlement, Crotona Park, in the Bronx. His brothers and his sister attended college, and his parents expected him to as well, feeling that baseball was "pretty rowdy." But Greenberg was extraordinarily tall for his age and felt conspicuous about his size. Sports, he said, "was an escape from all that. . . . A big, tall kid was almost required to be an athlete in those days, particularly in public school." Greenberg spent "about 85 percent of my mind and time" on athletics.[43]

In 1934 Greenberg first entered into the consciousness of the baseball world in a substantial fashion. Playing 153 games and hitting fourth in the lineup most of the year, he hit .340 with twenty-four home runs and 139 runs batted in. *The Sporting News* ran an article on him as the World Series opened, calling him the "young Tiger star" and emphasizing his Jewish antecedents. The article described his growing up in the Bronx, playing semi-pro ball, and signing with the Tigers. It then detailed a story of Greenberg's first declining to play on Rosh Hashanah, and then changing his mind when he was assured by some rabbis that playing would not necessarily be sacrilegious. He hit two home runs against the Red Sox that day as the Tigers won the game, 2–1. A writer for the *Detroit Times* had described the event as follows: "There was more than the mighty bone and sinew of Hank Greenberg behind those two home runs which went whistling out of Navin Field. . . . They were propelled by a force born of the desperation and pride of a young Jew who turned his back on the ancient ways of his race and creed to help his teammates. Greenberg said, 'The good Lord did not let me down.'"[44]

The Sporting News called Greenberg's home runs on Rosh Hashanah his "biggest thrill this season," noting that Greenberg had mentioned that in 1933 he had not played on both Rosh Hashanah and another Jewish holy day, Yom Kippur, and "nobody said a word about it." The article ended with a self-conscious description of Greenberg, stating that "there is little suggestion of the Jewish characteristics about his appearance, his nose being straight, and he speaks with more of a Harvard than a so-called East Side accent."[45]

Ten days later Greenberg elected not to play on Yom Kippur. By then the Tigers had increased their hold on first place, so his absence from the lineup was perhaps less vital. The *New York Evening Post* interviewed his family, however, and Greenberg's father was reported as saying that Hank "promised us when we saw him . . . that he would not play on Rosh Hashanah or Yom Kippur. He wrote us later that he was sorry he had played on Rosh Hashanah. . . . Yom Kippur was different. I put my foot down and Henry obeyed."[46]

Greenberg's decision to respect one of the Jewish holy days became a matter of national interest. He later recalled walking into a synagogue "and the place was jammed. The rabbi was davening [praying]. Right in the middle of everything, everything seemed to stop. The rabbi looked up; he didn't know what was going on. And suddenly everyone was applauding. I was embarrassed; I didn't know what to do." The newspaper writer Edgar Guest, who frequently wrote poetry for his columns, composed one on Greenberg's decision not to play, entitled "Speaking of Greenberg." The poem included the lines,

> The Irish didn't like it when they heard of Greenberg's fame
> For they thought a good first basemen should possess an Irish name
> In the early days of April not a Dugan tipped his hat
> Or prayed to see a double when Hank Greenberg came to bat
>
> . . . . .
>
> Come Yom Kippur—holy fast day world wide over to the Jew
> And Hank Greenberg to his teaching and the old tradition true
> Spent the day among his people and he didn't come to play
> Said Murphy to Mulrooney, "We shall lose the game today!"
> "We shall miss him on the infield and shall miss him at the bat
> But he's true to his religion—and I honor him for that!"[47]

The incident contributed to the modification of Greenberg's stance on ethnicity. He had gone from being unconscious of his heritage to, as he put it, "resent[ing] being singled out as a Jewish ballplayer, period." With time, however, he found "myself wanting to be remembered not only as a great ballplayer, but as a great *Jewish* ballplayer." He realized that he had become "a kind of role model" to "a generation of Jewish kids who grew up in the thirties." He had helped "the ballplayer become a respectable citizen," and in the process learned "that he had to set an example for young America, for the kids." Being the first Jewish star gave him his own special constituency, and he came to appreciate it. On one occasion he showed Bud Shaver of the *Detroit Times* a fan letter he had received from a thirteen-year-old Jewish girl, distraught because Max Baer had been defeated for the heavyweight championship by James Braddock and "begg[ing Greenberg] not to fail her or his people."[48]

All during Greenberg's triumphant prewar years he was subjected to regular abuse for being Jewish. Birdie Tebbetts, a catcher on the Tigers at the time, described the situation to Ira Berkow: "There was nobody in the history of the game who took more abuse than Greenberg, unless it was Jackie Robinson. . . . However, Hank was not only equal to it, he was superior to most of the people who were yelling at him."[49] In 1938 Harry Eisenstat, a left-handed pitcher, joined the Tigers. Eisenstat was Jewish and attached himself to Greenberg ("Hank introduced me to a lot of the Jewish people in the Detroit community, and he showed me how to dress"). In a conversation with Ira Berkow, Eisenstat recalled that Greenberg had once told him, "Don't ever use the term, 'because you're Jewish,' if you don't do well. You do well in playing ball, you'll never hear it come up. But if you don't do well, other people will use that as an excuse. It should be more of an incentive to be successful."[50] "Sure there was added pressure being Jewish," Greenberg wrote in his autobiography. "How the hell could you get up to home plate every day and have some son of a bitch call you a Jew bastard and a kike and a sheenie and get on your ass without feeling the pressure? . . . Being Jewish did carry with it a special responsibility."[51]

In 1938, as Greenberg chased after Babe Ruth's record of sixty home runs in a season, eventually hitting fifty-eight, he may have been concerned with the "special responsibility" of being Jewish, but he was unaware of the international implications of his ethnicity. "I didn't pay much attention to Hitler at first," he recalled, "or any of the political goings-on at the time. I was too stupid to read the front pages, and I just went ahead and played. Of course, as time went by, I came to feel that if, as a Jew, I hit a home run, I was hitting one against Hitler."[52] By 1941, in fact, Greenberg had come to realize that baseball paled in significance alongside the challenge of the Axis.

By the opening of the 1941 season Greenberg was an acknowledged star. He had hit .312 in 1939 with thirty-three homers and 112 runs batted in, then followed that up with a .340 average, forty-one homers, and 150 RBIs in 1940, winning the most valuable player award for the second time. As the Tigers began spring training in 1941, however, Greenberg's Detroit draft board classified him 4F, and thereby ineligible for the draft, because of flat feet. The news of his rejection, he remembered, "caused some consternation. The newspapers hounded me and reported that I had bribed the doctor to put me in 4F. They made such a big deal about it that I was reminded of how the press had hounded Jack Dempsey in World War I, trying to make a scapegoat out of him because he wasn't in uniform. He had been called a shirker. I thought that this was what they were trying to do with me."[53] Greenberg persisted, and the draft board reexamined him, pronounced him eligible, and inducted him on May 7, 1941. At the time the United States was not actively involved in the war and Greenberg was called up for only a year, expecting to return for the 1942 season.

After Pearl Harbor, Greenberg decided to reenlist. He told a reporter in Philadelphia on December 9 that "I have not been called back. I'm going back of my own accord. . . . Baseball is out the window as far as I'm concerned."[54] He was the first major league player to enlist after the United States declared war.

Greenberg joined the Air Corps, was sent to Officers Candidate School in Miami, and was commissioned a second lieutenant. For a year and a half he toured the United States for the Flying Training Command, inspecting training programs for aviators. Eventually, realizing he might never see any action, he asked to be transferred to Washington and was eventually sent to the Far East to help establish bases for B-29s in China. He stayed overseas until the middle of 1944, when he was recalled to New York, and spent the rest of the war visiting defense factories in New England. He was discharged in June 1945. In his autobiography he called his wartime service "a long hitch and a wonderful experience." He had played almost no baseball at all since the spring of 1941.

The newspaper reaction to Greenberg's return demonstrated his changed status. Instead of the first Jewish star, he was now the first returning serviceman. Press reports welcomed him back, praised his patriotism, and speculated on whether he could continue to play effectively after so long an absence. An account in the Associated Press, written about a week after Greenberg's discharge, was typical. Whitney Martin of the AP wrote, "The fans wish him well because he always was a gentleman and a credit to the game, and because they admire him for his army record. . . . He will be watched as a symbol of hope to all the other ballplayers in the service who fear their absence from the game might impair their effectiveness and their money-earning capacity."[55] Martin's account referred to Greenberg as "a symbol of hope," not as a Jew, but as a returning serviceman.

Greenberg slowly worked his way back into playing shape, and had the satisfaction of hitting a grand slam home run on the final day of the season to clinch the 1945 pennant for the Tigers. "The best part of that home run," he recalled, was hearing later that the Washington Senators' players, trailing the Tigers by one game and assembled in their clubhouse listening to the Tigers' game on the radio, said after Greenberg's homer, "Goddamn that dirty Jew bastard, he beat us again." "They were calling me all kinds of names behind my back," Greenberg said, "and now they had to pack up and go home, while we were going to the World Series."[56]

From that point on Greenberg's baseball career was largely anticlimactic. He retired in 1948, having saved $300,000 of the $447,000 he had earned playing baseball.[57] Although at the time of his retirement he was only thirty-six, and had played only nine full seasons in the major leagues, he was elected to the Hall of Fame in 1956.

Hank Greenberg was an unusual baseball player. He made the most of his relatively limited physical talents. He took on the "responsibility" of being the first Jewish star, making the insults of his adversaries motivation to maintain his high level of performance. He consistently sought to learn more about the game and to improve his performance. He was a single-minded and tenacious negotiator with owners at a time when players had limited bargaining power. As he matured, and especially after he left baseball for the service, he achieved a certain detachment from the game, so that by the end of his career owners were paying him very high salaries for the privilege of allowing him to retire when he chose. After his retirement he reentered the game from the management side. When he finally left he was financially independent, beholden to no one.

In Greenberg's autobiography he sought to minimize the effects of religion on his life. He pointed out that although he continued to be denied entry to certain clubs because he was Jewish, members of Jewish clubs were themselves prejudiced against non-Jews. He rarely attended synagogue and did not emphasize religion to his children. He suggested that religion had meant little in his own life: for his bar mitzvah, he simply memorized meaningless words in Hebrew.[58] But if "religion," strictly speaking, had not played a central role in Greenberg's life as a ballplayer, being Jewish certainly had. He had been, in many respects, the perfect antidote to anti-Semitic stereotypes; the ideal player to suggest that even Jews could become absorbed into the melting pot.

◆

In his autobiography Greenberg singled out two ballplayers of whom he was "always envious." One was Charley Gehringer, his teammate on the Tigers, who became a Hall of Famer. The other was Joe DiMaggio, who came up with the Yankees in 1936, a year Greenberg was out with a broken wrist. Greenberg said of Gehringer and DiMaggio: "They were just natural hitters, never had to work at it, or so it seemed. They were just born to hit. . . . Joe never went to the gym in the winter, he never worked out, he just kept his weight down and when spring training started, he was ready to hit. . . . Both were very quiet, not outspoken. You couldn't get much out of them, but on the ball field their playing looked effortless."[59]

Joe DiMaggio was in many respects the Italian analogue to Hank Greenberg. He was the first Italian star, establishing his status at precisely the same time that Greenberg came to prominence. His career, like Greenberg's, was interrupted for a stint in military service, which helped to confirm his role as an assimilated ethnic. He was portrayed in the popular press, during the early years of his career, primarily as an Italian ballplayer, and a host of ethnic stereotypes attached themselves to that portrayal. Because of his ballplaying accomplishments, his ethnic identity receded with time, and after his military service it virtually disappeared. Finally, like Greenberg, DiMaggio's persona was anti-stereotypical: he came to appear as an "ordinary,"

Hank Greenberg, far right, and Joe DiMaggio, center, at the 1937 All-Star Game in Washington, photographed with, from left to right, Lou Gehrig, Joe Cronin, Bill Dickey, Charlie Gehringer, and Jimmy Foxx. Notice Greenberg's conspicuous height and DiMaggio's deadpan expression. (National Baseball Library and Archive, Cooperstown, N.Y.)

extremely accomplished ballplayer, not as someone displaying "Italian" characteristics.

There was, however, an essential difference between the public perceptions of DiMaggio and Greenberg, one that reflected the different temperaments of the two players. Greenberg, although not college-educated, was bright, inquisitive, a voracious reader, and increasingly articulate. DiMaggio, a high school dropout, remained taciturn and nondescript his entire career, conforming to his early characterization as "Deadpan Joe." Although DiMaggio was a stubborn negotiator about contracts, he did not, as Greenberg did, write letters to management, propose ingenious financial arrangements, and act the part of the shrewd bargainer. When he retired in 1951 DiMaggio assumed the status of the "average" baseball retiree for his time, serving as a part-time hitting instructor and making ceremonial appearances. He never sought to enter baseball in an executive capacity, and he avoided controversy.

At the same time DiMaggio became a kind of cult hero. His unfortunate marriage to Marilyn Monroe dramatized his conspicuous unfitness for the world of Hollywood celebrities, underscoring his ordinariness. His oddly successful emergence in the 1970s as a spokesman for a drip coffee percolator called "Mr. Coffee" captured his innate lack of pretension. The key to DiMaggio's success as a cult hero after his retirement was that he seemed as modest, as "regular," and as limited a personality as he had as a ballplayer. The 1967 Simon and Garfunkel song, "Mrs. Robinson," from the movie *The Graduate*, contained these famous lines: "Where have you gone, Joe DiMaggio / A nation turns its lonely eyes to you." It suggested that DiMaggio was a hero and a symbol of a more innocent, less sordid past. "It has something to do with heroes," songwriter Paul Simon said of the couplet. "People who are all good and no bad in them at all. That's the way I always saw Joe DiMaggio."[60]

In searching for an explanation of the different perceptions of Greenberg and DiMaggio in the years after their retirement, it becomes clear that one dimension of the melting pot theory of ethnicity in baseball emphasized a blending of the player's ethnic identity in a stereotype of baseball averageness. In retirement DiMaggio made no effort to be seen as other than a former player. In a 1979 article he was quoted as saying, "For a guy whose only real talent was on the ballfield, I've made out fine." In a sense the melting pot theory expected that baseball ethnics would submerge their ethnic identity not just in the identity of an American, but of an American ballplayer. Greenberg had done more than that: he had sought to transcend ballplayer status. As a consequence he became, after leaving active playing status, something of a contentious figure. DiMaggio remained "humble" and beloved.

Unlike Greenberg's early struggles in the minor leagues, DiMaggio was a sensation nearly from the start of his career. In 1933, at the age of eighteen, he played his first full professional season for the San Francisco Seals, hitting .340 with twenty-eight home runs and 169 runs batted in. Most remarkable, he hit safely in sixty-one consecutive games. By July *The Sporting News* had discovered him, calling him a "phenom" and an "exceptional kid" and spelling his name wrong. When he reached fifty games he was referred to as "the find of the season." This was also the first characterization of him as "Deadpan Joe," "so-called because his face remains expressionless while he slams the ball to all parts of the field." The same article noted that DiMaggio "had never had a day's experience in any kind of professional baseball" before the 1933 season.[61]

Just before his second Yankee season, in March 1936, Dan Daniel of the *New York World-Telegram* described DiMaggio as being "from the spaghetti society of romantic San Francisco," and referred to him as "Giuseppe."[62] The next day the *New York Daily News* described DiMaggio as "the Italian rookie."[63] On March 18 Joe Williams wrote in the *World-Telegram*, apparently in an effort at humor, that Yankee manager Joe McCarthy "extended the hand of sympathy to Emperor Haile Selassie of Ethiopia today. It seems that the Italians are causing him some concern too."[64] Williams's reference was to DiMaggio's supposed inability to hit the ball to all fields. On May 2 the *New York Times* labeled DiMaggio "the Coast Italian." [65]

This treatment of DiMaggio culminated in a June 13 cover article in *Time*. The article stressed DiMaggio's membership in a large Italian family from San Francisco. It recalled his older brother Tom advising him to pursue baseball rather than work on his father's fishing boat, how he sent most of his salary home to his parents, how he had bought another brother, Mike, a fishing boat with his earnings, and how, in general, his attitude, "like many young brothers in large Italian families," was "characterized by a solemn, almost embarrassing humility which is exceedingly useful because it causes his elders and superiors to take paternal interest in him." *Time* asserted that DiMaggio, in his first season in the big leagues, was "already almost as much a hero as Ruth used to be," and that "most . . . of his fan mail . . . comes from Italian well-wishers."[66]

After the 1937 season DiMaggio capitalized on his new-found celebrity status by making a movie, called "Manhattan Merry-Go-Round." DiMaggio's role consisted of a cameo appearance in which he delivered, according to the *New York Times*, a "self-conscious monologue about baseball."[67] While working on the picture he met Dorothy Arnold, an aspiring actress, whom he would marry in 1939. He also resolved to secure a substantial raise from the Yankees, having clearly lived up to their expectations for his performance on the field.

We have seen that most of the publicized or protracted salary disputes between players and owners in the early years of baseball involved such stars as Ruth, Cobb, and Walter Johnson, who had reputations for being hard bargainers, as did Greenberg. The wonder, in fact, is how few stars engaged in protracted salary negotiations. Honus Wagner, Christy Mathewson, Lou Gehrig, and many others quietly accepted their clubs' terms, which in some instances involved pay cuts that bore no relationship to their performance. In the early 1930s Gehrig's salary was cut, after he had had a particularly impressive year, because of the Depression; Gehrig apparently did not protest.

DiMaggio was well aware of his status as a potential box-office draw, and in the early years of his career consistently agitated for more money. In 1938 the Yankees offered him $25,000, and he held out for much more, a reported $40,000. The Yankees declined to adjust their figure, and DiMaggio remained in San Francisco during spring training. Eventually he signed for $25,000, and when he returned to the lineup in late April was surprised to find the fans booing him. The fact that his salary was among the highest in baseball and most Americans were experiencing financial problems may have contributed to the situation. DiMaggio was puzzled and hurt by the fans' reaction, complaining to local writers and resolving, he said later, "never again to be [the] target" of fans. He was to have additional contract disputes in the future, but was not to miss spring training again.[68]

As the Second World War broke out DiMaggio was married, with a child, and seemed in little danger of being drafted. But, as in the case of Greenberg, pressure mounted on him and other baseball stars to join the war effort, and eventually, in February 1943, he enlisted in the Air Force. Unlike Greenberg, he neither sought nor participated in combat, spending the war playing baseball and making appearances before troops. The war years, during which his marriage to Dorothy Arnold collapsed, nonetheless took their toll on him, and he was hospitalized for a duodenal ulcer that had first surfaced in 1940.[69]

DiMaggio's participation in the war, and the ethnic implications of that participation, precipitated a decisive transformation in his public image. Before the war his Italian background had been consistently emphasized in articles, with the treatment regularly indulging in ethnic stereotypes. As the United States entered the war, with Italy on the side of the Axis powers, the full import of DiMaggio's being an Italian-

American was grasped, and his commitment to the Allied cause embraced as proof of the validity of the melting pot theory. DiMaggio's success as a major league ballplayer, and the associated success of his brothers Vincent and Dominic, who had both joined major league teams by the early 1940s, was offered as proof of the capacity of Italian immigrants to become "good Americans," and a resultant argument against making Italians on the west coast subject to being relocated to detention centers, as Japanese were in 1942. Then after the war, when DiMaggio returned to baseball and retained his status as a heroic celebrity, his ethnicity seemed to vanish: he was portrayed simply as a model ballplayer, an embodiment of the values of the national pastime, not as an Italian.

In January 1942 Congress considered reclassifying Italian-American aliens as "enemies" and restricting their movements, particularly on the west coast. In testimony before the Select House Committee Investigating National Defense Migration, Congressman John Tolan, committee chairman, asked Chauncey Tramulto, a San Francisco attorney, to describe the impact of reclassification on Giuseppe DiMaggio, Joe's father. Tramulto responded by noting that although neither Giuseppe nor Joe's mother were American citizens, they had reared nine children, eight of whom had been born in the United States and the ninth of whom was naturalized, and three of the DiMaggio brothers were major league baseball players. "To evacuate the senior DiMaggios," Tramulto concluded, "would, in view of the splendid family they have reared, . . . present . . . a serious situation." In October 1942, the executive order classifying Italian aliens as "enemies" was rescinded.[70]

When DiMaggio returned from service to rejoin the Yankees for the 1946 season, he was to have only six more years as a ballplayer. He did not play at his prewar levels, batting a cumulative .304 and averaging twenty-two home runs a season. He was beset by injuries, including bone spurs on both heels, a sore arm, and strained muscles. He continued to play through the discomfort at a respectable level, hitting under .300 in only two seasons. In 1947, coming back from a subpar 1946 season, he hit .315 in 141 games, made only one error in the field, and was named the league's most valuable player for the third time. And in 1949, after operations on his throwing arm and one of his heels, he hit .346, even though by the end of season he was ill with a viral infection. In 1949 he made $90,000 and the next year $100,000. A poll of

Yankee players taken before the 1950 season revealed that an overwhelming number of his teammates saw him as their "baseball model" and thought he was well worth his salary.[71]

◆

The transformation of DiMaggio's ethnicity in popular literature paralleled but did not duplicate that of Greenberg's. Although Greenberg's superstar status, his large size, his aggressiveness, and his involvement in World War II served to make him into an assimilated ethnic, he remained subject to anti-Semitic barbs and exclusionary practices, both as a player and as a baseball executive, and ultimately came to take pride in being a role model for Jews. Greenberg retained an edge in his personal relationships, one nurtured on self-consciousness and aggressiveness, that colored others' perception of him. Sometimes the prickliness of his relationships, and his conspicuous success, resulted in his ethnic identity never fully being submerged.

By DiMaggio's retirement his ethnic identity had been fully associated with assimilationist themes, so that he was no longer thought of as an "Italian" but as a "poor immigrant boy who had gained success through his baseball talents." Because of his own muted, reclusive personality, any strains or edges in DiMaggio's temperament that could have been attributed to ethnic stereotyping had disappeared from public view. He had, to all appearances, completely internalized the role of the "humble," team-playing superstar, uncomplaining, uncontroversial, leading by example. This role was so consistent with idealized expectations for the performance of baseball players—even superstars did not hold out in spring training—that DiMaggio's persona became virtually stripped of ethnic identity. The fact that he fought through injuries, never bad-mouthed his teammates or management, never let up on the field, and spoke in baseball clichés to the press made him appear as the personification of a stereotype, one that had no ethnic dimensions.

Greenberg and DiMaggio showed the strains as well as the rewards of the melting pot theory of ethnicity in baseball. Their ethnic status, the fact that they were the first conspicuously successful ballplayers from their ethnic group, helped propel them to stardom. Their apparent ability to slough off ethnic traces, to become assimilationist figures, helped them as well: they came to be seen as "great" ballplayers as well as Jewish ballplayers or Italian ballplayers. They acquiesced in the demands of the assimilationist ethic, such as enlisting in World War II when neither was compelled to and neither would probably have been drafted into combat. As a result they ended up being heroes and role models for persons not only within but outside their ethnic groups.

But Greenberg was never allowed to forget the fact that he was Jewish, and he spent much of his career trying to sort out how he felt about his religion and how he could most profitably deal with the constant ethnic abuse he endured. For a time he adopted DiMaggio's response of tunnel vision, concentrating his energies on baseball and not thinking about much else. When the Second World War came, at the height of his career, and he realized he was fated to participate, he approached the experience as an opportunity to broaden his horizons. The result was that he began to see baseball differently, and the benefits of star player status did not seem to outweigh the costs he encountered by being a player under the reserve system and a Jew in a game without any other Jewish superstars. When he came to those perceptions he began to think in terms of pride and independence. He found those values inconsistent with the status of being a Jewish baseball player.

DiMaggio's calibration of the costs and benefits of being a prominent baseball ethnic seems to have been less self-conscious. But it was clear that although he was prepared to subsume his ethnic identity in the role of an All-American baseball star, there were limits to the extent he would depart familiar and comfortable environments for ones more in keeping with the life of a celebrity. He hovered around those environments, venturing in and then recoiling. In another era, one in which ethnic assimilation and the melting pot theory were less dominant cultural presences, DiMaggio might have married someone reminiscent of his youth, carved out a conventional, familiar private life, and still maintained his status as an exceptionally accomplished ballplayer. That was not possible for him, or perhaps he was disinclined to go that route. In any event, in both him and in Greenberg a sense of vulnerability, associated with the strains of being a prominent ethnic pioneer, lingers.

For the national pastime, however, the official messages of Greenberg's and DiMaggio's careers were obvious enough. They had become superstars and Hall of Famers by demonstrating that, at one level, a man's ethnic status was inconsequential if the man could play ball. That message was a simple and, in some ways, a salutary one. But it had a tacit corollary, that recognizing the irrelevancy of a ballplayer's ethnic origins to his ability to participate at the major league level meant that ethnicity was entirely irrelevant to the ballplayer as well as to his contemporaries. That corollary was false, and the melting pot theory illusory, both in baseball and elsewhere. Hank Greenberg and Joe DiMaggio were both ethnics and ballplayers, and there were things to celebrate about them in both capacities. They were given a message that only one sort of celebration was appropriate.

9

The Enterprise, 1923–1953

IN THE WINTER of 1945–46 baseball executives surveyed what promised to be a new, and revitalized, landscape for their game. With the close of World War II a flood of players was expected to return to the major and minor leagues, and club owners anticipated an end to stopgap measures to maintain baseball as a profitable entertainment, such as the creation of a women's professional baseball league,[1] or the appearance on major league rosters of players not eligible for wartime service—including a one-armed outfielder, Pete Gray of the St. Louis Browns, and several players whose only claim to fame was that they were too old to be drafted. With peace, and hopefully prosperity, a new era in the economic history of baseball was perhaps anticipated.

Had the magnates of baseball been exceptionally prescient on surveying the landscape of their enterprise as World War II ended, they might have been both reassured and puzzled. In many respects the enterprise of Organized Baseball resembled, in the winter of 1945, the entity that had survived a challenge to its monopsonistic structure in the 1922 *Federal Baseball* case. The three organizing principles of the enterprise, the reserve clause, blacklisting of "ineligible" players, and territoriality, were still intact. Despite those principles, baseball still enjoyed immunity from the antitrust laws: it was still, in the parlance of *Federal Baseball*, sport rather than trade or commerce, a series of local rather than interstate exhibitions. The primary purposes of the 1903 National Agreement—to prevent "ruinous" competition by sanctioning "contract jumping," to maintain civic identity through the creation of territorial monopolies and the maintenance of relatively constant player rosters, and to avoid radical competitive imbalance by binding players to certain clubs unless those clubs sought to dispose of the players—were still being effectuated.

A hypothetically prescient club owner might also have taken comfort in noticing that in other respects the enterprise of baseball in the winter of 1945 looked very much like its counterpart in 1923. All of the original franchises created by the National Agreement remained extant: the American and National Leagues each contained the same eight clubs, in the same cities, that they had in 1903. With the wave of early twentieth-century ballpark construction, every major league city now had a concrete and steel stadium that had been built or significantly rebuilt since 1908. Only one of the early parks, Baker Bowl in Philadelphia, was no longer in use, although the Cleveland Indians would soon take up the option of playing in Municipal Stadium. Transportation around the leagues was the same, by train, and schedules the same, featuring regularized eastern and western swings by clubs, who took road trips in two- and three-week intervals. Finally, the hierarchy of Organized Baseball's officialdom was the same that had replaced the National Commission in 1921: a commissioner's office; league presidents; and the National Association of Professional Baseball Leagues, which governed the minors but accepted the commissioner's authority. Each professional club in Organized Baseball had a place in the hierarchy, and had its practices regulated by the enterprise's governing principles. Commissioner Kenesaw Mountain Landis had died in November 1944 and was replaced by Albert B. ("Happy") Chandler, but the arbitrary power of the office to make rulings "in the best interest of baseball" remained intact.

In short, in the midst of dramatic cultural changes through 1945, including two world wars, a major depression, and the emergence of the automobile and the airplane, Organized Baseball seemed to have maintained an essential continuity. At the same time, however, a magnate, had he looked closely around him in the winter of 1945, might have seen the foreshadowing of developments that threatened to alter permanently the state of the enterprise. Two such developments had already surfaced, although their impact was yet to be felt in massive proportions. Night baseball had been in the major leagues for ten years, although it had not yet become commonplace, transforming the schedules of players and fans and tying baseball more closely to the leisure hours of Americans on conventional work shifts. Baseball was now being broadcast regularly on the radio and had been shown on television, but the immense revenue potential of media rights had yet to be realized by club owners.

Black players were still banned from the game, and the Negro Leagues were at the height of their popularity, but integration of the major leagues and the subsequent collapse of the Negro Leagues was only two years away. Although some owners in 1945 might have suspected that integration was at hand, it is fair to say that none anticipated the tremendous impact black ballplayers would have on the game in the fifties and sixties, or the comparable impact Latin American players would have in subsequent decades. Nor could those club owners who came to endorse integration because of an anticipated upsurge in black fan attendance have seen that the upsurge would be only temporary, and that the great success of black players would not be matched in a longstanding attachment of urban blacks to the game.

By 1955 a suit by two Yankee pitchers who had been blacklisted for declining to agree to salary terms reached the Supreme Court, which reaffirmed the conclusion in the *Federal Baseball* case that baseball was exempt from the antitrust laws until Congress decided to include it within their coverage. Congress, for its part, took no action, preserving baseball's status as the only professional sport with antitrust immunity. It appeared that the essential continuity of the enterprise of baseball in the twentieth century would remain. But within twenty years the reserve clause and its blacklisting practices had vanished, free agency had been established in the major leagues, and the fifty-year territorial continuity of the American and National Leagues had been shattered. No outside agency had set the forces in motion that produced these massive changes: they had been initiated by developments within baseball itself.

At the same time that the owners of baseball franchises were straining to defeat challenges to the reserve clause and lobbying to retain the sport's antitrust exemption, they were willingly, even eagerly, encouraging one another to take advantage of the escalating value of media rights to their games and to move economically depressed franchises into more lucrative markets. After insisting on the integrity of the original territorial sphere carved out for major league baseball in 1903, they suddenly abandoned that sphere in 1953, allowing franchises to move at will. Several did, all to potentially more lucrative markets, tracking important shifts in the American population after World War II. Meanwhile the broadcasting and televising of baseball games grew at a rapid pace, and owners learned that at the major league level, at least, radio and television significantly added to their coffers.

New, enthusiastic groups of fans and new revenue from broadcasting and television rights also swelled those coffers in the fifties and sixties. The owners had more money to spend on player salaries, and they spent it. Baseball players began to realize that their earning potential was both considerable and finite: they and others, lawyers and sports agents, began to see themselves increasingly as salaried professionals. Following the lead of other groups in the labor force after World War II, they began to organize. Eventually they themselves began to see the potential advantage of a "market" system for player salaries, just as the owners had seen the advantage of comparable systems for media rights and franchise locations. Ultimately they mounted organized challenges to the reserve clause and blacklisting; ultimately those challenges were successful.

The result was that by 1953, when it appeared that baseball was very much the same enterprise it had been in 1923, or even, in some respects, 1903, it was in fact already on its way to becoming a radically different enterprise, one whose three governing legal and economic principles were already degenerating, and would disappear entirely in the next twenty years.

◆

In the relatively quiescent world of baseball labor relations between the 1920s and World War II, there was one persistent area of contention: the role of the minor leagues in the structure of the overall enterprise. The debate focused on two issues, the legitimacy of allowing major league clubs to draft players from minor league rosters and the appropriateness of major league clubs owning minor league teams outright, in a so-called "chain store" or "farming" arrangement.

The debate over the draft, which produced a number of inconclusive "agreements" and compromises between the minor and major leagues in the 1920s, is difficult to reconstruct or even to fathom today, especially because everyone involved in the debate conceded that the primary purpose of minor league clubs was to provide an ongoing supply of players to the majors. Nonetheless the debate continued apace, and with hindsight provides a good example of the economic assumptions from which participants in the enterprise of Organized Baseball viewed labor issues.

Minor leagues were already in place when the National Agreement was entered into in 1903, and they continued in existence throughout the twentieth century, rising and falling in numbers and affluence. The years before World War I represented the high point of the minors, in terms of the number of leagues in operation, and World War I their low point. In 1912 over forty minor leagues existed, but the number had fallen to nine in 1918, the precipitous decline a function of the emergence of the Federal League and the impact of the war on attendance.[2] Some minor league franchises, and some leagues, operated on shoestrings, fading in and out of existence; other franchises, such as the Baltimore Orioles and the Newark Bears in the International League, or the Los Angeles Angels in the Pacific Coast League, were conspicuously successful.

The entrepreneurial motives of minor league club owners were many and varied, but the value of their franchises was decisively affected by the value of their players. Although some minor league teams drew well at the gate, the largest share of their revenues came not from fan attendance but from the sale of their players to major league clubs. The minor leagues were indispensable to the majors for player development, since once a major league season started the clubs had no time to devote to developing prospects. Although baseball had been played in colleges since before the National Agreement, the number of players coming from college teams to the majors remained small, an interesting fact in itself.[3] Both the minor and major leagues, then, had an overriding common goal, that of funneling players from the minors to the majors.

Beyond that common goal, the interests of the minor and major leagues seemed not particularly compatible, and this combination of a common end and apparently clashing means fueled the longstanding debate over the minor league draft. Between 1921, when Landis assumed office, and 1931, when an enduring agreement was eventually reached, the minors and the majors periodically clashed over the issue of major league drafting of minor league players. Makeshift agreements were reached in 1921, 1922, 1923, and 1928, producing discontent from both sides and consequent agitation for change. Between December 1920 and December 1931 *The Sporting News* ran over fifty articles, columns, and editorials on the draft issue, more than any other single topic involving the enterprise of Organized Baseball in that time period.

The agitation over the draft issue at first glance seems out of proportion to its impact, since at no time during the debate was there a proposal to permit the major league clubs to draft any more than two players from any minor league club, and the number of players drafted in a single season never exceeded twenty. But the idea of a minor league draft touched off fundamental clashes about what baseball was all about. One perspective, typified by that of owner Jack Dunn of the International League Baltimore Orioles, treated a draft as inimical to the freedom of owners to buy and sell their players in the marketplace. Dunn had made a career of developing bright prospects and selling them to the highest bidder, and he resisted any efforts to institute a draft that affected the International League. A contrasting perspective was that of Commissioner Landis, who consistently advocated a "universal" draft (one in which any player from any minor league club could be drafted by the majors, subject to rules of compensation) as the fairest and most efficient way of securing talent for major league clubs and furthering the career advancement of minor league ballplayers. Between these two poles of opinion there ranged a variety of other views, reflecting the sometimes incompatible goals of player development and profits for minor league franchises.

From the early twentieth century on, the minor leagues had been divided into classified levels of franchises, allegedly approximating the caliber of play in a given minor league.[4] The classifications were designed to facilitate player development, but they also served to establish compensation rules for drafted players and limits on the number of players that could be drafted. In 1911 an agreement was reached dividing the minors into AA, A, B, C, and D-level leagues, fixing compensation levels ($2,500 for an AA player, $1,500 for an A player, and so on down to $500 for a D-league player) and limiting the capacity of the majors to draft more than a designated number of players from the higher minor leagues (only one player per team from AA clubs).

These agreements were repeatedly tinkered with through the 1920s, and in 1921 two new features were incorporated into the agreement established that year. In addition to being allowed to draft players, the major leagues, and the minors as well, were permitted to farm players off their roster to a lower level league club for a limited period. Moreover, certain minor leagues were permitted to opt out of the draft altogether in exchange for giving up their right to draft players from lower leagues.

In that compromise agreement one can clearly see the perceived incompatibility of the goals of player development and profit making. Those minor leagues who chose to opt out of the draft signaled that their primary interest was retaining control over all their players in order to sell them. The majors and some minor leagues, on the other hand, wanted the opportunity to farm players so they could develop more fully in a lower league. The agreement also demonstrated the superior bargaining position of the high minor league clubs. In addition to choosing to opt out of the draft, they were allowed to farm larger numbers of players than their lower-level counterparts. They also were protected from having the majors draft more than a designated number of players. Thus a high-level opting-out league, such as the International League, could sell players to the highest bidder, farm as many as six players to lower-level clubs, and keep all of its players from being drafted. On the other end of the spectrum, a class D-level league could not protect any of its players from being drafted, but could expect that many of the high minor league clubs would not draft those players.

Opponents of modified draft agreements argued that they had the effect of retarding player development, and one can see how this might have been so. Having given up their right to draft players from lower-level leagues, the high minors had committed themselves to having to buy as well as to sell players in the open market. They were thus less likely to pluck a promising player from a lower league, since that player was now going to be sold at the going rate. Although any league could buy and sell players in addition to drafting them, the major leagues could draft lower-level players at will. The system thus appeared to ensure that once a player appeared on a low-level league roster, he was only likely to proceed up to the level of drafting leagues, and then would either be bought by a high minor league club or be drafted into the majors. Unless a major league club had an exceptional scouting system, it was unlikely to draft a player from a low-level minor league team before he had seen some service in the high minors.

It became quickly apparent to the major league clubs that they were not faring well under the 1921 arrangement, and they sought to pressure the exempt high minors into allowing them to draft certain players from their rosters in exchange for agreeing to option or release a given number of players to those leagues. All the exempt high minor leagues except the International League capitulated to this pressure in 1923, and even the International League accepted the proposal beginning with the 1925 season. Nonetheless the majors continued to complain of the excessive costs of having to buy rather than to draft players from the high minor leagues for the rest of the decade.

Eventually, in 1931, taking advantage of the adverse impact on the minors of the depressed economy, the major leagues effectively forced the exempt high minors to reenter the draft, and established a "universal" draft. Their payment for these new privileges was of three kinds, reflecting the conflicting goals of the minor league system. To alleviate the high minors from the loss of revenue that followed from their power to sell players on the free market, the majors increased the compensation for drafted players to $7,500 for AA players. They also agreed only to draft one player per high minor league club per year, ensuring that a wholesale raiding of minor league rosters would not take place and that each player on such rosters was worth at least $7,500.

Those concessions were aimed at the use of minor league players as revenue devices. Other concessions were oriented toward roster continuity in the minors and player development. The majors agreed to option as many as fifteen players to the minors a year, and not to draft players from designated levels of minor leagues until those players had been in the minors for a certain length of time (four years for a Class AA player, three years for a Class A player). This meant that a promising minor league player would have to remain in the minors for a certain length of time before he could be drafted, thereby preventing minor league rosters from being depleted and hopefully ensuring that the minor leagues would have time and incentives to develop their players. If a minor league club had an exceptional player on its roster, it was not prevented from selling him, and could even attach as a condition of the sale that the player remain with his minor league club for a designated period. We have seen that although Joe DiMaggio was sold by the San Francisco Seals to the Yankees in 1934, he remained with the Seals for another year before entering the big leagues.

In the major leagues' anxiety to avoid having to pay exorbitant prices for minor league players, and the minor league club owners' comparable anxiety to maintain their freedom to gain the maximum amount of revenue from their player assets, two dimensions of minor league baseball seemed to be getting shortshrifted. One, of course, was the desire for players to reach the major leagues. The 1931 agreement actually made it more likely than any of the previous draft agreements that players would remain for long periods in the minors by prescribing a certain time of minor league residency before a minor league player was eligible to be drafted. Since players on major league rosters could be optioned to the minors as many as three times, a given player could remain in the minors for four years, be drafted by a big-league team, then sent back down for three more years before he could be claimed by another major league club.

The successive agreements between 1921 and 1931 also had the effect of making it clear that minor league teams would have continually fluctuating rosters, affecting the caliber of the teams' play and their capacity to develop a civic identity. Minor league entrepreneurs who shared the orientation and attitudes of Jack Dunn relied on their skill in scouting and player development to maintain their clubs at a high level of performance. In Dunn's case the Orioles consistently performed well. But the personnel on the Orioles at any given time was not constant. Baltimore fans were in effect given the promise of a regularly competent ballclub in exchange for continuity of personnel.

On the whole, the established baseball press favored universalizing the minor league draft over the course of the debate, citing the adverse impact of exempt leagues and a restricted draft on the opportunities of players to advance in their profession. *The Sporting News* made its position clear in a December 20, 1923, editorial, and never modified it throughout the subsequent lengthy debate. "There is one fundamental principle involved in the draft," the paper announced, "and that is a ball player entering upon his 'profession' and under the system that prevails signing his life away when he puts his name to his first contract, shall be 'guaranteed' an opportunity to advance to the highest pinnacle in his profession. Without the draft [a club] can by impossible demands block the player's progress."[5] On the other hand, three years later *The Sporting News* conceded that "one of the free and inalienable rights of baseball" was that of "any league to say that it will be drafted upon or not." Since this right conflicted with "the right of ball players to advance in their calling," the paper predicted that "this draft matter is not likely to be settled to the general satisfaction of everybody as long as there is baseball."[6]

It is interesting that in the debate over the minor league draft all of the participants, whatever their position, employed the language of "rights" and individualism. Players had the right to advance; leagues had the right to opt out of the draft; minor league club owners had the right to sell their players to the highest bidder; major league clubs had the right to protest being offered mediocre players for exorbitant prices. The use of rights language in the debate had two effects. First, as *The Sporting News* recognized, it rendered the draft issue an intractable one, since the rights of one side invariably conflicted with the rights of the other. Theoretically, it was not possible to resolve the draft issue without at least one set of rights being sacrificed. The issue might have been more profitably explored by seeing it as a practical problem of labor relations in which the interests of players, minor league owners, and major league owners were both complementary and opposed. Instead commentators on both sides fulminated about rights and Americanism.

Second, and more important, the use of rights language obscured two embedded features of the enterprise of Organized Baseball that were the driving forces behind the conflict over a universal draft. The first feature was the reserve clause and its attendant blacklisting practices. The reason that a player, once in the minor league system, was beholden to the whim of the club owner for his advancement was simply because he himself could not negotiate with any other club or owner for his services. He was "reserved" by the club: only the club could dispose of him. In short, baseball players had no rights of advancement. If it was un-American to keep a ballplayer from reaching the highest levels of his profession, the reserve clause was un-American.

The second feature was the ability of major league club owners to exercise ultimate control of the form of their arrangements with minor league clubs. The practical facts of player development in Organized Baseball were that the worth of a minor league player was principally dependent on some major league club wanting his services. If no major league team wanted a player, however attractive he might be to his minor league club and its fans, his value was significantly reduced. The minor leagues were dependent on the majors for their existence. The major leagues were not comparably dependent on the minors. They relied upon them for player development, but, as we will see, if the price of minor league players became too high, or their opportunities to secure good minor leaguers became too limited, they could resort to other development options.

In the debate over an unrestricted draft, then, the major league club owners were bound to prevail. Their self-interest in obtaining minor league players for the lowest possible rate coincided with that of the players in advancing their careers, but ultimately even the strongest minor leagues were too dependent on the majors to resist. There was extensive talk of rights in the debate, but in the end economic power prevailed. The minors were in too precarious a position to hold out against the majors indefinitely because they were too dependent on the majors for their revenues, and their dependency on the majors followed from the obvious fact that it was baseball at the major league level that most Americans cared about. Thus when Jack Dunn, who had "developed a great many great players at Baltimore," decided one year to "stand pat on a satisfactory team, refusing to even sell a player," John Sheridan of *The Sporting News* attacked the action as "an evil effect upon development and progression of baseball talent in half of Organized Baseball."[7]

◆

The power of major league club owners in the enterprise they had fashioned was made even more apparent by another development affecting the minor leagues that occurred as the debate over the draft was playing itself out. Sheridan had cited the "exorbitant prices" demanded by minor league clubs for "average prospects" as a reason for instituting a universal draft. Some major league club owners found "exorbitant prices" for minor league players not the worst evil of the system. A canny minor league owner, made aware of a major league club's interest in one of his players, could alert other, wealthy clubs about that interest, hoping to spark a bidding war for the player's services. In the resulting bidding less solvent clubs often found themselves unable to compete. This was particularly galling when they had invested time identifying the player in the first place.

One major league club that found itself too often in that position, in the years after World War I, was the St. Louis Cardinals, whose general manager (and briefly field manager) at the time was Branch Rickey. The Cardinals' economic situation was a result of the major leagues having wedded themselves so firmly to a geographically rigid version of territoriality. Drawing on a relatively small population base, especially in the years before interstate highways, and forced to compete with the Browns for fan support, the Cardinals, in the years immediately after World War I, were among the National League's less affluent franchises, still in the process of repaying debts accumulated by their previous owner, Helene Britton.[8]

Later in his life Branch Rickey recalled the frustration he encountered on first joining the Cardinals immediately after World War I, when the minor league draft was suspended for a time and a free market for minor league players' services governed. Rickey, a former athletic director at Ohio Wesleyan University, had numerous contacts in college baseball and was often tipped off about promising young players by those contacts. But when the Cardinals expressed interest in a minor league prospect, the owner of the club holding the player under contract often took that interest as a signal of his marketability and informed other clubs. Rickey could not outbid wealthier clubs, such as the New York Giants, Chicago Cubs, or Pittsburgh Pirates in his league, and frequently witnessed his discovery going to one of his competitors.[9]

Rickey resolved to address this problem by becoming, in effect, a minor league club owner himself. Modifying a practice already known as "farming" that had existed prior to World War I, Rickey began purchasing, on behalf of the Cardinals, limited interests in minor league clubs, beginning with Fort Smith, Arkansas, in the Class C Western League and Houston in the Class A Texas League. He received the interests for comparatively little money and quickly entered into informal agreements with the minor league teams—colloquially known as farming agreements—by which they would give the Cardinals right of first refusal on promising ballplayers. The purchase of interests in minor league franchises by major league clubs had been sanctioned by the 1921 agreement reinstituting the draft, but no one anticipated that a major league team would involve itself as widely and deeply in the minors as did the Cardinals under Rickey.

By 1925 the Cardinals had acquired a controlling interest in Syracuse in the International League as well as Fort Smith and Houston. By the mid-1930s they controlled two other AA clubs, Columbus in the American Association and Sacramento in the Pacific Coast League. By 1940 they owned fifteen clubs outright and had working agreements with seventeen others. At the height of their farm system

Branch Rickey in a characteristically didactic pose in the early 1940s, when his St. Louis Cardinal farm system, opposed by Commissioner Landis, was in its most expansive phase. (Bettman Archive)

expansion the Cardinals controlled over six hundred players and either owned or had a working agreement with a team in every Class D league in the nation. They also had made it clear that their interest in the minor league teams they owned or controlled was entirely in terms of profit and player development. This was brought home sharply in 1928, when Rickey moved the International League's Syracuse franchise to Rochester, attracted by the prospect of a new stadium financed by local interests. Rochester became a conspicuously successful International League franchise; Syracuse was left without a team for six years.

The key to the Cardinals' farm or chain store system, under Rickey, was the same as that of the Baltimore Orioles under Jack Dunn: successful scouting and player development. As the system became profitable, the Cardinals plowed money back into it, refurbishing ballparks, adding lights, and conducting widespread tryouts.[10] Their lowest-level clubs regularly lost money, but the system as a whole made up for it. Through their farm system the Cardinals developed a stockpile of talent at the minor league level, just as Dunn's Orioles had done. The difference between the two operations was less marked than it might have seemed. Both Rickey and Dunn wanted to produce winning baseball for their home teams and to make profits as well. In Dunn's case he achieved this through the discovery and grooming of good players, and their eventual sale to the majors. In Rickey's case his best players were intended for the Cardinal roster, but as the Cardinals' stockpile grew, Rickey found he could sell off minor leaguers in the Cardinals' system who had talent but whose prospects for the major league club were restricted by established players.

The success of the Cardinals under Rickey's general managership was impressive, both in terms of performance and profitability. The team won National League pennants in 1926, 1928, 1930, 1934, and 1942, winning three World Series in that time span, and were regularly in the first division. Rochester won International League pennants in 1928, 1929, 1930, 1931, and 1940. The farm system produced such major league stars as Jim Bottomley, Pepper Martin, Dizzy and Paul Dean, Tex Carleton, Joe Medwick, Johnny Mize, Mickey Owen, Terry Moore, Enos Slaughter, Mort and Walter Cooper, Stan Musial, Marty Marion, and Harry Walker. Most of these played for the Cardinals on championship teams, but others were sold at large sums to competitors. The Giants bought Mize for $50,000; the Cubs bought Dizzy Dean in 1938 for $185,000.[11] In both cases the cost of acquiring the players had been part of the cost of acquiring farm teams. By the late 1920s the Cardinals had demonstrated that their system could be made to pay its own way.

As the Cardinal farm empire expanded in the twenties and thirties, it precipitated two sharply divergent reactions. The established baseball press and Commissioner Landis attacked it as undermining the draft and infringing on the rights of minor league ballplayers to advance in their profession; Landis sought a way to use the powers of his office to dismantle it. At the same time other major clubs, notably the Yankees, Tigers, Indians, and Dodgers, began to adopt it. By the mid-1930s Landis had been forced to abandon his campaign to eliminate the farm system practice, although he continued to monitor the Cardinals' empire for abuses of the rights of individual players. Meanwhile *The Sporting News* had come to acknowledge that, as it editorialized in 1933, "the chain store system now has become a permanent part of the structure of baseball."[12]

It was in the late 1920s, noting the success of the Cardinals, that *The Sporting News* entered the debate over chain store baseball operations. In pointing out that the Cardinals' system may have violated, at least in spirit, the rule that no major league team should have control of more than forty ballplayers, *The Sporting News* conceded that by farming players off to minor league clubs in which they had an interest or with which they had a working agreement, Branch Rickey and Sam Breadon had technically stayed within the letter of the rule. Nonetheless it worried about the effects of the farm system on minor league franchises: "As long as the fans of a minor league city feel that the team, which they are expected to swear loyalty to, is not theirs at all, but merely a sort of ball playing company operated without regard for its success as a team, . . . there is going to be little loyalty to that minor club by the fans it looks to for support."[13]

In their critique of the farm system *The Sporting News* had brought some significant internal contradictions in the enterprise of baseball to the surface. Minor league franchises most clearly revealed the dual nature of professional baseball franchises. A minor league club was a business, oriented toward making a profit. A significant source of its profits, given the structure of Organized Baseball, was the value of its players on the major league market. In one sense, then, a minor league franchise was designed to develop players so as to realize their fullest market value. The most lucrative market for those players was the major leagues. But that meant that a minor league team was always grooming its players to send them elsewhere.

A minor league club was also, in a nation in which baseball was a recreational pursuit and a source of civic identity, a symbol of local pride. A minor league city's pride in its team was reflected in that team's won-lost record and in its players. Minor league players were to minor league cities as big-leaguers were to the cities of the majors: familiar figures with whom one could identify and for whom one could root. The constancy of those figures was part of their familiarity. When a major league team bought one of those players, his departure was typically a civic loss. One might nonetheless take pride, as a local resident, in the player's success. But when the minor league club was completely controlled by a major league team, when players were shifted willy-nilly to serve the goals of that team's organization, and when apparently no concern for the vicarious investment of the minor league city in its club was shown by the major league team, a dimension of baseball was lost.

It was this vein of emotional support for the minor leagues as miniature replicas of the civic-mindedness and partisan loyalty of the majors that *The Sporting News* had tapped in its critique of the farm system. And yet, in the end, critics came back to the same premise: the purpose of the minor leagues was to develop players for the majors. Despite the apparent cruelty and selfishness of the Cardinals' farm system, all Rickey and his lieutenants had done was create a more efficient system of player development. But by treading on the civic pride of the minors they had sullied a cherished ideal.

Sensing that its position on the farm system may have contained elements of wish-fulfillment, *The Sporting News*, as the twenties passed into the thirties, began alternating critiques of chain store minor league operations with stories, such as those of January 13, 1928, November 12, 1931, and November 19, 1931, documenting growing interest in major league clubs in acquiring minor league franchises and pointing out some of the advantages of the practice. It ran profiles on Branch Rickey, including one in which he made a lengthy defense of the farm system.[14]

As noted, Rickey's efforts to develop a farm system were consistently opposed by Commissioner Landis. Landis's position on the issue of major league–minor league relations was identical to that expressed by John Sheridan and *The Sporting News* in the 1920s. He believed in the civic autonomy of minor league cities and franchises, but he was opposed to any potential barriers to the advancement of players up to the major leagues. He thus supported a universal draft, assuming that it was the most likely system to facilitate player advancement. He made no effort to reconcile the goal of minor league franchise autonomy with the goal of promoting players as rapidly as possible.

Although Landis's positions were not necessarily consistent, they were diametrically opposed to Rickey's practices. Rickey's practices were not illegal, however, so long as the major league owners ratified ownership of minor league franchises by major league teams, as well as working agreements. In the December 1928 winter meetings Landis polled club owners on the legitimacy of the farm system, hoping to find opposition, but the owners declined to take any action.[15] The next year he again denounced the chain store system, stating that "we must solve the problem of the evil of common ownership if the little fellows are to survive." Perhaps aware that his views were running against the tide, he added that the 1929 annual meeting had been filled with "minor league owners looking for major league clubs to take them over."[16]

In 1933 Landis was summarily rebuffed by the major league owners on the farm system. By a vote of sixteen to nothing, they adopted a rule specifically permitting chain store arrangements, introduced by Landis's longtime foe Phil Ball of the St. Louis Browns. The rule provided that all agreements involving the purchase or transfer of players' contracts should be given full force and effect, notwithstanding the fact that some of the agreements were between clubs where one club controlled a majority of the stock of the other club. The only practice that was forbidden was the ownership of two teams in the same league.

In some respects Rickey may have been closer than Landis to the consciousness of those who were controlling the enterprise of baseball from the 1920s through the Second World War; he once said of the commissioner that "during his long term in office he has done nothing to extend baseball, nor has he ever shown any real understanding of the difficulties of baseball operation."[17] Landis, like John Sheridan, approached economic issues such as the draft and the farm system "on principle," but the principles affecting such issues pointed in contradictory dimensions, and in the end the major league club owners made decisions based on what they perceived to be their economic self-interest.

◆

As Organized Baseball struggled with the issues of player development, the minor leagues, and the farm system throughout the thirties and forties, its existing structure of legal and economic relations, with its core principles of territoriality and the reserve clause, remained undisturbed. But after the Second World War developments occurred that threatened that structure. We have seen that earlier in Organized Baseball's history the emergence of a rival major league, the Federal League, had had an unsettling effect on the economic and legal relations of the enterprise. Several players had jumped contracts with American or National League teams to sign with Federal League franchises, and the courts, despite their willingness to consider enjoining the jumpers from playing for new teams at the time of the Phillies' suit against Nap Lajoie, had treated jumping to the Federal League as a distinguishable, and permissible, phenomenon. A consequence of this attitude was that many ballplayers who remained with American or National League clubs, such as Ty Cobb and Walter Johnson, received large salary increases for the 1914 or 1915 seasons. Finally, the Federal League war had precipitated the *Federal Baseball* case, in which Organized Baseball's exemption from the antitrust laws was challenged in the Supreme Court.

In 1946 an almost exact parallel to the Federal League controversy appeared to be surfacing. Seventeen players from major league clubs jumped their contracts to sign with teams in the Mexican League, which after World War II was making a determined effort to expand and upgrade its operations. Among other things, the Mexican League hoped to attract large numbers of players from the American Negro Leagues and create high-level integrated teams. Waving cashier's checks, Mexican League representatives flocked to spring training camps.

Among the seventeen players who deserted Organized Baseball for the Mexican League before the 1946 season was Danny Gardella, an outfielder for the New York Giants. On learning of the players' departures, Commissioner Chandler declared that the jumpers would be ineligible in the major leagues for five years. Gardella played one year in the Mexican League, but in the spring of 1947 he sought to return to the Giants; he also approached a number of other major and minor league clubs. He was uniformly rebuffed.

Similar treatment was accorded to Max Lanier and Fred Martin, who had left the Cardinals in 1946 to play for Mexican League teams. During the summer of 1947, Lanier and Martin, along with other ex–Mexican Leaguers, formed an all-star team and sought to obtain permission to play exhibition games at ballparks. "Wherever we went," an affidavit from Lanier and Martin later alleged, "agents of [Organized Baseball] preceded us and threatened owners of baseball parks and players with the direst penalties, including suspension from Organized Baseball for five years, if they allowed their teams to play against us or allowed us to use their baseball park."[18]

As in the Federal League controversy, Organized Baseball's response was not limited to blacklisting and threats. They also sought to create additional incentives for players not to depart for the Mexican League. Among the incentives initiated in 1946, at the height of the Mexican League's contacts with American players, were a $5,000 minimum salary for all major league players; a limitation on salary cuts to 25 percent of the preceding year's salary; the creation of a pension fund for major league players, to be financed out of receipts from the annual All-Star Game; and the introduction of a system where each major league team would have a player representative who could communicate grievances to owners.

None of these actions prevented the last parallel with the Federal League war from surfacing in 1949. That year Gardella, Lanier, and Martin brought suit against their former major league clubs, the American and National Leagues, Commissioner Chandler, and George Trautman, the president of the minor leagues, asserting that the blacklisting practices amounted to a monopoly and a conspiracy in restraint of trade, violating the Sherman and Clayton Acts. Gardella asked for $300,000 in damages; Lanier and Martin, invoking the triple-damage penal clause in the Sherman Act for violators, demanded $2.5 million.[19]

Gardella's suit, filed in federal court, came to trial first and was treated as the leading challenge. The trial court, following *Federal Baseball*, dismissed the suit for lack of jurisdiction, reaffirming Holmes's holding that baseball was neither a subject of commerce nor an interstate activity.[20] Gardella appealed to the United States Court of Appeals for the Second Circuit, where the case was heard by a three-judge panel composed of Judges Harrie Brigham Chase, Learned Hand, and Jerome Frank. In a 2–1 decision, the Second Circuit reversed and held that Gardella had made out a cause of action against Organized Baseball.[21]

Each judge issued a separate opinion. In dissent, Judge Chase followed the *Federal Baseball* precedent, agreeing with the trial court that it had no jurisdiction to hear the case since baseball was not a subject in interstate commerce. He also maintained that no cause of action for restraint of trade had been made out because Gardella had not alleged that the reserve clause practices had any effect on the prices of baseball games in the market or on the rights to broadcast or advertise baseball games.[22] This argument was both formalistic and myopic. The practices clearly had a direct effect on the price Gardella and other players could ask for their services, and that price affected the prices owners needed to charge for games in order to make a profit.

The other two judges held that the trial court did have jurisdiction over the case. Judge Hand noted that in the years since the *Federal Baseball* decision, radio and television broadcasts of games had become commonplace, and Congress and the courts had agreed that radio and television were subjects in interstate commerce. Those facts were sufficient to distinguish *Federal Baseball* for Hand, and so he stopped there, declining to pass upon the legality of the reserve clause.[23] Judge Frank, however, entertained that issue and concluded that the reserve clause and associated blacklisting practices made baseball "a monopoly which, in its effect on ballplayers like the plaintiff, possesses characteristics shockingly repugnant to moral principles." He termed the status of ballplayers under the practices "something resembling peonage." He also pointed out that the Supreme Court precedents on which Justice Holmes had relied in *Federal Baseball*, decisions which gave a narrow reading to the meaning of "interstate commerce" for antitrust purposes, had been overturned by later decisions. He suggested that these developments had left the *Federal Baseball* decision "an impotent zombi."[24] Frank concluded that the reserve clause and associated practices were illegal, and that "the public's pleasure does not authorize the courts to condone illegality, and . . . no court should strive ingeniously to legalize a private (even if benevolent) dictatorship."[25]

The Gardella, Lanier, and Martin cases threatened to become epic after the Second Circuit's resolution in *Gardella*, but both sides had an interest in their not continuing in the courts. By 1949 all the players involved had found that life in the Mexican League did not compare favorably with their situation in the major leagues, and they wanted the opportunity to reenter Organized Baseball before they became too old to continue playing. On the other side, Organized Baseball did not want a test of the legality of the reserve clause in the Supreme Court, especially now that the radio and television dimensions of the enterprise had been made apparent. Thus an out-of-court settlement of all three cases was arranged in that year, under which the players were reinstated and paid an undisclosed sum in damages by Organized Baseball. Gardella was given his unconditional release by the Giants, and Commissioner Chandler arranged for him to be picked up by the Cardinals, who also agreed to take back Martin and Lanier. In 1951 Chandler testified before a congressional committee studying baseball's antitrust exemption that he had only reinstated Martin and Lanier after the district court judge in their cases had ruled that he was not compelled to do so, and that the cases had been settled because the players had seen that "the thing [in Mexico] was not as good as they thought it was, and they were sadder and wiser," and because "the lawyers [for Organized Baseball] thought we could not win the Gardella case."[26]

The settlements in *Gardella* and the companion cases did not prevent the antitrust implications of Organized Baseball's practices from resurfacing in the succeeding years. In the early 1950s baseball was attacked from two fronts. Congressman Emanuel Celler, the powerful chairman of the House Judiciary Committee, opened an extensive series of hearings in July 1951 before a subcommittee charged with the "study of monopoly power," calling a number of representatives of Organized Baseball and in effect asking them to justify their restrictive economic practices and the sport's exemption from the antitrust laws. And in that same year two players who had been blacklisted under the reserve clause rule filed suit in federal court for reinstatement and damages. Both were pitchers: James Prendergast, who had been blacklisted by the Syracuse club in the International League for refusing to accept his demotion from Syracuse to Beaumont of the Texas League,[27] and George Toolson, who had been blacklisted for refusing to accept assignment from Newark (Class AAA) to Binghamton (Class AA) in the New York Yankees' farm system.[28] Both suits accused the clubs

Three National League owners who would be pivotal figures in economic developments within baseball from the 1930s through the early 1950s, pictured at the 1934 winter baseball meetings in New York. From left to right: Philip Wrigley, owner of the Chicago Cubs, whose ownership of the minor league Los Angeles franchise was an important factor in the eventual breakup of major league baseball's original franchise map; Emil Fuchs, owner of the Boston Braves, the first franchise to relocate; and Sam Breadon, owner of the St. Louis Cardinals, who relied on the farm system to survive economically in the 1930s. (National Baseball Library and Archive, Cooperstown, N.Y.)

against whom they were filed of combining to monopolize professional baseball in the United States and of depriving the players, through the reserve clause and blacklisting, of their professional means of livelihood.

Toolson's suit and an additional suit filed in the Southern District of Ohio by another player, Walter Kowalski, challenging the reserve clause,[29] were dismissed for want of jurisdiction by the district courts, who cited *Federal Baseball*. In both cases United States Circuit Courts of Appeals affirmed the decisions.[30] In Prendergast's case the district court delayed consideration pending the outcome of the other two cases. The lawyer for George Toolson filed a petition for certiorari with the Supreme Court in 1953. The Court granted the petition, consolidated the Toolson case with the Kowalski case, and heard arguments in October of that year.

Those close to major league baseball, on considering their legal and economic position in the early 1950s, might well have concluded that they were being pinched from two sides. They might have feared that the courts would overturn the reserve clause and associated practices, and that if they did not, Congress might act to remove their "exemption" from the antitrust laws. Their concerns might have been accentuated by a closer examination of the legal and economic issues. In light of the burgeoning revenue from radio rights in the thirties and forties, and the rapid rise of television in the fifties, it was absurd to think of baseball as a "local" sport, and equally absurd to imagine baseball clubs suddenly severing their connections with the broadcast industry. And in light of the salaries paid baseball players, the revenue from concessions and broadcast rights, the ownership by major league clubs of minor league franchises, and the numerous other business activities engaged in by baseball teams, it was equally absurd to think of baseball as other than a commercial enterprise.

Furthermore, the growth of farm system arrangements seemed to have tightened the monopolistic aspects of baseball. Agreements among teams within a farm system overlapped agreements between individual clubs and players, binding players ever more closely to their teams. A certain unrest was developing among some minor league players who felt trapped by the farm system, as testimony at the 1951 baseball hearings would reveal. Increasingly, the ownership of baseball seemed remote from the men who played the game.

Finally, several interest groups had begun to focus on a cornerstone of "baseball law" that seemed to be creating some acute difficulties by the early 1950s: the territoriality principle. Territoriality had had two dimensions: a restriction on competition within geographic areas, and the freezing of major league franchises among originally designated cities. The first dimension had obvious antitrust implications, and baseball's inner circle was well aware that the Justice Department had announced, after the Second Circuit's decision in the *Gardella* case, that they were studying all of the antitrust implications of baseball's rules while *Gardella v. Chandler* was being remanded.

The second dimension was even more controversial. Beginning in the 1930s the Pacific Coast League, an established AAA circuit with cities from San Diego to Seattle, had been agitating for major league status. Between 1930 and 1950 the population of San Francisco and Los Angeles had both nearly doubled; by the 1950 census Los Angeles was the third largest city in the nation and San Francisco the seventh. The National Football League had added professional teams in San Francisco and Los Angeles after the Second World War, playing schedules against teams on the east coast and in the midwest. Moreover, by the 1950 census three additional cities without major league franchises, Baltimore, Minneapolis–St. Paul, and Buffalo, had populations greater than St. Louis and Cincinnati. Yet baseball continued to have two teams in St. Louis, as well as two teams in Philadelphia and Boston, cities in which, for most of the thirties and forties, at least one of those teams was the weakest or next to the weakest in its league in attendance. Territoriality seemed not only to be the equivalent of exclusivity, but to be an economically inefficient practice.

Thus the forecasts of those charged with anticipating the reaction of Congress and the courts to major league baseball's legal and economic practices in the early 1950s might well have been gloomy. Yet baseball survived the dual threat from the Supreme Court and Congress with its original structure virtually intact. The Court, after hearing the *Toolson* case, summarily affirmed on the authority of *Federal Baseball*, declining to reexamine "the underlying issues" in that case. "Congress has had the ruling under consideration," the Court noted in a per curiam opinion, "but has not seen fit to bring [baseball] under [the federal antitrust laws] by legislation."[31] Justices Harold Burton and Stanley Reed dissented, Burton pointing out what was entirely obvious to any observer of the enterprise of Organized Baseball in 1953:

> In the light of organized baseball's well-known and widely distributed capital investments used in conducting competitions between teams constantly traveling between states, its receipts and expenditures of large sums transmitted between states, its numerous purchases of materials in interstate commerce, the attendance at its local exhibitions of large audiences often traveling across state lines, its radio and television activities

> which expand its audience across state lines, its sponsorship of interstate advertising, and its highly organized "farm system" of minor league baseball clubs, coupled with restrictive contracts and understandings between individuals and among clubs or leagues playing for profit throughout the United States, . . . it is a contradiction in terms to say that the defendants in the cases before us are not now engaged in interstate trade or commerce as those terms are used in the Constitution of the United States and in the Sherman Act.[32]

Nonetheless a majority of the Court decided to leave to Congress the question of how to apply the arcane structure of baseball's labor relations to the business world of the 1950s. Meanwhile Congress, although conceding the interstate character of baseball, had itself decided to finesse the issue. The House subcommittee chaired by Emanuel Celler called a number of witnesses and raised a number of ticklish issues for baseball, such as the farm system, the reserve clause, territorial limits, the exclusion of west coast and other major cities from the major leagues, and the treatment of minor league players. Various individuals with agendas and grievances against Organized Baseball, ranging from disgruntled players to officials from west coast cities who wanted to lobby for big-league franchises, were given the opportunity to testify before the subcommittee, and baseball officials, including (now former) Commissioner Chandler, National League president and commissioner-designate Ford Frick, American League president Will Harridge, minor league president George Trautman, and Chicago Cubs owner William Wrigley were summoned and grilled by the subcommittee about potentially monopolistic practices. But in the end the subcommittee made no recommendations, and Congress took no action.

In retrospect, the inaction of both the Supreme Court and Congress may appear stunning. Not only was Organized Baseball undeniably an enterprise in interstate commerce, other "entertainment" industries, such as the motion picture industry, had been held to come within the antitrust laws.[33] The reserve clause, blacklisting, the territoriality rules, the farm system, and baseball clubs' effort to limit competition for their radio and television rights were obvious efforts to create a buyer's monopoly in player services and to restrict competition for baseball franchises. The rules limiting major league franchises to those cities who held them at the formation of the 1903 National Agreement

Larry MacPhail, testifying at the 1951 Celler subcommittee hearings. Several years before, MacPhail had criticized major league owners for being excessively traditionalist in their approach to economic issues. (Associated Press)

had the effect of excluding numerous cities and fans from the prospect of major league baseball in their locality. In the face of this evidence Congress and the Supreme Court did nothing.

Obviously something was present in the consciousness of policymakers, who considered the legal and economic situation of Organized Baseball in the early 1950s and implicitly concluded that the structure of the enterprise should not be disturbed. To get a sense of those elements, one can turn to the 1951 congressional hearings, where in the course of testimony several arguments on behalf of the status quo were advanced.

◆

One argument was that baseball, although concededly a business, was also a sport, and the mixture made it, as Philip K. Wrigley put it in his testimony before the Celler subcommittee, "a very peculiar business."[34] It was a business in which, Wrigley said, "your competitors are your partners,"[35] in which the "sport" elements of the enterprise affected its other elements. Whereas in many industries a particular firm could, through its superior product development or distribution methods or other techniques, achieve a greater share of the market than its competitors and even drive some of them out of business, in baseball keen competition among franchises was always desired. Competitive imbalance, with some clubs invariably dominating other clubs, actually hurt the game.

This led Wrigley to the supposition that competitive balance among baseball clubs was protected by the reserve clause. He stated to the Celler subcommittee that he believed that the reserve clause was "apparently . . . essential within organized baseball," and that he had not heard any players "ever complain about it."[36] He admitted that there was some player dissatisfaction with "the form which [the reserve clause] is in," but he believed "everybody recognized [that] apparently it is essential."[37]

If the testimony of players who were called before the Celler subcommittee was representative of their peers, Wrigley was substantially correct in his belief about the "essential" nature of the reserve clause. Seven current or former players testified or had their statements read before the subcommittee. Of those only one, former minor league player Ross Horning, did not support the reserve clause, and the most

Horning would say was "I think there is a need of change," and that "it is difficult to see how 16 owners should have complete control of America's national game."[38] In the context of Horning's testimony, however, his statement primarily referred to the condition of minor league players, whom he thought were being exploited by the clubs who had reserved their services.

All the other players, ranging from Ty Cobb to current major leaguers Fred Hutchinson and Harold ("Pee Wee") Reese, strongly endorsed the reserve clause.[39] Even players who had been brought before the subcommittee because they had been engaged in salary disputes with their teams, such as Al Widmar or Ned Garvey, or who had a list of grievances about the treatment of players in the minor leagues, such as Cy Block, admitted that at least at the major league level the reserve clause was necessary and not an undue hardship to players. This was even though some players, including both critics of baseball's labor economics such as Horning and defenders such as Reese, asserted that the "richest clubs" would be likely to obtain the best players whether or not a reserve clause existed.[40]

Crucial to the widespread assumption that the reserve clause was essential to maintain competition among baseball clubs, then, was the apparent belief, on the part of both players and executives, that limitations on the bargaining power of *the players* was the only feasible way to achieve competition. No one considered the variety of other alternatives that are now entertained in discussions of baseball labor issues, such as a free agency system for players but an established salary structure for all participants, or free agency combined with a cap on salaries for each major league team, or free agency and a salary cap combined with some method of sharing the total revenues generated by baseball among all clubs. As late as the early 1950s all those directly affected by baseball labor relations took as a starting point the premise that the only way to achieve close competition among teams was to restrict the options of the players.

In that respect, then, the consciousness of the participants in baseball labor relations in the 1950s was not very far from the consciousness of their predecessors in 1903. But although no one involved with baseball or examining the practices of baseball seemed inclined to dismantle the reserve clause system, and many endorsed Fred Hutchinson's view that "the minor leagues could not survive without continuation of the reserve clause, and I do not believe that the big leagues would last much longer than the minors,"[41] the other of baseball's fundamental and sacrosanct principles, territoriality, did not engender the same kind of reflexive support. By the early 1950s the territoriality principle was flying in the teeth of demographic and market trends, and the Celler hearings gave a fair amount of time to critics of the existing franchise structure of the major leagues. Defenders of territoriality, for their part, did not assign the same sacrosanct status to that principle that they had assigned to the reserve clause.

Cubs' owner Philip K. Wrigley was in a unique position among major league club owners in the early 1950s in that he not only owned the Cubs but the Los Angeles team in the Pacific Coast League. He was sympathetic to the Pacific Coast League's interest in achieving major league status, but at the same time he realized that if it did, he could own two major league clubs, something that the rules of baseball prohibited. As Wrigley put it before the Celler subcommittee: "I am on both sides of the fence. I am in a very unhappy situation. . . . I have been in partnership with these fellows [the major league club owners] for years and I can't go out and cut their throats."[42]

Wrigley's ambivalence was precipitated by his expectation that the city of Los Angeles itself, rather than the entire Pacific Coast League, would apply for major league status, citing its impressive population numbers and growth. The way for Los Angeles to acquire a team would be to have an existing major league franchise move to Los Angeles. "In your opinion," Wrigley was asked, "do you think it would be feasible to transfer franchises from, say, two-major-league clubs in towns where . . . one of those two teams might not be doing too well? Do you think it would be feasible from an economic standpoint to proceed in that way?"[43]

"It is feasible," Wrigley replied, "but I don't think it would be the best thing for baseball or for the territory in the long run." First, he maintained, transfers might not be necessary if major league baseball expanded. ("I don't think [the majors] should be limited to 16 clubs which [they were] in the early 1900's because of the growth of the country.") Second, however, new franchises outside the existing geographic circuit would mean that "your scheduling would be very difficult." He pointed out that unlike the case of professional football, where a game was played only once a week, allowing "plenty of time for travel," the baseball schedule "is practically continuous." Moreover, "over the years it has proven that the more closely associated clubs in a territory draw better."[44]

The first reason was hardly an argument for preserving the existing rules on territoriality, and Wrigley was subsequently drawn into a discussion of those rules. "I wonder if you feel," he was asked, "that the present rules with regard to territorial rights are essential to preserve what is good about organized baseball." Wrigley's first responded, "I do not think that anything that has ever been in force for any number of years without change can possibly be good. I think that you have to keep changing things to keep abreast of the rapidly changing world." Pressed, he said he "would favor changing the rules" about territoriality.[45] Apparently he had been influenced by his contact with Los Angeles, which at the time was faced with the near impossibility of getting a major league franchise, since the transfer of a club from one of the existing cities required the unanimous consent of all the other clubs in that club's league and the approval of a majority of the clubs in the other league.

The stated rationale for preserving the original 1903 circuit of clubs in the National and American Leagues was "to preserve and stimulate competition for the League Pennants and the World Championship."[46] Wrigley had alluded to that rationale in his suggestion that "closely associated clubs" fostered attendance. But the rationale hardly applied to all situations. One proposed franchise move in the early 1950s involved the St. Louis Browns, who considered moving to Baltimore (and eventually did). Given the proximity of Baltimore to Washington and Philadelphia, two of the original members of the American League, it would seem that the "close association" rationale would have supported a move.

More fundamentally, it was hard to imagine how retaining the original circuit of clubs in the major leagues preserved and stimulated competition among those clubs. If the magnates of Organized Baseball were concerned about one of their number "grabbing a club possibly to move into a territory, make a capital gain, and move out again," as Wrigley suggested,[47] that concern seemed more directed at the stability of franchises, or the continuity of civic associations, than at competition among clubs. In fact freezing the circuits at the original league cities had arguably retarded competition. As some original cities, such as St. Louis, Cincinnati, and Boston, lagged behind others in population growth, their franchises found it harder to attract a sufficient number of fans, more difficult to purchase new players, and consequently harder to field winning teams. The dismal records of the Philadelphia Phillies and Athletics, the Cincinnati Reds, the Boston Braves, and the St. Louis Browns in the thirties and forties, when contrasted with the winning records of larger-market teams such as the New York clubs, suggested that the rigidity of the major league circuits was actually retarding competition.

The Celler subcommittee, mindful of the claims of west coast cities and other cities in areas of population growth, issued a report that was severely critical of the existing rules on territoriality.[48] In response Organized Baseball modified its principal rules on territoriality, permitting the transfer of major league clubs from one city to another with only the consent of a majority of the club owners in the affected league, except where the transfer was to a city already occupied by the other major league, in which case all club owners in both leagues needed to consent. In addition, the transfer of major league clubs to cities that housed minor league franchises, previously permissible without any restraints, now required the consent of the minor league in which the relevant franchise was located and a payment of "just and reasonable compensation" to that franchise.[49]

These changes were eventually to result in the breakup of the original circuits, in both major leagues, which arguably set in motion forces that were to transform an enterprise whose structure had remained largely constant for fifty years. But at the time of the Celler subcommittee hearings an additional issue appeared to stand in the way of franchise shifts, at least those that involved sections of the country that had not previously housed major league teams. This was the issue of transportation, alluded to by Wrigley in his comment that "scheduling would be very difficult."

To understand why that issue was a barrier to franchise relocation, it is necessary to recall the scheduling arrangements for major league teams that had existed ever since the First World War. Travel by train on the existing circuits made scheduling a relatively routine process. The east coast teams in each league (Boston, New York, Philadelphia, Brooklyn, and Washington) would travel on a four-circuit railroad swing throughout the other cities (Pittsburgh, Cleveland, Cincinnati, Detroit, Chicago, and St. Louis), lasting from three weeks to a month, playing three or four games in each city. Then they would return home and await the coming of the midwestern teams. The schedule was "unbalanced" in that east coast clubs played more games against each other than against midwestern clubs: this cut down the number of long road trips in a season. There were rarely long journeys on trains from one city to another, although teams would be away from home for lengthy periods.

With this model of a schedule dominating their consciousness, major league club owners in the early 1950s could not see how west coast clubs, or even clubs in cities such as Houston or Minneapolis–St. Paul, could be easily accommodated. They did not think of flying regularly between cities; they did not think of the current "balanced" schedule, which allows teams to play an identical, but unevenly dispersed, number of games against each of their rivals. When they imagined Los Angeles or San Francisco joining a major league circuit, the club owners of the 1950s imagined those cities being part of an extended railroad network, stops on a "western swing." They could not see how the logistics would work out. It was no surprise that when franchise moves eventually came after 1953, the cities chosen—Milwaukee, Baltimore, and Kansas City, replacing Boston, St. Louis, and Philadelphia—were ones whose locations were not radically outside the existing railroad circuits.

Thus the Celler subcommittee hearings closed without any major action being taken to disturb the structure of baseball's enterprise, and the *Toolson* case demonstrated the Supreme Court's determination, even in the face of overwhelming evidence, not to invade baseball's prerogatives without congressional approval. But in the atmosphere that precipitated the player challenges to the reserve clause and the discussions at the hearings were the stirrings of a new order. And, oddly enough, those who initiated it were not those most disadvantaged by the status quo, the players. The collapse of the enterprise that had been carefully structured in 1903 was precipitated by the owners themselves.

◆

The atmosphere of the Celler subcommittee hearings and the player challenges to the reserve clause was accentuated, for major league club owners in the 1950s, by a puzzling decline in attendance at baseball games. In the years between 1946 and 1949 the average crowd at a major league contest was over 16,000, a jump from about 7,500 in the 1940–45 period and 6,500 in the decade of the 1930s. Then, for the next ten years, the average crowd declined to slightly over 13,000.[50] On its face, this statistic must have bewildered club owners. The 1950s was a prosperous decade for Americans, in which purchasing power dramatically increased and population growth continued. No world war or major domestic crisis was present to distract Americans from recreational pursuits, and several other professional sports, ranging from football to golf, enjoyed dramatic upsurges in their popularity. To many observers the quality of baseball being played in the major leagues appeared to have reached an all-time level of excellence. Yet the rise in the level of talent on the field was not paralleled by a rise in gate receipts.

Owners should have looked beneath the surface. Ballparks remained mired in the central city, the residential areas around them deteriorating as middle-and upper-income residents left for the suburbs. Their locations had been planned around public transportation, not the automobile. As they aged, the cost of maintaining them mounted, and in several cities their ambience began to deteriorate. Shibe Park, Ebbets Field, Forbes Field, and Briggs Stadium, once featured as elegant civic structures, became seedy and ugly with age.[51]

Television provided suburbanites with another reason not to venture from their homes in the evening. At the same time recreational sports increased, especially for youth: Little League baseball became entrenched in many communities in the 1950s. As more major league clubs began to televise their games, even into minor league cities, Americans were given the choice of staying at home in the suburbs to watch a ball game. The impact on the minor leagues was especially acute: minor league attendance declined from 49 million fans in 1949 to 15.5 million in 1957.[52]

While these developments were taking place, another one, noted by the Celler subcommittee, was also occurring. This was the dramatic movement of Americans from northeastern and midwestern cities to the southwest and far west.[53] At first blush this population growth, in cities which did not have major league franchises, seemed to be pointing in the opposite direction from the other trends, since it suggested the existence of potentially lucrative markets of new major league baseball fans. But, as noted, baseball's existing territorial structure did not seem well established to accommodate the expansion or transfer of franchises. The Celler subcommittee hearings had revealed the resistance of baseball's officialdom to alterations in the longstanding circuit of clubs. In addition to the comments previously discussed, American League president Will Harridge had testified that if he were a club owner he would not want his team to fly in airplanes,[54] and Washington Senators owner Clark Griffith had stated that "California is entirely out of the major-league circuit."[55]

Despite declining attendance, the demographic trends of the late forties and fifties presented major league baseball with significant political pressure to expand into new cities, or somehow integrate those cities into its established circuits. A game could hardly claim to be the national pastime if those who ran it deliberately excluded large numbers of Americans from the opportunity to participate in it directly as local fans of a hometown franchise. The Celler subcommittee had been responsive to this expansionist pressure in several respects, allowing advocates of west coast baseball to testify, grilling baseball officials on their views toward the Pacific Coast League and west coast cities, and allowing the interest of Los Angeles in securing a major league team to occupy an arguably disproportionately large space in their hearings. In their report they had taken the position that Organized Baseball should "get going" on broadening the geographic base of the major leagues.[56]

In response to pressure from the west coast, a committee from the National League, chaired by its president, Ford Frick, had compiled a report on "the Pacific coast and its baseball potentialities," which they introduced into evidence before the Celler subcommittee.[57] Their report considered three alternatives: the creation of major league status for the Pacific Coast League; the creation of a special classification for that league, in between major and minor league status, in which its draft rules would be modified to give it more power vis-à-vis both the majors and the existing minor leagues; and the expansion of the major leagues to include some Pacific coast cities, specifically San Francisco and Los Angeles. The Frick committee noted that it had rejected the first alternative as "not practical," considered the second to be "largely a matter of window dressing" and to raise equity problems with the other high minor leagues, and stated that although it considered expansion into Pacific coast cities "the most practical" alternative, "such a move cannot come from the major leagues" because it affected minor league interests.[58]

In fact the Frick committee was not being entirely candid about the reasons for its lack of enthusiasm for any of the alternatives it had sketched. Major league club owners did not like the first alternative because they did not want to limit their own opportunities to move into west coast markets should that prove feasible. They did not like the second because they thought it would limit their opportunities to control player development in the minor leagues. And they did not like the third because they were not clear they could agree on which leagues would gain access to which new markets: some markets appeared more potentially lucrative than others. They also did not mention, in the Frick committee report, a fourth alternative that they were discussing among themselves: the transfer of existing major league franchises to west coast cities.[59] The remarks of Griffith and Harridge at the Celler subcommittee hearings suggested that this alternative was far from being a popular one, but it was on the table, within official baseball circles, by the early 1950s. The club owners' alteration of Rule 1(c) on territoriality in December 1952 was a clear signal that franchise transfers were beginning to be taken seriously.[60]

Against this backdrop, attention within the ranks of major league owners began to focus on three two-city teams with significant attendance and financial problems: the Boston Braves, the St. Louis Browns, and the Philadelphia Athletics. Discussions about the possibility of transferring any of these teams were, from their outset, affected by the owners' growing consciousness that expansion of major league baseball into Pacific Coast League cities might well be a lucrative venture. The two major leagues approached the question of franchise transfers in quite different ways.

The National League was, from the outset, more enthusiastic about westward expansion and more interested in cornering the Los Angeles and San Francisco markets. This was because of the presence among National League owners of Walter O'Malley, who had assumed control of the Brooklyn Dodgers from Branch Rickey in 1950, and Wrigley of the Cubs. O'Malley had quickly become convinced that Ebbets Field was a chronically inadequate facility, especially for the automobile age, and had had no success getting the borough of Brooklyn to help him finance a new stadium. Wrigley wanted to capitalize on his ownership of the Los Angeles club in the Pacific Coast League and had come to believe, as early as the Celler subcommittee hearings, that major league baseball on the west coast was inevitable.

The American League, in contrast, had no owners (save maverick Bill Veeck of the St. Louis Browns) who were enthusiastic about west coast expansion, and some (represented by Griffith) who could not even conceive it. As American League owners considered franchise transfers or expansion, they regarded themselves as implicitly limited by two factors: circuit-consciousness and the availability of adequate ballparks. Since the building of Yankee Stadium in 1923, ballpark construction on a major league scale had become prohibitively expensive for private financing, and municipalities, backed by taxpayer-oriented bond issues, had emerged as the only entities deemed fiscally competent to build new stadiums.

That fact, in the eyes of American League owners, limited transfers or expansion to those cities that had major league-level ballparks. Neither Los Angeles's Wrigley Field nor San Francisco's Seals Stadium were large enough, and the huge Los Angeles Coliseum was regarded as improperly shaped for baseball (a belief that was confirmed when the Dodgers played there briefly after moving to Los Angeles in 1958). In actuality, the only non–major league cities with adequate ballparks in the early 1950s were Milwaukee and Baltimore, both of whose parks had been municipally financed. The availability of a ballpark, combined with a lingering circuit-consciousness accentuated by the caution with which major league baseball addressed travel by airplane, determined the direction of franchise transfers in the early 1950s. The west coast was, for those reasons, not to be the area initially chosen for inclusion in the major leagues; but the prospect of baseball's entrance into west coast markets, coupled with a growing recognition of the economic infeasibility of two major league teams in certain cities on the original circuit, was the force that eventually shattered the structure of the enterprise that had been created in 1903.

The details of franchise transfers, the expansion of both major leagues that those transfers precipitated in the late 1950s, and the increasing recognition among major league club owners that the division of consumer markets among various franchises involved not only a fan base for attendance purposes, but a radio listener and television viewer base, generating substantial additional revenue, are largely beyond the scope of this book.[61] They ushered in a new era of baseball, in which the shape of the enterprise, so remarkably constant for fifty years, would be altered beyond recognition.

It seems worth concluding this chapter, however, by briefly con-

Milwaukee County Stadium, where the Braves played after their 1953 move from Boston. One might compare its configuration and location with those of Shibe Park and Yankee Stadium. Note the space allocated to parking, the absence of adjacent trolley lines, the close proximity to superhighways, and the absence of any connection to the central city. Built with public funds, County Stadium was a prototype for ballparks for the next two decades. (National Baseball Library and Archive, Cooperstown, N.Y.)

trasting two sets of franchise transfers that took place in the 1950s. Those transfers, taken together, create a demarcation line that separates baseball's twentieth-century past from its present and future, and accordingly frames the scope of this book. The first set of transfers took place in 1953 and 1954, when the Boston Braves moved to Milwaukee, the St. Louis Browns to Baltimore, and the Philadelphia Athletics to Kansas City. The second set took place between 1957 and 1960, when the Brooklyn Dodgers moved to Los Angeles, the New York Giants to San Francisco, and the Washington Senators to Minneapolis–

St. Paul, and the American and National Leagues voted to expand by adding a total of four teams by 1962.

The 1953 and 1954 transfers were undertaken largely within the established structure of the enterprise, although they disrupted the established league circuits that had been a cornerstone of the territoriality principle. The first modern franchise shift, Boston to Milwaukee in the National League, was made with the unanimous consent of the National League owners by Lou Perini, who already owned the Milwaukee American Association franchise. The shift thus did not invade minor league prerogatives; it did not radically change the transportation circuit of the league; and, on the surface at any rate, it had the blessing of all of Perini's partner-competitors. It was also to a city with a ready-made, municipally financed, major league–capacity stadium. Finally, it involved an economically depressed club in a two-team city whose population base was comparatively small, the paradigmatic "problem franchise" identified at the Celler subcommittee hearings.

On the surface, the American League franchise transfers of 1953 and 1954 appeared to be similar. They both involved the weaker of two clubs in a two-team city; neither disrupted existing train-travel circuits; both had the blessing of American League owners. Behind the scenes, however, the American League moves were far more contentious and involved broader agendas. The Browns' transfer was blocked by a coalition of owners until Browns' owner Bill Veeck, who had alienated a number of his colleagues, was forced to sell out his interests in the club. (Veeck considered suing his fellow owners for blocking his proposed sale, but he was advised that the *Federal Baseball* decision would bar any antitrust suits.) In addition Yankees' owner Del Webb extracted an understanding from other owners that his support for the transfer of the Browns was predicated on the owners' agreeing to enter the Los Angeles market in the future. Neither of the latter grounds for American League approval of the transfer was made public.[62]

The Yankees were even more prominent in the move of the Athletics from Philadelphia.[63] Faced with paralysis in the front office because of the longevity and increasing senility of club owner Connie Mack and the incompetence of his two sons, and confronted with a deteriorating, inaccessible stadium in an increasingly run-down and dangerous area of the center city, the Athletics were a woefully weak and unprofitable franchise in the late forties and early fifties. After Connie Mack's forced retirement in 1950, at age eighty-seven, his sons Roy and Earle, after an unsuccessful effort to revive the team over the next three years, began to consider selling the team in 1954. They were encouraged to do so by other American League owners, who disliked having to visit Shibe Park, with its depressed conditions and poor gate receipts.

When a "Save the A's" campaign in the summer of 1954 failed to generate much fan interest, the Yankees proposed a sale to Arnold Johnson, who owned an interest in the Kansas City American Association franchise, a Yankee farm team. Johnson's plan called for him to sell the existing Kansas City stadium to the city of Kansas City, which would refurbish it and lease it back to him. With the proceeds from the first years in Kansas City, Johnson would eventually liquidate the Macks' debts that he had acquired in purchasing the Athletics. In October 1954, American League owners met and approved the transfer, but it was not formally consummated, and a group of Philadelphia businessmen subsequently convinced Roy Mack to sell the A's to them. In a symbolic meeting in New York, in which Connie Mack made a personal plea to the American League owners, the American League turned down the Philadelphia bid and reaffirmed the sale of the A's to Johnson. The Yankees would become a major beneficiary of the sale, because for the next thirteen years, until the Athletics moved again, this time to Oakland, the Kansas City franchise regularly sold or traded a series of outstanding players to the Yankees, the most notable of whom was Roger Maris, who was named the American League's Most Valuable Player in 1960 and 1961 and in the latter year hit sixty-one home runs, breaking Babe Ruth's 1927 record of sixty.

The A's transfer represented something of a break with the established territorial consciousness of the owners, in that for the first time in history a league voted to transfer one of its original franchises to a new city rather than to keep the team in its traditional location. But, once again, the move did not involve a major deviation from the established transportation networks, nor did it involve construction of a new ballpark. Moreover, it balanced the American League from the point of view of its traditional geographic distribution of clubs, replacing one of the eastern cities, which had grown to five with the Browns' transfer to Baltimore, with a western city, restoring the 4–4 balance.

Thus it could have been said that the first round of franchise transfers in 1953 and 1954 took place largely within the established consciousness, with respect to travel and franchise locations, of the enterprise. Moreover, it could have been said that the primary motivation of the club owners in approving the transfer was to shore up the fortunes of economically depressed franchises in two-club cities that, over the past fifty years, had grown too small to support two major league teams.

Neither comment could have been directed toward the 1957 moves of the Dodgers and Giants to Los Angeles and San Francisco. Those moves, initiated jointly, deprived the leading baseball market in the nation of two of its teams. Neither move was precipitated primarily by the declining condition of a ballclub. The Dodgers were not in decline at all, despite the inadequacy of their ballpark. The downturn in the Giants' fortunes after their World Series championship in 1954 was attributed to a combination of disappointing play and a deteriorating facility, and the Giants were not regarded as an economically disadvantaged franchise. Instead, the moves were calculated to take advantage of the burgeoning west coast market. Walter O'Malley of the Dodgers convinced Horace Stoneham of the Giants, who had considered moving to Minneapolis, that a joint move of the franchises would create a natural rivalry for their followers and ease the logistics of travel to the west coast for other clubs. Both the owners of the Giants and the Dodgers knew that there would be repercussions of their move, with pressure immediately created for a replacement National League team in New York, and as such they anticipated that their shifts would set off a chain of events that would result in expansion. Their goal was to be first into the west coast. In so doing they ignored the constraints of travel and ballpark availability that had figured so prominently in the earlier transfers. Neither Los Angeles nor San Francisco had an adequate existing ballpark; the Dodgers played in the Los Angeles Coliseum, the Giants in Seals Stadium, while new parks were being built (with significant municipal support). The two new National League cities were half a continent away from any others: the existing transportation networks of the league had been fractured.[64]

The moves of the Giants and Dodgers, then, reflected a new consciousness about major league baseball franchise ownership. The movers assumed that the fragmentation of the established National League circuit of clubs would not undermine the enterprise of major league baseball; on the contrary, it would save it. The moves were a tacit concession that the first generation of steel and concrete ballparks, built within cities, serviced by public transportation, drawing upon closely contiguous residents, had become obsolete. Baseball, the owners of the Dodgers and Giants believed, was now a game whose revenues would come from fans located in relatively large areas around a ballpark, driving to the games in cars, and from radio and television rights. California, with its extensive freeways, growing population, close connections to the entertainment industry, and its suburban lifestyles was the symbol of baseball's future; Boston, Philadelphia, and even New York, with their crowded streets, deteriorating inner cities, and inaccessible ballparks, the symbol of its past.[65]

Thus the enterprise of Organized Baseball, fifty years after the formation of the National Agreement, stood on the threshold of radical alteration. The territoriality principle had already been recast, and within twenty years the reserve clause and blacklisting principles would be altered as well. And as the enterprise changed, baseball's cultural status changed as well. Once the principal and arguably the only sport that served as a source of cultural identification and aspiration for Americans, baseball has found itself, from at least the 1960s on, as one of an increasing number of visible and successful American professional sports. The years between 1903 and 1953 thus, in retrospect, increasingly appear as an era unto themselves, an era in which baseball established itself both as a unique and "peculiar" business and as the national pastime. It remains to summarize the threads of that development and to speculate about the reasons for it.

10

The Decline of the National Pastime

IN MANY BOOKS on baseball, perhaps in most "serious" books on baseball, the historian Jacques Barzun, who was born in France but spent his scholarly career at Columbia University, is quoted for the proposition that "whoever wants to know the heart and mind of America had better learn baseball." But although the Barzun quote is regularly offered and just as regularly solemnized, its context is rarely given, and Barzun's reasons for his conclusion rarely analyzed. Here is a longer version of the Barzun quotation:

> Whoever wants to know the heart and mind of America had better learn baseball. . . . Baseball is Greek in being national, heroic, and broken up in the rivalries of city-states. . . . It fitly expresses the powers of the nation's mind and body. . . . [It has] the glory of being the most active, agile, varied, articulate, and brainy of all group games. It is of and for our century. . . . The idea of baseball is a team, . . . a twentieth-century setup of opposite numbers. . . . A kind of individualism thereby returns, but it is limited. . . . Accuracy and speed, the practiced eye and the hefty arm, the mind to take in and react to the unexpected, the possession of more than one talent and the willingness to work in harness without special orders—these are the American virtues that shine in baseball.[1]

When Barzun's celebrated sentence is set forth in context, one begins to get a sense of why those invoking him have tended to limit themselves to his opening remarks. His extended observations collapse as meaningful propositions, saying more about the self-image of academicians in the 1950s than the "national" dimensions of baseball. Other than Barzun's assertion, no reasons are advanced for why baseball is "the most active, agile, varied, articulate, and brainy of all group games," and the assertion is dubious. Almost any group professional sport offers its players more activity than baseball. The regular movements of professional basketball or hockey players are surely more agile than those of baseball players. Baseball's variety, when compared with football, basketball, or soccer, is actually a misnomer, stemming from the indirect way in which runs are scored in baseball, as distinguished form the steady, regular progress toward a goal line, a basket, or a goal that marks those sports. In terms of the activities of individual players, all of those sports are more varied than baseball; baseball is in fact distinguished by its repetitiveness.

As for baseball's celebrated intellectual dimensions, those are arguably deceptive. Baseball is unique among major American sports in having long periods of time elapse before significant action takes place. Because of these time intervals, it is easier to follow as a spectator once one is initiated into its intricacies, and very much easier to listen to on radio. The gaps between significant action also allow more time for strategizing—compare soccer, where at present the coach cannot even call a time out—and for vicarious involvement by spectators. But that is not to say that the game itself is more sophisticated than its counterpart. Football, for example, requires a much greater mastery of coordinated team drills and activities than baseball. Basketball and soccer have hundreds of set plays involving multiple team members at the same time; a baseball play rarely involves more than two players at once, and only occasionally, as with a double play or a throw and tag from the outfield, is there a sense of precisely coordinated roles. Baseball's appeal to intellectuals may in part be simply a function of the fact that its spectators have more time to think about forthcoming action, and intellectuals, by definition, like to think. This book suggests that the other reasons for baseball's special appeal to intellectuals, as well as other Americans, are cultural rather than intrinsic.

Barzun's observation that baseball "is of and for our century" of course requires some kind of agreement on the character of the twentieth century. His central point appears to be that the twentieth century has been one of "limited individualism," in which an individualistic past has given way to a "twentieth-century setup" in which "opposite numbers" of individuals are linked in groups, teams, outfits, and other collective bodies. Even if Barzun is right in his characterization of the twentieth century as less individualistic than previous ones, which seems problematic on its face (were nineteenth-century marriage and child-rearing patterns more individualistic than their twentieth-century counterparts?), his characterization of baseball as "a kind of individualism [that] is limited" seems to lack a comparative perspective. Nothing seems more individualistic than a basketball player driving to the basket, one on one, but the play is only a tiny moment in a collective, team game. The "individualism" of baseball rests heavily on the attention paid to isolated encounters between a player and the ball, of which the most prominent involves batters and pitchers. Such episodes differ from "individualistic" moments in other team sports because in baseball many other players remain inert while the episodes occur. All team games are marked by such episodes. Soccer, for example, is filled with them, yet that sport is rarely thought of as individualistic.

Finally, consider Barzun's comments about "the American virtues" that baseball supposedly brings to the fore. He lists among those "accuracy and speed," a "practiced eye" and a "hefty arm," an ability to "take in and react to the unexpected," "the possession of more than one talent," and "the willingness to work in harness without special orders." None of these qualities seems distinctively linked to baseball or uniquely American. It is hard to know what Barzun means by "accuracy," but if he means the ability to place the ball in a precise spot it would seem more important in basketball, football, or soccer than in baseball, except for one position, pitcher. Speed is clearly more important in soccer and football than in baseball, as is abundantly evident when professional athletes from different sports compete against one another in made-for-television events. A "practiced eye" and a "hefty arm" are simply euphemisms for athletic qualities important in all sports.

The generalizations get even more precarious when they are used to describe "American," as well as "baseball" virtues. How does Barzun know that Americans are conspicuous for possessing "more than one talent," or for exhibiting a "willingness to work in harness without special orders"? If anything, intuitive cultural stereotypes suggest the opposite. It is Americans who are characterized as conspicuously provincial and insular alongside their European counterparts, and as particularly resistant to authority, bureaucracy, or anything that curbs their ingrained belief in autonomy. Working in harness without special orders seems more stereotypically applied to citizens in cultures with strong totalitarian traditions.

And, of course, why should baseball be regarded as a game singularly inclined to bring versatility or "working in harness" to the fore? Long periods of time can go by in a baseball game in which an individual member of a team does not have to come into contact with his teammates at all, let alone "work in harness" with them. All professional sports require the performance, on a very high level, of a number of athletic functions, such as running, jumping, throwing, and catching or trapping a ball. One would be hard pressed to say that baseball is significantly different from other group sports in demanding multiple athletic talents. They all do.

In short, Barzun's generalizations about baseball and "the heart and mind of America" seem to be a collection of unfounded assertions, rampant overgeneralizations, and exercises in wish-fulfillment. Yet his memorable line persists, and is still given credence. Its enduring quality suggests that it contains a kernel of truth.

The overall effort of this book, in fact, has been to show that baseball unquestionably was, and may well still be, America's national pastime, occupying the status of more than a mere professional sport. But the argument of this book is not that there is something intrinsically American about the game of baseball, or that only baseball could have evolved from a sport to a pastime. It is, in fact, the reverse, that baseball became the national pastime because those at the upper echelons of the sport as an enterprise consciously, and unconsciously, transformed it from a working class, "rough," urban sport to a game that simultaneously embodied America's urbanizing, commercializing future and the memory of its rural, pastoral past.

Crucial to understanding the transformation of baseball from a sport into a pastime is the recognition that much of that development was haphazard, fortuitous, and, from the perspective of hindsight, often illogical, inefficient, or even perverse. As baseball caught hold as a "national game," it became a cultural mirror, however much its magnates sought to carve it out as a private, peculiar domain. It could not avoid being touched by the social issues that touched the rest of America in the twentieth century, issues ranging from race and ethnicity to the advent of electronic media and dramatic growths and shifts in the population. Despite affecting the image of a boy's sport, it became a lightning rod for gambling, racial and ethnic tension, labor disputes, and the relationship between cities and sports franchises. It faced these problems because they were at the center of American culture from 1903 to 1953.

Thus a book about baseball in the first fifty years of the twentieth century is to some extent a book about the nation as a whole. But this book has been centrally concerned with the special place that baseball, as a growing professional sport, occupied in the American nation, and why it, alone among its competitors, should have occupied that place.

In many respects, we have seen, baseball mirrored American society, as it evolved in the first fifty years of the twentieth century, rather than being isolated from it. When ballparks were built, their character and location reflected the ideals and concerns of growing cities. When radio became established as an important and widespread medium, baseball games became part of its programming, and baseball and the radio industry developed a symbiotic, lucrative relationship despite fears on the part of much of baseball's officialdom that the new medium would eventually result in vast home audiences listening to games broadcast from empty stands. When baseball was a "deadball" game, the sporting press popularized it as such; when it took on wider, more catholic dimensions in the 1920s, with the advent of Babe Ruth and the home run, the press was there to help create a new class of baseball celebrities. When wars came, players readily enlisted and teams drilled at ballparks. President Roosevelt allowed the major leagues to continue a full schedule during World War II on the grounds that having baseball around was good for American morale. For all its "peculiar" status as a business, a sport, and a pastime, baseball was regularly touched by the technological changes of the century. If anything, it was more reluctant to embrace those changes than many other enterprises. The electric light, the radio, the television, and the airplane made baseball executives, on the whole, uneasy when first introduced.

There were, however, two major exceptions to baseball's general tendency to mirror the larger culture rather than to function as a pastoral oasis in the industrializing, urbanizing, and increasingly technocratic landscape of the twentieth century. The exceptions lay in its approach to demographics and its approach to labor relations. In both areas baseball stood resolutely against trends outside it, seeking to freeze its structure at a point in time. In so doing it invoked the full power of its claims to be seen as a pastime as well as a business. And in so doing it arguably created its essential identity. When those two approaches eventually collapsed after 1953, making baseball appear identical to other economic institutions and other professional sports in America, one could argue that baseball surrendered the special qualities that had given it claim to being the national pastime.

Demographics came first. Convinced that the territoriality principle was the only way to protect club autonomy and foster civic pride, baseball's officialdom fiercely resisted any effort to alter the original distribution of franchises it had created in 1903. In many respects the Celler subcommittee hearings of 1951 were not so much about the reserve clause or the antitrust exemption, but about what baseball was going to do about the fact that very large centers of population existed, notably on the west coast, that under the present structure had no hope of securing major league teams.

At the time of the Celler subcommittee hearings it had become apparent that the territoriality principle had come to be at war, in certain locations, with the principle of civic aggrandizement and revival through major league baseball. Once sensibly tied to civic development in a relatively sparsely populated continent with a few metropolitan areas, territoriality had now become a synonym for barriers to entry. In the 1940s, Bill Veeck sought to buy the St. Louis Browns and transfer them to Los Angeles, and to buy the Philadelphia Phillies and transfer them to Milwaukee. In both cases the franchises were moribund, and the transfers likely to turn the club's financial prospects around. In both instances major league owners responded by blocking the sale until local ownership could be found. The franchises, safe in their existing homes, continued their financial and competitive decline.

Had the changing demographics of America in the 1950s simply been reflected in new communities of prospective fans, the territoriality principle might have endured longer. But it was clear that post–World War II demographics had not just changed the attendance base, but the entire revenue base of major league franchises. New population centers did not just mean new fans to attend games; they meant new listeners and new viewers, new opportunities for advertising revenue. With the astonishing rise of home television in the 1950s, baseball clubs realized that television contracts would be a very important part of their enterprise. The irresistibility of Los Angeles and San Francisco as major league baseball cities was as much a function of their potential as radio and television markets as any other factor.

Thus the territoriality principle collapsed in increments, with the failing Braves moving to Milwaukee and the failing Browns to Baltimore, both cities approximately within the existing territorial circuit; then the failing Athletics moving to Kansas City, pressing the boundaries of the circuit westward; then the Dodgers and Giants declaring a revolt against territoriality by moving their solvent franchises from Brooklyn and New York to Los Angeles and San Francisco. With their moves the demographic world of baseball finally began to track the demographics of America generally. It was now apparent that media markets, population shifts, and the airplane were the dominant factors driving franchise location. In this world the expansion of major league baseball was inevitable, and it swiftly came. Today expansion is still with us, and the location of a franchise is a product of its current profitability and the other options available.

Lost in the new world of baseball demographics has been one of the foundations for the older conception of territoriality. This was the conviction that the continuity of a franchise, both in terms of its personnel and its civic associations, was an important ingredient in fostering its civic identity. It was no accident that the first franchises that moved in the 1950s departed from two-team cities: their residents' civic pride was allegedly consoled by the fact that one team remained. Now that sense of continuity is apparently given less weight. When the Washington Senators moved to Minnesota in 1960, Organized Baseball scrambled to replace them with an expansion Washington club as quickly as possible. When that club moved again to Texas in 1971, no replacement was forthcoming.

In the original promulgation of the fundamental laws of baseball, territoriality harmonized with rules of labor relations in the promotion of continuity for a franchise. Not only did a club's location remain constant over the years, its roster could remain relatively constant. Both territoriality and the reserve clause fostered the civic dimensions of a franchise; both were essential parts of baseball's unique economic structure. But the territoriality principle was not, when it was promulgated in 1903, a startling innovation, out of phase with other enterprises. If anything, it was a sensible "anti-cutthroat" proposition that prevented ruinous competition in designated markets. Territoriality only became obsolete because the markets for baseball franchises changed in size, location, and definition.

The reserve clause was something else. From the *Lajoie* case on it was recognized as an unusual restriction on the bargaining power of employees signing personal service contracts. It was not treated as a decisive precedent, and when the emergence of the Federal League precipitated another round of contract jumping, courts and commentators declared that the reserve clause practice violated basic principles of mutuality in contract formation. The survival of the reserve clause for fifty years after *Lajoie* isolated the baseball industry from other labor forces in the American economy. Over the course of the twentieth century trends in labor relations had been in the direction of greater working benefits and more equal bargaining power between employers and their employees. Trends had also been in the direction of increased unionization and collective bargaining for workers. In the 1950s baseball stood nearly alone as a major, national industry in which contracts were still negotiated individually, in which radically unequal bargaining power existed between clubs and players, and in which unionization did not exist.

In the Celler subcommittee hearings several players were asked about the possibility of unionization in Organized Baseball, and none expected it to materialize. Commentators on the monopsonistic character of baseball took a similar view. Observers and the players themselves saw professional baseball players as too "independent," or too "individualistic" to embrace unionization. Most players, as we have seen, favored the reserve clause, citing its positive effects on team balance and the stability of franchises. Even commentators that found baseball's labor practices clearly inconsistent with federal antitrust laws hesitated to recommend the abolition of the reserve clause or the removal of baseball's antitrust exemption. Fifty years after the formation of the National Agreement the game retained its status as a "peculiar business" with its own unique labor practices.

Over the next twenty years, however, the forces that had contributed to the breakdown of the territoriality principle, gaining momentum from that breakdown, eventually altered the labor relations consciousness of the baseball industry. Franchise movement and electronic media revenues significantly altered the profitability of many baseball franchises. In addition to the increased gate receipts that followed relocation to a new city, at least in the short run, franchises benefited from lucrative radio and television contracts. As the popularity of television increased, and advertising space on the electronic media dramatically augmented in value, radio and TV stations could afford to pay large sums for the privilege of broadcasting games. In the fifties and sixties television and radio programs were saturated with baseball coverage, including competing national broadcasts and extensive local television broadcasts. In those decades it became commonplace for every major league club to air live radio broadcasts of all of its games, and some clubs televised nearly all their games as well. In those decades club owners discovered something they had not anticipated about electronic media coverage of baseball games: coverage did not decrease major league attendance, and actually appeared to help it.

Increased revenues from the electronic media, coupled with the ability to relocate financially troubled franchises and a more permissive attitude toward expansion into new markets, dramatically changed the financial structure of major league baseball. The inevitable result was an increase in the salaries paid to players. But for a time, because of the reserve clause, a growing gap existed between the revenues of successful teams and their expenditures on player salaries. Superstars of the fifties and sixties, we have seen, were still subject to the reserve clause, and were paid far less than they could have commanded in the open market.

Given the apparent upswing in baseball's financial picture that had been generated by new markets and electronic media revenues, and given the growing unionization of American professions in the fifties and sixties, it was perhaps inevitable that a new labor consciousness would take hold among baseball players. The beginnings of that consciousness can be seen as early as the years following World War II, when the retirement benefits of players became a labor relations issue. The situation of retired players had been a chronic complaint of baseball's labor force, since active baseball careers, compared with those in most other industries, were short, and for most of the early twentieth century retirement benefits were virtually nonexistent. We have seen that the first open recognition of the retiree problem came in the 1930s, when proceeds from the annual All-Star Game were directed to a pension fund established for disabled retired ballplayers, and later for all retirees. The idea of a pension fund, as noted, had come from a newspaper, not from owners or players, but it penetrated the consciousness of the baseball industry. One of the responses of Organized Baseball's officialdom, when confronted with the *Gardella* case in 1949 and the Celler subcommittee hearings two years later, was to take publicized steps to increase player pension benefits.

As late as the 1960s, however, owners were still able to argue that a player reluctant to sign a contract had only the option of quitting baseball and facing considerably reduced economic prospects. Faced with this option, Dodger pitchers Don Drysdale and Sandy Koufax staged a joint holdout before the 1966 season, hiring an agent, demanding significant raises, and announcing their retirement, in which they planned to make a motion picture. Walter O'Malley of the Dodgers responded by saying that he had never negotiated with an agent and did not expect to do so, but the Dodgers compromised, paying Koufax $130,000 and Drysdale $116,000 for the 1966 season. The Drysdale-Koufax incident played up the imbalance between increased owner revenues and the artificially depressed wages of players under the reserve clause.

Then, in 1966, the major leagues' Players Association, hitherto a loosely organized, passive body, retained Marvin Miller, former adviser to the United Steel Workers, as its executive director. Miller's background in labor relations convinced him that baseball was not essentially different from other industries in the later years of the twentieth century and that there were a number of issues on which club owners were vulnerable. He first concentrated on pension benefits, minimum salaries, and arbitration, stressing in particular an interest in tying pension benefits to television and radio revenues. This last was a masterstroke, because it simultaneously highlighted the extraordinary growth in those revenues in the fifties and sixties and the vulnerability of professional athletes caused by the short tenures of their careers. It also steered clear of the reserve clause at a time when the players were not yet united or powerful enough to mount a head-on attack against it.[2]

Aided by owner overreaction to his presence, Miller helped foster a growing "union" consciousness among major league players. Between 1966 and 1969 Miller secured concessions from owners on pension funds, negotiated a lucrative agreement between the Players Association and the Topps Chewing Gum Company to guarantee players royalties from baseball cards, and hammered out a Basic Agreement between players and owners in 1968, in which the major league minimum salary was increased, a formal grievance procedure for disgruntled players was created, and a "study" of the reserve clause was commissioned. In the spring of 1969, for the first time in over fifty years, the threat of a players' strike, precipitated by continued wrangling over pension benefits, surfaced. The owners were in a particularly weak position at the time, having fired their commissioner, General William Eckert, during the winter of 1968. One of the National League's lawyers, Bowie Kuhn, played a pivotal role in the settlement of the pension dispute and was rewarded by being named commissioner.

In agreeing to "study" the reserve system the club owners were signaling their desire to bury the issue from public consciousness, but their inaction on the issue was eventually to precipitate a series of developments that led to the abolition of the reserve clause and the transformation of baseball's labor relations. Those developments included a revised Basic Agreement in 1970 that provided for collective bargaining by the Players' Association, including the use of agents and binding arbitration of grievances beyond the commissioner's office. They also included a challenge to the reserve clause itself by St. Louis Cardinal outfielder Curt Flood, who sought to prevent being traded to the Philadelphia Phillies. Flood would eventually take his case to the Supreme Court and lose, in a bizarre 5–3 decision. But the same year the decision was announced, 1972, players went on strike, missing eighty-six games. And when a new Basic Agreement in 1973 retained the reserve clause, two players, Andy Messersmith and Dave McNally, challenged it after the 1975 decision and won before designated arbitrator Peter Seitz. In 1976 yet another Basic Agreement incorporated limited free agency, and the transition to a new era of baseball labor relations was complete.

The collapse of territoriality, itself brought about by changing demographics and the rise of the electronic media, had eventually fostered a new labor relations atmosphere within baseball that brought down the reserve clause itself. By 1976 none of the three fundamental laws of Organized Baseball remained intact. Baseball appeared indistinguishable from other professional sports or from other large "entertainment" industries. It was oriented around the "free market," collectively negotiated labor practices, and the electronic media. It was no longer a "peculiar" fiefdom affectionately shielded from the rest of economic life, but an industry subject to the same variables and uncertainties as other industries competing for the entertainment dollar.

Such is the present status of baseball. In light of dramatically inflated salaries, the allegedly chronic difficulties of small-market franchises, the inability of owners to hire a commissioner, and the 1994–95 players' strike, it appears that the transition from a "peculiar" to an ordinary entertainment business, although dramatically improving the financial position of players, has thrown the game into chaos. It is even possible that in transforming itself to resemble the paradigm of a contemporary professional sports industry, baseball has lost its status as the national pastime. It is possible, in short, that that status may have been linked, to an important extent, to baseball's economically and culturally anachronistic features. A brief consideration of that issue concludes this analysis of the unique place of baseball among American professional sports.

◆

There were many reasons why baseball became the national pastime, and some of them were fortuitous. The early twentieth-century owners that decided to merge competing major leagues and establish an overriding legal and economic structure to the enterprise did not make those decisions in order to give their sport a special status in the American pantheon. They made the decisions because they felt the economic health of the game depended on antidotes to cutthroat competition, in the form of player free agency, and to the competitive imbalance they expected to follow from widespread roster shifts. They also believed that if an entrepreneur had made the investment of buying a baseball franchise and operating it within a metropolitan area, he deserved some assurance that other competitors would not infringe upon his territory.

The founders of Organized Baseball thus created the structure of the game to preserve and protect their own interests. At the same time, however, that structure created a unique set of partnerships among players and club owners. Despite being competitors, club owners had a joint stake in the game's being as attractive, popular, and lucrative as possible. They had a joint stake in close, even hotly contested pennant races. Players had the same stake. They stood to make more money if their clubs drew well at the gate, and clubs tended to draw well at the gate if they were involved in close competition. Winning teams tended to draw better than losing teams, but when winning teams won too decisively, eliminating drama from a pennant race, their attendance tended to decline.

In short, all of the major participants in early twentieth-century baseball had considerable incentive to develop the game as a source of vicarious pride and satisfaction for fans. And we have seen that in nearly every phase of the game, civic pride and satisfaction were cultivated by those within major league baseball. Those who built ballparks, or reported on games in print or broadcast them on radio, or helped foster the status of ballplayers as celebrities, or sought to link the game to American youth and exemplary American values, or created a Hall of Fame of superstars were engaging in those tasks to cement emotional allegiances between baseball and its fans. In the fifty years after 1903 they pursued that goal with considerable success.

Alongside the particularistic economic concerns of an early generation of owners, then, lay mutual goals of promoting and selling the game that were held by both owners and players. This tended to create the impression that baseball's "peculiar" economic and legal structure, despite its patent one-sidedness, was endorsed by all of its participants. And to an important extent this was correct. In a world in which most baseball players could not have hoped to command the level of salary and benefits they received from playing baseball in any other walk of life, the reserve clause looked like a pretty good deal.

Over time those two overlapping dimensions of baseball—the particularistic economic agenda of the early owners and the joint goal of all parties in promoting the civic dimensions of the game—came to be run together, so that the civic status of baseball, the extent to which it transcended being a mere professional sport to become a metropolitan and subsequently a national presence, was linked with its peculiar economic status. Thus when the Celler subcommittee questioned the reserve clause and baseball's antitrust exemption in the early 1950s, players and club owners united in asserting that to dismantle the foundations of baseball law would be to dismantle the game itself. What they meant in making that argument, it turns out, was not that professional baseball would cease to be played in America if the reserve clause, blacklisting, and territoriality were eliminated, but that professional baseball would cease to be something special, something more than simply a sport played for money.

And in a sense that version of their argument may well have turned out to be correct. There is no question that a combination of the collapse of territoriality and the dismantling of the reserve clause structure has changed the civic dimensions of contemporary major league baseball. Players now routinely change rosters; the continuity of personnel on a club has been vastly curtailed by free agency. Franchises also are able to change cities with relative ease: even one-team major league metropolitan areas cannot be sure that they will retain a team if that team consistently loses money. One might compare the treatment of the Phillies and the Browns in the forties and early fifties, when the National and American Leagues intervened to keep losing franchises in a city, with arguments made recently about the Pittsburgh Pirates franchise. When confronted with the proposition that Pittsburgh was one of the original clubs of the National Agreement, and that it would be a shocking departure from baseball tradition to have no club in Pittsburgh, advocates of franchise relocation have pointed out that the Pirates could not fill their stadium in the last game of a recent National League championship series. In that argument there seems to be only one criterion for franchise continuity: success at the gate.

As baseball has settled into a routine of franchise relocation, expansion, and perennial changes in clubs' identities brought about through free agency, it finds itself duplicating the pattern of other contemporary professional sports. It finds itself appearing no different, in its economic and legal structure, from basketball or football or hockey, sports whose economic health has been dependent on a combination of media revenues and consistent gate attendance, and whose teams' civic identities are muted and variable. It is certainly ironic that baseball, having invested so much of its history in tacitly propounding its cultural uniqueness among professional sports, has engineered its own transition to ordinary status. No one made baseball evolve from the enterprise that still existed in 1953 to the enterprise that exists today. The courts, Congress, and the general public largely left baseball alone, despite its anomalous economic status. Baseball wrought the changes itself.

It seems far too late to return to the reserve system, or to restore antiquated definitions of territoriality. It may even be too late to restore the commissioner's office as an interventionist moral force, a check on owners as well as players. But it also seems that even if baseball solves its current economic and labor problems through some form of revenue-sharing among clubs and players, it will simply be acting like other contemporary professional sports. How, in light of this, will baseball distinguish itself, retain its special hold on the American citizenry?

Some commentators on the game have suggested that baseball owns a unique advantage over other professional sports in that its internal rhythms, consisting of a long season, played in daily stages over the spring and summer months, in outdoor arenas, give it an evocative, pastoral quality that touches its fans deeply and which no other sport can match.[3] That may be so—although there are now five domed stadiums in the majors—and the pastoral dimensions of baseball have already been identified as one of the elements that made it into the national pastime. But one may wonder how far the cerebral, pastoral, contemplative, timeless dimensions of baseball can be taken. As we have seen, the pastoral image of the game was itself a product of a particular generational consciousness, that of the Progressive Era. But generations come and go, and the practical problem facing all professional sports in America is how to attract the allegiance of new generations. Baseball has traditionally done this through the oft-cited ritual of fathers taking children to ballparks and teaching them the intricacies of the game.

One wonders whether these rituals will survive the next century. Because of its current salary structure, major league baseball is an expensive game to attend regularly. Young persons are bombarded with sports in contemporary America, both at the level of participation and observation. Many sports are easier to play than baseball. Many sports are easier to generate among small groups of children, requiring less space and fewer participants. As fewer young Americans play baseball because of competition from other sports, and fewer American families are financially able to attend games regularly, the time-honored customs of parents playing catch with their children or taking them to the park to watch their heroes may give way to other rituals, such as fathers or mothers coaching youth soccer for their sons and daughters.

So it may be that baseball, at the almost miraculously evocative level that has been the stuff of those who have written affectionately and probingly about the game—the baseball of dramatic pennant races, watched by knowledgeable fans intimately familiar with the personnel of their home teams and the opponents, conducted on sunny spring, summer, and early fall afternoons, generating endless discussions and critiques and tears and euphoria—will increasingly be the stuff of history. It may be that the twenty-first century will be one in which commentators gravely announce that baseball was, rather than is, the national pastime.

Notes

Chapter One

1. Lawrence Ritter, *Lost Ballparks: A Celebration of Baseball's Legendary Fields*, 91, 158–60 (1992); John B. Foster, "The Magnificent New Polo Grounds," *Baseball Magazine* (October 1911); John T. Brush, "The Evolution of the Baseball Grandstand," *Baseball Magazine* (April 1912); Eugene Murdock, *Ban Johnson, Czar of Baseball*, 63–68 (1982).

2. Brush, "Evolution of the Baseball Grandstand," 2.

3. Ibid., 3; Foster, "Magnificent New Polo Grounds," 100–102.

4. Ritter, *Lost Ballparks*, 160–62, 165; *New York Times*, June 29, 1911; Foster, "Magnificent New Polo Grounds," 100.

5. Municipal Stadium was built in Cleveland in 1931, not intended primarily as a baseball park but as an all-purpose "stadium" (a type of structure that Yankee Stadium had anticipated) designed for football, baseball, and other large-arena sports or entertainment events. The ballparks in other major league cities were designed exclusively for baseball. At the time the last of those was completed, Braves Field (Boston) in 1915, the only other professional sport that drew large crowds was boxing. For an excellent overview of contemporary reaction to the new concrete and steel ballparks, see Robert Bluthardt, "Fenway Park and the Golden Age of the Baseball Park, 1909–1915," *Journal of Popular Culture* (Summer 1987).

6. Stephen A. Riess, *Touching Base: Professional Baseball and American Culture in the Progressive Era*, 90 (1982).

7. See Peter A. Levine, *A. G. Spalding and the Rise of Baseball*, 5–7 (1985), for a description of the early game.

8. David Q. Voigt, *From the Commissioners to Continental Expansion*, vol. 2 of *American Baseball*, 102 (1970); James M. Kahn, *The Umpire Story*, 75 (1953).

9. See Ritter, *Lost Ballparks*, 94, for details of the October 10, 1904, game.

10. Ibid., 92–98.

11. *Brooklyn Daily Eagle*, April 9, 1913.

12. See *New York Times*, April 12, 1912; *Brooklyn Daily Eagle*, April 13, 1912.

13. See Riess, *Touching Base*, 88, 112 n. 9. The name "Dodgers," which replaced Superbas shortly after Ebbets Field opened, was a product of the play-

ers being thought of as dodging trolley cars on their way to Washington Park and Ebbets Field.

14. *Brooklyn Daily Eagle*, April 9, 1913.

15. Ibid.

16. Quoted in A. Yager, "Plans Revealed for Ebbets Field," *The Sporting News*, March 14, 1912.

17. Ritter, *Lost Ballparks*, 51; *Brooklyn Daily Eagle*, February 1, 1912; *New York Times*, April 7, 1912.

18. "New York's Major League Teams Ready to Start 1913 Season," *New York Times*, April 6, 1913.

19. *Brooklyn Daily Eagle*, April 9, 1913.

20. For details on Ben Shibe and the building of Shibe Park, see Bruce Kuklick, *To Every Thing a Season: Shibe Park and Urban Philadelphia, 1909–1976*, 15–29 (1991).

21. On the role of ballparks as cultural symbols in the early twentieth century, see Riess, *Touching Base*, 85–119.

22. For details on the identities and social origins of the ballpark builders see ibid., 53–77.

23. Kuklick, *To Every Thing a Season*, 25; Dale L. Swearingen in Philip J. Lowry, ed., *Green Cathedrals*, xi–xii (1992).

24. See Lowell Reidenbaugh, *The Sporting News Take Me Out to the Ballpark* (1983), for seating capacities.

25. See *The Sporting News*, April 1, 1909. A consideration affecting double decking in the Boston area was the fact that Fenway Park was built on filled land in the Back Bay. This meant that in addition to ordinary pillars, extensive piles would be required to support a double-decked structure. This consideration did not affect Braves Field, however, which was built on the site of a golf course in Allston, across the Charles River from Boston proper.

26. For the seating figures see Kuklick, *To Every Thing a Season*, 26.

27. See Ritter, *Lost Ballparks*, for capacities.

28. This section draws upon Harold Seymour, *Baseball: The Golden Age*, 42–71 (1971); Charles Alexander, *John McGraw*, 170–83 (1988); Harold Kaese, *The Boston Braves*, 136–59 (1948); William Curran, *Big Sticks*, 90–101 (1990), where a different sort of reconstruction of an early ball game appears; and especially the *New York Times*, August 16, 1914, pp. S 3–4.

29. See *New York World*, August 13, 1914, p. 8; *New York Tribune*, August 13, 1914, p. 10.

30. See David John Kammer, *Take Me Out to the Ballgame*, 106 (Ph.D. diss., University of New Mexico, 1982), citing articles in the New York press.

31. See ibid., 105–8, quoting articles in *The Sporting News* and the New York press.

32. See ibid., 118.

33. Ibid., 119.

34. For details see Frank Graham, *The New York Yankees*, 75–76 (1951).

35. See Kammer, *Take Me Out to the Ballgame*, 146.

36. See *The Sporting News*, January 31, 1929. The Cleveland Indians had experimented with numbers on the sleeves of uniforms as early as 1915, but abandoned the practice.

37. Ritter, *Lost Ballparks*, 9–17, 188–89. One could see the early-twentieth-century process of building ballparks, sinking capital into them, and failing to upgrade them over time as paralleling the process of "deindustrialization" in other large American industries during the same time. See Paul Tiffane, *The Decline of American Steel* (1988).

Chapter Two

1. For details on the Baltimore-Philadelphia opening game in 1902, see *Baltimore Sun*, April 24, 1902; and Charles C. Alexander, *John McGraw*, 88–89 (1988). Background on the Philadelphia owners and their connections can be found in Lee Lowenfish and Tony Lupien, *The Imperfect Diamond*, 58–69 (1980), and "The Front Office," 467–69, in *The New Phillies Encyclopedia* (1993). On Ban Johnson's role in the *Lajoie* case, see Eugene Murdock, *Ban Johnson: Czar of Baseball*, 54–55 (1982); Lowenfish and Lupien, *The Imperfect Diamond*, 67–69.

Johnson's special interest in the Cleveland franchise stemmed from the fact that its owner, Charles W. Somers, had been one of Johnson's major financial backers in his career as a baseball entrepreneur. Somers initially backed several of the American League franchises when that league sought to expand in 1900 and 1901, including the Philadelphia Athletics. See Bruce Kuklick, *To Every Thing a Season*, 14–15 (1991). Johnson was also close to Connie Mack, the original manager and part owner of the Athletics. See Murdock, *Ban Johnson*, 46–49.

2. A good source of team rosters and other information about major league baseball in the first decade of the twentieth century is Marc Okkonen, *Baseball Memories: 1900–1909* (1992), based on newspapers from the period.

3. Ed Delahanty is perhaps best known for the circumstances of his untimely death in 1903, when, in a state of excessive inebriation, he was dispatched from a train carrying the Washington Nationals from Chicago to New York. The conductor put him off the train at Fort Erie, Ontario, just across the Niagara River from Buffalo. Delahanty, in the course of attempting to walk from Canada to the United States across the "Peace Bridge" spanning that river, apparently fell off the bridge and was killed. His body was not found until several days later. For one account of Delahanty's death, see Fred Lieb, *Baseball As I Have Known It*, 17 (1977); for another version, see Sam Crawford's reminiscence to Lawrence Ritter in Ritter's *The Glory of Their Times*, 65 (1984).

4. Leach to Ritter in *Glory of Their Times*, 33.

5. The details of the *Lajoie* case are taken from *Philadelphia Ball Club, Limited v. Napoleon Lajoie et al.*, C.P. No. 5, Phila. Co. (trial court opinion), and

Phila. Ball Club, Ltd. v. Lajoie, 202 Pa. 210 (1902) (Pennsylvania Supreme Court opinion).

The work of David Montgomery on labor relations in the late nineteenth and early twentieth centuries provides context for my discussion of Organized Baseball's early-twentieth-century labor practices. See David Montgomery, *Workers-Control in America* (1979) and *The Fall of the House of Labor* (1987).

6. 202 Pa. at 212–13.

7. *Lumley v. Wagner*, 1 DeG. M. & G. 603 (1852). That case involved the opera singer Johanna Wagner, who had signed a contract with Benjamin Lumley to sing at Her Majesty's Theatre in London from April 1 to June 1, 1852, and to authorize Lumley to arrange her singing engagements in the future. Wagner subsequently entered into a contract with Frederick Gye to sing at Covent Garden, and Lumley sought to enjoin Wagner from singing at any theater other than his. The court, in an opinion by Lord St. Leonards, the Lord Chancellor of England, conceded that it could not compel Wagner to sing for Lumley, but nonetheless granted the injunction. *Lumley v. Wagner* was a particularly suggestive precedent for the *Lajoie* case, since Lumley's effort to reserve Wagner's services for the future paralleled the major league baseball clubs' use of the reserve clause in player contracts.

8. 202 Pa. at 217.

9. Ibid. at 219.

10. With one exception: between 1914 and 1917, when the rival Federal League sought to invade the National and American Leagues' "major league" domain, players were induced to jump contracts and some player salaries temporarily skyrocketed. The history of the Federal League and major league baseball's response to it, however, was, as we shall see, the exception that proved the rule.

11. Lowenfish and Lupien, *The Imperfect Diamond*, 61–66, 76–79. The Tiger players' grievance was neither an approval of Cobb's conduct (he had severely beaten a New York Highlander fan who was disabled) nor a protest against the severity of Cobb's suspension, but a response to the fact that Cobb had been suspended without being given a chance to "tell his side of the story." Apparently the fan, Claude Lueker, had been casting aspersions on Cobb's racial ancestry. The striking players were alleged to have felt that this sort of abuse, directed to a white native of Georgia such as Cobb, was overwhelmingly provocative. See *New York Times*, May 16, 1912, for a report of the incident.

12. *American League Baseball Club v. Chase*, 149 N.Y. Supp. 6, 17 (1914).

13. See Stephen A. Riess, *Touching Base: Professional Baseball and American Culture in the Progressive Era*, 95–96 (1982).

14. On the Federal League's origins and the "peace settlement" between the Federal League and the established major leagues, worked out in December

1915 and January 1916, see David Q. Voigt, *From the Commissioners to Continental Expansion*, vol. 2 of *American Baseball*, 114–120 (1970).

15. *American League Baseball Club v. Chase* at 15–16.

16. In 1940 the population of Los Angeles was 1,504,277; that of St. Louis 816,048. *Sixteenth Census of the United States: 1940, Vol. 2, Part 1.*

17. Albert G. Spalding, *America's National Game*, 3–4 (1911).

18. 259 U.S. 200 (1922), affirming the U.S. Court of Appeals for the District of Columbia Circuit's decision, 269 Fed. 681 (App. D.C. 1921), which reversed an unreported trial court decision.

19. It is important to distinguish the *Federal Baseball* case from another suit that the Federal League filed against Organized Baseball in January 1915, charging Organized Baseball with violating the antitrust laws and asking that their existing contracts with players be declared void. This suit was in response to major league clubs' efforts to prevent their players from jumping to the Federal League. It was filed in Judge Kenesaw Mountain Landis's federal district court in Chicago, and Landis held up a decision until the Federal League eventually sued for peace in December 1915. Landis played no role in the *Federal Baseball* case. See J. G. Taylor Spink, *Judge Landis and Twenty-Five Years of Baseball*, 29–40 (1947).

On Baltimore's nonparticipation in the Federal League peace settlement see Harold Seymour, *Baseball: The Early Years*, 243–45 (1960). Apparently Charles Comiskey and Charles Ebbets were the owners who insulted the Baltimore franchise during negotiations, Comiskey referring to Baltimore as a "minor league city" and Ebbets suggesting that there were "too many colored population" in Baltimore to provide an adequate fan base. Quoted in Seymour, *Baseball*, 244.

20. The language is from Holmes's dissent in *Northern Securities Co. v. United States*, 193 U.S. 197, 410–11 (1904).

21. *Paul v. Virginia*, 8 Wall. 168 (1869); *Hooper v. California*, 155 U.S. 648 (1894); *U.S. v. E. C. Knight*, 156 U.S. (1895).

22. 269 F. at 685.

23. Ibid. at 687–88.

24. Ibid. at 687.

25. *Federal Baseball Club of Baltimore, Inc. v. National League of Professional Baseball Clubs, et al.*, 259 U.S. 200, 208 (1922).

26. Ibid. at 208.

27. Ibid. at 208–9.

28. The mistaken attribution of ballplaying ability to Holmes may have originated with John Kieran's "Baseball Slaves and the Law Horrible," *New York Times*, April 21, 1937, from which the quotation is taken. On Holmes's lack of interest in sports, either as a participant or an observer, see G. Edward White, *Justice Oliver Wendell Holmes: Law and the Inner Self*, 469 (1993).

Chapter Three

1. Albert G. Spalding, *America's National Game*, 189–90 (1911).

2. Ibid., 535.

3. For more detailed discussions of late nineteenth-century gentry reform politics, see John G. Sproat, *The Best Men* (1968), and Geoffrey Blodgett, *The Gentle Reformers* (1966).

4. See Irving E. Sanborn, "The Slimy Trail of the Baseball Pool," *Baseball Magazine* (July 1925).

5. Comiskey in G. W. Axelson, *"Commy": The Life Story of Charles A. Comiskey*, 317–18 (1919).

6. Spalding, *America's National Game*, 129.

7. Ibid., 301, 308–9.

8. For more detail on the incidents between 1904 and the World Series of 1919, see Harold Seymour, *Baseball: The Golden Age*, 281–93 (1971).

9. After the Black Sox scandal broke in 1920, several players on the Phillies confirmed that they were offered bribes to throw games against the Giants but had declined the offer and kept silent about it. Seymour, *Baseball: The Golden Age*, 284–85.

10. Fred Lieb, *Baseball As I Have Known It*, 98 (1977).

11. Accounts of Chase's complicity in the July 25, 1918, incident and the subsequent actions taken by the Giants and the National League vary considerably. Compare Seymour, *Baseball: The Golden Age*, 291–93, with Charles Alexander, *John C. McGraw*, 206–7, 214–216 (1988). I am inclined to accept Alexander's account, which is based in part on articles in *The Sporting News*, August 22, 1918, p. 2; September 26, 1918, p. 1; November 4, 1920, p. 8; and November 11, 1920, p. 1.

12. The most authoritative source is Eliot Asinof's *Eight Men Out* (1963). Asinof's book, based in large part on interviews with former players in the late 1950s and 1960s, was deliberately undocumented. In his preface Asinof referred to "the complete privacy of many of [his] sources," who "chose to remain anonymous" (xiii).

13. Comiskey in Axelson, *"Commy"*, 318 (1919).

14. My account of the Black Sox scandal, except where otherwise documented, relies on Asinof, *Eight Men Out*.

15. Hugh Fullerton, *Chicago Herald Examiner*, October 10, 1919.

16. *New York Times*, October 11, 1919.

17. Quoted in Asinof, *Eight Men Out*, 133. See also *Chicago Tribune*, December 15, 1919.

18. Earl Obenshain in *The Sporting News*, October 16, 1919.

19. Grand Jury report to Chief Justice Charles A. MacDonald, November 6, 1921, quoted in J. G. Taylor Spink, *Judge Landis and Twenty-Five Years of Baseball*, 63 (1947).

20. *Chicago Tribune*, September 23, 1920; *New York Times*, September 25, 1920. The "boxer" mentioned in the *Times* article was clearly Abe Attell, and the article was remarkably accurate in its description of Attell's role in the fix, including mentioning Attell's approach to Rothstein, whom the article claimed turned Attell down.

21. *Chicago Tribune*, September 29, 1920; *New York Times*, September 29, 1920.

22. *Chicago Tribune*, September 29, 1920.

23. *New York Times*, September 30, 1920.

24. *Chicago Tribune*, August 3, 1921.

25. This account of Landis's career, except where otherwise noted, is based on Spink, *Judge Landis*, ghostwritten by Fred Lieb; Lieb, *Baseball As I Have Known It*, 115–25; Jules Tygiel, *Baseball's Great Experiment*, 31–34, 41–43 (1983); Seymour, *Baseball: The Golden Years*, 325–99; and Clark Nardinelli, "Judge Kenesaw Mountain Landis and the Art of Cartel Enforcement," in *Baseball History*, ed. Peter Levine, 103–14 (1989).

26. Quoted in Spink, *Judge Landis*, 35.

27. Jack Lait, subsequently editor of the *New York Daily Mirror*, quoted in Spink, *Judge Landis*, 26.

28. *The Sporting News*, January 15, 1920. See Spink, *Judge Landis*, 53–54.

29. *The Sporting News*, January 20, 1921.

30. See Spink, *Judge Landis*, 82–83.

31. See ibid., 86.

32. See ibid., 242–43, 277–78.

33. Arch Ward, "Talking It Over," *Chicago Tribune*, July 6, 1933.

34. *Chicago Tribune*, May 21, 1933.

35. Arch Ward, *Chicago Tribune*, September 1, 1933.

36. Ward, "Talking It Over."

37. It is interesting to compare the 1878 edition of *Spalding's Baseball Guide*, 5, in which Spalding accepted the theory of baseball's being derived from rounders, with the 1905 edition, 15–19, in which he rejected the theory. On the Spalding-Chadwick debate see *The Sporting News*, December 2, 1905; Robert Henderson, *Ball, Bat, and Bishop: The Origin of Ball Games* (1947); and Peter A. Levine, *A. G. Spalding and the Rise of Baseball*, 112–15 (1985).

38. Benjamin G. Rader, "Introduction," in Spalding, *America's National Game*, ix–xv (reprint; 1992).

39. See Levine, *A. G. Spalding*, 113–14.

40. A. G. Mills to Edward Fowler, December 20, 1907, quoted in Levine, *A. G. Spalding*, 114.

41. Spalding, *America's National Game*, 19.

42. Henry Chadwick to A. G. Mills, March 20, 1908, quoted in Levine, *A. G. Spalding*, 115.

43. See Spink, *Judge Landis*, 240–41.

Chapter Four

1. See John B. Holway, *Voices from the Great Black Baseball Leagues* (1975).

2. Janet Bruce, *The Kansas City Monarchs: Champions of Black Baseball*, 44–45 (1985).

3. Histories of the Negro Leagues have given more attention to Rube Foster and his Negro National League than to the Eastern Colored League, which was organized by owner Edward Bolden of the Hilldale club, originally a semi-pro organization from the Philadelphia area. The lack of information about Hilldale and the Eastern Colored League has been remedied by Neil Lanctot's *Fair Dealing and Clean Playing: The Hilldale Club and the Development of Black Professional Baseball, 1910–1932* (1994). Lanctot's book properly emphasizes the extent to which black baseball franchises typically fared better economically when operating as independent, barnstorming clubs, scheduling games against white as well as black teams, than as members of leagues. Lanctot also documents the strikingly low attendance at Negro League games (between 1926 and 1932 Hilldale averaged between 340 and 1,844 fans for Sunday and holiday games, the ones most likely to draw crowds), and the fact that an economic recession affected the black community as early as the mid-1920s, well before the more general recession that came after the stock market crash of 1929.

4. See Robert Peterson, *Only the Ball Was White*, 258–59 (reprint; 1984); Lanctot, *Fair Dealing and Clean Playing*, 232–33.

5. Art Rust Jr., *Get That Nigger off the Field*, 4–6, 8 (1974).

6. For details on the careers of Posey and Greenlee, see John B. Holway, *Blackball Stars: Negro League Pioneers*, 299–326 (1988); Donn Rogosin, *Invisible Men: Life in Baseball's Negro Leagues*, 53–55, 103–6 (1983).

7. Ted Page, quoted in Holway, *Blackball Stars*, 306.

8. See Rogosin, *Invisible Men*, 108.

9. Attendance figures are from Bruce, *Kansas City Monarchs*, 89, quoting the *Pittsburgh Courier*, and Peterson, *Only the Ball Was White*, 288–310. Where the *Courier*'s figures do not square with those quoted by Peterson, the *Courier*'s would seem more accurate, especially since some of Peterson's appear to be impressionistic estimates. In any case the numbers, when compared with the average attendance for a Negro League game (typically under a thousand), are impressive.

10. *Chicago Defender*, October 23, 1926, quoted in Bruce, *Kansas City Monarchs*, 58.

11. *Pittsburgh Courier*, July 29, 1933. From the 1920s through the 1940s, the *Courier* demonstrated a persistently "racial" perspective on the news. It made no serious effort at comprehensive coverage; instead it reported "black" fea-

tures, ranging from stories about black victims and perpetrators of crime to the comings and goings of local black socialites. It was uncompromisingly militant in its opposition to segregation and its championing of racial equality. A number of its stories involved lynchings in the south and other evidence of racism in the white community. A detailed study of black newspapers in the era of segregation would be a helpful historical contribution.

12. Ibid., August 12, 1933.

13. Ibid., August 19, 1933.

14. Ibid., August 26, 1933.

15. Ibid., September 18, 1933.

16. Ibid., September 1, 1934.

17. Bruce, *Kansas City Monarchs*, 89.

18. *Chicago Defender*, August 15, 1936.

19. See Rogosin, *Invisible Men*, 116.

20. See Bruce, *Kansas City Monarchs*, 88, quoting *Kansas City Call*, July 5, 1935; *Chicago Defender*, August 15, 1938; *Pittsburgh Courier*, July 13, 1935.

21. Bruce, *Kansas City Monarchs*, quoting *Chicago Defender*, August 5, 1944; June 2, 1945; August 17, 1945.

22. For Leonard's comments see Holway, *Blackball Stars*, 322–25.

23. Leonard, quoted in Holway, *Blackball Stars*, 325.

24. See Bruce, *Kansas City Monarchs*, 72–76.

25. For the Monarchs' dominance of the Negro American League between 1937 and 1946, see Peterson, *Only the Ball Was White*, 273–84; for the income of Negro League owners between 1942 and 1946, see Bruce, *Kansas City Monarchs*, 102, quoting *Pittsburgh Courier*, September 20, 1947. The average weekly wage for a black American in 1945 was under forty-five dollars a week. See Neil A. Wynn, *The Afro-American and the Second World War*, 14 (1976).

26. For the details of the incident see Bill Veeck, *Veeck as in Wreck*, 173–75 (1962).

27. Report of the Major League Steering Committee in *Organized Baseball*, Hearings Before the Subcommittee on the Study of Monopoly Power, House of Representatives, 82 Cong., 1st Sess., 1951. The steering committee report was never formally issued or made public. The major league owners sought to destroy all copies, but Commissioner Albert B. Chandler kept a copy in his papers. The steering committee report has found its way into several works on the Negro Leagues and the integration of major league baseball, including Jules Tygiel, *Baseball's Great Experiment*, 82–86 (1983).

28. Roy Campanella, *It's Good to Be Alive*, quoted in Tygiel, *Baseball's Great Experiment*, 125–26.

29. Leonard, quoted in Tygiel, *Baseball's Great Experiment*, 127–28.

30. Judy Johnson, quoted in Peterson, *Only the Ball Was White*, 81.

31. Leonard, quoted in ibid., 81–82.

32. See Effa Manley and Leon Hardwick, *Negro Baseball Before Integration*, 94–96 (1976); Bruce, *Kansas City Monarchs*, 116.

33. Rickey's comments are cited in the *Chicago Defender*, October 27, 1945, and in the *Pittsburgh Courier*, November 3, 1945. Manley's are from Manley and Hardwick, *Negro Baseball*, 72–73. See also Bruce, *Kansas City Monarchs*, 112.

34. For Wilkinson's comments, see Peterson, *Only the Ball Was White*, 102; for Baird's comments on Rickey, see *Kansas City Call*, January 28, 1949. The history of Manley's negotiations with Veeck and Branch Rickey over the contract of Monte Irwin are in Manley and Hardwick, *Negro Baseball*, 90–92. See also Bruce, *Kansas City Monarchs*, 114–15.

35. The 1942 *Sporting News* editorial is quoted in Peterson, *Only the Ball Was White*, 179. The 1945 reaction is in *The Sporting News*, November 1, 1945.

36. See John Holway, *Voices From the Great Black Baseball Leagues*, 103, 128, 267–68, 284, 312, 345 (1975).

37. For a fuller description of the meeting, see Arthur Mann, *The Jackie Robinson Story*, 160–64 (1951).

38. Quoted in Tygiel, *Baseball's Great Experiment*, 163.

39. *Boston Chronicle*, April 19, 1947; *Baltimore Afro-American*, April 9, 1947; Mike Royko, *Chicago Daily News*, October 26, 1972.

Chapter Five

1. "Baseball All the Year," *Cincinnati Enquirer*, June 20, 1919; "Night Base Ball," *Sporting Life*, July 24, 1909.

2. "Night Baseball A Success," *Chicago Tribune*, August 27, 1910.

3. "Night Ball At Reds' Park," *The Sporting News*, June 24, 1909.

4. *New York Times*, May 3, 1930. See also "Lights Satisfy in First Trial" and "Managers, Umpires, and Players Approve Contest," *Des Moines Register*, May 3, 1930.

5. Lawrence McAdams, "Twilight Baseball," *Baseball Magazine* (July 1930).

6. Frank C. Lane, "The Romance of Night Baseball," *Baseball Magazine*, 483–86 (October 1930).

7. See the comments by players in the *Des Moines Register*, May 3, 1930.

8. Quoted in Lane, "Romance of Night Baseball," 484.

9. See the comments of Dreyfuss in Harold Seymour, *Baseball: The Golden Age*, 361 (1971). Another owner, Sam Breadon of the St. Louis Cardinals, seems also to have been aware of the class implications of night baseball. He decided in 1930 to install lights in the Houston ballpark of the Cardinals' Texas League franchise. "Right now," Breadon was quoted as saying, "installing lights looks

like a minor league proposition and perhaps the salvation of the small circuits. There are so many counter attractions nowadays that baseball in the small towns has appeared to be dwindling in popularity. There are not enough of the leisure class in the small towns to keep the golf courses and automobiles busy and still make baseball a paying proposition. But night baseball will make it possible for the working people to attend a game whenever they want, without missing an afternoon from work." Quoted in J. Roy Stockton, "The Pros and Cons of Night Baseball," *Baseball Magazine* (August 1930).

10. Quoted in Lane, "Romance of Night Baseball," 484–86.

11. Ibid., 486.

12. *The Sporting News*, July 16, 1931.

13. Damon Kerby, "Night Game Dying in Minors, Novelty Wearing Off, Claims Lefty Leifeld," *The Sporting News*, November 12, 1931.

14. In recent years, when All-Star Games have been played on the west coast starting at about 5 P.M. to accommodate national television, the number of strikeouts in early innings has often been high.

15. *The Sporting News*, January 26, 1933.

16. *The Sporting News*, February 8, 1934.

17. *The Sporting News*, August 23, 1934.

18. *The Sporting News*, September 13, 1934.

19. *The Sporting News*, December 20, 1934.

20. Quoted in "Night Ball Dangers Steer Giants Away," *The Sporting News*, December 20, 1934.

21. My thanks to Chaplain Robert B. Payne, whose father Earl D. Payne was an illumination engineer in the Power Division of Cincinnati Gas and Electric at the time the Crosley Field lighting system was built, for supplying me with information about the process. Earl Payne was also a photographer who took thirty-three photos of the first night game, one of which is reproduced on page 177.

22. Edgar G. Brands, "Minors' Night Game Experience Lights Way for Majors," *The Sporting News*, January 24, 1935.

23. Landis is quoted in Michael Gershman, *Diamonds: The Evolution of the Ballpark*, 155 (1993).

24. *The Sporting News*, May 30, 1935.

25. *The Sporting News*, September 12, 1935.

26. "Installation of New $18,000 Lighting Plant Under Way at Birmingham Park," *The Sporting News*, March 5, 1936.

27. *The Sporting News*, November 12, 1936.

28. *The Sporting News*, November 26, 1936.

29. On Mack's interest, see *The Sporting News*, November 19, 1936; on Bradley's, see *The Sporting News*, September 16, 1937.

30. Tommy Holmes, "153,498 At Five Dodger Games Make Owl Ball Critics Blink," *The Sporting News*, August 11, 1938.

31. Edgar G. Brands, "Floodlights Turn Night Into Day at Cincy as McKechnie's Reds Brighten Crosley Field," *The Sporting News*, June 16, 1938.

Chapter Six

1. My discussion of *The Sporting News* is based on Lowell Reidenbaugh, *The Sporting News Take Me Out to the Ballpark* (1983), which is as much a history of the paper as of baseball stadiums, and Stanley Frank, "Bible of Baseball," *Saturday Evening Post*, 9 (June 20, 1942).

2. Frank, "Bible of Baseball," 9.

3. G. H. Fleming was able to produce a history of the 1908 pennant race in which he extracted details of every game the New York Giants played from New York newspapers, as well as specialized baseball weeklies. See Fleming, *The Unforgettable Season* (1981).

4. See Fred Lieb, *Baseball As I Have Known It*, 36, 217–18 (1977).

5. See Stanley Woodward, *Front Page*, 141 (1949).

6. Daniel M. Daniel, quoted in Jerome Holtzman, *No Cheering in the Press Box*, 2, 5–6 (1973).

7. Ibid., 9.

8. Ibid., 3, 6–7, 9, 12.

9. Marshall Hunt, quoted in ibid., 17.

10. Hunt quoted in ibid., 18.

11. Ibid., 20.

12. Ibid., 24.

13. Paul Gallico, quoted in ibid, 71.

14. Richards Vidmar, quoted in ibid., 104–5.

15. Abe Kemp, quoted in ibid., 166–71.

16. Shirley Povich, quoted in ibid., 125–26.

17. Walter W. ("Red") Smith, quoted in ibid., 244, 259.

18. John Drebinger, quoted in ibid., 217. On the origins of the "ideal of objectivity" in the newspaper profession (a late-nineteenth- and early-twentieth-century phenomenon), see Michael Schudson, *A Social History of American Newspapers* (1978) and *Origins of the Ideal of Objectivity in the Professions* (1990).

19. Woodward, *Front Page*, 142–43.

20. Ibid., 139–40.

21. The best treatment of Ruth's life and career is Robert Creamer, *Babe: The Legend Comes to Life* (1974).

22. Daniel, quoted in Holtzman, *No Cheering in the Press Box*, 2.

23. See Lieb, *Baseball As I Have Known It*, 216.

24. Woodward, *Front Page*, 140.

25. Ibid.

26. Daniel, quoted in Holtzman, *No Cheering in the Press Box*, 2.

Chapter Seven

1. Harold Arlin, quoted in Curt Smith, *Voices of the Game*, 7 (reprint; 1992).

2. For details of the 1922 World Series broadcast see Charles Fountain, *Sportswriter: The Life and Times of Grantland Rice*, 194–96 (1993).

3. Ibid., 196.

4. For Rice's and the listener's comments, see *New York Times*, October 1, 5, 1922.

5. Smith, *Voices of the Game*, 11.

6. For the Lardner comment see ibid., 12.

7. Erik Barnouw, *A Tower in Babel: A History of Broadcasting in the United States*, 1:186 (1966).

8. Ibid., 1:14–21.

9. In 1936 *The Sporting News* ran a brief profile of Reagan, which read as follows:

> A thorough knowledge of the game, a gift of narrative and a pleasant voice have won 25-year-od Ronald (Dutch) Reagan, sports announcer for station WHO, Des Moines, Ia., a wide following among fans, and the real scope of his popularity is brought out by his showing as a prominent contender in *The Sporting News* popularity contest for broadcasters.
>
> After graduation from Eureka College, Eureka, Ill., where he was active in athletics, Reagan was a life guard for seven years [this information does not seem credible, since Reagan began broadcasting at the age of twenty-one]. During his periods of cogitations between rescues, he decided he wanted to be an actor, but switched to radio when he applied for and obtained a job as sports announcer for WOC, Davenport, Ia., in 1932. Six months later, Dutch transferred to WHO, where he has since remained. Reagan is now completing his fourth season broadcasting, by telegraphic report, the games of the Chicago Cubs and White Sox under the sponsorship of General Mills, manufacturers of Wheaties. (*The Sporting News*, October 1, 1936)

10. Ronald Reagan to Curt Smith, quoted in *Voices of the Game*, 30.

11. Red Barber, quoted in Bob Edwards, *Fridays with Red: A Radio Friendship*, 51–52 (1993).

12. Fred Hoey, quoted in Edgar G. Brands, "Fred Hoey Moved to the Radio Booth From Usher, Player, Reporter Roles," *The Sporting News*, May 7, 1936.

13. "This Our Latest Problem," *The Sporting News*, April 27, 1922.

14. John B. Sheridan, "Back of Home Plate," *The Sporting News*, August 17, 1922.

15. Ibid.

16. "Baseball By Radio," *The Sporting News*, July 14, 1925.

17. Ibid.

18. "The Radio and Baseball," *The Sporting News*, December 17, 1931. A few months later *The Sporting News* echoed this position in another editorial, conceding that "the radio is here and will remain" but complaining about "a poor reporter . . . put[ting] a story on the air, which may be both libelous and false" or "a lot of very bad twaddle." "The Radio Again," *The Sporting News*, May 5, 1932.

19. "On the Air Lines," September 28, 1933. The "On the Air Lines" column in *The Sporting News*, which began that year, was a signal of the established status of radio broadcasts of baseball games.

20. Harry Hartman, "Defense of Radio Broadcasting by a Broadcaster," *The Sporting News*, November 17, 1932.

21. "On the Air Lines," *The Sporting News*, October 12, 1933. See also the discussion in Smith, *Voices of the Game*, 36–37, who incorrectly reports the year in question as 1934.

22. *The Sporting News*, August 16, 1934.

23. *The Sporting News*, February 28, 1935.

24. The Supreme Court of New York's opinion in New York Giants v. Tele-Flash, handed down February 21, 1936, was not reported. See "More Static in Radio Problem," *The Sporting News*, March 12, 1936.

25. Edgar G. Brands, "Broadcasts of Game Blanket America," *The Sporting News*, April 23, 1936. Brands also listed other cities in which major and minor league games were broadcasts, concluding that "a notable increase in the attention paid to baseball by radio" had taken place since 1935.

26. "On the Radio Airlines," *The Sporting News*, April 30, 1936.

27. "Bringing Radio and Game in Tune," *The Sporting News*, November 19, 1936.

28. *The Sporting News*, December 3, 1936, and December 21, 1936.

29. "National Splits With American Over Radio," *The Sporting News*, July 14, 1938.

30. *The Sporting News*, December 17, 1936.

31. *The Sporting News*, March 18, 1937.

32. "Scribbled by Scribes," *The Sporting News*, May 6, 1937, quoting Dan Goldberg in *Variety*.

33. Quoted in Edgar G. Brands, "Better, More Vivid Accounts Promised Fans, as Radio Refutes Barbed Charges," *The Sporting News*, April 14, 1938.

34. "Giving the Ear-Drums a Rest," *The Sporting News*, December 23, 1937.

35. Don Basenfelder, "Radio Broadens Baseball Broadcasts," *The Sporting News*, April 21, 1938.

36. Quoted in Edwards, *Fridays with Red*, 60.

37. "Compliments of Wheaties *et al.*," *Time*, April 17, 1939.

38. Ibid., 61.

39. *Pittsburgh Athletic Co. v. KQV Broadcasting*, 24 F.Supp. 490 (W.D. Pa. 1938).

40. Smith, *Voices of the Game*, 106.

41. Details on this group of radio announcers, unless otherwise noted, are from Smith, *Voices of the Game*.

42. Details of Barber's career are from Edwards, *Fridays with Red*, and Smith, *Voices of the Game*.

43. Barber's call is quoted in Edwards, *Fridays with Red*, 113.

44. Quoted in Smith, *Voices of the Game*, 134.

45. Vin Scully, quoted in ibid., 48.

46. Edwards, *Fridays with Red*, 173.

47. Quoted in ibid., 74.

48. See ibid., 45–49. Barber once got into a controversy with the author James Thurber, who appropriated "The Catbird Seat" as a title for his column in the *New Yorker* magazine. Thurber never asked Barber's permission to use the phrase, but when Barber sought to use it for a column in the *New York Journal American*, Thurber refused permission. Barber, in characteristically vivid language, "sent word to Mr. Thurber that that was gettin' the goose a little far from the gander," and Thurber apparently took offense. See ibid., 48–49.

49. Quoted in ibid., 62.

50. Quoted in ibid., 70.

51. Ibid., 116. For the details of the episode, see ibid., 114–17.

52. Quoted in ibid., 24.

53. See ibid., 167–70.

54. For the details of Allen's early career, see Smith, *Voices of the Game*, 484–88.

55. For the details of Allen's early career, see Smith, *Voices of the Game*, 54–61.

56. See ibid., 317.

57. See ibid., 263.

58. Quoted in ibid., 123. Allen's broadcasting a World Series in which the Yankees were not participating was itself unusual for the time.

59. See ibid., 141.

60. See Edwards, *Fridays with Red*, 160.

61. Quoted in Smith, *Voices of the Game*, 264.

62. Allen's comments are in ibid., 264; Barber's comments, originally in his 1970 book *The Broadcasters*, are quoted in Edwards, *Fridays with Red*, 160.

Chapter Eight

1. "A New Division in Baseball," *The Sporting News*, December 6, 1923.

2. G. H. Fleming, *The Unforgettable Season*, 65–66 (1981).

3. Quoted in ibid., 256.

4. See, e.g., C. B. Power, *Pittsburgh Gazette*, May 12, 1908, quoted in ibid., 65 ("Abby"); W. W. Aulick, *New York Times*, June 11, 1908, quoted in ibid., 92 ("Battey"). In his account Aulick added that Abbaticchio was "a gent with a serial name, called variously Abby and Battey."

5. See Jack B. Moore, *Joe DiMaggio: A Bio-Bibliography*, 130 (1986).

6. *New York World*, September 20, 1908, quoted in Fleming, *Unforgettable Season*, 232.

7. See Fleming, *Unforgettable Season*, 109, 132.

8. Joe Vila, *The Sporting News*, September 17, 1908, quoted in ibid., 224.

9. Gym Bagley, *New York Evening Mail*, Monday, September 28, 1908, quoted in ibid., 265.

10. Joe Vila, *The Sporting News*, October 7, 1908, quoted in ibid., 305.

11. "A New Division in Baseball," *The Sporting News*, December 6, 1923.

12. "The Challenge to the Jew," *The Sporting News*, September 15, 1921.

13. "Scribbled by Scribes," *The Sporting News*, March 16, 1922.

14. *The Sporting News*, June 22, 1922.

15. *The Sporting News*, September 6, 1923.

16. F. C. Lane, "Why Not More Jewish Ball Players?" *Baseball Magazine* (January 1926).

17. For an account of Moses Solomon's brief career, see Peter Levine, *From Ellis Island to Ebbets Field*, 110 (1992).

18. *American Hebrew*, June 18, 1926.

19. *American Hebrew*, April 20, 1928. The *New York Times* account is quoted in Levine, *From Ellis Island to Ebbets Field*, 111; details of Cohen's career can be found therein, 110–15, citing Tilden Edelstein, "The American Dream and the National Game," unpublished paper presented to the meeting of the Organization of American Historians, April 1983.

20. *The Sporting News*, November 23, 1929.

21. Westbrook Pegler, *Chicago Tribune*, April 13, 1928.

22. Ibid.

23. Los Angeles *B'nai B'rith Messenger*, April 12, 1929. It is interesting that a Jewish writer for a Jewish paper would refer to Jewish fans as "Yids."

24. Cohen's interview with the American Jewish Committee is quoted in Levine, *From Ellis Island to Ebbets Field*, 115. He returned to the major leagues as a coach in 1960 for the Philadelphia Phillies (see *New York Post*, March 29, 1960). The "three strikes for three balls" comment, originally made by New York sportswriter Dan Parker, is quoted in Levine, *From Ellis Island to Ebbets Field*, 116.

25. *The Sporting News*, August 20, 1925, December 31, 1925.

26. "The Sons of Caesar," *The Sporting News*, July 9, 1931.

27. "We Still Have the Irish," *The Sporting News*, June 8, 1933.

28. *The Sporting News*, July 21, 1932.

29. "His Bat Makes 'Em See Red," *The Sporting News*, May 19, 1932.

30. Harry T. Brundidge, "Ernie Orsatti, Utility Player of Cardinals, Gave Up Chance to Become Movie Hero for Diamond Career," *The Sporting News*, February 4, 1932.

31. "Dolph Camilli to Add Grace to Cubs' Infield," *The Sporting News*, September 17, 1933.

32. "Leaves From a Fan's Scrapbook," *The Sporting News*, May 24, 1934.

33. Dick Farrington, "Wolf at the Home Door Made Cavarretta Major Leaguer Early," *The Sporting News*, August 22, 1935.

34. "22 Nationalities Represented in A.L. Ranks," *The Sporting News*, June 11, 1936. Moe Berg, who had attended college and law school and spoke twelve languages, combined his interest in baseball with one in international affairs and later became an intelligence agent. See Nicholas Dawidoff, *The Catcher Was a Spy: The Mysterious Life of Moe Berg* (1994).

35. Fred Lieb, "Oi, Oi, Oh Boy! Hail That Long-Sought Hebrew Star," *The Sporting News*, September 12, 1935.

36. See Levine, *From Ellis Island to Ebbets Field*, 101–2, citing a letter from Mrs. Johnny Kling to Lee Allen, February 12, 1969, in the National Baseball Hall of Fame and Museum, Cooperstown, New York.

37. Harry T. Brundidge, "Levey, One of Few Jewish Lads Making Good in Big Show, Told to 'Beat It' at Polo Grounds," *The Sporting News*, December 1, 1932.

38. "Oi Gewalt! Make Way For The Weintraub Boy," *The Sporting News*, June 28, 1934.

39. "Star of David Shines," *The Sporting News*, August 23, 1934.

40. Daniel M. Daniel, "Yanks Hope To Dress In Myer As Tailor-Made Jewish Star," *The Sporting News*, October 24, 1935. Dan Daniel regularly wrote stories with an ethnic angle for *The Sporting News*: he was himself Jewish, having changed his name from Daniel Margowitz. See Levine, *From Ellis Island to Ebbets Field*, 114.

41. For Berkow's discussion of his participation in the Greenberg autobiography, see his introduction to *Hank Greenberg: The Story of My Life*, ed. Ira Berkow, xi–xxi (1988).

42. Ibid., 53.

43. Ibid., 4–7, 18.

44. Bud Shaver, quoted in ibid., 59.

45. Dick Farrington, "Greenberg, Young Jewish Star, 'Just Tumbled Into Game,'" *The Sporting News*, October 4, 1934.

46. Quoted in *Hank Greenberg*, 60.

47. Quoted in ibid., 61.

48. Quoted in ibid., 78.

49. George ("Birdie") Tebbetts to Ira Berkow, quoted in ibid., 103.

50. Harry Eisenstat, quoted in ibid., 104.

51. Ibid., 116–17.

52. Ibid., 117.

53. Ibid., 145.

54. Quoted in ibid., 149.

55. Whitney Martin, Associated Press, June 22, 1945, quoted in ibid., 152–53.

56. Ibid., 155.

57. Ibid., 197.

58. Ibid., 266–67.

59. Ibid., 93–94.

60. Paul Simon, quoted in Larry Merchant, *Ringside Seat at the Circus*, 12 (1976).

61. Articles on DiMaggio's streak in *The Sporting News* appeared on July 20, 1933, July 27, 1933, and August 3, 1933. DiMaggio had actually played three games for the Seals at the tail end of 1932. For details of DiMaggio's career, see Moore, *Joe DiMaggio*.

62. *New York World-Telegram*, March 2, 1936.

63. *New York Daily News*, March 3, 1936.

64. *New York World-Telegram*, March 18, 1936.

65. *New York Times*, May 2, 1936.

66. *Time*, July 13, 1936.

67. Quoted in Moore, *Joe DiMaggio*, 31.

68. See Dan Daniel, *New York World-Telegram*, May 5, 1938; Al Silverman, *Joe DiMaggio: The Golden Year, 1941*, 101 (1969), quoted in Moore, *Joe DiMaggio*, 35–36.

69. Moore, *Joe DiMaggio*, 56–57.

70. Tramulto is quoted in John Diggins, *Mussolini and Fascism: The View from America*, 400 (1972).

71. See Moore, *Joe DiMaggio*, 78.

Chapter Nine

1. Unlike the issues of race and ethnicity, the issue of gender did not play a significant role in the twentieth-century history of baseball's emergence as the national pastime. From its origins, Organized Baseball was assumed to be an "entertainment" whose participants would be male: indeed it was assumed that it would be "unnatural," and possibly in bad taste, for women to play the sport for profit. This assumption, although sexist, was apparently so clearly substantiated by physical evidence that throughout the 1980s no one sought to challenge it, despite the rise of gender equity and a heightened public consciousness about issues of gender discrimination. The National Women's Professional Baseball League, a creation of World War II, can be said to be the exception that proves the rule. Its players were expected to wear short skirts, learn etiquette, and otherwise demonstrate their femininity. They were the equivalent of "clowning" black barnstorming teams in the era of the Negro Leagues, whose clown acts purportedly demonstrated their racial identity and thus their "separateness" from white baseball.

It is, of course, significant that a game claiming to serve as the national pastime should exclude, on gender grounds, half the American population from its participating constituency. But the grounds of exclusion were not patently sexist. Organized Baseball courted female fans; the exclusion of female participants, for most of its twentieth-century history, was treated as simply confirming the principle that certain physical skills were required to play the game, and women as a class lacked those skills. No doubt there were early twentieth-century potential exceptions to that principle, but no evidence of commentary decrying the tacit exclusion of women players from Organized Baseball has been found. For this reason the existence of a women's professional baseball league, however great its intrinsic interest, cannot fairly be made part of the story of baseball's emergence as the quintessentially American sport of the first fifty years of the twentieth century.

2. For a good overview of the history of the minor leagues, see Harold Seymour, *Baseball: The Golden Age*, 400–422 (1971). Other books I have consulted for this portion of the chapter are The National Association of Professional Baseball Leagues, *The Story of Minor League Baseball* (1952); Robert Obojski, *Bush League: A History of Minor League Baseball* (1975); and Neil J. Sullivan, *The Minors* (1990).

3. Unlike professional football and basketball, major league baseball, even today, has not drawn heavily upon colleges as a source of player talent. In light of the tendency on the part of major league clubs to keep college-age players in the minors unless they show exceptional ability, one might well ask why Organized Baseball is apparently disinclined to let prospects develop on college teams.

Several reasons suggest themselves. Baseball practices, as noted, tend to become ingrained and resistant to change, and in the early years of the twentieth century the colleges were poor prospects for developing players. The coaching talent at most colleges was amateurish, and most young men who were financially and academically able to attend college were not likely to become professional athletes. No minor league professional football or basketball leagues existed in the early twentieth century, so aspiring professional athletes in those sports had to be trained in college or not at all. Baseball, on the other hand, offered the minor leagues as a source of potential profit as well as of player development. As a rule, a young man's decision to play professional baseball was made after high school, and for at least the first fifty years of the twentieth century the kinds of young men who chose to sign baseball contracts did so with a tacit understanding that their occupational prospects were better as a professional baseball player than anything else.

Today the situation is quite different, with the proliferation of college baseball teams, improved resources and coaching in college baseball, and a tendency on the part of exceptionally talented college players to leave their institutions early to sign professional contracts. Even so the inertia of past practices remains, resulting in Organized Baseball's probably not making optimally effective use of the colleges as a source of player development.

4. Details on minor league classification and successive "agreements" between the majors and the minors with respect to the draft are taken from Seymour, *Baseball: The Golden Age*, 406–9.

5. "After Chicago," *The Sporting News*, December 20, 1923.

6. "The Meeting of the Minors," *The Sporting News*, December 16, 1926.

7. John Sheridan, "Back of the Home Plate," *The Sporting News*, January 12, 1926, supra note 7.

8. For details on the Cardinals and their farm system under Branch Rickey, see Fred Lieb, *The St. Louis Cardinals*, 59–92 (1944); J. G. Taylor Spink, *Judge Landis and Twenty-Five Years of Baseball*, 226–40 (1947); Seymour, *Baseball: The Golden Age*, 410–20; Sullivan, *The Minors*, 93–114. Much of the information contained in those sources was confirmed and embellished by former Cardinals executive Vaughn P. ("Bing") Devine in two interviews with Michael D'Agostino, July 16 and July 20, 1994. My thanks to Bing Devine for sharing his experiences.

9. See Lieb, *St. Louis Cardinals*, 81–82, quoting a conversation with Rickey.

10. In 1927 *The Sporting News* reported that the Cardinals had purchased the Danville, Illinois, club, including its "spacious park located on the government reservation at the Soldier's Home on the outskirts of [the] city," and were converting the facility into a vast training camp, "the largest baseball training camp in the world." The paper noted that on March 30 eighty players were

working out at the camp, which was "within easy reach of St. Louis." The players were to be placed with the Cardinals' affiliates in the minor leagues. Red Hughes, "Where Did Rickey Dig Them All Up?" *The Sporting News*, March 31, 1927.

11. See Lieb, *St. Louis Cardinals*, 82–83; Sullivan, *The Minors*, 101–2.

12. "Chain Store System Endorsed," *The Sporting News*, December 22, 1933.

13. The Observer, "Casual Comment," *The Sporting News*, December 1, 1927.

14. Branch Rickey, quoted in Dick Farrington, "Branch Rickey, Defending Farms, Says Stark Necessity Forced System," *The Sporting News*, December 1, 1933.

15. "Landis Polls Major Owners On Farms, But No Action Is Taken," *The Sporting News*, December 20, 1928.

16. L. H. Addington, "Draft Differences Widen Breach Between Minor Leagues," *The Sporting News*, December 12, 1929.

17. Quoted in Lieb, *St. Louis Cardinals*, 89.

18. Quoted in *New York Journal-American*, March 12, 1949.

19. For an excellent account of the Gardella case and its labor relations context, see Jay H. Topkis, "Monopoly in Professional Sports," 58 Yale Law Journal 691 (1949).

20. *Gardella v. Chandler*, 79 F. Supp. 260 (S.D.N.Y. 1948).

21. *Gardella v. Chandler*, 172 F2d. 402 (1949).

22. Ibid., 403–7.

23. Ibid., 408.

24. Ibid., 409.

25. Ibid., 415.

26. Albert B. Chandler, quoted in United States Congress, *Hearings Before the Subcommittee on Study of Monopoly Power, Part 6: Organized Baseball*, 288, 290 (1952). Hereafter cited as *Baseball Hearings*.

27. *Prendergast v. Syracuse Baseball Club*, No. 3936, Northern District, New York, filed April 30, 1951.

28. *Toolson v. New York Yankees*, 101 F. Supp. 93 (Southern District, California, 1951).

29. *Kowalski v. Chandler et al.*, No. 2646, Southern District, Ohio, dismissed January 25, 1952. Kowalski's suit differed from the other two in that he had not been blacklisted. He claimed, however, that the value of his services had been reduced by a combination of the reserve clause and the farm system.

30. *Toolson v. New York Yankees*, 200 F. 2d. 198 (9th Cir., 1952); *Kowalski v. Chandler*, United States Court of Appeals for the Sixth Circuit, February 20, 1953.

31. *Toolson v. New York Yankees*, 346 U.S. 356, 357 (1953).

32. Ibid., 357–58.

33. See *United States v. Paramount Pictures*, 334 U.S. 131 (1948). For a summary of arguments that baseball's practices violated the antitrust laws in several respects, see Peter S. Craig, "Monopsony in Manpower: Organized Baseball Meets the Antitrust Laws," 62 Yale Law Journal 576 (1953).

34. *Baseball Hearings*, 735.

35. Ibid., 741.

36. Ibid., 732.

37. Ibid.

38. Ibid., 373.

39. See ibid., 11–12 (Ty Cobb), 553 (Al Widmar), 590 (Seymour Block), 601 (Ned Garver), 840 (Fred Hutchinson), 852 (Pee Wee Reese).

40. Ibid., 373 (Horning), 852–53 (Reese).

41. Ibid., 840. A good collection of player reminiscences from the period of the Celler subcommittee hearings, which reveals the general satisfaction of major leaguers with their economic lot, is Danny Peary, *The Played the Game* (1994).

42. Ibid., 721.

43. Ibid., 723.

44. Ibid., 724.

45. Ibid., 739.

46. Major League Rule 1 (c), quoted in *Baseball Hearings*, 1125.

47. Ibid., 740.

48. *Report of the House of Representatives, Subcommittee on Study of Monopoly Power of the Committee on the Judiciary*, 82 Cong., 2d Sess., 189–203 (1952). Hereafter cited as *House Report*.

49. See the discussion in Craig, "Monopsony in Manpower," 600–601.

50. See the table in Benjamin F. Rader, *Baseball: A History of America's Game*, 173 (1992).

51. A dramatic portrait of the decline of Shibe Park in Philadelphia can be found in Bruce Kuklick, *To Every Thing a Season* (1991).

52. Although the impact of television on major league games has not, over the years, revealed itself to be adverse, there is no question that the impact of television on the minor leagues in the late forties and fifties was detrimental. The Celler subcommittee, in its final report, cited a 1950 study of the entertainment decisions of fans living in minor league cities in which major league night games were televised. Fifty-three percent of the fans polled stated that they would choose to stay home to watch a major league game rather than go out to attend a minor league night game. See *House Report*, 78–80.

53. On the migration of Americans from the northeast and midwest to the southwest and far west after World War II, see Michael J. Greenwood, *Migration and Economic Growth in the United States*, 21–50 (1981).

54. *Baseball Hearings*, 954.

55. Ibid., 535.

56. Ibid., 125.

57. Ibid., 88–91.

58. Ibid., 90–91.

59. For a good discussion of the major league owners' attitudes toward baseball on the Pacific coast, see James Edward Miller, *The Baseball Business: Pursuing Pennants and Profits in Baltimore*, 14–15 (1990).

60. See *The Sporting News*, December 17, 1952, reporting on the American and National Leagues' relaxation of their requirements for franchise transfers.

61. It is worth pointing out, however, that the percentage of households in the United States with a television set went from 12.3 percent in 1950 to 87 percent in 1960, so that by the end of the 1950s it was abundantly clear to everyone in the baseball business that television was likely to be the principal source of publicity and advertising revenue, and possibly the principal source of revenue itself, for major league baseball clubs in the future. This has had, of course, incalculable consequences. The figures on television set ownership in the decade of the 1950s are from Miller, *Baseball Business*, 62.

For an overview of the franchise transfers of the 1950s, see Lee Lowenfish, "A Tale of Many Cities: The Westward Expansion of Major League Baseball in the 1950s," *Journal of the West*, 71 (July 1978).

62. See Miller, *Baseball Business*, 31–35.

63. For the details of the sale, see Kuklick, *To Every Thing a Season*, 120–26.

64. For a discussion of the Dodgers' move to Los Angeles, which supports the view that both the Dodgers' and Giants' franchise transfers were done primarily to gain a foothold in lucrative markets, see Neil J. Sullivan, *The Dodgers Move West* (1987).

65. In April 1958, *U.S. News and World Report* ran an article in which a number of baseball executives were polled about the future of the game. The article reported that they expected that "baseball is moving west," along with "the shifting pattern of the nation's population"; that "baseball owners are hunting for bigger stadiums, with more space for car parking"; and that "baseball . . . is reaching out for big new markets for television broadcasts." "Behind Baseball's Big Moves—Gate Receipts, Parking, TV Fees," *U.S. News and World Report*, April 18, 1958, 94–97.

Chapter Ten

1. Jacques Barzun, *God's Country and Mine*, 159–161 (1954).

2. Details of the Drysdale-Koufax holdout and Marvin Miller's emergence can be found in Marvin Miller, *A Whole Different Ballgame* (1991); James Edward Miller, *The Baseball Business: Pursuing Pennants and Profits in Baltimore*,

141–49 (1990); and Lee Lowenfish and Tony Lupien, *The Imperfect Diamond,* 195–202 (1980).

3. Many commentators have become quite carried away in their enthusiasm for this image of baseball. Consider Bartlett Giamatti, former president of Yale University and commissioner of baseball:

> Baseball is counterpoint: stability vying with volatility, tradition with the quest for a new edge, ancient rhythms and even new blood—an oft told tale, repeated in every game in every season, season after season. . . . If baseball is a narrative, an epic of exile and return, a vast communal poem about separation, loss, and the hope for reunion—if baseball is a Romance Epic—it is finally told by the audience. It is the Romance Epic of homecoming America sings to itself. (A. Bartlett Giamatti, *Take Time For Paradise: Americans and Their Games,* 95 [1989])

Index

Aaron, Hank, 157
Abbaticchio, Ed, 250, 255, 346n.4
African Americans. *See* blacks
agents, use of, 325, 326
air travel, 308, 322
A. J. Reach & Co., 22
Alexander, Grover Cleveland, 99, 120
Alger, Horatio, 199
Allen, Mel, 230, 231, 236, 237–42, 345n.58
All-Star Games: in Negro Leagues, 139–43; in Organized Baseball, 118–19, 121–22; pension fund and, 121–22; radio broadcasts of, 219
American Association, 134
American Broadcasting Company (ABC), 237
American Hebrew, 254
American League: contract jumping to, 48, 50; formation of, 47, 60; franchise transfers in, 312–13; night games in, 117; radio broadcasting of games and, 222–23; westward expansion and, 310
American League Service Bureau, 125, 257
America's National Game (Spalding), 124
Amsterdam News, 135, 156
announcing: radio, 208–14, 222–24, 226–31; television, 206, 239, 242
Anson, Adrian ("Cap"), 132
anti-Semitism, 261
antitrust laws: baseball's immunity from, 7, 8, 73, 275, 277, 295, 328; Congressional investigation into, 295, 297; lawsuits citing violations of, 69–81, 293–97, 335n.19, 352n.33; reserve clause and, 61, 66; territoriality principle and, 297–98
Arlin, Harold, 207
Arnold, Dorothy, 269, 270
Asinof, Eliot, 336n.12
assimilationism, 272–73
Astor, William W., 39
Attell, Abe, 98, 103, 337n.20
attendance, ballpark: decline of, in 1950s, 306–7; demographic trends and, 307–8, 321–22; ethnic identification and, 253, 254–55, 256, 259; night baseball and, 162, 166, 170, 175–76, 178–80, 185–86; television broadcasts and, 307, 324, 352n.52. *See also* seating capacity
Austrian, Alfred, 95, 103, 104
away games. *See* road games

Baer, Max, 263
Bagley, Gym, 250–51
Baird, Thomas, 144, 153
Baker Bowl, Philadelphia, 20, 276
Ball, Phil, 65, 67, 291
Ballantine brewing company, 236, 241
ballparks: ambience of games in, 29–37; construction of, 21–29, 39–41, 45, 46; deterioration of, 307, 313, 333n.37, 352n.51; early features of, 11–12, 18–20, 22, 26–27, 36–37, 40–41; installation of lights in, 173–74, 180, 182, 185, 187; perceived permanency of, 20–21, 25, 44, 45–46; safety of, 18; seating capacity of, 12, 15, 26–27, 44, 184; transportation to, 17, 19, 22, 29, 39, 42; urban growth and, 7, 20; westward expansion and, 310, 314. *See also names of specific ballparks*
ballplayers: corruption of, 86, 88–104, 105, 111–15; development of in minor leagues, 278–92; labor strikes by, 62, 325–26; pension fund for retired, 121, 122; sportswriters' relationship to, 193–200, 202–5; statistics of, 118, 213–14. *See also names of specific ballplayers*
Balt-Feds franchise, 66, 70–81
Baltimore Afro-American, 149, 156
Baltimore Elite Giants, 150, 157
Baltimore Orioles, 10, 47
Banks, Ernie, 157
Barber, Walter ("Red"), 212–13, 224, 225, 228, 229, 231–37, 241–42, 345n.48
Barnard, Ernest, 23

Barnes, Don, 181
barnstorming: during Great Depression, 137; in Negro Leagues, 128, 130, 137–38, 145–46, 174, 338n.3; portable lighting systems and, 144–46, 164, 174
Barzun, Jacques, 316–19
baseball: anomalies in emergence of, 5, 8; as business enterprise, 59–60; changes in after deadball era, 117–18; decline of, as national pastime, 329–30; emergence as national pastime, 3–4, 6–8, 327; gentry politics and, 85; as "heart and mind of America," 316–19; historical origins of, 123–24, 337n.37; pace of games, 33, 317; unique status of, 320. *See also* Organized Baseball
baseball card royalties, 325
Baseball Hall of Fame, 118–21, 125, 265; first players elected to, 119–21; first radio announcers elected to, 231, 242
baseball journalism: newspaper, 190–205; radio, 206–44; television, 206, 227, 321, 324, 353n.61
baseball "law": early challenges to, 69–81; revision of, 309, 322, 326; rules of, 60, 61–63. *See also* reserve clause; territoriality principle
Baseball Magazine, 11, 96, 97, 165–66, 192, 253
Baseball Players' Charity Fund, 121, 122
baseball pools, 85–86
baseballs: early use of, 14; practice of replacing damaged, 117–18
baseball "wars," 60
Baseball Writers Association, 125
Basic Agreements (1970/1973/1976), 326
batting. *See* hitting
batting practice, 30
Beckwith, Johnny, 141
Benswanger, William, 141
Benton, John ("Rube"), 99–100, 111, 114
Berg, Moe, 258, 259, 347n.34
Berkow, Ira, 260–61, 263, 348n.41
Bernard, Bill, 47–48, 50, 52, 55, 57
Bescher, Bob, 35, 36
Birmingham Black Barons, 158
Bissell, Herbert P., 66
Black, Joe, 157
blacklisting: challenges to, 278, 293–97; as response to reserve clause violations, 61, 66, 80
blacks: African Americans as, 127n; employment prospects for, 129–30; exclusion of, from Organized Baseball, 127–29, 147–49, 245, 246, 277; newspapers oriented towards, 133–34, 141, 142, 156, 338n.11. *See also* Negro Leagues
Black Sox scandal, 37, 91–104, 336n.9; purported connection of Jews to, 251–52; results of, 6, 7, 104–5
Block, Cy, 302
B'nai B'rith Messenger, 255, 347n.23
Bodie, Ping, 250, 255
Bolden, Edward, 338n.3
Boston Braves, 29–37, 169, 171; relocation of, 311, 312; uniforms of, 30–31
Boston Chronicle, 156
Boston Red Sox, 11, 15, 98
Bottomley, Jim, 288
Boyle, Harvey, 218
Braddock, James, 263
Bradley, Alva, 181
Brands, Edgar, 171, 175–76, 188–89
Brannick, Eddie, 224
Braves Field, Boston, 23, 27, 331n.5, 332n.25
Breadon, Sam, 181, 289, 296, 340n.9
Bresnahan, Roger, 249
bribery: baseball's association with, 87–89, 99, 111–12. *See also* gambling
Brickhouse, Jack, 228, 230
Briggs Stadium, 307
Britt, Jim, 230, 242
Britton, Helene, 286
Brooklyn Daily Eagle, 16, 17, 18, 19
Brooklyn Dodgers, 16, 197, 309; integration of, 148, 149, 150, 157; night baseball and, 182; radio broadcasts of games by, 224–25; relocation of, 311, 314, 353n.64
Brooklyn Eagles, 152
Brooklyn Superbas, 16
Broun, Heywood, 89
Brown, Edward, 17
Brown v. Board of Education, 148
Brundidge, Harry, 259
Brush, John T., 10, 11, 13, 15–16, 21, 23, 38, 42
Buffalo Buf-Feds, 66
Burke, Michael, 236–37
Burley, Dan, 156

Burns, Edward, 223
Burns, George, 34, 35
Burton, Harold, 298

Cahill, George, 161
California, expansion of major leagues to, 298, 303, 308–10, 314–15
Camilli, Dolph, 257
Campanella, Roy, 150, 153, 157
cantilever technique, 40
Caray, Harry, 228, 230, 242
Carew, Rod, 260
Carleton, Tex, 288
Cartwright, Alexander, 123
catchers, protection for, 14, 32
Cavarretta, Phil, 258
celebrity: of Babe Ruth, 37, 38, 163, 198–200; baseball journalism and, 198–200, 205; ethnic identification and, 254, 262
Celler, Emanuel, 295; Congressional subcommittee of, 295, 299, 301, 303–6, 307–8, 321, 323, 328
censorship, radio, 222–23
Chadwick, Henry, 123, 124
chain store system. *See* farm system
Chalmers Motor Company, 88
Chance, Frank, 89
Chandler, Albert B. ("Happy"), 105, 155, 276, 292–93, 295, 299, 339n.27
Chapman, Ben, 157
Charleston, Oscar, 138, 141
chart system, statistical, 213–14
Chase, Hal, 65–66, 89–91, 99, 336n.11
Chase, Harrie Brigham, 294
Chesbro, Jack, 15
chest protectors, beginnings of, 32
Chicago American, 102
Chicago American Giants, 131, 133, 142, 143
Chicago Cubs, 65, 87, 98–99, 183–84, 222
Chicago Daily News, 156, 211
Chicago Defender, 133, 139, 142–43
Chicago Exposition (1893), 37
Chicago Herald-Examiner, 96, 99
Chicago Tribune, 98, 99, 101, 121–22, 161, 223
Chicago White Sox, 31, 66; Black Sox scandal and, 91–105; photograph of 1919 "Black Sox," 94
Cicotte, Eddie, 93, 95, 97, 100, 101, 103
Cincinnati Enquirer, 161
Cincinnati Reds, 91, 171–75, 177, 178–80, 186, 188, 232
City Beautiful movement, 7, 64
civic loyalty, and connection to baseball, 64–65, 66–67
Clark, Edward, 122–23, 125
Clark, Stephen, 122
Cleland, Alexander, 125
Cleveland Broncos, 50
Cleveland Buckeyes, 157
Cleveland Indians, 276, 333n.36
Cleveland Stars, 138
"Coast to Coast" (radio show), 233
Cobb, Ty, 62, 88, 112, 114, 119, 120–21, 141, 148, 270, 292, 302, 334n.11
Cohen, Andy, 254–55, 259, 346n.19
Cole, Robert, 143
Coleman, Jerry, 236, 241
collective bargaining, 326
college recruiting, 349n.3
Collins, Eddie, 98, 120
Columbia Broadcasting System (CBS), 208, 237–38, 243
Columbia Park, Philadelphia, 22
Comiskey, Charles, 23, 86, 107, 335n.19; Black Sox scandal and, 92, 93, 95–97, 98, 101, 103, 104, 105; night exhibition game staged by, 161; photograph of, 100
Comiskey Park, Chicago, 20, 23, 122, 139, 142, 161
commerce: distinguished from "sport," 82–83, 275; "interstate" and baseball, 75–81, 294, 297–99; as legal concept, 74; media coverage as, 294
Commerce Clause of United States Constitution, 74
commercial sponsorship: of major league games, 220, 225, 229; of televised baseball, 353n.61; of World Series games, 218, 235, 238
commissioner, baseball: Black Sox scandal and, 6, 105; first appointment of, 6, 7, 92, 104, 105–8; influence of, 125–26; power assumed by, 108, 110. *See also* Landis, Kenesaw Mountain
compensation. *See* salaries
competitive balance: in Negro Leagues, 133; in Organized Baseball, 64, 81; reserve clause and, 301–2
construction, ballpark, 11–13, 21–29, 39–41, 45, 46

contract jumping: in Negro Leagues, 128; punitive actions for, 47–48, 57, 60, 113, 114; reasons for, 49–50, 334n.10
contracts: early lawsuits on breaches of, 47–48, 52–58; interleague wars and, 60–61; mutuality in, 48, 53, 54, 56–57, 66; reserve clause and, 49–50, 52–58, 60–61; salary disputes and, 270; ten-day clause and, 49, 53, 54, 55, 61
Coogan, James J., 10
Coogan's Hollow, New York, 10, 11
Cooper, Mort and Walter, 288
Cooperstown, New York, 118, 122–25
corruption, ballplayer, 86, 88–91; Black Sox scandal and, 91–104; punitive actions for, 105, 111–15
Corum, Bill, 180
Costas, Bob, 233
Costello, Jim, 90
County Stadium, Milwaukee, 311
Cowan, Tommy, 207
Cox, William, 147
Cronin, Joe, 267
Crosby, Bing, 111
Crosetti, Frank, 256
Crosley, Powel, 172, 212, 229, 231–32
Crosley Field, Cincinnati, 20, 23; night baseball at, 173–75, 176–78, 180, 186, 188
crowd control, ballpark, 16–17, 18
Cruisenberry, James, 98–99
Cuban ballplayers, 247–48
Cuccinello, Tony, 256, 257

D'Agostino, Michael, 350n.8
Daily Forward (New York), 255
Daniel, Daniel M., 193–94, 197, 200, 202, 205, 269, 347n.40
Danning, Hank, 258
deadball era: end of, 43, 117; style of baseball in, 14, 28, 33–34
Dean, Jerome ("Dizzy"), 146, 288
Dean, Paul ("Daffy"), 146, 288
Dearborn Independent, 251–52
Delahanty, Ed, 50, 52, 333n.3
demographic trends, relationship to baseball, 307–8, 321–22
Dempsey, Jack, 264
Depression. *See* Great Depression
Des Moines Demons, 164
Detroit Tigers, 62, 261, 264
Detroit Times, 261
Dever, William, 104
Devery, Bill, 10, 13
Devine, Vaughn P. ("Bing"), 350n.8
Devore, Josh, 35
Dickey, Bill, 267
DiMaggio, Dominic, 271
DiMaggio, Guiseppe, 271
DiMaggio, Joe, 235, 239, 247, 249, 258, 260, 348n.61; as ethnic baseball star, 266–74; photograph of, 267
DiMaggio, Vincent, 271
Doby, Larry, 153, 157
Dolan, Cozy, 111–12
Donlan, Mike, 249
Doubleday, Abner, 124, 125
double-decked grandstands, 26–27, 332n.25
"Doughertys, The" (security police), 18
Douglas, Phil, 111
Doyle, Larry, 35
draft system, as player development devices, 278–85
Drebinger, John, 196, 197, 342n.18
Dreyfuss, Barney, 23, 107, 166–67
Drysdale, Don, 325
Dudley, Jimmy, 228, 230
Dunn, Jack, 280, 283, 285, 288
Durocher, Leo, 226, 234
Dwyer, Bill, 211
Dyer, Bill, 228, 229

Easter, Luke, 157
Eastern Colored League, 133, 338n.3
Ebbets, Charles, 16, 17, 21, 23, 42, 335n.19
Ebbets Field, New York: construction of, 17; deterioration of, 307; features of, 18–20, 28; history of predecessor to, 16–17; night games at, 182, 183; opening of, 16, 18, 20; press box at, 202; radio announcing from, 234
Eckert, William, 326
economics: of draft system, 278–85; of farming system, 285–92; of franchise transfers, 306–15; of night baseball, 162, 164, 165–66, 170–72, 175–76, 178–80, 185–86; of racial integration in baseball, 151–52
Edison, Thomas, 160
Edwards, Bob, 233, 234, 235, 236
Edwards, Henry P., 125, 257, 258
Eisenstat, Harry, 263

electric light bulb: invention of, 160. *See also* lighting systems
electric scoreboards, in early ballparks, 41–42, 43
Elson, Bob, 230, 240
enterprise, baseball: legal character of, 69–83; roots of, 59–69. *See also* Organized Baseball
entertainment business, baseball as, 326–27
ethnicity in baseball: assimilationism and, 272–73; ballpark attendance and, 253, 254–55, 256, 259; media commentary on, 247–48, 250–59, 261–62, 269, 347n.23; melting pot theory and, 5, 246–47, 249, 257, 260, 268, 271, 272–74; stereotyping and, 245, 246, 247–48, 249–51, 253, 266, 272; World War II and, 260, 263–65, 270–71. *See also* Italian ballplayers; Jewish ballplayers
Evans, Nathanial ("Nat"), 103
Evers, Johnny, 35

Fallon, William, 103
farm system: development of, 115–16, 285–92; opposition to, 115–16, 289, 290–91; team improvement through, 64, 280–81
Farrell, Frank, 10, 11, 13, 89
fatalism, as economic perspective among early ballplayers, 63
Federal Baseball Club of Baltimore, Inc. v. National League of Professional Baseball Clubs, et. al., 70–81, 292, 335n.19
Federal Communications Commission, 208
Federal League, 37, 38; antitrust lawsuit by, 70–81, 106; collapse of, 89; contract jumping to, 48, 65–67, 292, 334n.10
Federal Radio Commission, 208
Felsch, Oscar ("Happy"), 93, 97, 100, 102–3, 105
Fenway Park, Boston, 20, 23, 27, 332n.25
ferro-concrete building process, 24–25
fielding practice, in early baseball games, 30
"filler" talk, by baseball radio announcers, 213–14
Fischer, Ray, 113, 114
fixing games, 86, 87–90, 111–12; Black Sox scandal and, 91–104
Flanner, Joe, 191
Fleischman, Julius and Max, 23
Fleming, G. H., 249–50, 342n.3
Fletcher, Art, 35
Flick, Elmer, 50
Flood, Curt, 326
"floor slab," as part of early ballpark construction process, 40
Florida Marlins, 184
football stadium construction, as model for baseball stadiums, 40
Forbes Field, Pittsburgh, 20, 23, 27, 137, 307
Ford, Henry, 251–52
Ford Motor Company, 218
Foster, Andrew ("Rube"), 131–33, 139, 164, 338n.3; photograph of, 132
Foxx, Jimmy, 267
franchises. *See* major league franchises
Frank, Jerome, 294
Fraser, Charles ("Chick"), 47–48, 50, 52, 55, 57
free agency, 302, 326, 328, 329
Frick, Ford, 105, 125, 177, 204, 243, 299, 308–9
Fridays with Red (Edwards), 234
Fuchs, Emil, 296
Fullerton, Hugh, 94–95, 96, 99, 204

Gaffney, James, 22–23
Galatzer, Milton, 258
Gallery, Tom, 233
Gallico, Paul, 196, 200
gambling: baseball's association with, 84, 85–92, 111–12; Black Sox scandal and, 91–104. *See also* bribery
games, baseball: contrasting pace of, 33, 317; "fixing" of, 86, 87–90
Gandil, Arnold ("Chick"), 93, 95, 96, 97, 100, 101, 102
Garagiola, Joe, 236
Gardella, Danny, 292–95
Gardella v. Chandler, 295, 298, 324
Garvey, Ned, 302
Gaynor, William, 16
Gehrig, Lou, 239, 259, 267, 270
Gehringer, Charley, 266, 267
gender issues, in Organized Baseball, 349n.1
General Mills, 220, 225
gentry reform politics, 85, 336n.3

Giamatti, A. Bartlett, 354n.3
Gibson, Bob, 158
Gibson, Josh, 138; photograph of, 145
Gillette Safety Razor Company, 235, 238
Gionfriddo, Al, 235
Glantz, Harry, 255
Gleason, Kid, 93, 95, 98
gloves, early twentieth-century, 14, 32
Godkin, E. L., 85
Gowdy, Hank, 35
Graduate, The (film), 268
grandstands, construction of in early ballparks, 26–27, 40–41
Graney, Jack, 228, 230
Graves, Abner, 124
Gray, Pete, 147, 275
Great Depression: ballplayer salaries and, 270; Negro Leagues and, 138, 144, 146; Organized Baseball and, 118–22
Green, Bernard, 40
Greenberg, Hank, 247, 249, 258, 259; as ethnic baseball hero, 260–66, 272–74; photograph of, 267
Greenberg, Stephen, 260
Greenlee, Gus, 137, 138–39, 142, 143, 146, 164
Griffith, Clark, 151, 166–67, 237, 308
Griffith Stadium, Washington, 20, 23; photograph of, 145
Guest, Edgar, 262
Gye, Frederick, 334n.7

Hall of Fame. *See* Baseball Hall of Fame
Hand, Learned, 294
Harlem Globetrotters, 143, 158
Harridge, Will, 121, 177, 299, 308
Hart, James, 87
Hartman, Harry, 218, 228, 229
Harwell, Ernie, 231, 242
Hasty, Robert, 251
Hedges, Robert Lee, 23
Heilmann, Harry, 230
Henrich, Tommy, 239
Herrmann, Garry, 71, 107, 108, 113, 160, 174; photograph of, 62
Herzog, Charles ("Buck"), 101, 250–51
Heydler, John, 90, 108, 114
Hilltop Park, New York, 11, 13–15, 26, 27; photograph of, 14
"hippodrome" effect, and night baseball, 167, 179, 184
Hitler, Adolf, 263–64
hitting: changes in, 118; during deadball era, 33–34
Hodges, Russ, 230
Hoey, Fred, 211, 213, 228, 229
Hogan, Frank, 255
Holland, John, 168
Holmes, Justice Oliver Wendell, 70, 74, 77, 78–80, 106, 294, 335n.28
Holmes, Tommy, 182
Holtzman, Jerome, 193–94, 196, 200, 202
Holway, John, 150
home games, radio broadcasts of, 206–7, 209, 211
home runs: inside-the-park, 15, 34; in-the-stands, 37, 45, 117–18; role in Babe Ruth's celebrity status, 37
Homestead Grays, 137, 139, 143–44, 151, 157
Hoover, Herbert, 208
Horning, Ross, 301–2
Hornsby, Rogers, 148, 254
horse racing, as analogy to baseball, 111
House of David team, 145–46
Howell, Harry, 88
Hoyne, Maclay, 103
Hoyt, Waite, 230
Huggins, Miller, 191, 194
Hunt, Marshall, 194–95, 198–99
Husing, Ted, 218, 228, 237
Huston, Tillinghast, 37–42
Hutchinson, Fred, 302

immigrants: in nineteenth-century American baseball, 4. *See also* ethnicity in baseball
Indianapolis Clowns, 157, 158
individualism, as theme in commentary on baseball, 317–18
infield, and early ballpark design, 15
integration of baseball, 146–59, 277, 339n.27; economics of, 151–52; media commentary on, 154–56, 158; opposition to, 127–28, 147–49. *See also* Negro Leagues
intellectualism of baseball, as typical commentator response, 317
interleague "wars," 60
International League, 71, 155, 282
interstate commerce: media coverage of

games as, 294; participation of Organized Baseball in, 75–81, 297–99
interviews with ballplayers, as a dimension of baseball journalism, 202–3
involuntary servitude, as analogy in baseball labor relations, 48
Irish ballplayers, 247, 257
Irwin, Monte, 157
Israel, Melvin Allen. *See* Allen, Mel
Italian ballplayers: assimilationism and, 272–73; ethnic commentary on, 250, 253, 256–58; in major leagues, 247, 248, 255–58, 260, 266–72; World War II and, 271. *See also* ethnicity in baseball

Jackson, Joseph Jefferson ("Shoeless Joe"), 93, 97, 101–2, 103, 105
Jackson, Rufus ("Sonnyman"), 138, 139
Jethroe, Sam, 157
Jewish ballplayers: assimilationism and, 272–73; ethnic commentary on, 250–55, 258–60, 261–62, 347n.23; in major leagues, 247, 248, 253–55, 258–66; as role models, 263. *See also* ethnicity in baseball
Johnson, Arnold, 313
Johnson, Byron Bancroft ("Ban"): ballplayer strikes and, 62; as baseball entrepreneur, 48, 50, 57, 60, 65, 333n.1; corruption in major leagues and, 89, 99, 101, 110, 112, 114; emergence of *The Sporting News* and, 190–91; *Federal Baseball* lawsuit and, 71; National Commission leadership and, 107–8; radio broadcasts and, 216–17
Johnson, Walter, 119, 120, 238, 270, 292
Johnson, William J. ("Judy"), 150
Johnston, Charles, 222
journalism. *See* baseball journalism
Jurges, Bill, 212

Kansas City Athletics, 311, 312–13
Kansas City Blues, 134, 135
Kansas City Call, 134, 142
Kansas City Monarchs, 131, 133, 144–46, 153, 157, 164, 174, 339n.25
Kansas City Star, 134
Kauff, Benny, 113, 115
Ken Rad Lamp Works Company, and first major league night game, 173
Keeler, Willie, 120
Kelly, Joe, 87
Kemp, Abe, 196
Kendall, Percy, 221
Keyser, Lee, 164
Kirk, William F., 249
Klem, Bill, 88, 177
Kling, Johnny, 259
Knickerbocker Club of New York, 123, 124
Koufax, Sandy, 325
Kowalski, Walter, 296
Kowalski v. Chandler et al., 351n.29
Kuhn, Bowie, 326
Ku Klux Klan, 245, 251

labor relations: ballplayer strikes and, 62, 325–26; minor league draft system and, 284; reserve clause system and, 302–3, 323–26; retirement benefits and, 324–26
Lacy, Sam, 149–50
Lajoie, Napoleon ("Nap"): as gifted ballplayer, 50–52; as Hall of Famer, 120; lawsuit against, 47–48, 52–60; photograph of, 51; suspicious batting championship of, 88
Lanctot, Neil, 338n.3
Landis, Kenesaw Mountain: appointment as baseball commissioner, 104, 107–8; character sketch of, 106–7; draft system and, 279, 280; farm system opposition by, 115–16, 289, 290–91; influence on Organized Baseball, 125–26; major decisions as baseball commissioner, 105, 110–15; night baseball opposition by, 116–17; photograph of, 109; racial attitudes of, 147; on radio broadcasting of games, 218, 238
Lane, Frank C., 166, 253
Lanier, Max, 293, 295
Lardner, Ring, 94, 97, 200, 209
Lasker plan (Albert Lasker), 108
Latino ballplayers, in early twentieth-century baseball, 247
Laux, France, 211, 228, 229
"law," baseball. *See* baseball "law"
lawsuits: antitrust violations and, 69–81, 293–97, 335n.19, 352n.33; on contract breaches, 47–48, 52–58
Lazzeri, Tony, 256
Leach, Tommy, 50–51
League Park, Cleveland, 20
League Park, Washington, 20, 23

leagues: bidding wars between, 60, 65–66. *See also names of specific leagues*
Leifeld, Lefty, 168, 169
Leonard, Buck, 143–44, 150, 151
Leonard, Hubert ("Dutch"), 112
Levey, James Julius, 259
Liberty Broadcasting System, 242–44
Lieb, Fred, 89, 94, 193, 197, 258–59
lighting systems: in major leagues, 173–74, 180, 182, 185, 187; in Negro Leagues, 144–46, 164, 174
Little League baseball, 307
liveball era, beginning of, 43
Lombardi, Ernie, 256, 257
Loomis, Fred M., 99
Lopat, Ed, 239
Los Angeles Dodgers, 311, 314–15, 353n.64
Lowden, Frank, 106
loyalty, regional, 64–65, 66–67
Lueker, Claude, 334n.11
Lumley, Benjamin, 334n.7
Lumley v. Wagner, 334n.7

MacDonald, Charles, 97, 99, 101–2
Mack, Connie, 21, 47, 52, 120, 181, 312–13, 333n.1
Mack, Earle, 313
Mack, Roy, 313
MacPhail, Larry, 149, 172, 176, 177, 182, 183, 186, 224–25, 232, 238; photograph of, 300
Magee, Lee, 90
major league franchises: draft system and, 278–85; farm system and, 64, 280–81; during Great Depression, 118; participation in interstate commerce by, 76–81; relocation of, 277–78, 305–6, 308–15, 329; territoriality principle and, 65–69, 297–98, 303–6, 321–22; transportation issues for, 69, 276, 305–6, 313, 314; westward expansion and, 298, 303, 308–10, 314–15, 353n.59. *See also* Organized Baseball
"Manhattan Merry-Go-Round" (film), 269
Manley, Abe, 152
Manley, Effa, 151–53
Mann, Leslie, 111
Manning, Jimmy, 23
Manning, Tom, 211, 228, 229, 230
Maranville, Rabbit, 35
Marion, Marty, 234, 288
Maris, Roger, 313
Marshall, John, 74
Martin, Fred, 293, 295
Martin, Pepper, 288
Martin, Whitney, 265
Mathewson, Christy, 35, 89–90, 94–95, 119, 120–21, 270
Mays, Carl, 107
Mays, Willie, 158
McAdams, Lawrence, 165
McAvoy, John, 210
McCarthy, Joe, 194, 269
McDonald, Arch, 225, 228, 230, 237–38
McEvoy, Leo Carl, 222, 223
McGraw, John, 31, 33, 36, 38, 47, 87, 111, 121, 249, 253, 259
McKechnie, Bill, 188
McKeever, Edward and Stephen, 17
McLean, Larry, 35–36
McLendon, Gordon, 242–44
McMullin, Fred, 93, 105
McNally, Dave, 326
McNamee, Graham, 209, 228; photograph of, 210
media: ethnic commentary in, 247–48, 250–59, 261–62, 269, 347n.23; franchise location and, 321, 322; as interstate commerce, 294. *See also* newspapers; radio broadcasts; television broadcasts
Medwick, Joe, 288
Melillo, Oscar, 256, 257
melting pot theory, of ethnic affiliation, 5, 246–47, 249, 257, 260, 268, 271, 272–74
Merkle, Fred, 35, 249
Messersmith, Andy, 326
Mexican League, 149, 292–93
Meyers, John ("Chief"), 35–36
mezzanine deck, in construction of early ballparks, 40
middle class, appeal of baseball to, 4, 8
Miller, Jon, 233
Miller, Marvin, 325, 353n.2
Mills, Abraham G., 123
Mills Commission, 123–25
Milwaukee Bears, 131
Milwaukee Braves, 311, 312
Milwaukee County Stadium, 311
minor leagues: attendance decline in, 307; development of, 115–16; draft system and, 278–85; economics of, 289–90; farm system and, 64, 115–16, 278, 285–92; major leagues' relationship to, 278–85;

Negro Leagues compared with, 150–51; night baseball in, 144, 167–68, 171, 174, 175, 185; radio broadcasts and, 219, 220; reserve clause and, 302–3
Minoso, Minnie, 158
mitts, early twentieth-century, 14, 32
Mize, Johnny, 288
"Monday Night Baseball," 230
monopolization, in major league baseball: Congressional investigation of, 295, 297, 299; lawsuits citing, 71–72, 293–97. *See also* antitrust laws
monopsony, baseball as, 63, 67
Monroe, Marilyn, 268
Montgomery, David, 334n.5
Montreal Royals, 155
Moore, Terry, 288
Morrissey, John, 144
"Mrs. Robinson" (song), 268
Municipal Stadium, Cleveland, 20, 45–46, 276, 331n.5
Murray, John ("Red"), 36
Musial, Stan, 288
Mutual Broadcasting System, 243
mutuality, in baseball contracts, 48, 53, 54, 56–57, 66
Myer, Buddy, 258, 260

Nashville Elite Giants, 143
National Agreement (1903), 6, 12, 57, 60, 62, 65, 81, 191, 275, 279, 323
National-American League, 108
National Association of Minor Leagues, 219
National Association of Professional Baseball Leagues, 276
National Broadcasting Company (NBC), 208
National Commission: creation of, 71n; decline of, 107–8; gambling investigations by, 87, 88
National League: contract jumping from, 47–48; franchise transfers in, 312; night games in, 117; radio broadcasting of games and, 222; westward expansion and, 309, 314–15
National Women's Professional Baseball League, 275, 349n.1
Native American ballplayers, 247, 252–53
Navin, Frank, 23
Navin Field, Detroit, 20, 23
Negro American League, 139, 146, 158
Negro Leagues: All-Star Games in, 139–43; barnstorming in, 128, 130, 137–38, 145–46, 164, 174, 338n.3; calibre of ballplayers in, 149–51; characteristics of, 128, 158; demise of, 146, 152–53, 158, 277; establishment of, 6, 131; histories of, 338n.3; "inferiority" of, 135–37; integration of Organized Baseball and, 146–59, 277, 339n.27; newspaper coverage of, 133–34, 192; night baseball in, 144–46, 163–64, 185; numbers business and, 138–39; organization of, 128, 130–33; salaries in, 130, 132, 143–44, 339n.25; as source of black employment, 129–30; World Series in, 139–40. *See also* blacks
Negro National League, 130, 131–33, 134, 138–39, 158, 164, 338n.3
Newark Call, 207
Newark Eagles, 151–52, 157
Newcombe, Don, 157
New Deal, 169
newspapers: baseball's relationship to, 7, 190–205; decline in status of, 203–4; ethnic commentary in, 250–52, 254, 255, 347n.40; on integration of Organized Baseball, 154–56, 158; Negro Leagues coverage in, 133–34, 139–42; racial commentary in, 133–34, 141, 142, 156, 338n.11; sports pages in, 192–93. *See also* sportswriters
New York Age, 142
New York American, 249
New York Amsterdam News, 133
New York Black Yankees, 135
New York Cubans, 158
New York Daily News, 194–95, 199, 201, 269
New Yorker, 345n.48
New York Evening Mail, 250
New York Evening Post, 262
New York Giants, 10, 29–37; "fixed" games and, 87–88, 99; Jewish ballplayers on, 253–55, 259; night games and, 173; relocation of, 311, 314; uniforms of, 31–32
New York Herald, 252
New York Herald Tribune, 192, 196, 197
New York Highlanders, 13, 15–16
New York Journal, 180
New York Journal American, 345n.48
New York Press, 193, 200

New York Sun, 198
New York Telegraph Company, 220
New York Times, 18, 38, 95, 101, 102–3, 164, 196, 254, 269
New York Tribune, 89
New York World, 96
New York World-Telegram, 200, 269
New York Yankees, 37, 235–37, 270, 312
night baseball: arguments for, 162, 164, 165–66, 170–72, 175–76, 178–80, 185–86; class implications of, 340n.9; early exhibitions of, 160–61, 164–65; imposed limitations on, 172, 181; in major leagues, 175–89; in minor leagues, 144, 167–68, 174, 175, 180, 185; in Negro Leagues, 144–46, 163–64, 174, 185; resistance to, 44, 45, 116–17, 161–63, 166–70, 179–81, 184–85, 188; sportswriters and, 201–2
Nugent, Jerry, 147
numbers business, 138–39

Oakland Athletics, 313
O'Connell, Jimmy, 111–12
O'Connor, Jack, 88
O'Connor, Leslie, 177
O'Malley, Walter, 235, 236, 241, 309, 314, 325
"On the Airwaves," 192, 344n.19
Organized Baseball: All-Star Game and, 118–19, 121–22; as anachronism, 8, 327; antitrust immunity of, 7, 8, 73, 275, 277, 295, 298–99; college recruiting in, 349n.3; cultivation of, as national pastime, 327–28; defined, 5n; draft system in, 278–85; economic and legal structure of, 59–69, 327–28; ethnicity in, 245–74; farm system development in, 115–16, 285–92; first commissioner of, 6, 7, 92, 104–17; franchise transfers in, 308–15; gambling's association with, 84–104, 111–12; Hall of Fame and, 118–21, 125; integration of, 146–59, 277, 339n.27; journalism and, 7, 190–205; Judge Landis's influence on, 125–26; lawsuits against, 70–81, 293–97; minor leagues and, 278–85; night baseball and, 44, 45, 116–17, 161–89; racial segregation in, 5–6, 127–28, 147–49; radio broadcasting and, 206–44; territoriality principle and, 63, 65–69, 297–98, 303–6, 321–22; women's exclusion from, 349n.1. *See also* baseball
Oriole Park, Baltimore, 47
Orsatti, Ernie, 257
Osborn Engineering Company, 39, 40
outfield: in early ballparks, 36, 44; seating of fans in, 15, 26
Owen, Mickey, 288

Pacific Coast League, 298, 303, 308, 309
Paige, Leroy ("Satchel"), 138, 142–43, 153, 154, 157
parity, in sports franchises, 64
parking facilities, ballpark, 42, 43, 44, 311
partisanship, regional, 64–65, 66–67
Patterson, Joseph, 194
Payne, Earl D., 177, 341n.21
Payne, Robert B., 341n.21
Pegler, Westbrook, 254–55
Pennsylvania Supreme Court, 54–55, 59
pension plans: All-Star Games and, 121–22; labor relations and, 324–26
Perini, Lou, 312
Perry, Scott, 107
Pesky, Johnny, 240
Petwig, Bruce, 141
Philadelphia Athletics, 12, 21, 47–48, 50, 57, 311, 312–13
Philadelphia Ball Club v. Lajoie, 51, 52–58, 60, 323
Philadelphia Phillies, 47–48, 50, 98–99, 147, 178, 321
Philadelphia Tribune, 133
"Pigtown," Brooklyn, 17
Pinelli, Babe, 257
pitchers: ban on trick pitches by, 117–18; pace of games and, 33; post-deadball era statistics for, 118
Pittsburgh Courier, 133, 141–42, 156, 158, 338n.11
Pittsburgh Crawfords, 138, 142, 146
Pittsburgh Pirates, 329
Pittsburgh Post-Gazette, 218
Pizzolo, Francisco Stefano. *See* Bodie, Ping
players. *See* ballplayers
Players' Association, 325, 326
Polo Grounds, New York: ambience of game in, 29–37; burning of, 10, 11; features of, 11–12, 26–27, 36–37; seating capacity of, 12, 27
population changes, U.S., 307–8, 321–22

portable lighting systems, 144–46, 164, 174
Posey, Cumberland, 137–39, 144
Postal, Frederick, 23
Potter, William P., 55–58
Povich, Shirley, 196
Prendergast, James, 295, 297
press box, photograph of, 202
Prince, Bob, 228, 230, 242
Professional Baseball Players Fraternity, 62
Progressive Era, 6–8, 126, 330
Protective Association of Professional Baseball Players, 62
Pylon Construction Company, 17

Quinn, Jack, 107

racial segregation, 5–6, 127–28, 147–49. *See also* integration of baseball; Negro Leagues
radio broadcasts: announcers for, 208–14, 222–24, 226–42; ballpark attendance and, 324; censorship of, 222–23; commercial sponsorship of, 218, 220, 225, 229, 235, 238; early history of, 206–9; "filler" talk and, 213–14; impact on major league baseball, 207, 208, 214–19, 243–44; re-created games and, 211–13, 220, 243; regional bans on, 219, 220, 243; television broadcasts vs., 206, 239, 242; of World Series games, 207–9, 218, 219. *See also* television broadcasts
Ralston, Robert, 52–54
Reach, Alfred J., 50
Reagan, Ronald ("Dutch"), 212, 227, 343n.9
re-created game broadcasts, 211–13, 220, 243
recreational sports, and ballpark attendance, 307
Reddy, Dick, 141
Redland Field, Cincinnati, 23, 28, 141
Reed, Stanley, 298
Reese, Harold ("Pee Wee"), 302
Reese, Jimmy, 259
Reichow, Oscar, 108
reporters. *See* sportswriters
reserve clause: abolition of, 326; ballplayer support for, 302, 323; blacklisting practices and, 61, 66, 80; challenges to, 277, 278, 293–97, 301–2, 324–26, 328; competitive balance and, 64, 81, 301–2; interleague wars and, 60–61; labor relations and, 302–3, 323–26; lawsuits pertaining to, 52–58, 70–81, 293–97; origination of, 49, 53; reasons for, 63–65, 77; as rule of baseball law, 61–63; territoriality principle and, 66–69, 297–98, 322, 326
retirement benefits: All-Star Games and, 121–22; labor relations and, 324–26
Reulbach, Eddie, 253
Reutlinger, Harry, 102
revenue-sharing, 329
Rice, Grantland, 208–9
Rickey, Branch, 152, 153, 154, 155–56, 235, 238, 285–91; photograph of, 287
Risberg, Charles ("Swede"), 93, 95, 97, 102
Rizzuto, Phil, 236, 239, 241
road games: major league transportation for, 69, 276, 305–6, 313, 314; radio broadcasting of, 211, 220, 226, 238
Robertson, Dave, 36
Robinson, Frank, 158
Robinson, Jackie, 148, 149, 152–57, 192, 263
Rogers, John I., 50, 52, 59
Rookie of the Year award, 157
Roosevelt, Franklin, 117, 176
Roosevelt, Theodore, 85, 106
Rosh Hashanah, 261–62
Rothstein, Arnold, 98, 103, 111
rounders, 123, 337n.37
Rowswell, Rosey, 228, 230, 242
Royko, Mike, 156–57
running stories, in newspaper coverage of baseball, 201
Runyon, Damon, 200
Ruppert, Jacob, 37–42, 254
Rust, Art, Jr., 135–36
Ruth, Babe: batting style of, 150; celebrity of, 37, 38, 163, 198–200; as Hall of Famer, 119–20, 121; news coverage of, 194–95, 199–200; paternity incident of, 195, 198, 199; Yankee Stadium design and, 41

Saam, Byrum, 230
salaries: of baseball journalists, 205; contract negotiations and, 270; labor relations and, 324–26; in Negro Leagues, 130, 132, 143–44, 339n.25; reserve clause and, 49–50, 56, 324–26; of star ballplayers, 194, 270, 271–72

Sand, Hennie, 111–12
San Francisco Bulletin, 196
San Francisco Examiner, 196
San Francisco Giants, 311, 314–15
San Francisco Seals, 268, 282
Saperstein, Abe, 143, 147
Saturday Evening Post, 191
Schacht, Al, 258, 259
Schalk, Ray, 100
Schneider, Pete, 90
Score, Herb, 240
scoreboards: electric, 41–42; rudimentary, 30, 32–33
scorecards, in early games, 30, 31
Scully, Vin, 231, 233, 235, 242
seating capacity: in early twentieth-century ballparks, 12, 15, 26–27, 44, 184; of Polo Grounds, 12, 27. *See also* attendance, ballpark
Second World War. *See* World War II
segregation. *See* racial segregation
Seitz, Peter, 326
Shaughnessy, Frank, 223
Shaver, Bud, 263
Sheridan, John, 216, 226, 285, 291
Sherman Anti-Trust Act, 61, 66; lawsuits citing violations of, 71–81, 293–97. *See also* antitrust laws
Shibe, Ben, 21–22, 23, 27, 42, 50; photograph of, 62
Shibe Park, Philadelphia: construction of, 21–22; deterioration of, 307, 313, 352n.51; opening of, 20, 45; photographs of, 25, 28
shin guards, 14, 32
Simon, Paul, 268
Sinclair, Albert, 65, 67
Singer, Isaac, 122–23
single-decked grandstands, 26
Sisler, George, 107, 120
Slaughter, Enos ("Country"), 239–40, 288
Smith, Craig, 235
Smith, Curt, 237, 241
Smith, Gene, 212
Smith, Red, 34, 196, 260
Smith, Wendell, 147, 158
Smyth, Constantine J., 72, 73, 75, 76–77, 82
Snodgrass, Fred, 34, 35
solidarity. *See* unionization of baseball
Solomon, Moses, 253, 259
Somers, Charles W., 333n.1
Spalding, Albert Goodwill: on "America's National Game," 69, 123; on gambling in baseball, 84, 86–87; photograph of, 68
Spalding's Official Baseball Guide, 123, 124, 337n.37
Spanish ballplayers, 247
Speaker, Tris, 112, 120, 141
"Speaking of Greenberg" (Guest), 262
Spink, Al, 190
Spink, Charles, 190–91
Spink, Taylor, 191–92, 204
Spink, Thomas, 157
spitball, outlawing of, 37
sponsorship. *See* commercial sponsorship
sport: interracial, 148; as pastime, 319; trade vs., 82–83, 275
Sporting Life, 161
Sporting News: on ballpark construction, 18, 38; on commissioner Landis, 108, 110; as dominant baseball periodical, 190–92; ethnic commentary in, 5, 245, 246, 250, 251–53, 254, 256–60, 261, 262, 347n.40; on integration of major leagues, 154–55, 158; on major league scandals, 88, 96, 97; on minor league draft and farm systems, 279–80, 283, 284, 285, 289, 290–91; night baseball debate in, 161, 167–71, 173, 175, 178–79, 180–81, 182, 187–89; on radio broadcasts of games, 213, 214–15, 216–17, 218, 220, 222, 223, 224, 344n.18; Ronald Reagan profile from, 343n.9
Sportsman's Park, St. Louis, 20, 23, 181
sportswriters: daily schedule of, 200–203; relationship to ballplayers, 193–200, 202–5. *See also* newspapers
stadiums. *See* ballparks
Stafford, Wendell P., 71, 72
Stallings, George, 33, 89
Standard Oil Corporation, 106
standing room, 26
statistics, ballplayer: post-deadball era, 118; radio broadcasts and, 213–14
Steele, Joseph, 21, 22, 24, 27
Stengel, Casey, 194
stereotyping, ethnic, 245, 246, 247–48, 249–51, 253, 266, 272
St. Louis Browns, 65, 88, 180, 304, 311, 321
St. Louis Cardinals, 87, 285–89, 350n.10
Stock, Milton, 36
Stoneham, Charles, 173

Stoneham, Horace, 38–39, 111, 238
strategy, in deadball era, 14–15
strikes, labor, in baseball, 62, 325–26
structural steel construction, in early ballparks, 25
Sullivan, William ("Sport"), 103
Supreme Court of the United States: *Federal Baseball* case, 73, 76, 83, 277; *Toolson* case, 297, 298–99, 306

Taylor, John, 23
Taylor, John W., 87
teams. *See* major league franchises; *names of specific teams*
Tebbetts, Birdie, 263
Tele-Flash, Inc., 219–20, 226
telegraphy, re-created game broadcasts via, 211–13, 220, 243
television broadcasts: ballpark attendance and, 307, 324, 352n.52; presentation of baseball, 206, 227, 321, 324, 353n.61; radio announcing vs., 206, 239, 242. *See also* radio broadcasts
ten-day clause, in baseball contracts, 49, 53, 54, 55, 61
Tener, John K., 71
territoriality principle, 63, 65–69; challenges to, 297–98, 303–6, 321–22; collapse of, 309, 322, 326; reserve clause and, 66–69, 297–98, 322, 326
Terry, Bill, 225
Texas Rangers, 184
"This Week in Baseball," 242
Thomson, Bobby, 230, 232
Thompson, Chuck, 231
Thompson, Hank, 157
throwing games. *See* fixing games
Thurber, James, 345n.48
Tiger Stadium, Detroit, 20, 23
Time, 225, 269
Tolan, John, 271
Toledo Tigers, 131
Toolson, George, 295–97
Toolson v. New York Yankees, 297, 298–99, 306
Topping, Dan, 194, 237, 238, 241
Topps Chewing Gum Company, 325
Totten, Hal, 211, 228, 299
trade: as legal concept, 74; across state lines, 75–81, 294, 297–99; sport vs., 82–83, 275
Tramulto, Chauncey, 271
transportation: to ballparks, 17, 19, 22, 29, 39, 42; interstate, 77–81; for major league teams, 69, 276, 305–6, 313, 314
Trautman, George, 293, 299
trick pitches, ban on, 117–18
triple-decked grandstands, in early ballparks, 27, 40–41
Trumbull, Walter, 252
twilight baseball, 163, 165–66, 169, 341n.14
"Twilight Baseball" (McAdams), 165
Tyler, Lefty, 35–36
Tyson, Ty, 211, 228, 229

umpires, 14, 32, 222
Unforgettable Season, The (Fleming), 249
uniforms: addition of numbers to, 42, 333n.36; early twentieth-century styles, 30–32
unionization of baseball: beginning of, 323–25; early failures of, 62–63
U.S. News and World Report, 353n.65
United States v. Paramount Pictures, 352n.33
universal draft system, in minor leagues, 280, 282–83, 284, 291
urban growth: emergence of baseball and, 7; new ballparks and, 20, 64

Vander Meer, Johnny, 182, 183
Variety, 168, 223
Veeck, Bill, 147, 153, 310, 312, 321
Veeck, William, 98–99; photograph of, 100
Vidmar, Richards, 196
Vila, Joe, 250, 251
"village mentality," as persistent in early twentieth-century urban America, 64

Wagner, Honus, 119, 120–21, 122, 249, 270
Wagner, Johanna, 334n.7
Walker, Charlie, 138
Walker, Harry, 240, 288
Walsh, Christy, 204
Ward, Arch, 121–22
Washington Park, New York, 16–17, 22, 26
Washington Post, 196
Washington Senators, 50, 144, 311, 322
Weaver, George ("Buck"), 93, 97, 105, 111, 114–15
Webb, Del, 238, 312
Wedge, Will, 197–98
Weeghman, Charles, 23, 65, 67

Weintraub, Phil, 258, 259
Weiss, George, 180
Western League, 48, 60
Western Union, 243
Westinghouse Network, 208
westward expansion, 298, 303, 308–10, 314–15, 353n.59
"Why Not More Jewish Ballplayers?" (Lane), 253
Widmar, Al, 302
Wilkinson, J. L., 131, 144, 153, 164
Williams, Claude ("Lefty"), 93, 95, 100, 102, 103
Williams, Joe, 269
Wilson, Bert, 230
Wilson, Tom, 143
women: exclusion of, from Organized Baseball, 349n.1; professional baseball league of, 275, 349n.1
Wood, Joe, 112
wooden ballparks, replacement of in early twentieth century, 12, 13, 16, 20, 26
Woodruff, Harvey, 98
Woods, Jim, 233, 241
Woodward, Stanley, 192, 197, 201–2
working class: early American baseball and, 4; Negro League fans as, 164; night baseball and, 340n.9
World Series: Black Sox scandal in, 91–104; commercial sponsorship of, 218, 235, 238; of Negro Leagues, 139–40; radio broadcasts of, 207–9, 218, 219
World War II, and ethnicity in baseball, 260, 263–65, 270–71
Wright, George, 177
Wright, Harry, 177
Wrigley, Philip K., 296, 301, 303–4, 309
Wrigley, William, 222, 299
Wrigley Field, Chicago, 20, 23, 157, 183

Yankee Stadium, New York: construction of, 39–41, 45; features of, 40–42, 45, 184; opening of, 12; photograph of, 43; radio announcing from, 235–36; symbol of transformation from deadball to liveball eras, 43–44
Yom Kippur, 262
Young, A. S. ("Doc"), 158
Young, Cy, 120
Youngblood, Albert, 252–53